ROAD, FIVE MILES FROM BOSTON.

VOICES
OF
BROOKLINE

Washington Street Firehouse decorated for Brookline's bicentenary (1905).

VOICES
OF
BROOKLINE

BY

LARRY RUTTMAN

PETER E. RANDALL PUBLISHER LLC
PORTSMOUTH, NEW HAMPSHIRE
2005

This book and jacket were designed by Grace Peirce. The text is set in Galliard. Printing and binding are by Sheridan Books.

The photograph on the dust jacket showing Devotion School students and teachers in front of the Edward Devotion House in the year of Brookline's bicentennial (1905) was taken by Armstrong and George of Boston and provided courtesy of the Brookline Preservation Commission, as was the image of the Brookline Town Seal in the front matter.

The front endpaper illustration, "Brookline from Parker Hill, 1855," was provided courtesy of the Brookline Public Library.

The back endpaper photograph was taken by the author during the 1974 running of the Boston Marathon at Coolidge Corner, Brookline.

The photograph of the author on the dust jacket and in the front matter was taken by Dr. John B. Little.

Library of Congress Control Number: 2005905604

ISBN: 1-931807-39-6

Printed and bound in the United States of America.

Published by:
Peter E. Randall Publisher LLC
Portsmouth, New Hampshire 03802
www.perpublisher.com

For my late mother and father,
Doris Grandberg Ruttman and Morris "Moe" Ruttman

and

For my wife, Lois Raverby Ruttman

Seal of the Town of Brookline.

The town then exists in all nations, whatever their laws and customs may be. It is man who makes monarchies and establishes republics, but the township seems to come directly from the hand of God. Town meeting and primary schools are the science, they bring it within the people's reach. They teach man how to use and how to enjoy it.

From *Democracy in America* by Alexis de Tocqueville

CONTENTS

Book III: IMMIGRANTS

Book IV: DOGS

Books V – X: THE FABRIC OF BROOKLINE'S UNIQUENESS A MICROCOSM OF DEMOCRACY

Book V: BROOKLINE HIGH SCHOOL

Book VI: POLITICS

Book VII: CITIZEN PARTICIPATION

Book VIII: PUBLIC SERVICES

Book IX: PRESERVATION

Book X: TOWN MEETING AND GOVERNANCE

Books XI - XVI: FACETS OF BROOKLINE COMMUNITY

Book XI: 9/11

Book XII: BUSINESS

Book XIII: MUSICIANS

Book XIV: PUBLIC FIGURES

Book XV: PROFESSIONALS

Book XVI: CLUBS — Dateline: BROOKLINE, Mass., USA

ABOUT THE AUTHOR

Photo by Dr. John B. Little.

LARRY RUTTMAN has lived in Brookline since the age of two, attending and graduating from Devotion School and Brookline High School. He received a B.A. in English from the University of Massachusetts at Amherst, and holds a Juris Doctor from Boston College Law School. Larry never seriously thought he would write a book, and is grateful to have written one about Brookline. He loves words, music, and the Boston Red Sox in equal measure. Larry continues to practice law in Brookline, where he and his wife, Lois, have lived for many years.

FOREWORD

WHAT DOES ONE SAY when asked to write the foreword to Larry Ruttman's extraordinarily entertaining and historical *Voices of Brookline* about his and my hometown on its three hundreth birthday — as a town father? I love this book because I share the same love and admiration for the town that helped to shape me that you find in virtually all of Larry's interviews and stories, which I have read and reread.

I was the young reformer for so long that taking on this new role is a real switch. But at seventy-one years of age, with both a Social Security and a Medicare card and the right to ride Boston's venerable public transportation system for thirty-five cents, it may well be time to assume that role.

I was born, like so many older Brookline residents, at the Boston Lying-In Hospital on Longwood Avenue in Boston. Every day, as we used to say, was Labor Day at the Boston Lying-In. I left there at the age of six days; took up residence in a brick two-family house at 397 Boylston Street with my then three-year-old-brother and my parents; moved to South Brookline — what the Townies called "the Country" — six years later, and with time off for college in Pennsylvania and military service in Korea, have been a proud resident of the town all my life.

Like so many of the people about whom you will read in Larry's book, I owe a great deal to the community in which I was reared, which I served in both local and state government, and where Kitty and I grew up, married, raised our kids, and still reside. Actually, although she was a freshman and I was a senior at the high school, I don't remember ever meeting her there, although she says we met once briefly in the hallowed high school quadrangle. In fact, I used to chide Johnny Grinnell, my basketball coach and political mentor, Kitty's home room teacher, and the first teacher who ever encouraged me to run for office, because he never introduced us when I was in high school. Of course, had he done so, I probably wouldn't have been interested. I was a Big Man on Campus, and I would hardly have been interested in a freshman woman!

Fortunately for me, we met years later, and I fell head over heels in love. By that time, however, I was gearing up for my first run for legislative office, and I made sure she was in front of St. Mary's Church for thirteen hours working the polls for her intended in the Democratic primary in September of 1962. When the votes were counted in that precinct and I had won by a decisive majority, I knew Kitty was the girl for me! And she has been ever since we took up residence as man and wife on Perry Street; raised three terrific kids, all of whom are products of the Brookline school system; and continue to live on the same street where we began our married life together in 1963.

Why do I love Larry Ruttman's stories about me and my fellow citizens? Because it informs us in a flowing style of all the facets of Brookline life going back as far as the eldest among us. Reading Larry's *Voices of Brookline,* it is clear that three things among many stand out about those of us who have had the great good fortune to live in our town. First, the town's commitment to educational excellence is absolutely fundamental. It is why our parents moved here. It is why there was no question when we were married that Kitty and I wanted to live here, too.

Read, for example, Larry's story on Bob Weintraub, headmaster of Brookline High School, and you will discover what it is about this terrific educator that makes him the man he is — a commitment to children, an instinctive sense of optimism, a powerful belief that good people, working together, can make a difference in the lives of children and the lives of their fellow citizens.

Bob is not alone. The best teacher I ever had was Kate O'Brien, my French teacher, and the longtime head of the Department of Modern Foreign Languages at the high school. What a woman! And what a teacher! If you didn't come out of her classes with a perfect French accent, there was something wrong with you.

The second thing that stands out about the town, and which comes through so loudly and clearly in Larry Ruttman's stories, is the commitment of its citizens to their community and the opportunity the town meeting form of government has given us to participate actively in its governance. I teach these days during the winter months at UCLA in Los Angeles. It's a great place to teach and a great place to spend the winter, but Los Angeles has only fifteen city councilors, each representing districts with approximately two hundred and fifty thousand people! How does one get into the politics of Los Angeles and run for office when it costs hundreds of thousands of dollars just to run for city council?

In Brookline, as Larry and I both know, all it takes is a comfortable pair of walking shoes, a bunch of brochures, and the energy to knock on the doors of your neighbors and greet them at the polls for thirteen hours on election day. If you do those things, chances are you will be elected to a town legislature of two hundred and forty town meeting members, participate actively in the government of the community, and represent your constituents in your neighborhood to the best of your ability.

But you don't even have to be a town meeting member. As Larry's informative and anecdotal stories on citizen participants like Chobee Hoy, Roger and Arlene Stern, Owen Carle, Ethel Weiss, and Ira Jackson make clear, there is probably no other community in which more people are more deeply involved in its civic life. Parks, schools, libraries, children's services, the senior center, the Coolidge Corner Theater, the Brookline Arts Center in an old town firehouse – you name it, the people of the town are engaged and involved. We hope the town benefits, but in our heart of hearts we know that we are doing this for ourselves as well.

Finally, as you can quickly sense from these pages, especially in Larry's story, *Giuliani, Baseball and Brookline*, which my good friend and former congressman representing Brookline, Father Robert J. Drinan, called "nostalgic, illuminating, and indeed inspiring," baseball played a huge role in the lives of all of us. Back in our youth, we had two professional teams in Boston, and many of us were within easy walking distance of both Fenway Park and Braves Field. I saw my first Red Sox game when I was four and a half, so waiting for the Sox to win a World Series has been a long ordeal indeed. But I also saw my share of games at Braves Field, including one during World War II where there were so few ballplayers available that the Braves first baseman wore a left-handed fielder's mitt, and there was a one-armed center fielder playing against the Red Sox at Fenway.

This was in the days before the Little League, and we used to play ball on our local diamonds literally every day of the season.

Each elementary school had sixth-, seventh-, and eighth- grade teams, and we played, and played hard. In fact, my brother Stelian and I were perhaps the only brother battery in Brookline school history — he pitched and I caught — and I remember we beat one team — I think it was Pierce — 27–0.

Do I have concerns about the future of our community as Kitty and I live out our golden years? Yes, I do, but, then, I wouldn't be a true son of Brookline if I didn't. When we bought our house on Perry Street in 1971 in which we still live today (where else can one grow tomatoes and cucumbers in his front yard?), we paid twenty-five thousand dollars for our half of a brick duplex that consisted of two ten-room units with a common fire-wall. And that price at the time was not a bargain. In fact, the bank thought it was slightly overvalued. With today's inflated values, what happens to the kind of solid middle class that lived in Brookline in our youth? What happens to young couples like us who today couldn't possibly afford to live in the town? What happens to our teachers and cops and firefighters who increasingly must look elsewhere for housing?

That worries the hell out of me. I want other young couples coming along to have the same opportunity Kitty and I had to live in and bring up their families in this vibrant town. But we will continue to work together with commitment, as we always have, to make our community the very best place we can make it, and try the best we can to open it up to people of all incomes, faiths, and colors.

The future of Brookline will flow from the quality and variety of its citizenry rather than from accumulated bricks and mortar. That said, how better to understand the ever-developing character of our town in this tercentenary year than to listen to its citizens in *The Voices Of Brookline* as told by Larry Ruttman, my friend of close to fifty years. This book provides a window to the extraordinary fabric of a very special place at this very special time.

Michael Dukakis
Los Angeles, California
February 19, 2005

PREFACE

PROVIDENCE MOVES IN STRANGE WAYS, when a moment seemingly prosaic ultimately proves to be poetic, permanently metamorphosing one's life in a way one could not have imagined, let alone hoped for. Such a moment occurred in my life late in the winter of 1998, and its progeny is the book you are about to read, completed in the waning days of December 2004 only hours before the commencement of Brookline's tercentenary year of 2005.

That providential moment came when Cathy Jenness, my talented legal assistant and friend of twenty five years, stepped into my office, to ask if she could take vacation time in early May to accompany her husband, Mike Jenness, captain of the Team Saquish gig rowing crew out of Plymouth, Massachusetts, on a trip to compete in the annual international regatta in the Scilly Isles, off England's rocky and windswept Cornwall coast. I coupled my ready agreement to her request with questions to satisfy my curiosity about what sounded like a romantic and adventurous voyage to a wild and wonderful locale.

Knowing career police officer and former Northeastern University football star Russell "Mike" Jenness for the gentlemanly gentle giant that he is, and instinctively feeling that the entourage he would draw about him for the venture would consist of unassuming, plain-spoken, and hardworking folk — and being somewhat of a romanticist myself — I spontaneously said words to this effect: "It sounds like a great trip. I wonder if I might come along." Equally romantic, and somewhat unrealistic, was the inchoate idea that if I brought along my hand tape recorder and camera, I could write a story about the venture worthy of publication — even though that seemed hardly likely, as I had never thought of myself as a writer except of legal briefs and the like.

Although it was unrecognized by me then, I am now persuaded that a mystical and powerful force entered my life at the precise moment that Cathy came into my office.

Indeed, I went along with Cathy and Mike Jenness, the Team Saquish crew, and their many friends to the Scilly Isles that May. The experiences of that trip far exceeded my bold expectations. The camaraderie I found in the company of our crew and the hundreds assembled for the races, not only gave me one of the best times of my life, but also inspired me to record many interviews and take numerous photographs. In the summertime afterglow of those sanguine days, I fashioned my first-ever literary attempt, an illustrated story about camaraderie and competition. Its title, *Row Hard, No Excuses* is the motto of Team Saquish, and it was published as the cover story in the February 15, 1999 issue of *Messing About in Boats*, a national magazine for the boating trade.

Unaware that my life was taking a new direction, I took satisfaction in the congenial experience I had shared, and in my new-found ability to convey that experience to a reader. I returned to the relatively routine practice of my profession, asking Cathy from time to time whether Mike was projecting another expedition. Word finally came that indeed he was; he planned to take Team Saquish to the fourth running of the Dutch Open Gig Championships at the Royal Netherlands Yacht Club, in the seas off the picturesque coastal castle town of Muiden, a few miles from Amsterdam, in early November 1999. Mike Jenness was happy to have me come along again with my tape recorder and camera, and I was more than happy to go. That trip had the same heady flavor as the first, a combination of good fellowship, adventure, and competition that spurred me to write a cover story entitled *Row Hard, No Excuses II*, appearing in *Messing About in Boats* on March 1, 2000.

Returning from Amsterdam, approaching my sixty-ninth birthday, ensconced in legal practice in a nice suite with collegial associates, I was as yet dimly (if at all) aware — despite my serendipitously successful forays into writing — that a convergence of forces, past and present, were pushing (perhaps guiding) me away from myself, as it were, toward an outward-looking endeavor I hoped would be of value to others and my hometown of Brookline. Always loving history and biography, and prone like most of us to the fantasy of wearing another hat, I had toyed with the notion of being a historian, knowing all the while, in my heart of hearts, that I probably lacked the discipline to hide myself away in the library for a few years to produce a worthy effort in the usual historical mode. That fantasy included oral history, having been fascinated long ago by Lawrence S. Ritter's classic *The Glory of Their Times* (1966), in which Ritter captured the words of some of the legendary major league baseball stars of the early twentieth century.

Later, I became enamored of the works of Studs Terkel, whose string of oral histories preserving the words of mostly ordinary Americans seemed to me likely to be read far into the future, illuminating, as they do, what life was like at the grass roots during this time, a view that no past historian had given us about his time. In my fantasy, I wanted to emulate Terkel's work, especially given my professional and personal experience in dealing with and talking with people from all walks of life, and my long standing dilettantish interest in practically everything.

Not long after returning from Amsterdam, landlord problems made it apparent that within months my associates and I would be dispersing and looking for new quarters, a prospect that naturally sparked a self-inquiry as to what direction I wanted to take. Thinking to try my hand further at writing, yet viewing with some trepidation even a partial withdrawal from a profession that had given me interest and sustenance for so long, I hovered in a state of indecision for some weeks, until an impulsive act on a Sunday in February set me firmly on the course I have followed since. On that day, returning along Harvard Street from a talk given by Sarah Boyer at the Cambridge Historical Society about her oral history work recalling that city's past, I pulled over to the curb, almost before knowing why I did so, in front of the Kehillath Israel on Harvard Street, almost directly abreast of Irving's Toy and Card Shop. Then and there, the idea popped into my mind of interviewing Ethel Weiss, the card shop's proprietress of more than sixty years (Ethel sold me candy when I was a kid attending Devotion School), as my first attempt to become an oral historian. Ethel (whose story appears in this book) heard my proposal and quickly agreed. Later, I sat with her in her store for a few hours tape-recording in some detail her life story, between the customers and visitors, young and old, who streamed in. Without exception, she treated each of them, and they treated her, with respect and affection.

The intrinsically valuable information Ethel Weiss related to me in that interview about her life in Brookline, and the spirit that flowed between us during and after it, persuaded me to curtail my legal practice, seek smaller and more private quarters, and pursue in some fashion — still without shape — a career as an oral historian.

Within a few weeks, the "fashion" presented itself the form of an idea "to preserve the history of ordinary Brookline citizens of the twentieth century as the world spins out of community and into cyberspace," as I put it rather grandiosely in my program proposal to Brookline Access TV Station Manager Karen Chase in late April, 2000. I think the grandiosity reflected the fragility of my latecoming notion about myself as a historian, so that had Karen thrown cold water on my proposal, I might still be practicing law full time. Instead, Karen — in her enthusiastic and engaging style — said, "That's a great idea!" a response I will remember gratefully forever.

In the ensuing months, I served the internship sensibly required at Brookline Access TV to learn the ropes in front of and behind the camera preliminary to being allowed to produce one's own show. On September 22, 2000, I hosted my first program, interviewing for one hour my good friend and lifelong Brookline resident Bernard "Bunny" Solomon, a well-known politico, businessman, and Northeastern supporter, whose range of friendships and contacts has no equal. Bunny Solomon's wit, story telling ability, and love of Brookline made him an ideal guest to get the show off the ground.

I chose as my next guest a man of much more sober demeanor, the late Charles J. Kickham, Jr, Esq., whose legal abilities I had always admired from a distance. I was delighted to experience a rapport with Charles, first in meeting with him at his office to prepare and then in the actual hourlong TV interview itself, out of which came not only interesting Brookline history, but revealing, even humorous, facts about his personal life as well. Charles' warm expression of satisfaction with the interview further impelled me to believe that the anecdotal method of gathering recent Brookline history was workable and valid. That belief was reinforced by positive comments from people who viewed the show.

Although at that point I had no idea of writing a book, it somehow occurred to me that the contents of the interviews might be written up as a feature-type article in the *Brookline Tab*. Providence once again was smiling on me. Then *Tab* editor Rebecca Lipchitz readily accepted my proposal. She published the stories I submitted in the following year or so, practically without excision or editing, allowing me more and more space. Rebecca's friendship and support catalyzed my dreams, which coalesced over that year into the notion of combining the stories into a book — an idea also supported by several Brookline citizens.

My fellow producer at Brookline Access TV, Dan Berman, asked me to be a guest on his media show in August 2001, in the bright summer days immediately preceding the cataclysm of 9/11. I can do no better than to quote my own words, spontaneously spoken during that interview, to convey how by that time the quest of capturing Brookline's history over the last seventy-five years or so had captured my imagination:

> I do want to preserve our history. It seems to be a gathering force, and I love it. It's something of value that I think I'm doing, or at least I hope I'm doing, and that makes me feel good. Not monetary value, but value for my own town. I love all these people [I'm interviewing]. I talk to them a lot. And just getting to know them has been wonderful. I have a good feeling about all the shows I've done — a warm and comfortable feeling with the people I've interviewed. I try to prepare beforehand, and as it goes along on the program, it's nice to hear their stories.
>
> My hope is to keep going, and I hope the effect it will have is that it will interest people and tell them more about their own town. In a future sense, I want to preserve it. And as time goes on, and we're gone, I want people to know about what the town was. I'm forming in my mind the making of a major project to go with the tercentennial of the town — 1705-2005. Three hundred years is a long time, and Brookline is a remarkable town. It's a unique place, and we have a story to tell. I want to tell the Brookline story not only to us, but also to all those out there.
>
> In writing the *Tab* articles I use whatever writing abilities I do have to give meaning to what the person has talked about. Often, you find that there are various strands of meaning in the interview. But usually there is a particular strand. Like with Michael Dukakis. We all

know about him, he ran for president, and he is a great person. But from what he said, he remembered all the influences in his life, especially his teachers at Baker School and Brookline High School. That says a lot about a person if he can remember everyone who influenced him in the past. When I wrote the article, I made mention of the affectionate way that Mike spoke about all the influential people in his life. I put that strand into the story, which brought life to this person and to those teachers, all of whom are part of Brookline history. I try to take meaning from the people on the programs, and, on my own part, to put it in the article.

Reading my own words, spoken more than three years ago, I now realize that at that point I was beginning to believe that I could fashion an interesting history of Brookline by telling stories about Brookline's plethora of fascinating people from all walks of life, whom I was now interviewing on a regular schedule. At the same time, I was stunned and mystified — as I continue to be — that at age seventy some force beyond myself was moving me away from myself and toward others to do my life's best work.

From that point forward, the idea of writing this book took on a life of its own, evolving as I went along, taking form as an endeavor to cover as many facets of Brookline life as I could, now embodied in the sixteen "books" within this volume. As time went on, the venture progressively captured more and more of my time and interest, drawing from me a focus, intensity, and commitment I had never before known.

How grateful I am that such an idea should have come to me at this relatively advanced stage of life, and that I should have had the opportunity of capturing Brookline's history in this way. If the reader finds something of value and interest in these pages, I will have been able to fulfill my dream of giving something of value back to Brookline and my fellow citizens. It has been a privilege to meet for the first time so many interesting and fascinating people, and to get to know better those people I had known less well previously.

Larry Ruttman
Brookline, Massachusetts
January 20, 2005

ACKNOWLEDGMENTS

I COULD NOT HAVE ACCOMPLISHED the writing of this book without the loyalty, friendship, and exceptional professional talents of Cathy Jenness, who over the last thirty years has aided and abetted me without fail in the practice of law and my literary efforts.

My very special thanks go to Michael Dukakis for writing the foreword and for his encouragement and support all the way — first being one of my early guests, and for making it possible for me to obtain several other guests; for meeting with me in his home the day after Thanksgiving 2004, to provide historical background about Brookline necessary for me to write the historical overview which follows; and for never responding to my many requests for help with a question but always with an immediate yes.

Thanks to Bob Hicks, editor of *Messing About in Boats,* who published my first two stories; Rebecca Lipchitz, former *Brookline Tab* editor, who published many of these stories practically without editing and without space limitations under a title of her invention, *Brookline Then and Now;* and Heidi Masek, my editor at the *Brookline Bulletin.*

I am especially grateful to Karen Chase, former station manager of Brookline Access TV, for enthusiastically encouraging my idea for a show on Brookline history, and Tom Bellotti, present station manager at Brookline Access, and all the other people there who have helped me over the last four years or so in the production of the programs from which these stories are drawn. I want to name some of them: Jamie Traynor, Paul Abrego, Erin Dalbec, Dan Foster, Ed Sweeney, Tracy Chen, and Andy Macbain.

I also wish to thank two of my fellow producers at Brookline Access TV for their support and encouragement from the beginning, Ruth Abrams and Dan Berman. During the first year I was producing my own show, Dan invited me to be a guest on his show, where I heard myself articulating, in answer to Dan's questions, my love of my quest to know more about Brookline's history, fanning the flame of my passion.

Special thanks go to Brookline High School seniors Mariana Folco and Samantha Cheng, whose more than capable help in transcribing many of the TV shows was invaluable, not least of all the transcription of the show on which they appeared together and provided a perspective on Brookline that only such articulate members of the teen generation could give.

Many Brookline citizens encouraged my efforts, and I thank them all. I wish to name a few: Bunny Solomon, Ethel Weiss, Betsy Shure Gross, Owen Carle, Steve Jerome, Ruth Dorfman, Jean Kramer, Sumner Kaplan, Arlene Stern, Timothy Sullivan, Maureen Flynn, Bob Sperber, and Ran Blake.

I must thank Afrika H. Lambe, daughter of acclaimed American tenor Roland Hayes, for going out of her way to provide to me the Bachrach portrait of him which appears in this book, and for telling me the story of how, in 1925, her father was obliged to buy the house in Brookline in which he raised his family and lived for over fifty years — gracing us by his presence — through a white proxy.

I would be remiss not to acknowledge each and every guest who has appeared on my TV show, all of them fascinating, each of them speaking freely, stories about all of whom appear in this book, which would not have been possible without them.

I must acknowledge reference librarian Ben Steinberg, archivist Anne Clark, and the other librarians at the main branch of the Brookline Public Library, whose help was indispensable in preparing the TV shows and in the writing of this book.

Many thanks go to Brookline preservation planner Greer Hardwicke for her aid in uncovering several of the antiquarian photographs and prints which appear in this book, including the dust jacket photograph of Devotion House.

For a novice writer like myself, the encouragement and expertise of people in the literary and publishing field eased the path from idea to reality. My thanks to Justin Kaplan, editor of *Bartlett's Familiar Quotations;* Marshall Smith and Dana Brigham, of Brookline Booksmith; William M. Fowler Jr., director, Massachusetts Historical Society; writer and publisher Ira Wood; publisher Tom Hallock; copy editor Doris Troy; copy editor Barbara Altman; acquisitions editor Edith Craft; and my own publisher, Peter Randall.

Special thanks for easing that path go to longtime friend and publishing guru Eugene R. Bailey, whose wise counsel and encyclopedic knowledge imparted to me unstintingly over several months provided not only a basic education in the fascinating art of the publisher, but also the ability to make this a far better book (whatever may be its merit) than it would otherwise have been. From him I learned the truth of the tenet that every writer needs an editor. Gene Bailey, acting in my behalf in that capacity, saved me from many of my own excesses.

From the first day I met Father Robert J. Drinan as a student at Boston College Law School, he was always supportive. Now as a lifelong friend, his latest encouragement has been in the writing of this volume.

Repetition of an often used maxim tends to dull its meaning, but many a truth remains in words like *A friend in need is a friend indeed.* I think of friends like John Caulfield, Melvin Glusgol, June Johnson Wolff and Richard Wolff, Albert Newell, Paul Sugarman, Steven Hoffman, and my best friend of almost forty-two years, my one-of-a-kind generous Gemini wife, Lois Ruttman.

AN OVERVIEW OF RECENT BROOKLINE HISTORY

FROM A LILY WHITE TOWN OF YANKEES, JEWS, AND IRISH that voted heavily Republican to the richly diverse and polyglot town of today that votes heavily Democratic, is an apt way to describe Brookline's transformation from the years of FDR to the tercentennial year of 2005. With such a profound change in the demographics and politics of the town, Brookline's essential character could have changed too, but that has not been the case. Now as then Brookline demonstrates a commitment to fine public schools and public services. Its citizenry still dynamically participates in the governance of the town, most notably in its representative Town Meeting, but also on the many boards and committees that comprise Brookline government.

There is a trade-off, of course, which is that the increasing expense of living in Brookline has forced out people of moderate means, including seniors, to some extent, but especially public service people, many of whom previously lived in Brookline. The result is that Brookline might now be described as a town comprising an economically and educationally elite diverse population, in which the lack of affordable housing, combined with the lack of developable land on which to build very much more, destines Brookline to retain this elite characteristic. Obviously, something is lost when the policeman or the fireman who works for the town can no longer afford to live in the community, depriving Brookline of the strong sense of personal commitment those people would have if living here.

Put another way, Brookline is ethnically and racially much more diverse but socioeconomically much less diverse — giving up affordability, as it were, for diversity in this shift. Brookline has been fortunate in its geographic location close to the center of burgeoning Boston, able to attract many people in the upper-middle-class income bracket who work in the city of Boston, yet want to send their children to Brookline schools. Generally, these are people who are highly educated, public spirited, and desirous of participating in Brookline governance, much as people who have been here for a longer period of time do.

Not unrelated to this shift is the other major change in Brookline in those years since the FDR era — that being the transformation of Brookline from a heavily Republican enclave — to a Democratic bastion by a margin of perhaps five to one. That itself makes a fascinating story.

Back in those years when Brookline was lily white, Yankees ruled the roost over the Jewish-Irish divide, holding practically all the vital political offices. Brahmin Yankee names like Daniel Tyler, chairman of the Republican Town Committee; Ned Dane, president of the Brookline Trust Company; and Stanton Deland, Esq., were the names one heard, along with other prominent Republicans, such as Hibbard Richter, Richard Allen, the Bowker brothers (Philip and Everett), James Henderson, Owen Carle, and Joseph Silvano, many of whom held political office, some of them being referred to as Swamp Yankees to differentiate them from their Brahmin cohorts.

At or a little before mid-century, Republicans of German descent such as Alan Morse, Benjamin Trustman, and Reuben Lurie became the first Jews to participate in town governance, generally holding moderate, enlightened, and thoughtful views.

In the early 1950s, rent control was the defining issue that metamorphosed Brookline political history, and Sumner Kaplan, who ran on rent control, was the agent of that change. He became the first Democrat in Brookline's history to be elected as a representative in the General Court, and drastically altered the style of electioneering in Brookline.

Sumner Kaplan was a politician in a mold Brookline had never seen before. Growing up in Roxbury, attending Harvard Law School, and then Mass. State (now the University of Massachusetts), he emerged from an Eastern European Jewish family, as opposed to those German Jews who had entered Brookline politics not long previously. Kaplan returned from World War II carrying with him liberal notions of what might be accomplished in the town of Brookline, which magnetized to him younger politicians of similar mind native to Brookline, like Michael Dukakis.

Perhaps the most telling weapon in Sumner Kaplan's political arsenal was his tough-minded approach to campaigning, a style his

Republican opponents disdained to use. Kaplan's campaigning revolution marked the first time ever in Brookline that candidates were out at all the MBTA stops, standing in front of supermarkets for a full afternoon, over and over again, night after night, all day Saturday and Sunday, and ringing doorbells personally in every neighborhood, along with forming precinct organizations. The Republican opposition refused to meet the challenge on its own ground, and looked askance at Kaplan and his campaigners.

Sumner Kaplan's victory, and the carrying of rent control, had a huge impact on the politics of Brookline. It represented the defining difference between the growing Democratic/liberal ethic of one segment of the population and the more conservative beliefs of those citizens who had been living in Brookline for a longer time. There is no question that the political transformation of Brookline from Republican to Democratic grows directly from the fight over rent control, and indirectly from the attendant changes during that period in people's attitudes and philosophy toward allied social issues, such as fair housing and civil rights.

Capitalizing on these events, Sumner's adherents, led by Michael Dukakis, formed a slate to take over the Brookline Democratic Town Committee in 1960, from which perch Dukakis sprang to several terms as state representative, three terms as governor of the Commonwealth of Massachusetts, and finally his nomination as Democratic candidate for president of the United States in 1988.

In this new era of Brookline politics, Sumner Kaplan and Michael Dukakis were followed by other outstanding Brookline Democrats, elected to serve in public office. During a noisy period in the sixties and seventies marked by great activism in civil rights and other social issues, Michael Dukakis, Jack Backman, and Beryl Cohen served together in the General Court. Other Democratic legislators of note were Peter McCormack, James Segel, and John Businger.

Brookline's representative Town Meeting, then and now, is without doubt the most important political institution here. Town Meeting serves one valuable purpose in simply involving many people in the governance of the town in a formal way, and — as in the case of Michael Dukakis and others — giving young people starting out in politics a chance to run for elected office, and to find each other to act in a concerted way.

More important, Town Meeting gives voice and authority to the citizenry of the town, acting as it does as the legislature of Brookline, having the last word on practically every major issue that arises. On those occasions when Town Meeting has voted down proposals that others important in town government supported, sentiment has been expressed that Town Meeting is an anachronism that should be replaced by a mayor or town manager form of government, a sentiment that has never gained much of a foothold against the deeply entrenched feeling among most people in Brookline that Town Meeting preserves democracy and the rights of her citizens to know firsthand what is going on in the governance of their town, and makes it possible to have the final say on all major issues.

Of course, Town Meeting, with its two hundred and forty voices, many times does not move in a straight line, which, combined with the fact that Brookline has no single elected chief executive, causes the grinding effect often associated with the democratic process. This has been alleviated to some extent by giving the board of selectmen appointive authority over many of the heretofore elected boards and commissions, following the recommendations of the well-known Committee on Town Structure and Organization, designed to increase centralization of authority in the board of selectmen. Still, Brookline does not have a particularly strong executive, preferring what might be described as a multi-headed part-time executive, including an appointed professional town administrator, whose day-to-day hands-on expertise has helped Brookline town governance to run more smoothly.

Appropriately, the town administrators have limited themselves to be administrators only, so that it may be said that the dominant influence in the governance of Brookline is the activism and dynamism of the people who run for office and volunteer to participate on the many boards and committees in town government. It must be noted, however, that over a period stretching back before mid century, Brookline has been fortunate to have had only three town administrators, all men of exceptional qualifications: the legendary Arthur O'Shea, his disciple, Richard Leary (legendary in his own right), and the highly competent present town administrator, Richard Kelliher.

There is no question that over the past fifty years, Brookline governance has become more consolidated and centralized. Yet it remains vaguely amorphous, with some lack of accountability and no real center. If any center can be identified, it remains the Town Meeting, together with the greater consolidation of power in the selectmen, town administrator, and town boards. Whatever one might say, the fact is that it works as a democracy. The town continues to be successful in its schools and services, with never a hint of corruption, and those schools and services are still the attraction of the town for those who can afford to live here.

A consistent theme in Brookline — perhaps the most important one in the retention of its essential character — is the quality of its schools. This has been markedly enhanced by the long tenures of three legendary school superintendents: Ernest Caverly, Robert Sperber, and James Walsh. No matter how many changes Brookline has experienced in the last three quarters of a century — whether demographically, ethnically, racially, or in terms of citizens' income — that quality has not waned. Indeed it has waxed, a pillar of strength in the community. There can be no question that students of this writer's generation got a fine education in the Brookline schools, but there is no question that the education youngsters receive now is far better with respect to quality of teaching and range of subjects, reflecting, and going beyond, the national trend in improvement in public education in the United States over the past fifty years. Current statistics at Brookline High School reflect that trend, as well as the richly diverse Brookline demographic. There are students from seventy-five nations, speaking forty-seven languages, having an average SAT score of 1167, with 86 percent of the student body going on to college, according to a recent statistical analysis.

As late as the 1960s, Brookline was heavily a rental community, so much so that Michael Dukakis says he would be "on the doorstep of Town Hall the day the new voter list came out because there would be somewhere between four thousand and five thousand new voters every two years in the town." The rise of the condominium has resulted in much less renting and turnover, providing a new element of stability and a reservoir of younger people whose interest in the schools and Brookline community provide the continuation of broad citizen participation for which our town is known. Another desirable effect of condo development has been a lessening — if not an eradication — of the rabbit warren effect, where family-size units were converted to accommodate overstuffing of tenants, usually students (on one occasion seventeen or so kids were found in one modestly sized apartment).

An argument can be made that Brookline is unique. First there is the form of Brookline's governance and broad citizen participation. Then there is the fact that Brookline, having successfully fought off annexation by Boston in the nineteenth century, remains its own self, although practically surrounded by Boston and very close to its center. Those factors attract many of Boston's elite in many fields to take up residence in Brookline. Adding to Brookline's appeal is that it retains somewhat of a small-town atmosphere. In large part, that may be accounted for by the conscious decision Brookline made a quarter of a century ago to resist the lure of the shopping mall, major credit for which must be given to Brookline's first hired planner, Justin Gray. During a time when there was some thinking that a mall might be constructed on Route 9 between Sumner Road and Chestnut Hill Avenue opposite the Brookline Reservoir, Justin Gray argued that if it was desired to kill Brookline Village and Coolidge Corner as business communities, the way to do so was to develop malls along Route 9. At that time shopping malls were coming into vogue and were surrounding the town.

However, when the first Chestnut Hill Mall was built in Newton, no part reached into Brookline; that mall was zoned out as a result of a deliberate planning decision encouraged and inspired by Justin Gray, relegating Hammond Pond hidden behind Chestnut Hill Mall and its parking lot, while Brookline Reservoir still gleams in the sun along Boylston Street, a victory of beauty over booty. That decision, along with factors such as more affluent people moving into Brookline with more disposable income, Brookline's signal accessibility by public transportation to downtown Boston, and the restoration of Brookline Village, revitalized the Village and Coolidge Corner shopping areas.

It must be said that Brookline Village, the backwater of the town at midcentury, now exists as a charming, restored, and historic shopping area due mainly to the reinstitution of the Riverside Line against bitter opposition from citizens in other areas of Brookline through which that line now runs. Also helpful to the rebirth of the Village as a neighborhood center was the infusion of significant state funds on Michael Dukakis's watch as governor, to accomplish the preservation, refurbishment, and beautification there.

Certainly allied to the exclusion of shopping centers in Brookline has been the choice to retain the low density that gives Brookline its small-town affect. A few transit-oriented exceptions have been made over the years, usually on the edge of town, or in appropriate places within the town, such as Brook House and the recently approved one-hundred-foot-plus laboratory and office building at 2 Brookline Place, both between Brookline Village and the Boston line, and the recently constructed Marriott Hotel on Webster Street in Coolidge Corner.

It is true that Brookline is the only separate community contiguous to or near Boston to be so close and so accessible to the city center by public transportation, a factor contributing in myriad ways to Brookline's success, ranging from the vitality and viability of its business centers, to the ease with which Brookline residents can work in Boston and live in Brookline — and the resulting accretion in Brookline land values.

Consistent with the idea of retaining its small-town atmosphere, Brookline has been jealous in guarding the remaining open space within the very highly developed town. During the craze-to-pave era of the 1960s, when the MDC proposed to construct an inner belt directly through Frederick Law Olmsted's Emerald Necklace, running, in part, between the "farm project" (where Brook House now stands) and the Muddy River all the way to Jamaica Pond, legal maneuverings carrying all the way to the Supreme Judicial Court were employed by Brookline opponents to successfully stop the MDC. Much later in that location, the riverside and adjacent lands were planted, landscaped, and otherwise improved to create the now beautiful stretch of parkland there.

At this writing, efforts are continuing to take advantage of state and federal funds to restore to its formerly pristine state that part of the Emerald Necklace and the Muddy River coursing through it that lies between Brookline's Longwood area and Boston's Riverway, between Park Drive and Boylston Street. Those efforts have so far been confounded by the continuing controversy over the reopening of the Carlton Street Footbridge into the Emerald Necklace.

Generally, however, Brookline has become very sensitive to the importance of open space, paralleling the reawakened environmental ethic nationally, resulting in small but important touches, such as better maintaining existing playgrounds, sanctuaries, and other open-space areas. This sensitivity is most notably captured in *Open Space 2000: An Analysis And Plan For Conservation, Parks and Recreation,* published by the Town of Brookline Conservation Commission in February 2000.

Open Space 2000 continues Brookline's long heritage of preserving open space for present and subsequent generations, whether as the gift of concerned citizens looking ahead or by the town investing in its own future. An example of the former is Larz Anderson Park, given to the town in 1949, in the tradition of Longwood Mall, Linden Square, and other green spaces. In 1961, the town received funds under the will of D. Blakely Hoar to purchase land for a bird sanctuary, resulting in the Hoar Sanctuary.

Acting on its own, the town, in the custom of the acquisition of its public golf course, Putterham Meadows, at the turn of the century, in recent years combined its own funds with state and federal grants to purchase Hall's Pond and Amory Woods Sanctuary.

Many open-space areas are under some degree of public control, including such sizable private tracts as The Country Club and Allandale Farm, the latter locked in by the actions of the Lawrence family as a working farm on beautiful land ten minutes from downtown Boston.

Undoubtedly the most expressive example in Brookline's history relating to the advancing American sensitivity to the importance of historic preservation over the last fifty years is the counterpoint between the demolition of the old town hall in the 1950s and the preservation of the main branch of the Brookline Public Library in the last few years. One has only to walk into the main branch today to realize how the restoration, preservation, and improvement of a classic, beautiful, and soundly constructed old building can more than meet the needs of today. To Brookline's detriment, the functional box that is the Brookline Town Hall of today replaced the solid, classic, three-foot granite-walled, late-nineteenth century town hall, whose vast amounts of space could have been modernized and transformed into a town hall satisfying all of Brookline's present-day needs. This turnabout in the attitude toward preservation is reflected in the private realm as well, most notably, at this writing, in the strenuous efforts to preserve the home of H. H. Richardson, the celebrated nineteenth-century architect who designed Trinity Church in Boston.

No overview of Brookline history since the time of FDR would be complete without mention of Brookline's senior population, once comprising the highest percentage of any city or town in Massachusetts, now somewhat diminished, but still significant. The relatively large amount of senior housing in Brookline has, to some extent, stemmed the flow of the senior population to the South or elsewhere, as has the recent addition of the senior center on Winchester Street, signaling the town's responsiveness to its elder citizens. The sum total of this is that a significant number of wise old heads remain here, counseling the rest of us, still participating in Brookline's governance and still a viable political constituency.

These introductory words are intended to be an overview of recent Brookline history and how the town has changed while retaining its essential character over the last seventy-five years. In reading the stories in this book, it will be found that what has been discussed generally here is fleshed out more specifically and more vividly through the *Voices of Brookline*.

Larry Ruttman
Brookline, Massachusetts
January 27, 2005

BOOK I

SISTERS

Jane Holtz (Kay) and Ellen Holtz (Goodman)
with their parents Jackson and Edith.

ELLEN GOODMAN

*Syndicated Columnist and Author, Pulitzer Prize
Winner, Lifelong Brookline Resident*

ELLEN GOODMAN COMBINES WIT WITH WISDOM to alter our perceptions of the personal and political with an élan and style peculiarly her own. Her acumen was long ago recognized when she was awarded the Pulitzer Prize for Distinguished Commentary in 1980, before she had reached the age of forty, obliterating the long-held notion that wisdom is the province of those advanced in age and experience. How did Ellen become the singular woman she is and how much did her upbringing in Brookline have to do with that? I sought answers to these questions when I was fortunate enough to steal a few moments to interview her in October 2004, amid the engrossing and enervating baseball and political days cascading toward the Red Sox victory and the Kerry defeat. Ellen provided some clues:

Brookline Access TV interview, October 8, 2004.

"My dad [Jackson Holtz] ran for Congress when I was a teenager in what is now the Tenth Congressional District. That was a really remarkable experience for a young person to go through. We are forever being told how hard it is on the families of people in politics. But the other side of the coin is what a wonderful experience it is! It's the opposite of a sheltered childhood. My sister, Jane, and I were exposed at a very young age, partially by my father running, but also because at the dinner table conversation turned to politics. My dad was the sort of person to whom you couldn't just give an opinion; you had to back it up. From a very young age, both of us learned that you had to back up your opinions, which is good training for journalism.

"Then when my father did run for Congress, we saw all parts of the Tenth Congressional District as it was then configured. We went to many different parts of communities that perhaps more-sheltered children had never gone to. It was a terrific, extraordinary experience, even though he lost. It would have been better if he'd won. We couldn't believe he would lose. You know, my father, who would not vote for him? The year he was running for Congress I was thirteen and working the polls at the Runkle School. Someone came up to me, looked me in the face, and said, 'I wouldn't vote for your father if he was the last person on Earth.' I went, 'Oh.' So maybe that too was part of the experience, because in my profession when you tell people what you think, they tell you what they think of what you think. An important part of being an opinion writer is to be able to take criticism, and to speak when you know people are going to disagree with you. So I watched that as a child, and I think I became stronger from it."

It may be that Ellen also gained strength and her feminist resolve from her experience as a slave girl in Brookline: "Nancy Brooks lived in our apartment building on Washington Street. She and my sister [Jane Holtz Kay, preservationist and author of *Lost Boston* and *Asphalt Nation*] were very good friends. They played house, and I had to be the baby going to sleep in the crib. It was their way of dumping me. That happened a lot. My sister got me to play the slave girl in a game called Pirate Ship. That was my other major role in our childhood."

Apparently playing roles came naturally to Ellen, as she sang and danced her way through Radcliffe, just as she has entertained and enlightened us with her column every week of every year for so long now:

"When I was in college, I was in several musical comedies, including *Guys and Dolls.* I wouldn't say that this was a great career option. My parents came to see me in *On The Town* one year. I had the role of the girl on the subway. If you remember, the play is about three sailors in New York. One of my lines was, 'So I says to Mr. Godolfin, I came here to deliver the brassieres, not to model them [dramatically delivered by Ellen on my show in a heavy New York accent]!' My father was in the audience, and he said, 'For this we sent her to Radcliffe?' He enjoyed it tremendously. My father had a great sense of humor. My parents were very engaged and open about our lives. My mother was the type of person who would listen to your problems until you were bored with them. I think my mother was very much that kind of a mother growing up."

It's no joke that performing runs in the blood in the Holtz family. Sister Jane went in for baton twirling, Ellen sang and danced, and Ellen's daughter, Kate, does stand up comedy. Ellen spoke humorously of how Kate has expanded the family's theatrical horizons: "Katie and her husband run a small theater company in Montana. Katie brought a show to Boston called *Broad Comedy.* She has a small feminist comedy troupe. They did the whole college tour, and they're just hilarious. They are truly funny. She does sing and dance. I, on the other hand . . . It's a good thing I have a fallback."

Seeking to catalyze Ellen's thoughts about Brookline's influence on her development, I read to her from her first book, *Turning Points* (1979), which detailed the effect of the changing roles of women on the family. Ellen had said there, "I wanted to live in the same house, go to the same school, and keep the same friends forever." Ellen's response tells us a lot about her professional *modus operandi,* and about Brookline itself:

"When I was a child, I think I was very rooted. One of the things that's been really lucky in my life and career, but one of the things that I've also worked at, is being able to write broadly while maintaining my roots. Most syndicated journalists, most opinion journalists, live in New York or Washington, mostly in Washington.

I'm one of the very few who didn't make that move. I think it keeps you centered in a very different way than if you do go to Washington. If you move to Washington, all the journalists talk only to each other, and they don't know what else is going on in the world. I live at home. I've written for my hometown newspaper for the vast majority of my work life. But you know, it keeps me centered in many ways. It keeps me connected. I believe in being a person of roots, in living in a time and place, and not being one of those people who live in cyberspace, or in some sort of non-connected way."

Having titled the show on which we were appearing *From Community to Cyberspace* with that same idea in mind, I concurred with her thought about keeping connected, remarking that "person to person, face-to-face is one thing, and cyberspace with chat rooms and cell phones is another thing."

Ellen continued, focusing sharply on community: "Obviously I live in cyberspace the way that we all do, and work in it. But you can live widely or you can live deeply, and in many ways I have chosen to live deeply. So there are some wonderful things I have observed, having lived in Brookline my whole life. I have observed these incredible transformations. I mean there are now way more sushi bars than delis in my hometown. I have seen Jack and Marion's become one thing after the other, and now Zathmary's. I've really lived through a very vibrant community, and a community that has become increasingly diverse throughout my life here. I think it's been great to stay in the same place. My mother went to Devotion School and my daughter went to Pierce School. I went to Driscoll and Runkle, then to BHS [Brookline High School] for two years. So we've lived here.

"In some ways Brookline is an even better community now because it is a more diverse community. We have people from so many different cultures and so many different ethnic backgrounds. When I was growing up there were three distinct ethnic groups. There was an upwardly moving middle-class Jewish community, an Irish Catholic community, and there was a Yankee community, which wasn't even in the public school system. Most of the Yankee kids went elsewhere to school. I think that is demographically, statistically true. Now there are way more Asian Americans, African

Americans, spillover academic kids, who are here, coming from immigrant communities from everywhere. There's a whole Russian community. So it has changed tremendously. My daughter went to school with many children from more different backgrounds than I did.

"Brookline still has all those advantages. It's a city suburb. It's a great place for working mothers, working parents, it's so easy in, easy out. The school system is much friendlier for working parents, and it had to be because, again, the community changed. When my daughter was little, there were no after-school programs, there was very little day care, and all the parent-teacher conferences were scheduled when you were at work still. So that has all changed, probably not as much as we might like, but significantly."

Ellen Goodman believes that "values" is what she writes about, and in talking about this, it becomes plain that those values spring from her own "very vibrant community."

"Oh, Larry, I've always had opinions [she laughs]. My editor at the *Globe*, the wonderful late Tom Winship, used to laugh and say he was trying to get my opinions out of the news hole, and that's why he gave me a column. You know, if you've been a reporter for ten years, pretty soon you want to say what you think about what's going on, about what you see, and not just say what the police chief said, what the victim said. I think if I had to put a label over what I write about, the label would be 'values.' In some way or other, everything I write about seems to come out of and reflect back on this word *values*. It is, on the one hand, a kind of cliché that's been grabbed by the right wing and, on the other hand, a real word. It's a word about how we look at the world, what we care about, and what has meaning. I'm in the 'What does it mean?' end of the business. Journalism has two ends: 'What's happening?' and 'What does it mean?' I'm in the 'what it means' end of the business.

"I think my values come from a variety of places. Certainly from family, certainly from community, but also from being a person in the world thinking about what you see and putting it into context. Being a parent as well as being a child produces a sense of values. Paying attention to the things going on around you. It's a complicated question where my values come from. You know, it's like how do you become the person you are? How does your brain take form? But certainly it's also interesting to figure out what things mean. It gives energy to my life and work."

It may be that Ellen has no peer in figuring out for us what things mean across a staggering spectrum of subjects, including parenting, divorce, alternative lifestyles, male-female employment roles, gay marriage, the uses and misuses of cyberspace, and seemingly mundane subjects like summer vacations, gardening, and the natural world around us, all becoming miraculous under her pen. Probably the most striking characteristic of Ellen's commentary is her ability to cast practically any subject in personal terms, an ability that immediately became evident when she, as she puts it, "met the women's movement on the job" more than thirty years ago, that social upheaval being the subject most associated with her then and now:

"I think of the women's movement as literally the movement of women from one life to many lives. I haven't written to or about one segment of women because in our lives most of us have been many different things. Some of us have been at work, some of us at home, we've changed careers, we've been working mothers, we've been working daughters. Life has been quite varied and the changes have really been significant."

Remarking to Ellen that there seems to be a parallel between her work and the work of Studs Terkel because both speak in terms of the ordinary person, the homemaker, the person you don't usually read about, I quoted to Ellen her previous trenchant observation, "Try to find the obituary of a homemaker — there's almost no voice for private lives in the newspaper." Ellen responded:

"I've been very conscious of that. I think part of it is because when I started writing, the women's movement slogan was in the air, and it was a slogan that said 'The personal is political.' In many ways I really wanted to break down the lines, because newspapers, if you remember, were very much segmented. They broke down the news into hard and soft news. They broke down the news into what men were interested in, which was politics, foreign affairs, et cetera. Then what women were interested in was always way back in the women's pages, which was family, furnishings, fashion. I always thought that life didn't stay in these nice little places, and I always wanted to write across the retaining walls and talk about things in a way in which they were both personal and political.

"A lot of the things that have been most important, like families, are personal and political because they entail big questions. Are you going to get child care? Are you going to get health care? Will women have the right to choose? What about the food we eat? What does all that mean? So I spent a lot of time and energy trying to break down those artificial categories. I believe all those personal things do have a political context, and the political ones have a personal context."

Ellen Goodman's "voice for private lives" sang out in duet with her longtime friend Patricia O'Brien in her second original book (as opposed to the several books Ellen has published over the years compiling her many columns), *I Know Just What You Mean: The Power of Friendship In Women's Lives* (2000).

"Patricia and I interviewed many friends. That was a wonderful kind of interviewing to do because, in fact, no one ever asks people about their friendships. We're asked about family, asked about work, but women were rarely asked about this thing that was so crucial to their lives, which was friendship. So when we sat down and did interviews with two people at a time, it was great fun. It was just wonderful! Some of the people we interviewed said they'd never had anyone ask them about their friendships. It was just a wonderful experience for them to get to talk about their lives as friends.

"Pat and I started to write this book because we felt that friendship was the third leg of the stool in life. Freud said that what makes people happy is work and love, but he missed the third leg, which I think is friendship. So we set out to put a spotlight on it and to really talk about friendship, because it is such a sustaining part of women's lives. Your friends may be the one thing that carry you through the whole life cycle. We found that to be really true for the women to whom we talked. Pat and I were pleased that the book was successful, partially because it's nice to have a successful book, but partially because it struck such a chord with the women we spoke to. Friends bought it for each other, so that was a particularly nice part."

Ellen Goodman sounds a clarion call for simplicity, decency, and humor in the foggy cyberspace of today: "Obviously I live in cyberspace in the way that we all live and work in it. I think that a lot of that stuff becomes so much more complicated that we're all spending too much time trying to figure it out. A computer should work like a refrigerator—you open it, it keeps your food cold, and you close it, period. But instead we're all stuck in techno hell, and I think that's true for everybody. Everybody spends so much more time on this stuff than you remotely want to!"

In a similar vein, Ellen, in one of her recent columns, made what she titled *A Call for Cellular Decency*. She humorously expanded on that column: "Haven't you been down the supermarket aisle with somebody beside you calling because they can't make a decision? 'Honey, I'm at the avocados.' My sister, Jane, was next to somebody ranting on a cell phone, and while on the phone that person gave out their number. My sister called that cell phone number and told the person to be quiet [she laughs]. I thought that was another step up."

Indeed, in her amusing yet persistently enlightening style, Ellen Goodman has always been and continues to be in our eyes and ears, exhorting us to take "another step up."

Photo courtesy of Jane Holtz Kay.

JANE HOLTZ KAY

Earth in the Balance

LISTENING TO JANE HOLTZ KAY TALK of her upbringing, education, and the rearing of her own children in Brookline, one can readily understand how she became the renowned and controversial critic that she is, concerning problems of transportation, environment, preservation, architecture, and planning in America.

Jane's father was, of course, Jackson Holtz, who came within a whisker of defeating Laurence Curtis in a famous congressional election here in 1954, at a time when Brookline had been for eons solidly Republican. Jane describes her father as a "great man and a fabulous father," and her household as "very quiet; I don't remember my mother or my father ever raising their voices, but they were very firm and set high standards."

It appears that Jane's father was shrewd both as a politician and as a lawyer: "When I was a high school student," she says, "he

Brookline Access TV interview, January 1, 2001. *Brookline Tab*, August 2, 2001.

would say to me when I came home with three A's and two C's
that if that's the best you can do, okay . . . I knew it wasn't the
best I could do and that it really wasn't okay. There was that kind
of influence. And he was funny and he danced. Both my parents
were great, and I think we [referring to her sister, syndicated *Globe*
columnist Ellen Goodman] were lucky to have them."

Jane's father influenced her to become a writer and to be
socially conscious, she says. "If I didn't know a word, he would
say, 'Go look it up in the dictionary.' He was really a person of
words. His family were German immigrants, and they all learned
elocution when they lived in Boston's West End. Dad was molded
politically when the West End was flattened, and as a lawyer then,
he represented ousted shopkeepers there. It was a political family
culture."

After Radcliffe (magna cum laude in history), Jane worked as
a journalist for the Quincy *Patriot Ledger*, writing obituaries. As
she says, "The women wrote the obituaries and the men went to
the police station." She then became, in turn, an arts reporter, an
architecture critic for the same newspaper, and after that the ball
started rolling and "one thing led to another."

Speaking of her sister, Ellen, she says, "We were close, and
read all the time. I can remember taking a flashlight and a going-
under-the-bedcovers kind of thing because it was after hours."

It almost goes without saying that Brookline schools had a lot
of influence on Jane's career path: "I do remember the assignments
we had at the Driscoll School from Elgie Klukas [later principal of
that school] in the seventh and eighth grades. We had to write an
autobiography. Can you imagine that? I wrote a fifty-page autobiography. I think I had chicken pox then, and nothing else to do.
I mean, I couldn't do it now. I illustrated it, and the title I gave
it was 'Steady Steps.' I mean, how steady can a kid's steps be?"
Modestly spoken, but obviously thirteen-year-old Jane was already
exhibiting the talent that would take her far.

"Miss Klukas also had us present speeches, so I memorized
'Paul Revere's Ride,' and it was one hundred and forty lines. I still
remember that chore. I also had a great American history teacher
at Driscoll in the eighth grade, Mrs. Thompson. She was fabulous."

At Brookline High, Jane exhibited a nascent, but ultimately

unrealized, athleticism: "I remember actually practicing to be a cheerleader—jumping up and hitting the back of my head with my feet and coming down in a split. Then came the day of really going out to be a cheerleader, and I didn't even have the guts or the nerve to go out for it."

Jane was still a schoolgirl when her father first ran for Congress in 1954. Chuck Colson, of Richard Nixon fame, was the manager of the Curtis campaign. Jane makes no accusations of "dirty tricks," but it is a fact that Dad's campaign headquarters was broken into and his campaign brochures disposed of.

More significant, Jane describes that campaign as a "fabulous experience for a kid because the district was so diverse, comprising Mission Hill with the housing projects, Back Bay, Hyde Park, Roslindale, and all of Brookline and Newton." This introduced Jane early to Boston's diversity, and perhaps accounted, in part, for her classic work, *Lost Boston*, published to acclaim in 1980 and updated only a few years ago, in which she laments the loss of and celebrates Boston's rich architecture and landscape.

Of course, that election of 1954, in which Jackson Holtz was the first Democrat to carry Brookline since FDR, presaged the soon-to-come turnover of Brookline from Republican to Democratic, under Sumner Kaplan and later Mike Dukakis.

Most meaningful may be Jane's memories of growing up on Washington Street near the Pierce School, which she describes as "the fun of my childhood. The place was populated with children. My best friend lived downstairs. There was that sense of community, and we would play in the front courtyard, and the back courtyard too, where we would play stickball, and my mother would drop down carrots from the roof for a little snack. It was very much what Jane Jacobs, the great urban theorist, said, that there were 'eyes on the street'. There was always someone there, always someone who could see you. You could walk to the corner and get something. You didn't need a car. My whole mobility going to the Driscoll School was quite exceptional in today's America."

"I was thinking about the story hour — you could just cross the street [to the library] and go to the story hour and sit in that nice little room with everybody — no computers — and there was an intimacy about the whole town, an attachment — it was a really freeing experience to be here. You could mark the ages of your life by the period when you could go to the park alone, or to the playground alone, or when you could walk home from school alone, and stop at Sharaf's on upper Washington Street, and have an ice cream and a root beer and then meander on home. My mother was a stay-at-home mother, but she wasn't a chauffeur — that's America now, but not Brookline, because people can move around pretty well."

Continuing her elegantly eloquent remarks, Jane says, "Things aren't easier now than they were then. There are more cars, and it is a struggle for parking. The composition of the town has changed — someone with our family's income could not live here now. There is a real loss of affordable housing, and that's a real problem. One of the first things I would do if I were God—am I allowed to be God on this program? — is that I would take over Harvard Street in a benign way and fill in the blanks there with dense housing, and even a streetcar line going all the way from Brookline Village up into Brighton, and then you wouldn't need the cars."

"The nineteenth-century city was a very progressive city. It's still the way it works in Europe. The new urbanism is that living densely is the way to do it. There's an article I wanted to write to be called 'The Underground Boarder.' It would call for the town to call every dwelling in town a two-family house. If you had more density, you could have more people and more public transportation and fewer cars. I would have been run out of town on a rail if I wrote that, but it makes a lot of sense."

But Jane sees a lot of good things about Brookline still: "The thing that distinguishes Brookline from Boston," she says, "is that there are good schools—when I raised my own children, we were living on Beacon Hill, and then moved back to Brookline because I wanted my kids to go to Brookline public schools." Showing her love of open space and greenery, in making that move Jane chose to live on Weybridge Lane [near Griggs Park] at the end of a dead end.

Jane talks about Boston's attempt to annex Brookline late in the nineteenth century in *Lost Boston*, as well as on my program. "Boston was providing all these municipal services — water, electricity, streetcars — and everybody wanted to hook onto Boston, and Brookline would have none of it," she says. "Brookline said annexation was a dragon waiting to be slain and maintained its independence, and the rest, as they say, is history."

Jane's preservationist instinct was probably touched off by her experience as a Town Meeting member, when she voted against taking down the old town hall: "At that time I was at Radcliffe, only twenty-one, ran for Town Meeting member and won. I was the youngest Town Meeting member, so my college paper, *The Crimson*, took my picture in front of the old town hall. I wasn't particularly a preservationist then, but I thought it was a fine building, which it was."

My question to Jane about the condos recently built at the Longyear Foundation site at the top of Fisher Hill catalyzed Jane's thoughts about the urban environment, including that of Brookline.

"I have mixed feelings about condo development as long as it maintains some integrity," she says, "because I don't believe we should live so high off the land. The opposite is the tear-downs we see in all these suburbs, and people build these mansions and they're gluttonous — hey max out the SUVs — and fill it with all that stuff at the Costco and come home to their three-car garage. It's the stereotype of the over-consumptive America." These problems are taken up in Jane's latest book, *Asphalt Nation: How the Automobile Took Over America and How We Can Take It Back* (1997).

Warming to her subject, Jane continues: "I consider rail one of the linchpins of a mobile and environmentally sound society. The Europeans use trains, and it is disgraceful that we have such poor train service. Hopefully Acela will accelerate."

Including Brookline in this thought process, Jane says that "I think Brookline is poor about bicycles. I think there could be more bicycling here. It's not a toy, but a means of transportation."

Jane relates Brookline's walkability to the influence of Frederick Law Olmsted, perhaps Brookline's most famous resident of the nineteenth century and the founder of the art of landscape architecture, whose home and office were here at Fairsted, on Warren Street, now administered by the National Park Service. Olmsted designed Boston's Emerald Necklace, Franklin Park, Central Park, Prospect Park in Brooklyn, the Green in front of the Capitol in Washington, D.C., and other public and private projects.

Jane says, "Brookline is a walkable town. All the Olmsted

communities had that same kind of accessibility and intimacy with nature, a sense that greenery is the 'lungs of the city.' I never knew the Olmsted house was within a five-minute walk from my house. At last, I discovered it. People are appreciative of Olmsted, but not always of his values. I'm thinking of the issue over Olmsted's Muddy River Bridge in Brookline connecting to the Emerald Necklace, where some of the neighbors don't want to reconstruct that bridge. That is distressing, and an outrageous example of NIMBYism [*not in my backyard*]. In fact, the one urban lesson is that if there are more 'eyes on the street', those woods that can be a little scary are no longer scary because you have people. That's an Olmsted message too."

Sure, there are problems, but Jane still sees Brookline as having a certain Olmstedian character. "When I was bringing up my kids," she says, "we were right near Griggs Park, which was wonderful, and near to Devotion School too, where there was always a lot going on. I think Brookline is a good town now for many of the same reasons that existed in the nineteenth century when H. H. Richardson [the architect of Trinity Church in Boston] and Olmsted came here to live."

Jane, drawing on her reservoir of historical knowledge, tells an amusing story of Olmsted staying at Richardson's house one night in winter, a story that tells a lot about the difference between Brookline then and now: "It snowed that night, and Olmsted woke up to that snow and, as the story goes, to the sound of plows. All the streets were plowed, and I would assume all the sidewalks as well, probably having something to do with Olmsted coming to live in Brookline. I think about that story a lot because when I was a kid in Brookline, they plowed the sidewalks. During all my life living in Brookline, I would see the kids walking down Park Street after snowstorms — carfree kids — and in some ways, another linchpin of a civilized society is if they can make it a walkable society."

Jane describes Olmsted's Fairsted as "sort of a scaled version of his approach toward the landscape — the slope of the hill and the planting of the rhododendron s— all of that was just the way he had defined it."

I might add to Jane's remarks that Fairsted is right around the corner for any of us here in Brookline; indeed, viewing this combination home and workshop, where Olmsted and his sons after him practiced landscape architecture well into the twentieth century, tells us a lot about the antithesis to the "paving over of America."

As one might expect, Jane Holtz Kay wishes for a return to the principles Frederick Law Olmsted used in his development of Boston's Emerald Necklace (of which Brookline's Muddy River is a part), believing that would be an anodyne to the "asphalt nation," and the sprawl it represents, remembering that before Olmsted came along, the Fens were a fetid and brackish mess. To Jane "it is so relevant that what was there before is what we now call brownfields, a toxic, polluted, and pernicious piece of the earth. Olmsted transformed that whole area into a different ecology, a different way of using the landscape in which each element in the chain [all the way from the Public Garden to Franklin Park] was distinct."

As we know, over the last century, a lot of the Emerald Necklace fell into disrepair, but "there has been a lot of cleaning up in the last ten years," says Jane. "The Boston Parks Department has done a wonderful job, and Olmsted people like Betsy Shure Gross [well known in Brookline for her activities in improving that part of the Emerald Necklace lying between Brookline and Jamaica Plain] have been very active in caring for those kinds of places. I believe landscape architects and planners are the ones who should be doing this work — they are the ones who can say that this is how we should deal with the land, but they can do it only if we have planning that says 'This far and no farther,' because if we continue to sprawl, then what difference does it make if our own front lawns are in good shape?"

So can Brookline retain its character into the future? "Brookline's problem is lack of diversity and lack of affordability," she says. "The town as an island can probably function, but sooner or later, if we don't act as a region and as a global community addressing global warming, the waters will continue to rise, and I have to wonder about somebody living in the Back Bay if the Charles River Dam would break. I paraphrase Thoreau, who said, 'What good is a pleasant piece of turf if you have a despoiled planet?' I think Brookline is good in terms of looking beyond itself, but I think it's a really critical time in our efforts to sustain our town and our earth."

As we concluded the tour de force on which Jane's prolific and versatile mind had taken us, she alluded once again to her Brookline beginnings: "It's a special town, which had a special kind of education when I grew up, and is a model everyplace." Jane herself is the proof of that.

Photo courtesy of Historic New England / SPNEA.

Upland Road in winter around Frederick Law Olmsted's time.

Susan Maze-Rothstein   *Lisa Wong*

SUSAN MAZE-ROTHSTEIN
AND LISA WONG

Two Women of Color Growing up in Brookline

BROOKLINE HAS NOT BEEN IMMUNE to the racial blight that has infected America for three hundred or more years, almost resulting in our dissolution in the Civil War, but on balance Brookline comes off a lot better than most places in the United States, if we listen to Susan Maze-Rothstein and Lisa Wong.

Each of these accomplished women went all the way through the Brookline school system, lived here as a single mom, and has chosen to remain here during her adult years, despite some unpleasant (but formative) experiences as each moved from childhood to maturity. Each of them is now highly successful in her own right: Susan is an administrative appeals law judge in the Department of Industrial Accidents (DIA) and a professor at Northeastern University Law School, where she teaches a first-year required course

---

Brookline Access TV interview, July 20, 2001. *Brookline Tab*, August 23, 2001.

entitled "The Law, Culture, and Difference Community Lawyering Program," and Lisa is the Coolidge Corner branch manager of the Brookline Savings Bank.

Even this brief sketch of their respective backgrounds raises multiple questions about Brookline: What is it like for a woman of color to grow up in Brookline and go through the Brookline school system? Did that help or hinder her development? How have these women managed to succeed so well in the world? Has Brookline been a help or a hinderance in that? Why do they continue to live here? Is Brookline really an enlightened community vis-a-vis race (as we like to think)? What can we do to improve our attitude (official and otherwise) toward racial issues?

To start off, I asked Lisa why she avoided a certain stairwell at Brookline High when she was a freshman there.

"My overall experience in the Brookline school system was positive as I went through Devotion, Baker, and BHS," she says. "As a freshman at BHS there was a particular stairwell where there was always a certain group of children loitering . . . These children were from the Whiskey Point area of Brookline. They would make derogatory comments — racial comments — as I navigated that particular stairwell, things like 'Hey, Chink' or mimicking the Chinese language, and that was very intimidating when you are a new student. So I just learned to avoid the stairwell from that time forward. During the one or two future times that I used that particular stairwell, out of necessity, I just learned to develop a thick skin, and to try and run up those stairs as quickly as I could, and think nothing more of it. It was horrifying when you're thirteen years old."

Susan's first formative experience along these lines was when she was in the kindergarten or first grade at Pierce School, playing house with a small group of children in class:

"They were playing with dolls and I said, 'I want to be the mommy.' One little girl looked at me and said, 'You can't be the mommy.' I said 'Why can't I be the mommy? I want to be the mommy,' and she said, 'You're not the same color as the doll.' And it was at that moment that I looked down at my skin for the first time with an awareness that there must be something about my skin coloration that made this an impossibility. I remember feeling hurt because I couldn't be the mommy. So that was one of my early Brookline school experiences.

"I learned quite a bit about human nature growing up in the projects on Egmont Street, " Susan says, "and I also discovered my athletic talents while living there, not because I was enjoying playing with the kids so much — I learned about those talents running away from children who were trying to whip me with their jump ropes and saying 'Go back to Africa.' They were Irish Catholic project kids. Because we were the first family with any color beyond white that had moved into the project, I was running away from children who were running after me trying to whip me back to Africa and yelling over my shoulder, 'I was here before you.' "I'm part American Indian, and I would run and run, and learned that I was quite quick.

"That was the kind of experience that helped me get an understanding of power relationships — of social dynamics — and to really understand at a very fundamental level that life is not a level playing field.

"However, I also found that when you identify your skills, you can find ways of using them. Actually I drew on that resource all the way through school, because in the eighth grade at Devotion, I became the person who got the award for being the most athletic eighth grader, and at BHS I got the award for being the most athletic female at BHS, having belonged to the gymnastics, track, and diving teams."

Susan's dearly loved and recently deceased mother was white and WASP, later converting to Judaism, a religion Susan now follows. Her father died when Susan was an infant, but his racial mixture of Native American and African American gives Susan a wide spectrum of racial, ethnic, and religious traditions, all of which she keenly appreciates. But as Susan herself notes, her dark skin has resulted in the world seeing her as an African American, from which base she has ventured forth with good and great spirit to help ameliorate the discrimination and inequity that continue to plague our social milieu.

Susan goes on about the experience of her family in the project: "My mother — when she saw how the children were treating us in the project — went to the pastor at St. Aidan's, asking him,

'Could you say in your sermon how important it is for children to treat each other equally, because my kids are being tormented by the kids in the project,' to which he said, 'Kids will be kids,' and he refused to say anything in any of his sermons."

"So with that support, my mother then decided on her own to create little community gardens, because she thought if she could get the kids engaged in something creative, that would change the focus of their attention and they would stop tormenting us. In fact she was successful in getting them very involved in those gardens, and it made our lives a little easier."

"Nonetheless," she says, "during that time, teenage boys in the project tried to run my brother over in a car, and I still would do a lot of running to get away from those kids. It wasn't a very comfortable and embracing childhood."

Lisa's experience, when her family bought a house and moved to South Brookline, where she attended Baker School, was somewhat more comfortable, but it still had racial overtones.

"I remember being aware of the lack of Asians attending Baker School. I remember in third grade there was only one other Asian. I was painfully shy, and that made me even more shy, feeling I couldn't identify with anyone."

But Lisa went on to make friends in heavily Jewish South Brookline, attending several bas mitzvahs. "I was exposed to a different culture as a result of that," she recalls, "which was wonderful."

Susan's diverse cultural and racial background, not to mention the economic and geographical differences from Lisa's situation, made the row Susan had to hoe difficult and daunting, ironically more so after Metco arrived during her Devotion years:

"At the time Metco arrived, I learned very quickly that not only was I not particularly acceptable to my white counterparts because I was too black, but I was also unacceptable to my inner-city Boston counterparts because I was too white, because I spoke the Queen's English, and because I did not have the same body and language mannerisms. So there was a cultural divide on that side as well."

"It was another kind of awakening to find myself in the middle, not fitting in any of these pictures, really."

So did Susan get support from her teachers?

"What support?" Susan asks. "I never had a teacher take an

interest in me as a learner. It could best be characterized as 'civil inattention.' No one attended to me as a learner, several teachers reporting to my mother along the lines that 'She's so bright, but she's just an underachiever,' with a wringing of the hands [Susan demonstrated this on TV]. We don't know why."

So I asked Susan the logical next question: Did she believe that this teacher 'civil inattention' was racial?

"That's an open question. I'd have to say it is a combination of things, as most things in life are. My Jewish-counterpart kids from the Coolidge Corner area were no more embracing than the project kids. All of these children come from somewhere. They come from families. Somehow subtle messages or blatant messages were being transmitted to these children. It was that adult population that actually was teaching in the school system. So I would have to say this, reflecting on the children population — that the adult population probably wasn't far different, so I would think there probably was some race in it."

Susan adds, "Certainly as a child, one hopes that the adults in the system are looking at multiple issues and trying to be as supportive as possible. That was not the experience I had."

Not quite agreeing, but certainly not disagreeing, Lisa says about her teachers, "I wouldn't say that I was completely ignored by them."

Listening to the accounts of Susan and Lisa, one might think that when they got out there on their own, they would leave Brookline. Not so. Both of them remained here, are prospering here, and are bringing up their children here — so I wanted to know why.

When Lisa became pregnant in 1985, she left her parents' home and "found a nice little place," right here in town.

"I think there is a little bit of stubbornness in me that I probably inherited from my father in that if I get myself in a jam from a societal standpoint, I will take care of the problem myself. I will deal with any adversity on my own. I love Brookline, and I was working for the Brookline Savings Bank. They granted me my maternal leave during the time I moved out."

"I now was a mother. I now had to be concerned with certain issues, with the crime rate, with the health of the school system, with day care issues, and Brookline was ideal, absolutely ideal! My daughter Daniella still attends the Brookline school system. She will be a junior at BHS this year."

After a failed first marriage left Susan stranded in New York City with a young child, she too returned to her mother, still living on Egmont Street, to attend Boston College Law School, deciding that, "This would be the best family system I could have as a single parent. Brookline is a walking community. I knew that the schools here have solid academics to offer, and those were very, very important to me as a parent, and as a young person trying to figure out what to do with limited resources. So that's why I came back to Brookline."

Susan, "the underachiever," was a star student at BC Law School, going on to clerk at the Massachusetts Appeals Court (a position reserved for only the most brilliant students), then worked for a few years as a civil litigator, ultimately (at a very young age) becoming a judge, and then a professor at Northeastern University School of Law.

Turning the negatives of her early experiences in Brookline into the positives of today, Susan has become a "bridge" person, exposing first-year law students to the complex relationships among law, diversity, values, and our multicultural American society in an effort to address unmet legal needs within America's diverse society.

"I truly think of myself as a bridge person," she says, "bridging between cultures and bridging between lenses. Each person has her own individual lenses that come from everything that person brings to the table. And because I bring a number of different lenses to the table, it helps me to work across barriers."

Hearing this, I described Susan as a "cultural optometrist," working on issues of social justice, such as one of the projects at Northeastern Law School focusing on predatory lending in minority, immigrant, and low-income communities — the client, in that case, being Boston Community Capital, whose goal, Susan says, was "to uncover the complicated impact of predatory lending on various types of borrowers, so that when they come to the lending table they are not going to get bilked."

Susan says her students, "in doing that, learn tremendous amounts about how law affects people across lines of power, race, and gender."

It seems to me that Susan's bitter experiences here in Brookline could well have led her in other and very negative directions. Can Brookline take credit, at least in part, for Susan becoming the positive and healing person she is? Perhaps, but obviously more has to be done.

Lisa, although a bit more oblique in her remarks, comes to similar conclusions.

"Brookline Savings Bank has been wonderful to me. I try to work very hard in return. I sometimes feel as if I have to work twice as hard because I am female, and other times I feel as if I have to work three times as hard because I am a minority female. And it grows exponentially when I think of every nonconventional personal matter that I have to deal with — I'm Asian, I'm female, I'm a single parent still.

"And there's a certain glass ceiling that may exist at Brookline Savings Bank. It's an unspoken glass ceiling that I'm not certain whether I can rise above. I love my employer. They have been very good for me, but I'm not one to sit quietly, unlike what my parents taught me. I will be brash. I will be loud. I will be a troublemaker, but it feels as if you have to be sometimes, as a minority, as a female, in order to be heard."

After listening to Susan and Lisa, I asked each of them my final question, which is that we often tell ourselves that Brookline is a wonderful community regarding race. Is it or is it not?

Judge and Professor Susan Maze-Rothstein says: "I think it is a work in progress. First of all, I'm very thankful for my life in Brookline, and for my present life in Brookline. Both of my children have gone to the Brookline public schools. But also I'm a very active member of the Diversity Committee in the Driscoll School, and because Brookline thinks so well of itself, it's very unwilling to look at and acknowledge where it needs to do work."

"I'm very hopeful about our new superintendent, Mr. Silverman. He seems to have a strong eye toward issues of diversity. I'm looking forward to dialoguing with him about that. But we certainly still are experiencing the concept of students of color not achieving at the level of their white counterparts. Is that because of some genetic flaw or is that because of the nurturing they receive — or is it because of something that's in

combination together with what is happening in the school setting itself?"

Coolidge Corner branch manager Lisa Wong agrees: "It is a
work in progress," she says. "Brookline is a wonderful place to live
in. It's a melting pot. It's an extremely diverse community. Since all
of us have lived in Brookline, you can definitely see the improvement
in the community from the time we were children until the time we
are adults. There's no place like it, and it can only get better."

It may well be that Susan's face and Lisa's face, too, represent
the America of the future and the Brookline of the future. If that
is so, I say bring it on, that's what America is all about!

Photo by author.

SARAH SMITH

*Chaser of Shakespeares, Mystery Writer, Sister in Crime,
Discoverer of "The Secret History of Brookline"*

PERHAPS ONLY A SISTER IN CRIME LIKE Brookline writer and resident Sarah Smith could be sufficiently steeped in mysterious spheres to be able to unravel both the mystery of who wrote the Shakespeare plays and "The Secret History of Brookline."

In fact, in Sarah's fecund imagination, woven together in sort of a seamless web are Brookline's library and its secret history, life's mysteries in general, and the Shakespeare mystery in particular.

As to life's mysteries, it is no mystery why Sarah is a Sister in Crime. She has written three historical mysteries, *The Vanished Child, The Knowledge of Water,* and *A Citizen of the Country,* the first two of which were named *New York Times* Notable Books of the Year and sold well all around the world. That accounts, in large part, for why Sarah has served as president of the New England

Brookline Access TV interview, December 10, 2003.

chapter of Sisters in Crime, and probably has a lot to do with Sarah's sisterly friendship with another Brookline writer, Linda Barnes, the creator of the Carlotta Carlyle mystery novels.

Obviously, mystery and crime are well entrenched in fair Brookline, and Sarah Smith is more than qualified to unlock "The Secret History of Brookline," as she did under that title in *The Fruitful Branch*, a book published a few years ago by the Brookline Library Foundation, in which twenty-one Brookline authors wrote warmly about their mostly Brookline library experiences.

As Sarah put it there, "The stacks, the old books, are a library's memory and a town's secret history."

But all of us remember that the stacks were off limits to most of us, for reasons romantic and otherwise. So how did Sarah Smith gain admittance? "One day no librarian was available," she says, "and I was told that if I left my library card at the desk — and didn't move any other books — and was careful on the stairs, because they were steep — and watched out for the trolls — I could go downstairs and get my book myself."

That *carte blanche* was tantamount to an air ticket to France for the adventurous and resourceful Sarah. She descended carefully, and by the time she emerged, she had unlocked Brookline's secret history and mined a wealth of nuggets for her 1996 novel about the devastating Paris flood of 1910, *The Knowledge of Water*. Sarah tells us about that:

"The reason we have these books in the stacks about Paris in 1910 is that Brookline was, as it remains, largely a very well-off town, and the Bostonians and Brookline people would go off and take their summer vacations in Europe, often in Paris. Of course, they brought back reminiscences of all of these lovely places they had been, and collected books written by expatriates, later giving them to the library. Around the beginning of the First World War, there were a lot of Americans writing memoirs, writing about what it was like to be in Paris. I read all of them. It was great! Now, I have to write another novel, this one about the first days of World War I in Paris — a mystery, of course!"

Once admitted to the stacks, Sarah discovered the diversity that characterizes Brookline then and now. Its residents have shown their interest in art, decorating, photography, gardening,

automobiles, sports, politics, and much more. As Sarah put it in
"The Secret History of Brookline": "We're political, liberal, rather
distrustful of big government, but strongly Democratic (say the
spines in the stacks). And, from the 1890s on, we have been a
town of strong women who made their political voices heard, from
Minna Hall to Donna Kalikow and Betsy Shure Gross."

Sarah is a lover of diversity, not only in the depths of the
Brookline Public Library, but also in the Brookline Village area
where she lives, and beyond. That love comes naturally to her. She
was raised as an Army brat by parents who originally lived in Brookline but moved on to Wisconsin, New Mexico, Japan, and New
York City. Sarah returned to Boston to attend college. Sarah mysteriously speaks of the diversity in her own neighborhood:

"It's marvelously multicultural. We have Russians, South
Americans, people from Poland, China, and Japan. We have a
block party every year, and the food is so good, and the neighbors
are so good. I love to see the diversity in Brookline, . . . including Pombo, our latest cat. Pombo means "pigeon" in Brazilian
Portuguese. My daughter is married to a Brazilian man. Pombo
is gray, and he has that pigeonlike cat meow, so obviously he was
a pigeon, hence Pombo."

Sarah solved for us the mystery of why it is that so many writers find Brookline a great place to live: "We have one of the
nation's best bookstores," she said, "the Brookline Booksmith,
which was named Bookstore of the Year by the American Book-
sellers Association a couple of years ago. Dana Brigham and the
staff at Brookline Booksmith are wonderful people, and very good
at supporting writers. And then there's the Brookline library, which
I use for a lot of my research. I do research in the newly refurbished main branch on Washington Street. It has an enormous
number of books, some very rare. I find the most marvelous stuff.
So I'm a huge fan of the Brookline Booksmith and the Brookline
library, and so are a lot of my writer friends. The present-day
Brookline library has a long shelf of material relating to Shakespeare; the stacks have more material than some college libraries."

Without doubt that "long shelf" was one of the sparks that
ignited Sarah's investigation into the perennial question of whether,
indeed, William Shakespeare of Stratford-on-Avon was the true

author of the Shakespeare plays. That question is explored in
Sarah's engrossing recent novel, *Chasing Shakespeares*, which takes
us on a romantic trip from Boston to London to seek the answer.
But a strange thing happened along the way, thrusting Sarah
squarely into that controversy for real. At the end of October
2000, when Sarah was touring England publicizing *The Knowledge
of Water*, she spent several days at The British Library researching
Chasing Shakespeares.

Sarah had reached the point in the novel where her hero, Joe
Roper, chasing down the long-held notion that the Earl of Oxford
(Edward de Vere) wrote the Shakespeare plays, visits The British
Library to investigate the Elizabethan writer (and Shakespeare contemporary) Anthony Munday, Oxford's secretary. There Sarah
found a poem attributed to Munday called *The Paine of Pleasure*,
the "last poem in a rather dull volume," she says. "The title was
far from promising. I handed it in unread, then gave way to
twinges of conscience and asked for it back."

At this point Sarah's whodunit deepens: "*The Paine of Pleasure* was way too good to be Munday's. But I didn't have time to
read it. I managed to talk The British Library into Xeroxing it for
me, and got it just before I had to leave to fly back to the United
States."

Sarah was flying into a hurricane: "The wind is whipping, and
the plane is jumping around, and I'm sitting there reading the
poems to take my mind off my immediate demise, and saying,
'This is good, this is really good! This isn't Munday! Don't let
me die! I have to tell someone about this!' "

In this scary atmosphere, Sarah had discovered a poem by
Oxford in a style very much like Shakespeare's. "It was like Shakespeare in a number of distinctive ways," she says, "ways that are
very hard to imitate, like the use of rare words associated with
sports, such as *crank*, *bias*, *dredge*, words that I had never heard
before."

So the obvious question was, Could Oxford be Shakespeare?

"An interesting question," Sarah replies thoughtfully, "and
very difficult to find the answers to. Shakespeare may have worked
for Oxford, Oxford may have been Shakespeare, Shakespeare may
have used Oxford as a potential source in a character. But the

interesting thing about the poem, which I discovered by accident in The British Library, is that it is certainly by Edward de Vere, the Earl of Oxford, and written before the time Shakespeare and Oxford could have known one another, yet remarkably 'Shakespearean.' It's 'Shakespearean' in many sorts of ways that are difficult to mimic, and look forward to some of the characteristic ways in which Shakespeare expressed himself when he started writing poetry many years later. So it's a very exciting poem to add to the whole mix of who wrote the Shakespeare plays and poems."

Sarah talked about Shakespeare's education: "We know that Shakespeare the playwright read over two hundred books, because he quoted them in the plays. Some of these books were very rare. Some were manuscripts. Shakespeare read French, Italian, and Spanish. He wrote a scene in French. He describes details of French and Italian geography. He even describes Dubrovnik! It's easier to explain how Edward de Vere knew these things—he had an education and the kind of opportunities that the ordinary person in Brookline would have now."

Sarah considers herself to be very lucky to have discovered the poem and to be in the midst of the mystery of the Shakespeare authorship. She has offered a paper on the subject, prompting several scholars to study *The Paine of Pleasure*. "The scholars believe me that it's by Oxford," Sarah tells us. "As to whether Oxford was Shakespeare, the most one can say is that the poem looks a lot like the sort of thing Shakespeare would write."

I suggested to Sarah that she might agree that the answer really doesn't matter because we have the plays, that great repository of human understanding, knowledge and enjoyment. Sarah's answer was layered, subtle, mysterious, and elusive, as befits this complex lady.

"I think it does, it matters tremendously. I love Shakespeare because he wrote the plays. I love Shakespeare the playwright, Shakespeare the poet. Because I love him, I want to know more about him, and I want to know the right things about him. I want to know what really is true. Why else does it matter? Because we used to think we knew who Shakespeare was, and he was the poster boy for so many unpleasant things, like British imperialism. And now we don't know who Shakespeare is, but it's a wonderful time not to know. We have big computerized databases that we didn't have even ten years ago. We have access to libraries and library catalogs online. We can read primary materials, and there's so much exciting work getting done from the Elizabethan period, because there's all this new stuff available.

"If we knew tomorrow that William Shakespeare of Stratford didn't write the plays and that the Earl of Oxford, Edward de Vere, did, then we would still know nothing! Obviously, William Shakespeare of Stratford was involved in some way. His name is on the plays, and we don't know why and how this happened. There are more questions than answers. I love anything where there are more questions than answers. It's such an exciting and interesting time to be studying the whole Elizabethan period, which seems now very modern and very full of ambiguities, questions, conspiracies, spies, and terrorists, very twenty-first century. Yes, it matters to me who wrote Shakespeare, because if I knew who wrote Shakespeare, I wouldn't be nearly as interested in this time as I am."

Still chasing, I asked Sarah whom she prefers to be the writer of the Shakespeare plays, William Shakespeare of Stratford or Edward de Vere the Earl of Oxford?

"The only reason I have for preferring the Earl of Oxford is that the mystery case for the Earl of Oxford is so much better," says Sarah. "He has access to everything we'd like Shakespeare the playwright to have access to. He's been to the right places, he knows the right people. For William Shakespeare of Stratford, we cannot prove many of those things, and quite a few of them would have been hard for him to do. So as a mystery writer, I think it's much more likely that Edward de Vere, the Earl of Oxford, did it."

Spoken like a true mystery writer, but I was curious as to Sarah's emotional preference as to who wrote the plays, remarking, "From what I know about your politics and your love of diversity and egalitarianism, I'm suspecting that from an emotional point of view, if the shroud of mystery could be taken away, and it was proved that it was indeed William Shakespeare who did the whole damn thing, you'd like that."

Sarah's answer connected some dots from Elizabethan England to twenty-first century Brookline: "My emotional preference is why the book is called *Chasing Shakespeares* instead of "Chasing

Shakespeare." Everyone has their own Shakespeare, everyone has his own idea of the great man who wrote these wonderful things. That idea inspires them, leads them to find out more. I would love that great man to have been a common man — it gravels me that Edward de Vere was an earl. But there's another Shakespeare in de Vere's story, a Shakespeare created by education as well as genius. If we believe in that Shakespeare, we'll appreciate education more — and our great Brookline schools."

In an hour that passed in a trice, Sarah Smith, her feet always anchored in the Brookline community, had transported me on the wings of her labyrinthine imagination from the deep recesses of the Brookline library to the England of Elizabeth, Shakespeare, and Oxford, deepening my appreciation for the mysteries of life.

Photo by author.

LINDA BARNES

Mystery Writer, Sister in Crime, Brookline Citizen,
Red Sox Aficionado

AS I SIT HERE WRITING THESE WORDS on October 22, 2003, less
than a week after that fateful eighth inning at Yankee Stadium, I
am surprised, yet not so surprised, that the renovations to the
Brookline Public Library, the yet-to-take-place renovations of
Fenway Park (which may or may not at this point include a new
skipper), and the life of a famed mystery writer can be woven
together to tell us a lot about Brookline history in the twentieth
century.

In 2002, when the Brookline Library Foundation produced
The Fruitful Branch, by twenty-one Brookline authors, on literature, libraries, and life, it knew what it was doing when it led off
the volume with two stories by Linda Barnes. The first is entitled
"Reflections on the Library" and the second is "Stealing First," the

Brookline Access TV interview, June 9, 2003. *Brookline Bulletin,* January 15,
2004.

locale of which is Fenway Park, and which entertainingly tells of the solving of a crime there by Carlotta Carlyle, Linda's six-foot-tall redheaded private investigator heroine.

Reading those stories, and the disparate moods created by each of them, convinced me that Linda would be a fascinating person to interview about Brookline and its history.

In the first story, Linda talks of when she was a student teacher at Brookline High, deciding even then that "this was a town in which a parent could raise a child." In describing the library, she writes that later, living in Brookline and writing her novels, there were days during which she needed "the light that filters through the high windows of the fiction room."

As she says about the library: "It is not rushed or hurried or driven by the constant getting and spending of the marketplace. It is a workplace, a sanctuary, a storehouse of our collective knowledge, and a testament to our values."

In "Stealing First," we meet another Linda, this one presciently describing that special feel of Fenway Park: "The gate was jammed as usual, noisy as usual, edgy with the special tension that means the hated Yankees are in town, jacking each game to play-off intensity."

On the show, Linda talked about growing up in tough Detroit. She credits her mother with her love of reading and libraries: "My mother was a first-grade teacher and she was a reading specialist. The thing she did was make sure children read, and so in my house every book was the bible. If it had pages, it was glorious, it was wonderful. It is a debt I can never repay for the way she introduced me to books."

Later Linda student-taught at Brookline High School, and her time there convinced her to make Brookline her home:

"I had a great experience at Brookline High School. I was looking for a drama-teaching job. I still talk to students that I had, and, of course, they were sixteen and I was twenty, and several of them sort of adopted me and I'm still in touch with them. They live all over the country. I did a one-act play with them and the drama teacher at BHS really let me do whatever I wanted to. It was a great and vibrant school."

Linda, whose son is presently a student at Runkle, tells us

as well as anyone can why a young parent chooses Brookline to live in:

"There was a lot of diversity, it was close to Boston, but it had great schools. I had lived in Cambridge; I'm a big public school supporter. I had looked at the Cambridge schools and I thought, nope, I don't think I can do this. I had a close friend who was a professor at Simmons. I was talking to her and she said if you move to Brookline, go to the Runkle school district."

Linda Barnes has written nine Carlotta Carlyle mysteries, the last one *The Big Dig*, published in 2001. She has won many honors, including the Anthony Award for her short story "Lucky Penny" in 1985. Yet it is here in Brookline, with its infrastructure and convenience, that Linda finds the comfort level needed to provide the great world beyond with the fruits of her art, reasons that draw many writers within Brookline's borders. As she said in *The Fruitful Branch*, the staff at the library guides her through the "archival maze," finding her ". . . books on firearms, psychological deviance, and techniques of arson investigation, without once managing to raise the eyebrow of the librarian."

In our interview, Linda expanded on the charms of creating in the library: "It's close enough to my house that I can walk there. Sometimes working alone can be very, very difficult. . . . That's when I can walk down the hill and go to the library. It's a different kind of silence. There are people there and they're all engaged in some sort of pursuit, they're looking for things in books. There's a smell to a library. There is an atmosphere to the library. There is a quality to the light that I find very stimulating and restful at the same time."

Describing the multiplicity of shopping malls in our society, Linda says that she is "very troubled by the fact that . . . we don't have enough money to put into libraries and schools. I think one of the reasons I live in Brookline is because a lot of the people feel that way here." As Linda spoke, I thought with pleasure that to this date (and let's hope always) Brookline has no shopping malls.

Just as Brookline people love libraries and schools, so too do they love baseball, many of us (this writer included) growing up in the shadows of the now extinct Braves Field, and Fenway Park, just as Linda grew up in the shadow of now extinct Tiger Stadium, the

Briggs Stadium of her youth. As she said, "I went to high school within walking distance of Briggs Stadium. I used to cut school and go see the Tigers. Hank Greenberg was, I think, the guy my dad talked about all the time. I grew up with Al Kaline. He was great. Baseball speaks to me."

Suggesting to Linda that perhaps perversely the Red Sox losing is a good thing, because it teaches you how to lose, teaches you to be a man, Linda is not so sure:

"I'm married to someone who grew up as a Cubbies fan, which is just terrible [even more terrible after the 'fan interference' that might have cost the Cubs the pennant]. I'm a little uncertain about my son with this heritage of the Cubs and the Red Sox together. We're teaching our child how to lose at a very young age, which I'm not entirely comfortable with. Every once in a while he goes 'Why, why do we do this? Can't I just be a Yankee fan?' I go, 'No, no you'll be a traitor, you cannot be a Yankee fan.'"

Having done my interview with Linda a few months before the latest Red Sox demise, I am sure that Linda's uncertainty has now reached the acute stage, and perhaps by now her son has become a Yankee fan.

Whether or not that has happened, one thing is for sure: The contiguity of big-league baseball to Brookline, as practiced by the Red Sox, has had an effect on the outlook and personalities of Brookline folks growing up and living here. Of her son, Linda says, "Someday, he'll relax and enjoy baseball," and treat the game's impact as an artist might.

"First of all, it alters time," she says. "A baseball game can last forever, as long as the score is tied, and that's a wonderful concept. It has very firm rules, and yet those rules get pushed and pulled and reshaped through time. It's a game of inches, and the difference between success and failure is so poignant in baseball. You know if the ball had just gone that much farther, if he had not jumped and made that splendid catch, the whole game would be different. So it's like life. How can I say this? Life is very unpredictable. It has rules but it's unpredictable."

Even in peaceful, if not bucolic, Brookline, life can be unpredictable and move in strange ways, as our talk showed. As Linda put it, "A lot of people look at me and the town of

Brookline, and say, 'Crime novels, why do you write crime novels?'
To me it always seems I've had no choice but to write crime novels.
First of all, I grew up in Detroit and that's where I learned about
crime. I have a lot of memories of that. I grew up living next to
a police officer. One of my major memories of my childhood is of
hearing something in the night and my mother coming into my
room and saying, 'Don't go near the window.' God, of course,
nothing could have got me to go to that window faster than that!
There were police sirens and there were cherry flashing lights outside. I watched and I watched. The next morning I heard people
discussing what had happened the night before. The cop that lived
next door to me had shot a teenager to death on our front lawn.
It was a very involved story. At the time our block, which was a
white block, was being 'block-busted.' There were black families
moving in and there were a lot of feelings about this. The white
cop had shot this black teenager who had a tire iron, he was guilty
of carrying a tire iron, and the cop said he thought it was a gun. . . .
I think it was a totally unjustified shooting."

I had my own Brookline story about the unpredictability of
life, in this same vein: "You know this resonates in my own mind
a little bit. I used to live at 26 Gibbs Street, near the corner of
Naples Road in north Brookline. I used to take care of Whitey
Hurwitz's kids when I was eleven or twelve years old. He seemed
like an ordinary guy to me, a businessman or whatever, but apparently on the wrong side of the law. There is a big area where
Naples Road comes into Gibbs Street. It is a wide intersection, and
one night Whitey was shot to death in the middle of that intersection. You can imagine how it was when I woke up the next morning. It was a gang murder in the middle of Brookline, not what
you expect. He must have done something the guys didn't like."

In fact, Linda believes there has been a flowering of the crime
novel genre from the 1980s on, comparable to the thirties and forties in England, and she relates this to the most famous Brookline
citizen of the twentieth century, JFK: "I think it has to do with the
murder of Kennedy. So many people were so taken by those images
and the questions that were asked and not answered. We have a
whole bunch of people who lost a father figure at an early age, and
they are writing about it. I believe that's why we have so many

crime novels right now. Most of the crime novelists I know have some secret death in their past."

Talking closely to Linda for an hour brought out her originality, openness, and humanity.

I say "originality," in that she persistently sought to introduce a female leading lady into the mystery genre and ultimately succeeded: "I felt that I was forging my own path for most of the way," she says. "It's hard to realize now that there were no American women in the detective fiction. Now there are many, but at that time Carlotta was in select company."

Linda's openness and humanity, not to mention generosity, are seen when she talks about her characters as bits and pieces of herself, whether heroes or villains. As she says, "I'm not interested in writing about cardboard characters. I'm not interested in people who represent good or who represent evil. I don't know those people. The people that I know have different facets to their personalities. . . . I don't have evil gangsters. I don't have great policemen, and Carlotta herself is flawed. . . . I think that people's flaws are certainly as interesting as their good points. Those are the things that I like to explore. . . . Carlotta tries to find a way to live in the modern world and that's a challenge. She's trying to raise a child in the modern world and that's a challenge. She's trying to do the right thing when it's not always clear what the right thing is. . . . I frame questions, and when I don't find the answers, I know I'm doing the right thing."

Whether sitting with her Red Sox cap on her head at Fenway Park or with her thinking cap on at the Brookline Public Library, Linda Barnes (or is it Carlotta Carlyle?) is another one of the myriad fascinating and wonderful people who make up the Brookline community.

Photo courtesy of Ruth Shapiro.

From left: Ruth, Bobbi, and Dolly.

THE "FABULOUS" BAKER SISTERS

Dolly and Bobbi, and their
"Sister-in-Blood" Ruth Shapiro

ORDINARILY ONE MIGHT NOT CONJOIN LOCALES and venues with such seemingly disparate connotations as Brookline, Tokyo, Greenwich Village, Brooklyn, the 1939 New York World's Fair, the Catskills, Scullers Jazz Club, Ohabei Shalom, and Kehillath Israel, but one would, to properly convey the fifty-year saga of the "fabulous" Baker Sisters and their "sister" Ruth Shapiro.

Dolly and Bobbi Baker and Ruth Shapiro were all children of the Roaring Twenties. The Baker sisters were born in Greenwich Village and Brooklyn, respectively, and Ruth Shapiro grew up in Brookline, where all now live, separately but together, as it were, near the house on Carlton Street where Ruth grew up and fell in love with show business, a path which led Ruth to becoming a "blood sister" to Dolly and Bobbi. Ruth talked about those long-ago days:

Brookline Access TV interview, January 30, 2004.

"I lived in a big house on Carlton Street. My grandfather built that house, then sold it, and many years later my father bought it back. After I got married and had my own children, my father gave me that house. So I lived there for many years with my children, as I had done before as a teenager. At that time, every Sunday, the performers who were in town, playing the Latin Quarter, the Bradford Roof, and the Mayfair, came to our house for brunch — performers like Jackie Leonard, Jackie Miles, Sophie Tucker, and Harry Richmond. The house is the one at the corner of Carleton and Ivy Streets. I live only three blocks away from there now."

I told Ruth a bit of show business history from my own family — my uncle Max Rutman danced his way around the country on the old Keith Circuit around that same time.

Ruth said she "fell in love with show business because my father, Ralph, had theaters and hotels while I was growing up. I remember that one of his vaudeville theaters was in Providence. I used to go every Saturday and hang around backstage with bandleaders. I remember Tommy Dorsey was performing with Frank Sinatra, who was sort of a skinny, pimply faced kid. I remember asking him, 'Would you go out and get me a sandwich please?' That's how far back I go! And I had a fascination for show business. On the Bradford Roof, my father played all the big stars. I mean there wasn't a big name that didn't come to Boston! The Bradford is now the Tremont House, across from the Wang Center. All the performers were my friends."

Listening to Ruth's account, you'd imagine that her path into show business was easy. Not so! There was more than a little resistance to that, as Ruth explains it:

"When I grew up, a nice Jewish girl from a well-to-do family was not allowed to go to work. And all I wanted to do was go to work. I would get these jobs with agents, and my father would find out and nix it right away. I wasn't allowed to go to work, I couldn't do that. But it's what I wanted to do in my life.

"Finally, when I got divorced, I had to go out and make a living. I went into the record-promotion business. That's when I met Dolly. I was hired to promote a record for her in 1954. A few months later, I met Bobbi. That's how we got together, and

I put them together as the Baker sisters. We've remained very close, like sisters. The other day I was going through a very old file. I came across a piece of paper and I started to laugh, because there it said: '1954, the Baker sisters have adopted me.' And we had *signed in blood*.! And the paper was witnessed by my daughter Susan."

The sanctity of such a covenant would naturally run in Ruth's family; she informed us that "my grandfather, Ben Snider, built what is probably the oldest temple in Brookline, the Ohabei Shalom, and my other grandfather, Joseph Rudnick, built the Kehillath Israel."

Before the powers that be intertwined their three destinies, Dolly and Bobbi sang and danced on stages in and around their native New York City. Dolly's world opened up while singing under Mike Todd's direction at the 1939 World's Fair, and Bobbi later made a comedic splash in the Borscht Belt, acting out a family tradition. In fact, Dolly and Bobbi did sort of a song-and-dance act on my TV show, as they talked about their growing-up years.

Dolly Baker: Dad, Pop, we called him Pop, he was a great trumpet player.

Bobbi Baker: Can I interject one thing? When we were growing up, as a trumpet player he would have to rehearse every day. We had a canary. Our father used to hit such a high note that the canary dropped dead!

DB: It was E above C, he always tried to hit that with the trumpet.

LR: And the canary actually died?

BB: Died. We had to have a funeral in the back of the house in Brooklyn. We made a little hole there, and our father played taps.

DB: Yes, and we cried while eating lamb chops.

LR: Well, I think everyone should know that this is the effect of the Fabulous Baker sisters. If you come to a performance, you're liable to pop off. Or at least liable to turn into a canary.

BB: (Laughs.)

DB: (Laughs.) I broke a glass of wine once in Tokyo.

LR: We'll wait for that. We're going to talk about that later.

DB: Back to the family.

LR: So he played The Palace, right?

DB: Yes, and he used to save all the playbills. Pop played the Palace and Bobbi saved all the playbills.

BB: Yes, I saved every playbill from 1928 to 1932 when The Palace closed. I just sold them all on eBay. I love to shop, and I love to sell, I'm going crazy on eBay. We grew up with Dad playing the acts of all the famous stars for us on the trumpet. So even though we were very young at the time, we knew the acts of all these stars. It was fabulous.

DB: May I . . . ?

BB: Jump in?

DB: Thank you.

LR: If you hear laughter in the background, it's Ruth in the control room laughing. This is a crazy TV show. We've got sounds in the studio and sounds outside the studio.

DB: This is Baker the younger, so she has to get in there.

BB: Yes, well, you're five years older.

DB: Mom was . . .

BB: She was a dancer . . . and her mother was a snake charmer. She had a snake, but the snake was stuck on both ends. She wanted to take precautions!

The "blood" pact formed among Dolly, Bobbi, and Ruth in 1955 prospered for several years, the Baker sisters recording for Mercury, and entertaining in supper clubs and hotels in the United States and Canada. Then dramatic, if not theatrical, events in Dolly's personal life forced upon her a long march to Tokyo: "I had three children with my first husband, who owned French restaurants in New York City. But I still had to go out and work. Things were not that good in the late forties and the fifties. I was working for the guys who owned the clubs in New York, the same clubs that Frank Sinatra and Tony Bennett played. The same thing they did, I did, and I had to. I was working for the mob. One of them was an Irishman, whom I went out with after my husband and I split up. He was a gentleman in every way. He and the girl in his club were knocked off, *boom boom*, and if I had been there that night, I would have been gone too!

"I had three children, and I was in danger. I decided I better get out of town, and along came this fellow. He was from the Far East, and we got together. He was a Portuguese and Philippine mix, a mestizo, an international person, very, very rich. He was very nice to me and my children, so I decided I have nothing left here, I have to get out of this town. He invited me to marry him and go to the Far East. He had homes in Manila, Tokyo, and Hong Kong. I handed Bobbi the key to my apartment in New York, leaving everything behind. I took off in a hurry with my three children. My second husband had a child by his first marriage, who became my stepson. I raised all four children in Tokyo. My husband died in 1977. I became very comfortable living in Japan. I was married to a very wealthy man, living very well, I belonged to all the clubs, including the American Club in Tokyo, had cars, the kids were in the best schools, I was protected. I guess that's the feeling. I could walk anywhere. I could do anything, because there was always someone who spoke Japanese to go along with me. Most of my close friends were Japanese. I didn't go to Japan to sing, I just went there to be a wife, and the mother of these four children."

But talent will out, as the saying goes, and Dolly's talent made her the Toast of Tokyo, winning the award there for Best Female Jazz Singer in 2001. Dolly spoke of how that happened:

"I used to do shows for the clubs, and also for the schools that my children were in, St. Mary's and Sacred Heart. Finally, the Japanese musicians grabbed me and said, Will you do this? Eighteen-piece bands would come along, and I'd be doing a show with them. I'd be singing Dixieland. I got to do everything all over the place, and I was teaching a lot of the Japanese singers. During some shows, I remember thinking, 'Oh, my God, I'm dying here.' But at the end of the show the Japanese gave you such an ovation — and they would throw flowers! The flowers would cover the stage! Bobbi, who was traveling around the world during those years entertaining, once performed in Japan at a huge theater. I went over and there was a thirty-or-forty piece orchestra. At the end of the show, Bobbi got these huge bouquets of flowers. We couldn't even carry all of them home. But that is how the Japanese respected performers."

During those years, Bobbi Baker's comedic and commercial

talents coupled when she and Ruth Shapiro operated the well remembered and fashionable, Bobbi Baker Limited in Chestnut Hill, from 1966 to 1984. During that time, Bobbi tells us, "I would do all the resorts around here. Ruth and I would close the store at six, get in the car, and drive up to Mount Washington, or do a show in Connecticut."

Bobbi's peripatetic life finally exhausted her. Little did she know that the relatively inactive life she then took up would lead directly back to standing in the spotlight once again with Dolly: "I retired about five years ago," she said. "I had been working on cruise ships for about eighteen years, packing my bags, traveling to India, doing a show on the ship, flying to Australia, picking up another ship, doing a show, getting off and flying. This is what my life was. Finally I said, 'I've had it! I am burnt out!' So I got my poodle, and I retired. I came into the twentieth-first century, bought a computer, learned what eBay was, and I started selling. I decided to join the Brookline Senior Center. I wanted to play mah-jong. I met a whole bunch of fun people. I joined Golden Age as well and took bus tours everywhere."

By the time Dolly returned from Tokyo in 2002, taking up her career here once again under Ruth Shapiro's management, Bobbi was well settled into her retirement, little suspecting that soon theatrical lightning would strike again. Bobbi told us about that:

"Ruthie did all the driving, and she would set up a microphone for Dolly, and I would come along once in a while to keep them company. I would sit in the back. It was fun for me to listen to my sister singing. I was so proud of her! One day somebody made a request but Dolly didn't know that song. So she goes, 'Well, my sister is sitting here in the back. Maybe she knows the song — why don't we get her up here?' I had told Dolly, 'I don't want to be in show business! Don't you ever dare ask me to get up! I've had it with show business. I'm burnt out!' They started applauding and you know what, I climbed over the heads of everybody — including the canes and the walkers—to get to that microphone! Because there was something inside of me that wasn't dead yet! I opened my mouth to sing — I hadn't done anything in five years — and it was like somebody had cleared me out, like the nasal passages opened up. I was alive again! I was hooked! So Dolly and I decided to team up. Ruthie had made us team up in the fifties, and now we did it again. Then we went into a studio and recorded a CD. We will be appearing at Scullers to give Ruthie the best birthday present we could think of."

Perhaps the best birthday present of all is that the Fabulous Baker Sisters now put on their revivified act for delighted seniors at the same Brookline Senior Center where only recently Bobbi was sedately shuffling mah-jong tiles, but at other venues too. Bobbi spoke of that: "We entertain in New England at many of the rehab places and retirement homes. Over the holidays, we put on four shows for busloads of people from Connecticut, Massachusetts, and New Hampshire at the Marriott. We were performing for four hundred people. The audiences were fabulous! We're back in the fifties again, riding high now. We have survived!"

Certainly *survival* is the word that most aptly applies to Brookline's large and thriving senior population. It might aptly be said, as well, that setting the bar for those survivalist seniors are the Fabulous Baker Sisters, Dolly and Bobbi, and their "sister" Ruth Shapiro.

Photos by author.

Linda F. Gavin   *Ellen K. Wade*

LINDA F. GAVIN AND ELLEN K. WADE

Brookline Attorneys, Each a Same-Sex Marriage Spouse

BROOKLINE AND NEWTON HAVE BEEN RIVALS on football and other fields for an eon, but on Monday, May 17, 2004 the openness and diversity that characterize both communities were on display for the rest of America, when festive parties were held at Brookline Town Hall and Newton City Hall to celebrate the first day that same-sex marriages could be performed in Massachusetts following the decision the previous fall by the Massachusetts Supreme Judicial Court that not allowing same-sex marriage was unconstitutional. Those celebrations included Linda Gavin and her now spouse psychologist Priscilla Hoffnung in Brookline and Ellen Wade and her now spouse Maureen Brodoff, vice president and general counsel of the National Fire Protection Association, in Newton.

Under the guiding and beneficent hands of Town Clerk Pat Ward in Brookline and Mayor David Cohen in Newton, the

Brookline Access TV interview, July 7, 2004.

governance of each community welcomed the new spouses with smiling faces and open arms, in marked contrast to those in our society who seek to use the issue of same-sex marriage to wedge the electorate apart.

Both Linda and Ellen have recently sat in the right-hand office to mine, Linda at my present office on Cypress Street and Ellen at my previous office in the S. S. Pierce building in Coolidge Corner, for me the word right denoting their geographical location and connoting the correctness of their cause. Indeed, it has been my pleasure to know and interview each of these wonderful women.

Linda and Ellen talked about the nuptials.

Linda: "We had a wedding at Brookline Town Hall. It was wonderful! The staff was lovely. There was a brunch and chamber music and flowers. People were very happy! Everyone we saw was very welcoming."

Ellen: "Mayor David Cohen invited us to be married in his office at Newton City Hall. There was a big party at Newton City Hall afterward to celebrate the day, not just us. There was a big crowd outside, seven hundred to eight hundred people. There were no protesters. The police were ready, measures were taken, but nothing happened. It was wonderful!"

For many years, Linda Gavin has successfully practiced criminal defense in Brookline, residing for a good part of that time with Priscilla in the Washington Square area, assisting in raising Priscilla's son, Aaron, by a prior marriage, since the time the boy was four years old. In recalling that experience, Linda sheds light not only on the quality of Brookline as a community, but also on the quality of nurturing that same-sex couples are able to provide:

"Aaron went to Runkle School, and a few years to Brookline High School. Those were positive experiences for us, especially the interaction with the principal and the teachers at Runkle, as well as the general feeling in the community. There were a lot of little shops in the Washington Square area, village meat markets, fruit stands, and the like. We knew all the shopkeepers and all of them were very accepting. It was really a great place to live, and a great place for Aaron to grow up. He loved it. He participated in the children's theater group in Brookline Village. At Brookline High he was on the wrestling team. He really enjoyed Brookline. Along the way, there was a group of bullies bothering him. Aaron was good about that, he dealt with it. Priscilla wanted to protect him and call the principal to call off the bullies. Aaron had a figurative coronary about that at the tender age of ten! He told his mother that whatever she did, not to do that, and he would deal with it in his own way. And he did. He finally called their bluff and they sat back down. He did quite well!"

Thinking that Aaron must be a pretty normal guy, I asked Linda to tell us what Aaron is doing now: "He's an emergency room physician," she said. "It looks like he'll be getting married next year. He still likes theater, jumping out of planes, and he's really excited about being part of his emergency ward team and getting to fly on a helicopter on rescue missions. All of us continue to have a very good relationship."

Ellen Wade, an accomplished and athletic woman who hails from Corpus Christi, Texas, winner of the Women's Bar Association's Pro Bono Attorney of The Year Award for 2001 in her field of elder law, told a similar story in response to my tongue-in-cheek suggestion that her fifteen-year-old daughter, Kate, must be an underachiever, getting bad grades, not taking part in school activities, and having no male admirers: "Kate is getting great grades, a big softball and volleyball player and has lots of male friends. Kate has been in Newton schools since kindergarten and is a sophomore in high school this year. I can't say enough good things about her experience in the Newton schools. Every step of the way her elementary school principal and her elementary school teachers have been great. Her principal and many of her elementary school teachers showed up at Newton City hall the day we got married to congratulate us and her. It was really nice."

We've never had any bad experiences," she says. "We've been very welcomed by the Newton community. We have wonderful neighbors. Even Little League baseball, a generally male environment, has been welcoming to Kate. I've coached everything I could get Kate to play. In her younger years, I coached Little League for many years, then I coached softball, soccer, basketball, and just about anything else. But it was different from if Maureen and I were heterosexual parents of Kate. We sort of ran interference. Before she started kindergarten, we went to her principal and explained that we were lesbians, that Kate had two mothers, and that we wanted her experience to be positive, to make sure that if problems arose with other kids, we'd know. We wanted people to be alert and aware. We always made sure we addressed the issues, and made sure the teachers knew. On Mother's Day, Kate made two things. And on Father's Day, she made something for her grandfather. Kate's teachers always made sure it turned out well."

Of course, family goes beyond spouses and children, so I asked Ellen and Linda about their respective relationships, and those of Kate and Aaron, with the families as a whole.

Ellen: "All of us go down to Texas; Kate and I go more often than all three of us. My father is down there. In the winter, it's nice down there, no snow! So we spend a fair amount of time there. We just spent a vacation with Maureen's family down on the Cape. All her sisters and her parents were down there. We enjoy each other's family."

Linda: "We get together with Aaron's father, Rob, around social occasions, like Aaron's graduation from medical school and various parties we have had in his honor, such as when he was finishing his residency. When Aaron was growing up, the adults needed to work at it. You need to put the child's needs first. Whatever those difficulties are when people get divorced, the interest of the child becomes the focus of the family. After time, things smooth out, you get along. Once upon a time, Priscilla and Rob were married and the best of friends, and over time, those things came back, even though you aren't necessarily best of friends after the divorce. Over time you find common alleys and pathways. Rob and I always got along, we never had a problem. It's worked out relatively well."

It might be said that the phrase "relatively well" is an understatement for how well Linda and Priscilla, and Ellen and Maureen, have raised Aaron and Kate, respectively, despite the burdens forced upon them by the discriminating status of the law prior to the groundbreaking decision of the Massachusetts Supreme Judicial Court in *Goodridge vs.* the *Department of Public Health*, in which Ellen and Maureen were one of seven couples who participated as plaintiffs. In very real human terms, Linda and Ellen tell of the big difference that decision has made in their lives.

Linda: "For one thing, it's made factual changes. I will be able to get on Priscilla's health care insurance. That will save us six thousand dollars a year. I will be placed on Priscilla's pension, as she's a state employee. It makes a considerable amount of difference both quantitatively and qualitatively. Not only does it feel different, but it has made a difference."

Ellen: "It's made a big difference. Just being able to say you're married is a big thing. Everyone knows what marriage means. And when you describe someone as your partner, it sounds like a business relationship. Now, the marital deduction is available in Massachusetts, but it's still an issue federally, same-sex marriages not being recognized for purposes of Social Security and taxation. I would expect these things to become recognized. It's great for kids to have married parents. I think it will be great for children to be clear that both parents are parents."

Ellen then shared a very personal story of her bout with breast cancer to emphasize the salutary and life-enhancing effects of the SJC decision: "I was diagnosed with breast cancer and had to have surgery. It was frightening having to go to the hospital. Everyone was very respectful of Maureen, and it was clear she would be included. I did have a health care proxy, but even with that in place, Maureen and I weren't married and she was not my spouse. She was really a legal stranger to me, except for the documents in place. It's scary to think what might have happened if we ran into the wrong health care provider, who was not disposed to honor the documents. They might have done that, but it didn't happen. Now we are next of kin. Now there is no problem here in Massachusetts."

Of course, all the returns are not in yet. Less open minds among us are attempting to snuff out the lamp lit by our highest court. Here's betting that the freshening zephyrs that have long characterized the currents in Brookline, Newton, and the Commonwealth of Massachusetts will prevail to the benefit of Linda, Priscilla, and Aaron, and Ellen, Maureen, and Kate, and of all of us.

BOOK II

THE HOLOCAUST

*Holocaust Survivor at Yad Vashem Memorial, Jerusalem
(1973).*

Regina Barshak

Holocaust Survivor, Conscience of Our Community

Edward J. Barshak, Esquire

Lifelong Firebrand Fighter for Civil Rights

DURING THE BITTER YEARS OF WORLD WAR II, when Regina Barshak was hiding out from the French police, who were collaborating with the Nazis in hunting down Jews in the Paris of her native France, and Edward J. Barshak was beginning his emergence from his native Fitchburg to become one of Boston's most respected advocates, one could not reasonably have predicted that some day these two remarkable people would blend their still now separate and significant lives into a marriage of uncommon vitality, interest, and fruition.

My own first view of Eddie Barshak came in 1958 when my first boss, well remembered Brookline attorney and civil rights

Brookline Access TV interview, April 27, 2004.

activist Morris Michelson, enlisted me to serve on the Commission on Law and Social Action of the American Jewish Congress, a venue at which, on many occasions, I was moved by Eddie's passionate pronouncements in favor of the extension of civil rights and liberties in Massachusetts and America. Indeed, six years prior to the Supreme Court's landmark 1963 decision in *Gideon* vs. *Wainwright,* which established the right of indigent defendants to counsel, Edward J. Barshak, Esq., had convinced the Supreme Judicial Court of Massachusetts to establish that right in Massachusetts in the case of [*Ivan*] *Brown* vs. *Commonwealth,* a case brought to Eddie's attention by the American Civil Liberties Union.

From that day to this, Eddie has continued in the same vein, now writing a friend-of-the-court brief for the Boston Bar Association in the case of *Comfort* vs. *Lynn School Committee,* opposing what is perceived to be residential racial segregation in that city, still practicing law full time, trying jury cases, soon to enter his fifty-sixth year of practice.

At the same time, Regina Barshak, the proponent of Brookline's Holocaust Memorial Committee more than twenty years ago, and still serving as its co-chairman, rose from the ashes of war to emigrate to the United States and adopt, since 1959, Brookline as her hometown, where she experienced a rebirth of her faith in humanity, ("I was not aware of the word *faith* when I left France, Regina says), and contributes in many constructive and concrete ways to the Brookline community.

Regina's mother's resourcefulness was the key to Regina's survival at the same time that her parents disappeared into the maw of the Nazi genocide. Regina's mother, Ida, and father, Abraham, were Polish nationals. Arriving in France in the early 1920s, they were never able to surmount French roadblocks to naturalization, although Regina and her brother, Max, both born in France, were French citizens. All of them were living together in the fourth *arrondissement* in central Paris in 1942 after the German occupation.

Max and others warned that a roundup of Jews by the French police was imminent. On the very next day, while Max was out of the apartment, the police came and detained Regina and her parents in a camp a few miles outside the city. As they were led away, Regina recalls that a neighbor yelled after them, "*C'est bien fait pour les juifs*" ("It serves them Jews right.") After three weeks in the camp, Regina's mother came to find out that the roundup was for Jews from other countries, not French Jews (whose turn would come), and went to the French camp commandant, pleading that Regina, born in France and seventeen years old at the time, should be released. Surprisingly, the commandant provided Regina with a release certificate. She left the camp, never again to see her mother and father, although Regina received two postcards from them on their way east, ostensibly to "work," but ultimately to Auschwitz. Displaying the pluck that still characterizes her, Regina went to the local police station near the family's Paris apartment, brazenly demanded the key to the apartment, got it, and returned to the apartment, remaining there alone without food. Within two days the French police appeared again, claiming the apartment was abandoned and demanding possession, which Regina successfully resisted. After another day alone in the apartment, Regina, guessing that Max might have taken refuge with their uncle in hiding in Yerres, a small town outside Paris — and with no way to communicate with Max to find out if her guess was correct — ventured out into the open to make the trip. Fortuitously, Regina's guess was the right guess, and she and Max lived out the war and the Holocaust in hiding in Yerres.

Regina told the story of the pair's emigration to the United States in September 1947: "I was twenty-two years old when I emigrated from France, my native country, after World War II," she said. "I insisted that my younger brother, Max Winder, emigrate with me. Max was a talented violinist and I was a budding French teacher. As Jews, both of us had been evicted from the institutions of learning we had been attending in Paris. Since we lost most of our family and friends to the Nazi and French rage against the Jews of France, and the rest of Europe, our ambition was to leave our native country. However, being admitted into the United States was a long, tedious process. It took almost three years to obtain visas. My brother Max was welcomed into the Cleveland Orchestra, then the Houston Orchestra, and finally the Boston Symphony Orchestra, where he played for twenty-nine years. Max passed away in 1991. It was comforting to me that he and his family lived in Brookline for many years."

As a natural outgrowth of the education of Eddie and Regina's three children in the Brookline school system, Regina early on became involved in various aspects of education in Brookline. From that, it seems, Regina's overarching interest in many facets of Brookline life took wing — to the benefit of all of us.

The Barshaks' first child, Danielle, was born the year the couple came to Brookline in 1959, and Rachelle-Aida and Joel followed soon after in 1961 and 1963, respectively. Regina tells of the good experience her children had in Brookline schools, including the story of what must have been one of the first of her many objections to the voice of authority, exhibiting even then her energetic and continuing practice of the right of free speech in letter, word, and action, which characterizes and defines her, and about which Regina says, "If I didn't have that, I would emigrate somewhere else."

Regina tells us: "Danielle started as a kindergartner at age five. In fact, she was almost put into the first grade but I objected, because she was so small that the difference between her and her comrades would be too great. They had excellent teachers who placed a lot of emphasis on reading and writing. That was a freedom that was different from French schools, where military discipline prevailed. Here, children sat on the floor and it was more like groups socializing, except for a purpose. The teachers were friendly to the children. I'm speaking from the point of view of a former student in France. They did not try to put any authority, horrible discipline, or regimentation on the children. My daughter read very serious material. She has become very literate."

Plainly, Regina's involvement in the education of her children in Brookline reintegrated and energized her faith in people: "Oh yes! There were many people then who were our friends. We had neighbors who were Jewish and non-Jewish. In those years the topic of the Holocaust did not come up. Human destruction was not what people talked about. I sensed that there was a general warmth among Jews and among the diversified community. Brookline feels like a big and varied family, a collection of friends.

We enjoyed the growing variety of people of different backgrounds and origins, as well as the wide scale of age ranges and diversity of professions and interests. We have also enjoyed the excellent school system and sophisticated teachers throughout our children's school lives in Brookline, all the way through Brookline High School."

Regina did much more than mark time with regard to public issues during these early years. She became involved in various aspects of education, joining the League of Women Voters, lobbying successfully for observance of Jewish religious holidays in the Brookline school system, and becoming active in environmental problems and women's reproductive rights issues. Certainly the centerpiece of her public life arose when, in the early 1970s, the world finally recognized the historical significance of the Holocaust. Regina talked about that:

"That was a period in which the subject of the Holocaust began to be broached in a more direct way. Well into the seventies, there was a diffidence among most people, and most survivors sensed it very strongly. But somehow something happened; perhaps it was the literature by historians on the subject, like David Wyman's book, *The Abandonment of the Jews*. Little by little, the Holocaust became more and more discussed. In 1981 a World Gathering of Holocaust Survivors was called in Jerusalem, gathering together survivors from all of the countries to which they had eventually emigrated. Thousands came to the gathering in 1981 in Jerusalem. Elie Wiesel was one of the main speakers. I was one of the very large crowd of approximately fifteen hundred Holocaust survivors. It was there that I met with Serge Klarsfeld, who published a book the size of a telephone book that contained the names of eighty thousand people who were deported from France and killed in such concentration camps as Auschwitz."

After that gathering in Jerusalem, Regina became part of an interviewing team of Brookline Holocaust survivors, for the very station on which I later sat interviewing the Barshaks, Brookline Access TV (BAT). Regina tells us, "At the time, I was part of an interviewing team. We made an appeal for people to volunteer, and I would say that at that time about thirty-two Holocaust survivors lived in Brookline. There were probably more."

"The survivors were interviewed here, on Brookline Access TV. We had interviewers like Laurence Langer [emeritus professor at Simmons College, National Book Award winner, author of *Holocaust Testimonies* and other Holocaust studies], and Stephen Bressler [for many years project coordinator of the Brookline Holocaust Memorial Committee and director of Human Relations/Youth Resources in Brookline]. Steve is a really wonderful human being. He's fully cooperative, fully understanding of the emotional aspects of this unusual subject, full of good ideas and initiatives, and very eloquent on the subject of the Holocaust. It's been a piece of luck as far as I'm concerned to have the kind of person Steve is in town government. Of course, Professor Langer is most eminent in this field."

It is the story of the formation of the Holocaust Memorial Committee that illustrates most forcibly Regina's moral commitment and tenacity. As she relates the story of the committee's formation, it is apparent that it was an idea whose time had come, but which might not have been realized without Regina's initiative.

"Around 1985," she tells us, " I wrote to the town government that there should be a Holocaust memorial committee. My letter was transferred to Brookline's Department of Human Services. My ideas were immediately and enthusiastically approved at a meeting of the board of selectmen. A decision was made that I was to become chairman. I had never been the chairman of anything in my life. I didn't know what to do! In any event, a group was formed to be a committee. In the first two years, eighty-six and eighty-seven, there were public ceremonies of remembrance, one time at the Devotion School and another time at the Brookline Public Library, places where people could come and attend. And they did! I'm also thankful to Brookline Access Television. Every year on the anniversary of Yom Hashoah, Brookline Access TV has put on segments of the interviews as part of the commemoration."

"We also had the hearty assistance of a number of Brooklineites who had served with the U.S. Army in World War II in Europe, some of them having witnessed the horrendous results of the Nazi rage. These brave men came forward. One of those soldiers who had served in Europe, a witness at Dachau, Leon Satenstein, has served with me as co-chair of the Holocaust

Memorial Committee for many years. A remembrance has taken place in Brookline each year since 1985. I have been fortunate to participate in many interviews on the subject of the Holocaust with many elementary school pupils, high schoolers, and college students."

Relating Regina's work in gaining recognition of Jewish holy days as holidays in the Brookline school system to Eddie's work in civil rights and liberties, Regina enthusiastically responded this way: "I married a civil rights lawyer. We want equality of treatment. I am very proud of Eddie. He was my hero from the first day I laid eyes on him. When the Americans came to France, I thought, 'Oh, they are nice!' I am not sorry I came to America."

I wondered aloud whether Eddie Barshak's development as a man and as a lawyer had been affected by marrying an unusual woman like Regina. Eddie agreed that it had. "It's an extra perspective that I wouldn't have if I stayed in Fitchburg and married one of my earlier girlfriends." I persisted, asking Eddie what that extra perspective was.

By now all of us were smiling, as Eddie replied. "Regina just said to me under her breath, in Yiddish, 'Don't answer.' " But Eddie did: "She's not just a Holocaust representative, she's unique. Being unique has rubbed off on me, pleasantly, most of the time."

Surely Eddie's answer, as well as the whole colloquy between Regina and Eddie closing the interview, speaks to the frictions in any marriage, but far more importantly to the powerful dynamic animating the union between Regina Barshak and Edward Barshak, people who together and apart have made a difference.

Photo by author.

ELLSWORTH "AL" ROSEN

Holocaust Educator, Volunteer, Author, and Filmmaker

WHEN TEENAGER ELLSWORTH "AL" ROSEN volunteered his services as an infantryman to the U.S. Army in World War II, he not only marked himself as a member of "the greatest generation," but also set the tone for a lifetime of giving to others, that quality set deeply and permanently in his soul by his experience late in the war, personally, twice, within days, coming upon the effects of Nazi genocide near Dachau in southern Germany.

Many-faceted Al Rosen talked about his ten-year service on the Brookline School Committee, his thirteen years as a trustee of the Brookline Public Library, his literary, film, and professional careers, and his rich family life.

As any writer will attest, getting published is no easy task, but for Al Rosen, success came in a trice, all as a result of wanting to

Brookline Access TV interview, April 21, 2004.

allay his younger daughter's fear of spiders. Al spun a web of his own, telling that story.

"It all started when my younger daughter, Susan, who now works at WGBH, was five years old and said she was afraid of spiders. I said to her, 'Susan, I'll go to the library and we'll get some books on spiders, because you shouldn't be afraid of them.' So I went to the library, and there was nothing for five-year-olds. The books about spiders were much more complicated. So I said to Susan, 'You know what? I'll write a book so that you'll understand all about this.' I was toying around, and wrote a book about spiders in verse, calling it *Spiders are Spinners*. It wasn't a big book, but it was all about the different kinds of spiders, and how they spin, and other ways they trap their prey. I was very friendly at that time with Roy Brown, a neighbor, now gone, who worked at Houghton Mifflin. He said, 'Why don't you send it in? I don't have any influence, but just send it into the science department as a children's book.' A couple of weeks later I got a notice back, 'Great idea! We're going to print the book.' No rejections, no agent, no nothing. To show you how bizarre this is, I found out later that at that time Houghton Mifflin got fifteen hundred or so manuscripts for children's books every year, of which they printed nine or ten, most of them from previously published authors. I was too naïve to know what a good deal this was. It sold for about ten years. Another book, *To Be a Bee*, was also published by Houghton Mifflin. I said, 'Oh, I'm onto a series, so I wrote *A Glance at Ants*, and *To Tattle on Turtles*. As to those, Houghton said, 'We don't do this any more,' so I have a couple of books that were not published as well as the ones that were published."

Al's innovative thinking was also on display when he was appointed to fill an unexpired term on the Brookline School Committee in 1969, during the height of the Vietnam War protests, when he found a solution that allowed Brookline high schoolers, including his older daughter, Joy, to strike yet continue with their schoolwork. Al tells the story:

"Joy was an activist among those Brookline kids who protested the Vietnam War. They wanted to go on strike and be able to devote full time to the protest. I had just been appointed to the school committee, not really knowing the ropes, and up came a hearing on the issue at the high school auditorium. Joy challenged, 'What are you going to do, Dad? We want to strike, and your vote as a member of the school committee is very important.' I was put in a real dilemma. I kind of supported her, but at the same time I was concerned with the kids' studies. After some discussion, I was the one who proposed a compromise along the lines that we would support the strike, but even being on strike the students would still be responsible for their schoolwork. When I came home that night, Joy was not happy, saying, 'What did you do to us? Now I have to study, now I have to be prepared for the exams!' Within a day, the strike had disappeared, so I sort of had the best of both worlds, supporting my daughter at the same time she continued at school. It was fun!"

The sagacity that Al displayed in his leadoff role on the school committee appears to be only one in the panoply of fine character-istics that mark his character, significantly formed on the fields of south Germany as Al and his comrades of the 36th "Texas" Division advanced toward Austria in April 1945, during the closing days of World War II.

Al Rosen, pointing out the appropriateness of our interview being in April 2004, practically fifty-nine years to the day after he and his fellow soldiers started coming across the Nazi concentra-tion camps, observed that at first "we didn't know what we were seeing," sort of a parallel to the world not waking up to the over-riding and overwhelming significance of the Nazi Holocaust in the long arc of human history.

"Between April 8 and May 8 is when the Allies discovered the camps. We had no orders to go liberate the camps. We weren't told the camps existed, and even when we saw them, we didn't know what we were seeing. A profound influence on the rest of my life.

"I had two experiences, which is kind of unusual, because most soldiers did not. We were in the front lines, and we were the first ones chasing the Germans. The first experience had to do with a train, not a camp — a train in the middle of a field. It was guard-ed by some German troops. We had a brief fight, but we solved that problem fairly quickly. In that fight, as I recall, some of the German soldiers were killed, some may have surrendered. It all happened very fast.

"As we advanced, we didn't know what the cars were. They were locked, and we shot off the locks. We knew that there were people inside because as we were approaching, I could hear moans from inside the cars. So we knew that there were people inside. We opened up the doors, and in each car there were prisoners in striped uniforms, prison garb, lying on straw mats, probably a third of them already dead. They hadn't had anything to eat or drink for six days. We didn't know if they were being taken to Dachau, or away from Dachau, which was nearby.

"Of course, I had never heard of Dachau at that time. We didn't know it existed, but we saw these people, and they were all Jews. How do I know? Because I spoke a little Yiddish, and they started speaking with me. I remember one guy who came out of the freight train, speaking in Yiddish to me, saying, 'You are a Jewish soldier.' You can imagine that was a big deal for him. We gave these prisoners the water that we had, chocolate bars, some pieces of clothing. My recollection is that maybe we were in that setting for only about an hour. It was not our job to liberate. Our job was to keep moving on."

A few days later, Al had another experience, perhaps even more haunting: "We saw a camp, a group of barracks surrounded by barbed wire. Coming in, we were fighting the SS guards, who had set fire to the barracks with the people inside. We found out that they were Gypsies. A few of them had been able to get out, and that's how we knew. The most traumatic part of that was that these SS guards didn't surrender, even though this took place a couple of weeks before the end of the war. Germans were surrendering every day. They knew the war was coming to an end. It was that kind of atmosphere."

Al continued, "We didn't take prisoners that day. There were no orders that you're not going to take prisoners, but everybody couldn't stand to see what was happening, especially so close to the end of the war when the Germans could have just walked away.

"So those were two experiences that had a very profound effect on my understanding of what happened, and what we have to do to prevent things like that from happening again."

Asked whether he had "personally accounted for the end of the life of some of the German SS that were doing these things,"

Al replied, "Yes, which isn't a nice thing to admit, I must say. When you're firing at a distance to an amorphous target, that's war, but this was so much closer up, and for a guy who's against the death penalty on principle, it's kind of traumatic. But in that kind of situation, had I been asked if I would do it again, I would have."

Al Rosen's war experiences planted a seed that has grown, and continues to grow, and which can be summed up in a quote of his recently printed: "I felt it was very important that this be told and retold." Al expanded on that idea:

"Well, there are two aspects that I try to communicate about those experiences, not just my experiences, but the importance of the world knowing about the Holocaust. The Holocaust was not just about six million Jews, but about many others whom the Germans killed. There were an estimated eleven million, which included Jehovah's Witnesses, homosexuals, Gypsies, political prisoners, and Communists. The Jews were given special treatment, obviously."

Al continued: "I've done two things that I'm quite proud of in connection with the Holocaust. One, is that I've had a hand in starting Facing History and Ourselves [the now world famous Brookline based organization that teaches tolerance to young people around the world through studies of the Nazi and other genocides]. Up to the 1970s, nobody wanted to talk about the Holocaust, except a few people like me, and nobody wanted to listen if I talked, because it was ancient history.

"Margot Strom, then a Brookline teacher, was very much interested, and came to the school committee at a time when I was either chairman or vice chairman. Margot said she'd like to develop a curriculum on the Holocaust, and that to do so she would need a semester sabbatical. By unanimous vote, the school committee voted taxpayer money, in effect saying, 'Let's do it.' A semester later, Margot came back and said, 'I have a good curriculum, the other social studies teachers would like to be trained in it, and for that we need fifty thousand dollars and a semester of training.' Okay, we'll do fifty thousand dollars.

Margot came back a semester later, saying, 'Other social studies teachers and other communities want to learn about it.' Eventually, seeing that the program was expanding beyond

Brookline's borders, we said, 'The time has come to raise your own money.' Now Facing History and Ourselves is raising ten million, twelve million dollars a year, and it's the most important organization in the United States that teaches about the Holocaust. This is something I had a little part of, and it's something I feel very good about."

In the last few years Al Rosen, approaching eighty, continued his lifelong passion to bring home the meaning and significance of the Holocaust to his fellow men.

"When I retired about ten years ago," he said, "I noticed there were about five hundred films about the Holocaust, in large part telling the important story of the survivors, most of them an hour or an hour and a half long. I thought, 'Let's make a video that is short enough to be shown to kids in one period, still leaving time to have a discussion.' We have now completed the video, which is about American soldiers, like myself, who were involved in the liberation. It's called *Bearing Witness: American Soldiers and the Holocaust*, twenty-one minutes in length, made at a cost of more than one hundred thousand dollars."

Al Rosen, for twenty-three years the assistant director and director of public relations for the Combined Jewish Philanthropies of Greater Boston, and for eight years after that director of the New England Region of the American Friends of the Hebrew University in Israel, used his connections made there, in Brookline, and elsewhere to raise the money.

The film, now in general circulation, forces middle and high school students to think through the tough moral questions related to the Holocaust, work in a similar vein to the work done by Brookline's Facing History and Ourselves. Al spoke of that:

"It did win four first-place awards. We sold quite a number of copies, we've given away a few, and I've had the opportunity to speak to mostly eighth graders and up, and college kids too. The reaction of the kids is particularly interesting. They and their teachers really don't know much about the Holocaust, so it really is an important educational tool. One question that has come up often during the discussion period is, 'Did you want to go to war?' Another question is, 'How did the American public feel about the war?' The kids have the mind-set of the Vietnam and Iraq experiences, and seem to have doubts as to the validity of World War II. When I tell them that I was a volunteer, that many people were volunteering, that people wanted to fight, this is sort of a revelation to them!"

As a youth, Ellsworth "Al" Rosen first volunteered to fight, and if necessary to bring death, to free the world from the Nazi yoke, then spent a lifetime volunteering, so to speak, for *life*, within Brookline and in the greater world, practicing the peculiarly American trait of volunteerism with skill and generosity.

Photo by author.

BARBARA YONA SOIFER

Holocaust Child, Artist, Brookline Activist

She, the most beautiful from her village, with family destroyed, survived. He, remained a skeleton from a family shot and buried alive.
—from *On Living On,* Barbara Soifer, 2004

BROOKLINE IS WELL NOTED for its high level of citizen participation and activism, and over the last several years, perhaps Barbara Yona Soifer, owner and jewelry design artist at The Little Swiss House/Yona Jewelry Design Gallery in Washington Square, is the prime exemplar of that quality. A suggestion of why Barbara gives back so extravagantly to Brookline arises from her public expression a few years ago that she "got involved in Brookline committees and causes because of my historical background. It was second nature to me to be an activist. My father, Emanuel, was in the

Brookline Access TV interview, June 20, 2002.

World War II underground. He saved lives, and was never captured. Several friends from his Ukrainian town had come to
Brookline." Barbara talked about that horrendous Holocaust
history:

"I was born in Belgium, after World War II. My parents met
in Poland after the war. My father was from the Ukraine and my
mother from Poland. During the war, each of them was almost
captured, but each managed to escape. I didn't know all the details
because my mother always tried to protect us. She didn't want my
father to talk about the war. Only a few years ago, I learned the
amazing story about my father's escape from the Ukraine."

Indeed, it is amazing that Emanuel Soifer survived the war,
and then came to settle in Brookline. His family lived in the town
of Zdolbunov. During the German occupation, the family decided to stay and die together; Emanuel, however, chose to run away
with the Cyker brothers. They hid in a swamp for a few weeks.
Emanuel then ventured back into the town. He actually witnessed
his whole family being shot and buried alive, his mother and father,
four brothers and sisters. Shocked, he ran away again, this time
staying away for two weeks, unable to speak. During that time,
Emanuel found out that the name of the Ukrainian collaborator
was Smolka. Wanting to escape, he approached the town once
again, hoping to take the train from the station there, when he was
captured by a Ukrainian guard.

The ensuing events might make a believer of the most jaded
among us. Nearby, in the station, was another Ukrainian "guard,"
who turned out to be a gentleman by the name of Michael Kramer,
in disguise. As Emanuel was arrested, Michael whistled some notes
of the Yom Kippur service. Emanuel whistled back a few notes.
Then Michael Kramer took him away from the arresting guard, saying something like, "I'll take this dirty Jew to the Germans myself."

What Michael actually did was to take him to Romania to hide
from the Germans. Emanuel Soifer hid in hayfields and all manner
of other places in nine countries during the rest of the war.
Sometimes he hid with the Cyker brothers, who later settled and
established themselves in Brookline.

The Cyker family sponsored the Soifers when Barbara's mother, Mala Kanar, decided after the war that America was a better

place to live than Europe. During the war Mala took a false name, Marisha, an Aryan Polish name that translates as Maria or Mary, and false papers too, so she survived. Apparently Mala did not look Jewish. During the war, a Polish nobleman in her village came to Mala's family, telling them they had to escape. At that point, Mala obtained the false papers and made her escape.

Emanuel's retribution came later, during the 1950s, when the Soifer family was living on Fuller Street in Brookline. One day he read in the newspaper that the German Consulate in Boston was looking for information about a suspected war criminal by the name Smolka. Emanuel remembered, of course, and immediately took a streetcar to the consulate, where he testified about his family's fate. His testimony was presented at the Nuremberg Trials and was the key to Smolka's conviction.

Despite Barbara's youthful resistance to her father's instruction in the fine art of Swiss watchmaking and repairing, it might be observed that her altruistic activism stems from the workings of his traditional trade:

"My father was a very lovely man," she says. "He was self-educated and descended from a line of Orthodox Hasidic rabbis in Hungary. During the war he was not able to go to university because he was running from the Germans. But he learned many languages. I believe there is a line of genius on my father's side. In European families, often the trades were passed on generation to generation. In my father's family, when anyone reached the age of ten, that person was asked to take apart a watch. If that person could then put it together, he or she would automatically be in the family watchmaking business. My father said one of his sisters was the best watchmaker in the family.

"When I was around ten years old, he passed on that tradition to me, at the first location of The Little Swiss House at 33 Court Street in Boston. I was asked to work after school, and I wasn't too crazy about that. Like most kids, I wanted to do other things. He made me take apart a pocket watch, and then he had me put it together again. I was bored. I said, 'So what?' I didn't know that it meant a lot. Knowing I didn't want to do that kind of work, my father wisely said he wanted me to come to the store regularly and watch out for stealing. And in watching for stealing — we had never had any stealing — I learned the trade, because I was exposed to all of the comings and goings in my father's store. So many years later, in 1976, long after my parents died, when I was ready to settle down to work, I knew the trade, and all that time I had spent in my father's store paid off."

The sensitivity and subtlety with which Barbara's father eased her into the watchmaking art characterizes the manner in which both of her parents brought her to maturity, better to realize their own dreams, cut short by the Holocaust, gifting Brookline with Barbara's activism and unique artistry.

Barbara spoke of that progression: "I was five when we moved to Brookline. My mother had heard how great the Brookline school system was, so that's what brought us here. I actually went to Brookline High School when the first and second grade was there. I didn't speak a word of English. I spoke French! I was provided with a Canadian French-speaking teacher, but I couldn't understand a word because I spoke Parisian French. Actually, I learned English very quickly, even though there was no English as a Second Language program at that time. For the third grade, I went to Driscoll School, then to Devotion School through the eighth grade, and then to Brookline High School. In 1964, I graduated from BHS as a member of the National Honor Society.

"Many of my classmates were children of Holocaust survivors. What was very characteristic of those parents," she remembers, "was that their children were the fulfillment of all their broken dreams, all the things they could not do. So they invested in their children, giving them the best education, the best of everything. We were referred to as "the gifted class." One of my English teachers at Devotion School was Dorothy Ellis. Later, when she was in her eighties, she told me more about those years.

Miss Ellis was a maiden lady, a real lady, a real teacher in the best sense of the word. She went to Brown University when very few women did [went to college]. Before she passed on, she recalled to me that the biggest problem the teachers had with the Holocaust kids was that they were so smart, it was hard to know what to do with them. So Miss Ellis personally went out and bought, from her own pocket, several copies of *A Midsummer Night's Dream*. There was a much smaller school budget in

Brookline then. We learned the entire play, and we performed it in its entirety at Devotion School. Pretty amazing, because we were just seventh- and eighth-graders! We did a really good job. A lot of the actors were children of Holocaust survivors, a lot of them very smart kids, many of whom went to Ivy League schools. It was because their parents made them study."

Study, and the strands leading from her parents' lives to her own, early on drew Barbara Soifer into the community activism that distinguishes her life today, catalyzed by JFK's assassination:

"Growing up, like many young people then, I was mesmerized by John F. Kennedy's message and charismatic qualities, and became a civil righter in a youth group called United Synagogue Youth at Kehillath Israel. I was devastated on the day JFK died. Within a few days, I and others formed a group that came to be called READ (Reading for Education and Development). All of us wanted to do something, and what I chose was to form a book drive, since there were so many books around my community. I was sixteen when we started, and worked on this book drive during my junior and senior years at Brookline High. Not long after my graduation, we sent seven thousand books down to Rust College in Holly Springs, Mississippi, delivered by the Teamsters Union. It was a huge and wonderful project!"

Barbara's mother and father were gone within a few years after that time, she says, and thinking she "didn't really want to work in the store," there occurred a hiatus in her life, until, magnetized by the spirit and teachings of her parents, as Barbara puts it, she "realized I belonged in the store, so I went back in." Describing The Little Swiss House as the wheel from which the spokes of her community activism come, from that time on Barbara followed the path leading to her creation of Brookline's First Light Festival, the Snowflake Winter Lighting Program, and the organization of the drive for the eighteen-foot, four-sided Washington Square Victorian clock, marking Barbara's beloved Washington Square as a center of Brookline commerce.

Along the way, Barbara has become a vice president of the Brookline Chamber of Commerce, the Brookline Chamber of Commerce Businessperson of the Year 2001, a principal in the Washington Square Merchant's Association, and a vice president of

Brookline Access TV (BAT). There, she created her own show, *Hidden Talents*, discovering people who either live or work in Brookline whose hidden talent is not that person's primary source of income.

Anything can happen, and usually does, when Barbara Soifer looks out to Washington Square from the confines of The Little Swiss House, on the same spot where her mother and father stood so many years earlier.

"When business is quiet, I tend to look out the window and come up with new ideas," Barbara says. "I started to see things that were lacking. It started to become evident to me that there was a correlation between what was going on outside my store and what was possible to happen inside my store, and that is how I started to get involved in the Brookline Chamber of Commerce and in more community events. These community events had a special dynamic that might also help the business community. It was sort of a multifaceted dynamic. If I looked outside my window and I saw that the sidewalks weren't nice, I said to myself, 'I don't see too many people walking. Why aren't they walking? Why don't we have much foot traffic? Maybe if we made it nicer, they would walk here.' So many years ago, we put down whiskey barrels all over Washington Square, and we planted flowers. The idea was that if we improved in a subtle and pleasant way, people might stroll on the white and wide, Parisian-like sidewalks.

"Then we realized that Washington Square was sort of a stepchild. People knew where Coolidge Corner was," she says, "but they didn't know where we were. So we decided to throw street fairs and, in time, that gave Washington Square name recognition. Over the years we have been involved in flower projects, and most recently in a big flower-planting project in Washington Square called the Washington Square Green Thumbs. In 1995, I created the First Light Festival to launch the holiday season, to make the businesses and their windows ready with winter decorations. We put up snowflakes on lanterns all around town, nonsectarian holiday lighting. First Light started in Washington Square under the chamber of commerce. It became a big project, and we had to turn it over to the town. Now we work with the town, and each year it gets bigger and better. It generates money that is given to the town for certain worthy causes. It's a community event. It's just a big party. It's fun! There are lots of projects that I am involved in that improve the community."

Perhaps the best example of how Barbara's activism benefits not only Washington Square, but also the whole of Brookline community, is the erection of the Washington Square Victorian clock in 1994, the fruition of work by Barbara and others in the Washington Square Merchants Association. Barbara tells the story:

"Washington Square needed a landmark. People used to call up and ask, 'Washington where?' At that time the Washington Square Merchants Association had put on street fairs for nine years, renting out sidewalk space to the artists. So we had a quantity of money on hand, we were nonprofit, and our mission statement at the association is that we give back to the community. We found this beautiful clock and put it up. It's the Washington Square clock, it's a wonderful clock! Now if someone calls up for directions, you say, 'We're located before, after, around, or near the clock!'"

"When I was growing up and I was in grammar school," Barbara says, "Brookline was a smaller community, and people stayed longer." She believes the challenge facing Brookline today is to preserve its traditional high level of community participation and activism and to involve its large youthful and diverse population, now generally disengaged and non-voting. Barbara's activist experiences give her a keen perspective on the problem:

"Brookline is logistically blessed, being near world-class educational, medical, business, and cultural institutions, able to draw people who either want to go to them or actually work at them. We are getting some fantastically qualified people who live in Brookline. That's like raw material, a natural resource, and we are foolish if we don't figure out how to meet them and engage with them. Many of those people come, buy property, stay a short time, and flip it over. How does that lend to community spirit? A very tiny percent of those people come out to vote. That's the challenge.

"I have found that if you have a project that is good, you can get people involved, like the Washington Square Green Thumbs. I left some notices around and got all kinds of people who wanted to volunteer to help, either financially or manually, with plantings and physical work. Brand new people! I believe that the issue of involvement in the community is not so much a function of longevity in the town as it is that the project needs to be stimulating and encompassing. We have to get that dynamic going! It is the responsibility of the people who have the ability to stimulate that kind of enthusiasm. I can do it because I've been doing it since I was a kid, I was sort of trained for it, and I like it. There are other people who can do it. There's a lot of potential in Brookline. I think there are wonderful people living here. We need to get them hooked up. Brookline is wonderful. I think it's the hub of the wheel. It's from there we get so much inspiration. There's a lot of potential in this town, and I encourage everyone to try to get involved."

Observing Brookline, and posing the major challenge that it faces in the future, from a historical and family perspective that stretches back to the Holocaust and forward to the present, Barbara Soifer has placed her "green thumb" squarely on the dilemma, the resolution of which will determine whether Brookline remains the special town it has been for so long.

MARGOT STERN STROM

Executive Director of Facing History and Ourselves

MARTIN SLEEPER

Associate Director of Facing History and Ourselves

"FACING HISTORY IS A BROOKLINE STORY of which Brookline can be very proud — really a program that was started in two Brookline classrooms by two master teachers," said Marty Sleeper, associate director and senior director of the New England Region of Facing History and Ourselves (and previously for twenty-one years principal of Runkle School from 1979 to 2000).

Indeed, Facing History is a fantastic Brookline story of a community of educators and communicators working right here on Hurd Road in Brookline, using all the techniques of pedagogy, including cyberspace, to get its message to millions of people here and abroad. These committed folks use the history of the Holocaust and other genocidal events in an interactive way among

Brookline Access TV interview, June 13, 2001. *Brookline Tab*, July 19, 2001 teachers, students, parents, and members of the community to get youngsters to think dynamically about issues of violence, discrimination, and categorizing of people, so that different everyday choices are made. In this way, lives are changed, as students think about these issues critically with regard to the present and future conduct of their own lives, so that, hopefully, they will act differently from how they might have done, thus reducing violence and discrimination in our society.

The two master teachers of whom Marty speaks are Margot Stern Strom, now the executive director of Facing History, and William Parsons, both eighth-grade social studies teachers back in 1976 when Facing History got off the ground, Margot at Runkle and Bill Parsons at Lincoln School. Marty tells us, "They worked with a terrific director of social studies, Hank Zabierek — and all of them worked under the guidance and sponsorship of a wonderful superintendent of schools, Bob Sperber — and with their vision and their idea of what could come about, they put together a program that is now educating students and teachers all over this country and in Europe."

Marty was right there on the ground floor too, since around that time, he says, he came in to teach seventh- and eighth-grade social studies at the Baker School. "I was not there long. When Hank Zabierek said to me that one of the things we are going to ask you to do and going to train you to do — it was recognized from the outset in Facing History how important teacher training was in order to do this work — is to teach a curriculum called Facing History. It's going to be part of eighth-grade social studies, and its basic content is teaching the Holocaust. It's a piece of history that needs to be taught."

Marty goes on: "I was fascinated, interested, and in all honesty I have to say I was also hesitant and a bit timid, because I didn't know a lot about the Holocaust. In the 1970s, the Holocaust was not taught in schools and universities, and I wondered how I and other teachers would be able to really engage students in thinking about the Holocaust in relation to their own lives, and not simply as a distant, albeit awful, event in history . . . How was I going to get my students to see the real significance of this history, and that it encompassed issues about human behavior that really are the same issues with which they were grappling on a daily basis, such as peer pressure, categorizing, and discrimination? Those were the questions I had to face as one of the first group of teachers trained in Facing History."

I was interested to know how Marty overcame his timidity and hesitancy, and his answer shows us how Facing History, now twenty-five years old, has trained thirteen thousand educators to teach Facing History to one million students in this country and abroad.

"The first thing is to teach the teachers the history," Marty tells us. "That is done by working with scholars like Larry Langer, Larry Fuchs, and Paul Bookbinder, all recognized Holocaust experts. That, along with listening to the testimony of Holocaust survivors gives Facing History teachers the historical background they need."

Marty also was taught the methodology of how this subject is presented to kids, and "how to get kids to become engaged with this material and how it relates to their own lives," he says.

Perhaps most important in training a teacher for this job is to get each teacher to think about himself or herself. As Marty says, "It was important to examine my own feelings about the Holocaust and the choices people made before that event, with times in my own life when I might have been a bystander rather than participating, or taking a stand, or when I might have succumbed to peer pressure rather than to think through a choice."

Thus, Marty faced himself and history, emboldening him to teach youngsters to face history and themselves.

With this training, Marty's hesitancy soon ended. Breakthroughs came during his first year of teaching Facing History at Baker School. One such event was when a "survivor spoke and the kids would not leave when the period ended — the class went on for ten minutes." Another moment was, as Marty tells it, "walking into a classroom in which we were deep into the subject of scapegoating, and how that can lead to violence, and also discussing the danger of judging a person by that person's religion. Three kids were gathered around and taunting a student who was having difficulty learning, and a fight was breaking out. I stopped the kids and told them that you have to stop what you are doing, you have to think about this. They did, and the kids started to make connections between the history and their own lives!"

So what really happened back there around 1976 to get Facing History started, and how and why did such a landmark program go forward here in Brookline? Was it by serendipity or was it something deep in Brookline's soil?

"It really came about through Dr. Sperber," Marty says, "and his belief that the Holocaust is a piece of history that should be addressed. He went to Hank Zabierek, and asked 'Do we teach this?' The answer came back 'no.' Then Dr. Sperber said that 'we should.' This resulted in certain teachers, Margot Stern Strom and Bill Parsons among them, going to a conference then taking place at Bentley College on Holocaust scholarship. Margot and Bill came back energized and said, 'We need to teach this history as part of a Brookline education, not as an add-on, not an elective, but fully integrated into the Brookline curriculum.' "

Marty goes on: "Dr. Sperber agreed, and it was put to the school committee, who took a courageous stand, agreeing readily that the Holocaust should be taught as part of the core curriculum in eighth-grade social studies in all Brookline schools. It was also recognized that this was an important step, requiring preparation not only in the schools but by outreach into the community as well. Also a decision was made that no teacher would teach Facing History unless trained to teach it. In fact, it used to be a condition of employment to be an eighth-grade teacher in Brookline that you had taken an institute in Facing History, since it was recognized that without that training this subject could be mistaught, and thus the ability to teach it had to be built into the professional development of Brookline teachers.

"It was also recognized that education in the community was required — letters were sent to parents inviting them to a parent meeting to tell about the teaching of Facing History, and to advise that the teacher was always available about the concerns and fears students might have as a result of the subject being taught.

"A six-to-eight week adult education course also was started, mirroring what was taught in the classroom.

"This was a community endeavor supported by the superintendent of schools and the school committee as a way of engaging the community — that was a courageous decision, a lighthouse decision in terms of forming an educational model for other systems around the country."

Marty Sleeper thinks it was no accident that all of this happened right here in Brookline: "The reason is that Brookline is an enlightened community, quite apart from the fact that Brookline has a large Jewish community, and that the main subject to be taught was the Holocaust. Facing History got off the ground in Brookline because it's a community, it's a school system, it's a leadership that really values the notion of training kids for participation and for citizenship. The whole Brookline community really understands what education is all about."

This is underscored by the make-up of the diverse and courageous school committee that beamed its bright light and voiced its unanimous votes on this innovative curriculum back in 1975 and 1976. Its members were Ann Wacker, John Connorton, Brian Conry, Viola Pinanski, Joseph Robinson, Ellsworth "Al" Rosen, Natalie Zuckerman, Jacques Dronsick, Roger Stern, and Barbara Senecal.

Marty speaks admiringly of Executive Director Margot Stern Strom, calling her "an inspiration in terms of the whole vision of Facing History." He tells of Margot's Memphis upbringing, where early on she discovered that the word *colored* in front of a water fountain did not refer to the color of the water. Perhaps that childhood discovery was the beginning of the end of any bystander role for Margot and the start of her development into the passionate and groundbreaking educator she is now.

In answer to my question whether Facing History can be used to change human nature for the better, Marty gave a hopeful answer: "If democracy is going to continue, we have to give children a sense that history is not inevitable — that terrible things that happened in the past, happened as a result of little choices made or not made — a sense of thinking about participating, by which I mean choosing to participate, to step in and made a choice, and that the best choices are thoughtful. In that way, democracy can go on."

Indeed, that is what Facing History is all about. Many of us can recall when history was taught by names and dates, coming

alive for some but falling flat on its face with others. Facing
History causes kids to think, to find "a civic voice" (in the words
of Harvard's Michael Sandel) — that is, in a way that leads to "justice for all people." As Marty says, "History is choice. To exercise
that civic voice, to make those choices, can make a difference."

This ability of Facing History to relate the Holocaust and
other genocidal events, such as what happened in South Africa, the
Manifest Destiny doctrine invoked in our own westward expansion,
and the eradication of whole populations around the world in the
twentieth century, to schoolyard pranks and prejudices is to show
youngsters that "you can participate in your own world. Those
opportunities are all around you, but it does require a certain civic
voice, a certain courage, a certain kind of thinking and judgment."

Now Facing History will come full circle, to be taught as a
senior elective at Brookline High School under the auspices of the
21st Century Fund for the endowment of Brookline High School,
the brainchild of the current BHS headmaster, Bob Weintraub.

"Dr. Weintraub has had the idea of endowing BHS in important ways," Marty tells us. "As part of that, Dr. Weintraub and others in his group have seen Facing History as a Brookline program
that really has something to offer BHS, so what we're planning is
a senior elective course at BHS in which individual students will
take a Facing History course. We want the students to think about
what this means for their diverse communities, and ways in which
there can be a community-service component of the course. The
students will not only be learning Facing History, but also finding
ways of going out into the community to mentor others and work
in agencies. Doing this, high school seniors will be able to see how
they can make a difference. Facing History has this power to bring
all that together to maximize students' education. We see it as a
way in which Brookline is growing along with Facing History."

My response to Marty was natural enough — that going out
into the community to participate in civics is really social studies
coming alive. I also thought to myself that in the past, Facing
History broke new ground here in Brookline by teaching kids to
relate history to their own present to change future choices, and
will again be breaking new ground in Brookline by sending out the
diverse student body at BHS into their various communities to help

others make the difference that Facing History has demonstrated can be made.

It may be true, as Marty Sleeper says, that Facing History And Ourselves "is the natural outgrowth of Brookline's traditional and deep respect for education," and that this is a story of which "Brookline can be very proud," but Brookline knows that Facing History has been on its own for a long time now, and that our pride is not only reflected in our own image, but also shines on Facing History in its own right, which Marty says is "a story that hasn't ended. There is a lot to do in this world, a lot of challenges, for which Facing History needs support."

BOOK III

IMMIGRANTS

Photo by author.

Photo by author.

DR. WOLFGANG KETTERLE

Physicist from Germany, Nobel Prize Winner,
Brookline Resident

IN BROOKLINE, YOUR NEXT-DOOR NEIGHBOR may be a Nobel laureate. Take, for example, Wolfgang Ketterle (Physics, 2001), who plies almost daily between his home in Brookline and his office at MIT, where his work on the observation of Bose-Einstein Condensation (BEC) in an atomic gas (a new form of matter predicted by Albert Einstein in 1925) won the Nobel Prize together with E. A. Cornell and C. E. Wieman.

Other Nobel laureates, who now or recently have lived in Brookline are Saul Bellow, who gave us *Herzog, The Dean's December, More Die of Heartbreak,* and other novels (Literature, 1976); Sheldon Glashow (Physics, 1979); Eric Chivian (Peace, 1985); Norman F. Ramsey, Jr. (Physics, 1989); Jerome I. Friedman (Physics, 1990); and Derek Walcott (Literature, 1992).

Brookline Access TV interview, August 26, 2003.

Lest one think that Dr. Wolfgang Ketterle's mastery of the seemingly arcane science of physics marks him as a man unable or disinclined to speak to us clearly about his field in particular and life in general, one might think again.

Any such notion I might have had along those lines was quickly dispelled once Wolfgang began speaking about his youth in Heidelberg (at whose famous university, founded in 1386, he first studied physics) and the start of his scientific inquiries under the encouraging guidance of his parents:

"My mother and father were always active. My father worked long hours, and when he came home, he maintained the house or worked in the backyard. The atmosphere was that if you work hard toward something, and finish something, you can be proud. My father always took time for vacation, so for me it was a balance between working hard on something and enjoying it, and relaxing.

"My father went to the drugstore and bought me some chemicals," he recalled. "I could make some fiery powder and ignite things and marvel at the flames. Or I could create chemicals that made some terrible odor or, more harmless, make chemicals that could change colors. My mother and father actively supported my curiosity about nature and about trying things out. No one in my family was into science. I was the first scientist in the family."

Wolfgang, replicating his experience in Germany with his own children, and demonstrating the balance between town and gown springing from it, spoke of his life in Brookline:

"I have three children. Jonas is the oldest, my daughter, Johanna, is in the middle, and the youngest is my son Holger. They are all doing well. They are all good in school, Jonas and Johanna at BHS and Holger at Baker School. I don't know whether they will follow me in science. I don't really have any expectations, or put any pressure on them. The most important thing is that they are fulfilled in life, that they feel satisfied when they work on something, and feel a sense of accomplishment. I'm very happy whatever they choose to do, whether in science, music, or something else, as long as they work hard. Jonas is a very gifted musician. He plays the clarinet very well. In his courses at Brookline High he shows an interest in chemistry and biology. He spent a month at MIT doing summer research. I think he will head toward science or engineering."

It is easy to imagine Wolfgang Ketterle setting off sparks in the minds of his own children, knowing how he enthralled the tenth-grade honors algebra class at Brookline High School, when he taught in the Educator for a Day program recently. Demystifying the work he does at MIT and relating it to real-world problems, Wolfgang catalyzed his gifted students to believe it when he told them, "Math is about more than solving high school problems. It's about real life." One of those students, sophomore Adam D'Agostine, spoke for the group: "Dr. Ketterle's class was extremely interesting. Kids taking math after eighth grade always ask, 'When are we ever going to use this?' Getting the small and large pictures helps."

Wolfgang expanded on the lesson about taking risks that he inculcated in the students at Brookline High School that day:

"Some people feel the challenge in math or physics is to make certain calculations. That is pretty much learning a technique, learning how to multiply or divide, to solve somewhat more complicated problems. I know my children and other students are struggling with that, but it's merely a technique. The real challenge in physics is to observe and to quantify. To realize that you can go to the next level, and observe and describe. That you can look at something, take it apart, describe the different parts, and put it back together. For that, you use the tools of math. Mathematics and physics are really much more interesting than high school students might think, because what it's really about is discovery, creativity, learning, and finding the description. I see it as art, imagination, and discovery."

The mystery of genius, and the "art and creativity" that animate it, always intrigues us. As only one person in twenty-five million becomes a Nobel laureate, it seems fair to count Wolfgang Ketterle under that heading, as we do another Wolfgang — Wolfgang Amadeus Mozart — who must have known he was a genius as early as age four or five, by which time he was composing and playing his own works in the presence of Europe's royalty. It seemed fair to ask Wolfgang when that realization came to him.

"That realization came in stages," he told us. "I was the best student in my high school class, and I knew I was academically talented. But I went from university to university, met other smart people, and for many years you don't know how good you might be. And that affected my career choices. As an undergraduate, my career goal was to go to industry and do some research there. Early on, I wasn't pursuing the career of an academic, and that is the kind of science I am doing right now. I was not convinced that I would be good enough to do that. After I got my Ph.D., I realized that I very quickly got to the heart of the matter and was able to take leadership. Suddenly, I stopped being afraid and experienced growing self-confidence. Even if you are the best in high school, and even if you have top grades in college and obtain a Ph.D., it's really hard to self-assess that you are able to do something bigger. So it's a growing realization.

"In 1989 I made the decision to work in the Department of Physical Chemistry at Heidelberg University to work on combustion research, with the goal of making combustion more efficient and cleaner. That was something very concrete, where you know what your work is good for. During my time there, I became aware that I had to work on something more abstract, and that I had the self-confidence to do that. I came to believe that if I were to work in some more abstract area of science where the goals are not well defined, I would be able to succeed and make discoveries — that this would be a worthwhile commitment and would not waste my life. I came to think that this would be the place where I belong and where I would be at my best. The consequence of that was that I left a secure job in Germany and went to MIT with no guaranty for employment, which was a risk for me and my family. I was thirty-two years old and I started in a new field."

Confidence breeds risk, and in 1990 risk brought to Wolfgang Ketterle a position in the Department of Physics at MIT under his enabling, instructive, and challenging mentor, Professor David E. Pritchard. This was the springboard to his current eminence. That led to the observation of ultra-cold atoms (i.e., Bose-Einstein condensation), for which he won the Nobel Prize, a purely scientific discovery that some day may be used to measure time and motion more precisely. Wolfgang spoke of that continuum from pure science to practical application:

"The discovery is about a new form of matter made of very cold atoms, the coldest matter in the universe, more than a million times colder than outer space. So that is one exciting aspect of it. It is unimaginably cold. I'm a fundamental scientist. I try to work at the frontiers of knowledge. If I feel that there is something new to be discovered, I try to go there. I sometimes feel like an explorer who puts his foot on a new island. Mainly one is driven by curiosity, but at the same time I think that if I do this curiosity-driven research, I will find new knowledge, which will become the foundation for new technology. I will work to finalize certain research. I'm not too concerned that I can point to some killer application that will lead to some new product or new devices. By working with cold atoms, we control the building blocks of nature. It may lead to better clocks, better navigation, better metrology — that is, the science of measuring things. Those are dreams and goals that may be accomplished with cold atoms. Whether these will materialize will take decades to find out. It takes years from conceptual idea to a prototype or product. So, I'm there for the long haul. I work on ideas that are the basis for our technological future."

The "long haul" of which Wolfgang Ketterle speaks applies equally to family, social issues, and sports, identifying him as a man who has achieved balance between the theoretical of his work and the pragmatic of his personal life. Speaking of sports, Wolfgang says, "I am that type of person who is intrigued by having challenges, and can concentrate and focus on those challenges. I love to bike, I like to jog. I love to exercise. I feel better when I exercise. I did long-distance running, and became excited by running marathons. I was running several marathons in Germany, finishing all of them in under three hours. I have participated in soccer, basketball, and pole vaulting. It was something special. You had to take a pole and catapult yourself into the air! You had to overcome your fears, and that is also something I enjoy. It's something you're a little afraid of, but with the power of your will, you can do it. That still characterizes my work — to attack the impossible and make the impossible possible. I like hiking for a few reasons. One is that hiking takes you to the high mountains, and whether it's the Alps or the Rocky Mountains, you are rewarded with wonderful views. Another is the exercise. You see, I'm in the valley and I want to walk up the hill. It's steep and it's a challenge. You work hard for it, and you enjoy your accomplishment. I did some skiing in the Alps, and I do some cross-country at the Putterham Golf Course." Whew!

But all of that work and play does not keep Wolfgang from his children, despite some round-the-clock experiments: "Whether I stay at the lab depends," he says. "If I don't have any other commitments, and if I know that my children don't need me, I can stay for long hours to finish something, but if I know my children are waiting for me, I have the discipline to stop working and go home. So even doing the most interesting work, if you have a commitment, especially a commitment to people you love, you will stop, and will resume even the most interesting work when there is time. So there is a passion, but you have to set your priorities."

Social consciousness came early to Wolfgang Ketterle, as a student in Munich in 1982, when he joined a peace movement opposing American nuclear proliferation, an issue that still haunts us: "I was against the philosophy that if you put up more arms, you stabilize peace. For me this was contradictory. If you put up arms, they eventually will create their own dynamics, and maybe trigger some preemptive attacks. So I was very concerned, and I rallied against the deployment of these missiles in Germany. Now, I'm deeply concerned that war has become a part of politics. I grew up in Germany, after the terrible experience of World War II. There were radical changes there. German policy focused on peaceful politics, and Germany self-terminated as a military power, until recently. When I came to the United States, I experienced it as the biggest military power in the world. I saw the United States using its military power to practice politics in various regions of the world, most recently Iraq. I saw a real difference in what I experienced in the first part of my life and what I am experiencing here."

Having always thought that man has difficulty controlling what he creates, I wondered whether Wolfgang saw mankind as threatened by products that his fellow physicists had brought into the world, especially the bomb.

"I share your concerns," he says. "I think knowledge, to understand the world, is positive. It reflects the human desire to understand who we are and what is around us. Now, this knowledge leads to technology, and technology can be used for the sake of mankind. We can prolong life, fight diseases, and produce food in a more efficient way. There is a large population of the world that is not starving anymore. That population has enough to eat and the basic necessities of life. This is an accomplishment of technology. Technology can also be used against mankind, by polluting the environment, or by creating arms of mass destruction that can be turned against mankind. This is where it becomes ambiguous — the same knowledge that can be used for mankind can also be used to threaten mankind. But I'm always an optimist about the future."

That optimism enables Wolfgang to view his adopted country in full, even if flawed: "Coming from Germany to the United States, I never felt like a complete stranger. Boston and Brookline are international communities, so I felt at home and respected. There are many foreigners here, but their peculiarities are regarded as richness. That is what my children have experienced in school. At Christmas, all the children are encouraged to talk about their traditions. It's a very rich way of sharing. The schools in Brookline, and the environment generally, make people proud of their heritage. Germany is not as open to integrating foreigners as the United States is. For me, it was an interesting experience to come as a foreigner to this country, to feel respected and welcome and to settle down."

When next you look out your window in Brookline and see that neighbor you don't know romping with his kids, mowing the lawn, or planting some flowers, look again and think twice; that man may be harnessing the atom and changing your life forever.

Photo by author.

COSTAS XANTHOPOULOS

Master Tailor: An Odyssey from Greece to Brookline

HAVING KNOWN COSTAS XANTHOPOULOS for more than thirty years, since he opened his custom store as a master tailor in Brookline, it was no surprise to view his sartorial splendor as he sat opposite me on the day of our interview. Costas, a handsome and elegant man, wore his signature white handkerchief against a dark suit of his own making, a white shirt, and a tasteful tie, an outward appearance belying the hard work that brought him to his high station in his adopted country.

Costas put it this way: "I never go out without my handkerchief. I feel naked if I go out without it. When I do the fitting to the customer, I'm with a jacket. But when I go to my workshop inside, I take off my jacket and sit down at the machine and work," a metaphor for the story of a man whose odyssey has taken him

Brookline Access TV interview, July 24, 2002. *Brookline Bulletin*, November 20, 2003.

from a small town in Greece, where at times there was hardly enough to eat, to his success here.

Costas' story is truly an American story — the story of immigration, which has always been the lifeblood of America. Speaking with him, I was interested in discovering how he traveled from there to here, thinking his story would shed even more light on how the people who come to our shores always seem to inject more of the ability and desire that continue to enrich our country and our town.

Costas grew up in the small agricultural town of Tirnavos. When he reached the age of thirteen, his father said he had to go to work to help support the family, even though Costas wanted to go to high school where all the other kids were going. His father gave him the choice of what job he was going to do, and the youth knew what job and how to go about getting it.

"I wanted to be a tailor because I admired good clothes," he said. "I used to see the lawyers and the doctors dressed in white linen suits, and I loved it. I said that's what I'm going to be one day — a doctor. Since I couldn't become a doctor, I became a tailor so I can make my own suits.

"I just went to the tailor shops. There were about ten of them in Tirnavos and I picked out the best one. It had a good name. I went over there and asked if they can hire me to teach me, not hire me to work, because I didn't know anything. In three years I became a tailor. I wanted to go a little farther. I wanted to go to Athens," he said, where he felt he could become a master tailor — that is, not only a tailor who could fit, fix, and finish a suit, but one who could cut it as well.

Naturally, his parents — his father, Yanni, and his mother, Caterina — were leery that Costas was too young at sixteen to go to the big city, but finally arrangements were made for him to stay with a cousin there for a short while, and his odyssey continued. In a short time, not only was Costas living in Athens, but also had his own place to live and the job that made him a master craftsman. "I was so proud to work for Alexandros Voudouris," he told us. "He used to go to Paris every year to get the new fashions, and he had a very good clientele in Athens. So I was proud to work for him."

Working hard for Voudouris, Costas became a master tailor

before the age of twenty, when army service beckoned. This reminded me that my paternal grandfather was a master tailor who came from Odessa in the late nineteenth century to ply his trade and raise a large family in Revere. When I told him this, Costas remarked on the many fine tailors that came from Eastern Europe, usually of Jewish descent. "There are not going to be any more," he says, "because it's a dying art. No one goes like I went at thirteen years old to learn the profession."

Returning to Athens from his army service, Costas worked a few months for Voudouris, looking around to start his own business.

"When I was ready, I opened my own shop — that was my dream." Thus, by age twenty-three, Costas had the first House of Costas, in Athens. Always a quick study, it took him only about three months to acquire his own customers.

Not long after, in 1964, Costas met Angela, the lady who would become his wife in 1965. Angela proved to be an angel in more ways than one, bearing Costas four fine children, helping him out in his shops there and here, and being the person who got Costas to America through an odd twist in our immigration laws.

Even with a child at home, Angela found a way to help Costas. As he says, "Well, nothing is impossible, Larry. If you want to do it, you'll do it. We had a machine at home, and I used to take work home, and Angela helped me out in this way."

During the late 1960s, Greece was ruled by a military junta that sharply curtailed the freedoms that Greeks prize so much, and made life there relatively unpleasant. Costas says, "The future in Greece was questionable, and we didn't know how long the junta was going to last."

Serendipitously, at that very time one of Costas's customers, a lawyer, told Costas that word had come from the American Embassy that a law was in effect that Greek kids born in Greece of parents who had spent time in the United States were considered American citizens, a law apparently born of the need for skilled labor. The aptly named Angela was a child of such parents. Quickly, application was made and granted. Angela went first, and within weeks the family was reunited at a cousin's home in Belmont.

In America, yes, but what were the prospects for Costas and

his family — he spoke no English, had little money, and was living in somebody else's home. Yet within two years, Costas not only had become a respected tailor at the exclusive men's store Louis, but had also opened his custom shop in Washington Square, Brookline, which is there to this day. How he did that is the story of American immigration over the years.

Within weeks after his arrival, with the few dollars he had, Costas moved his family to an apartment in Brighton, began taking classes to learn English, and had his first tailoring job at Demarco of London, a store that went out of business shortly after he became employed there. He sought employment at Louis, working there for a year and one-half, all the while holding tight to his dream of having his own House of Costas in this country: "I always was looking for a tailor shop, my own shop. That was my dream." he says, "but I didn't have money. I was looking around Brookline because I was told that Brookline was a nice area, close to Boston, with lots of good people, and that I could make a good living there."

Costas found the place he wanted, on Beacon Street near Washington Square, right next door to where his House of Costas is now.

The rest is a story in survival, resourcefulness, and success. Costas gave the only three hundred dollars he had as earnest money against the lease, borrowed one thousand dollars from a good friend, used another friend's credit to borrow one thousand dollars from the Shawmut Bank, and had a custom cutting table made, a table he uses to this day. For twenty-three hundred dollars, Costas was in business for himself.

"The first month I was panicked," he recalls. "I said, Where are the customers? So what I did was to get in touch with and chase some customers of Louis." Costas had cards made, sent them off to some of these customers, and even went so far as to go down to Louis and distribute them to customers there whom he knew, as they went into and came out of that establishment.

"You have to do it, Larry," Costas says. "It's life or death. I found a way to work on my own. I mean, what can I do? I had to do something. I don't know if it was bad, but at that time I had to do it. I took some customers of Louis. The next month, they started coming in!" Of course, it didn't hurt that Costas's work was on a par with Louis but far less expensive.

The name of Costas's first shop in Brookline was Fits Fine Tailoring. Costas said he got the name from working at Louis, where he often heard it said to a customer — "This fits fine."

A few years later, when Costas moved next door, he named it House of Costas, completing the circle begun in Athens. Never employing more than a few people at a time, over the years Costas has had some twenty or more employees, generally hired through ads on Greek language radio, giving a chance to other immigrants from Greece and elsewhere to make it here.

Costas believes that English fabrics are the best: "England was, it is, and will be forever the best cloth maker. I suppose it's the soft water that makes the fabric quality. They have very good fabric designers too."

Costas sees the patterns that he has cut over the years as the link between himself and the Brookline community: "The procedure is like this. We take measurements to cut the fabric. Then I sit down at the big [custom] table and I make the patterns on paper and then I cut the fabric. Each customer has his own pattern. I have about two hundred patterns hanging in my shop, and I'm really very proud of that. I see names going back three generations. This is a beautiful thing, starting with the grandfather, then the children, and now it is the grandchildren. Well, it's for the House of Costas. I love it!"

In 1990, Costas was chosen Best Tailor in Boston by *Boston Magazine's* Best of Boston. More customers came, but Costas resisted the lure of expanding his business: "You can't control the quality of the workmanship. The bigger you become, the less quality. So I kept it as a small operation like now, and I'm happy the customers love what I am doing, and they come back, and they recommend me, on and on," as the odyssey of Costas reaches its penultimate point.

In 1971, about a year after he arrived in this country, Costas became a U.S. citizen. Having spent half his life in Greece and half in America, and going back each year to spend some time with this sisters and family still in Greece, he naturally has some views about how life goes in each country:

"It's hard to decide where to live and which country you love most. I love them both. I love the country where I was born, the culture. I am very proud because, as you know, Greece was the first democracy in the world over two thousand years ago.

"Then, I love this country. It's a powerful and rich country, and with a little guts, anyone can make his place here. I'm mostly a craftsman and make things. I'm not so much a businessperson to make a billion dollars, but I'm happy the way I am."

Costas has some thoughts about community and the pace of life here: "Here life is a little fast, perhaps a little too fast. People wear themselves out faster than in Greece. Over there life is a little slower and they enjoy the days a little more than here. Many immigrants come here to accomplish something, and we work more than play. You're supposed to play a little more than work, and that's the way we are. Then I go to Greece, I fit in right away. I have my father's house in the town where I was born."

For Costas Xanthopoulos, as for many other immigrants to America, this is how it goes: loving his adopted country but not forgetting his roots. As Costas says about his Newton home, "My favorite thing is my garden," which goes a long way back to his farmer father in Tirnavos: "My father was very particular about the house garden. I learned a lot from my father there about gardening, and now I am proud of my vegetable garden here."

Whether you cite his love of country, love of family, love of the land, or love of craft, one thing is for sure — taking them altogether, Costas and his family and other families like his are among the ingredients that contribute to and sustain the energy and community of America, allowing its unprecedented success to continue.

Photo by author.

ELIAS AUDY

Chairman of the Brookline Chamber of Commerce,
Immigrating from Lebanon and Succeeding and
Ascending Against All Odds

COMING HERE FROM LEBANON, Elias Audy has succeeded and
ascended in Brookline (he is now president of the Brookline
Chamber of Commerce), much as Costas Xanthopolous did when
he came here from Greece years before. Elias's forward and friendly qualities were obvious when I interviewed him, and do much to
explain how a Lebanese Arab succeeded in predominantly Jewish
Brookline. Of course, the story of Elias's growing up in Lebanon
goes a long way in explaining how he became the Brookline community leader he is now.

   Part of that story has to do with the diversity of the Lebanese
community in his hometown of Kura (near the famous Cedars of
Lebanon). Elias tells us there was "lots of education, affluent

Brookline Access TV interview, December 26, 2002. *Brookline Bulletin*, December 31, 2003.

people, and community work. I grew up in that region exposed to different cultures and ethnicities, and that is what I like about Brookline. I come from a big family, a family that cared, and a family that got involved in a lot of civic work."

Elias arrived in the United States in 1969, and first went to the University of Houston, then came to Boston and attended Northeastern. Here he met his wife, Laurde, also now active in the Brookline community: "I knew her a little in Lebanon, but we had no real relationship. It so happens that my brother is married to her older sister, so here we are two brothers married to two sisters and we keep teasing each other about who married the better-looking one [he laughs]. She is a member of Brookline Rotary too."

There is no doubt that Elias's civic-mindedness springs from his family life. "Every single morning," he says, "at least two of my brothers and sisters come by to have coffee with us before we all go to work. This is the kind of family life we have, because of my parents being here with us."

With all this good stuff behind him, it was natural that Elias would combine his work and family into total immersion in the Brookline community. As he tells it, back in 1987 and 1988, when he started to work at his Mobil station on Boylston Street, he learned that Mobil had a program that would give money to schools if the local dealer provided assistance in the giving. Elias went to the town hall and asked how he could go about providing a grant from Mobil to the Brookline schools, and the rest is history: "They sent me to the Brookline Foundation where Deborah Brooks was the director," he says. "She arranged a meeting with [Brookline activist and realtor] Chobee Hoy, and I was so impressed with the way Chobee presented her idea of giving to the town of Brookline that since then, not only have I continued giving to the town of Brookline, but I have been involved in almost every civic program that is in Brookline."

Elias has special feelings for Chobee Hoy, who will follow Elias as president of the chamber of commerce. "She does a lot of good work, and she has a unique way of leading people to do the right thing. At the same time, Brookline is a magnet that attracts me to continue doing what I feel is the right thing to do. There is always something exciting to do in Brookline, there is always a project."

Previously, Elias was president of the perennially active Brookline Rotary Club.

"Here in Brookline, Rotary helps in many ways. We have a budget of over thirty thousand dollars. Two years ago we gave the senior center ten thousand dollars, and this year we are giving the library ten thousand. Right now we are doing a library building project in our sister city in Nicaragua. Brookline Rotary is committed to help match the grant to equip the library in Nicaragua with computers and furniture, which might come to a twenty- to thirty-thousand-dollar project. It is a way to promote peace and understanding between people, and I wish that every community would act in that fashion."

As president of Brookline Chamber of Commerce, Elias sees a natural affinity between business and community in Brookline: "The Brookline business community is a big part of the community, and I always felt there should be a greater communication between them and the community of Brookline at large. The chamber is a great organization, and is a great resource to schools, nonprofits, and other entities in the Brookline community, so the chamber should be supported and maintained in good standing."

Obviously, open-faced and open-hearted Elias Audy has a natural gift for combining profit making with community making. Not only has he used Mobil for charitable giving to the town, but also through his business he relates in a personal way to his customers. As he says, "It's a service industry. You need to believe in two things. First, you need to believe in serving people and trusting people, and second, customer service, and I believe that we have them both . . . .

"The exposure to meeting people is just tremendous. Our customers are varied, and from all walks of life. And people know a good thing when they see it. Especially in Brookline! You don't have to go to the dealer for everything. There are certain things for which you need to go to the dealer, but it's a waste of time and money to go there for certain other things. A smart consumer would know."

Well, I don't know whether or not I'm a smart consumer, but my wife and I take our Toyotas to Elias and have never been sorry. The service is friendly, the work successful, the charge reasonable!

It seems that Elias's community pursuits in Brookline are legion. He is on the board of directors of the Brookline Music School. "Music should be in every household," he says. "There should be an opportunity for every kid to learn music. It sets minds into different horizons." As a Mozart lover and an inveterate concertgoer, I can attest to the truth of Elias's words.

That interest in children extends to Elias's work with the Kids Clothes Club. "It's an organization that gives coats to kids of need. A very generous and good-natured lady, Faith Michaels, is the one who started that organization, buying one or two coats at a time, and now they give over three thousand coats a year, all over greater Boston, not just in Brookline."

In the same vein, Elias has received an award from the Brookline Educators Association. Elias comments, "Education is a great wealth, and Brookline values it so much that you can't ignore it. I support education through the Brookline Foundation and I teach a day program, and go and judge the eighth-grade speech contest every year."

I asked Elias what makes Brookline so special: "It is a special place, and I wish I could point to one particular thing that makes it special, but everything that goes on in Brookline contributes, the nonprofits, Kids Clothes Club, chamber of commerce, the Rotary Club, town politics, the schools, the citizens of Brookline — all those things together," he said.

It seems to me that Elias Audy's success in America, both before and in the face of 9/11, is a testament to the notion that a smiling face, a good heart, and compassion for one's fellow human beings wins the day against whatever odds. Elias puts it this way, showing himself to be a natural-born humanist:

"If you act normal, who you are, don't pretend, then people will respect you for what you are. I just traveled to Las Vegas. I was very, very scared about how it would go, going through the airport. I look Arab, my face. Nobody bothered me. I was not picked to go to the side, except in one stop I was picked to step aside, and I knew why. I had something in my pockets that activated the sensor. They were very polite and they searched me like they would anyone else. I don't think I was singled out. There may be some cases, but I believe it is a society that tolerates differences, and we are judged by who we are, and not where we are from.

"We are all just human beings. I believe in that. That is probably why I never experienced something like that. There were some gestures that were at certain times made toward me, but if you react similarly to those gestures, a confrontation will arise. But if you don't, it will just go away. You can defuse things very easily, instead of letting them elaborate."

Could it be that the actions and words of Elias Audy offer a simple anodyne to the world's continuing and deadly troubles, a prescription missed by our more "profound" thinkers?

Elias carries this attitude back to his home country, which he visits every year or so, doing a project through Brookline Rotary to build a home for the elderly in Lebanon: "I made a point to tell them it came from a Rotary where sixty percent of the members are Jewish. That is how you bring people together. Show the good side of things. How do you think they feel when the Jews of Brookline contribute to a kitchen in Lebanon? In general, if things like this keep happening, I think that brings peace and brings people together. Once you do the right thing, differences will disappear and people will come together."

Would that such a spirit existed in all of us. I was moved to conclude the interview by saying, "It doesn't surprise me that you would do that. You just strike me as the kind of person who does things like that. To end the program, since we're both on camera, I'm going to lean closer [I wanted to be closer to this fine man], so that we can both shake hands." And we did.

Perhaps a metaphor for peace.

Fred Dinov with his children   *Samir and Prakruti Majmudar.*
Gabi and Philip.

FRED DINOV AND LILLY SHLAYEN
FROM RUSSIA AND
SAMIR AND PRAKRUTI MAJMUDAR
FROM INDIA

Restaurateurs, American Citizens

AS I WRITE THIS STORY, during the hectic days of the Democratic
National Convention taking place in Boston in July 2004, it strikes
me that recent events have left many Americans unsettled about
how the rest of the world views our values, even casting among us
some doubt as to how we view ourselves. Perhaps the best pallia-
tive for this troublesome, if not troubled, state of mind is to speak
to recent immigrants, who are able to see our country with clear
eyes and a keen appreciation for what it offers. I recently had this
opportunity when I interviewed Fred Dinov and his wife, Lilly
Shlayen, from Russia, and Samir and Prakruti Majmudar, from
India, on the same day in separate programs, surely a good example of the purpose of local access TV — that is, to show the character of a community and give voice to its diverse elements.

   If one believes that diversity, along with the infusion of new

Brookline Access TV interviews, March 8, 2004.

and different blood, reinvigorates and reinvents America as time goes by, then the last few decades have been such a time, not only in Brookline, but also around the country. The demise of the Soviet Union in 1991 has brought millions of Russians to these shores, including a substantial contingent to Brookline. During that same period, millions of immigrants from other countries around the globe have landed here, bringing with them their own customs, traditions, and language, yet eager to learn and adopt our ways. This is a story repeated again and again in our history, which, it might reasonably be argued, accounts for America's continuing success. The stories that Fred, Lilly, Samir, and Prakruti told lend credence to the concept that America — at least so far — remains a beacon of hope in the world, a land where everything is possible, where anyone can become anything.

Fred Dinov, the proprietor and chef at the Café Europa, in Brookline Village, ventured into the unknown to come here a dozen years ago, rising in that short time to be his own master and to form a thriving family with Lilly Shlayen, whom he met here. Lilly, too, is from Russia; she came with her parents at age eight from Odessa.

Fred had started his studies in the culinary arts in Russia. Arriving in New York, he worked at a Russian restaurant and went to the famed French Culinary Institute in Manhattan, where he honed his art and formed friendships with celebrated chefs such as Jacques Pepin, André Soltner, Alain Sailhac, and Daniel Boulud. Is it any wonder that Fred, laconic in word, but expressive in culinary presentation, answers the question of how he likes the United States by saying, "Oh, it's beautiful" and that he finds it a "land of opportunity"?

My appetite to do a program with Fred Dinov had been whetted by my first eating experience at Café Europa a few years before. I was working late at my office one night and needed time out to refuel. Chancing into Fred's restaurant, I was entranced to find uncommonly delicious continental cuisine served in a European ambience amid tables buzzing with conspiratorial but indecipherable conversations spoken in foreign tongues. That experience brought me back many more times, always with the same result, so when I got around to thinking of combining the immigrant and ethnic food experience in Brookline on my local access TV program, I naturally gravitated to Fred. As I sat with him at Café Europa to prepare, Fred took down a picture from the wall showing himself and Jacques Pepin, Fred resplendent in his tall white chef's hat, which I persuaded him to wear on the program. I called him "Brookline's best-kept secret," as he described his way of preparing a rack of lamb, called, in the Russian style, *karski*.

Lilly Shlayen, busy raising Gabriela, six, and Philip, three, helps out her husband from time to time at Café Europa, and advises him on further expansion from behind the scenes.

Lilly and her family have found a good life in America, not only from their point of view, but also from ours. Lilly tells the story:

"My experience here has been very positive. Of course, I arrived as a child, so it's very different for me, but for my parents, it's very positive and they love America. They are native Russians, but they are citizens here, and they consider themselves American. They live in Waltham, and are working, and are very successful. My father owns a business, Odessa Shoe Repairs. He has been very successful with that, and now has new locations. My mom works in Wellesley, where she has a manicure salon, so they are still working, thriving, absolutely living the American Dream. Most of my immediate family is here in the United States, and I have a lot of Russian friends."

Hearing that, I thought Lilly could accurately describe the experience of Russians immigrating to this country. She told us: "I think for most it has been very positive. This is the land of opportunity, especially for the Jewish community to be able to practice their religion, so yes, I think it's been positive for most. Fred is not Jewish, and I don't think he plans to become Jewish. But he does value my belief. We do practice Judaism, we did have a Jewish marriage ceremony, and our kids are Jewish."

Thinking to myself that this is diversity within diversity, I suggested that it sounds like a good relationship, but that Fred's culinary talent must have something to do with it. Lilly agreed: "Yes, he won me over with his food, absolutely! I always say it was the duck that won me over." Fred, a man of few words, but not without humor, added, "A table for two."

In a conflict not unknown as generations of new Americans

climb the ladder of American society, it may be that that table for two will remain a table for two, as Fred and Lilly's children make their own choices going forward. Lilly, while acknowledging that "Fred hopes our children go into the restaurant business, I have somewhat different hopes for them, perhaps college, but it's up to them, whatever they choose. I want them to be happy and successful in whatever path they choose."

This prototypical pattern has already shown itself in the lives of Samir and Prakruti Majmudar, proprietors of Rani Indian Bistro in Coolidge Corner, whose two eldest daughters, Meghna and Aparna are both graduates of Harvard University, the former an anthropologist and the latter an economist, both working in their respective fields. It is an open question whether their youngest and latecoming daughter, Sanskruti, now a seventh-grader at Driscoll School, will complete the cycle or follow in her parents' footsteps, a not unlikely answer considering the continuing path of success Samir and Prakruti are enjoying.

As in all immigrant stories, it is interesting to trace how the Majmudars came from there to here, now having been U.S. citizens for the past ten years or so. Samir tells of the day when a friend, who had worked in one of the few good hotels in Bombay, took him there: "Just the whole ambience, and the feel of the hotel looking from outside, made me want to work in that kind of environment, and that drew me to the business."

The die was cast. Samir went to a well-known hotel management and catering technology school in Bombay, worked in the Hotel President in that city for a few years, married Prakruti around that time, and, he says, "I was then offered a better job about five hundred miles away from Bombay at the Cama Hotel in Ahmedabad," where he spent five years.

Then an opportunity arose that further developed the cosmopolitan demeanor that characterizes Samir: "A friend of mine drew me to run his restaurant in Malta. He had just bought a pub and did not know how to manage it. He said, 'Samir, you've lived long enough in Bombay. How about going out and exploring the world?' and I thought it wouldn't be a bad idea! It was a great opportunity to run a restaurant in Malta, an independent island country about two hundred miles south of Sicily."

Returning to Bombay, a chance came for Samir to visit the United States to attend summer seminars at Cornell University in restaurant management. Despite having been raised and working in democratic India and Malta, Samir's first impressions of America, while attending classes at Cornell and a short time later visiting Prakruti's relatives in Needham, were powerful and prescient: "Very exciting," he remembers. "It was the summer of 1982, great weather. America already existed in my imagination. I had seen American movies. I'm a big movie buff. I felt like I knew the country because of the movies, but it was quite exciting seeing it; it was new, very different from Europe and India. I thought, 'Wow, this is very nice!' I felt that there were many more opportunities. If I wanted to do something over here, it was very easy for me to do it, rather than trying to do it in Bombay, where no bank or financial institution would lend money to a restaurant or small private business at that time."

Shortly after arriving in Boston, it looked like Samir's passage to America would be much smoother sailing than E. M. Forster's *Passage to India,* when his impressive restaurant credentials resulted in an offer to run the beautiful Boston Indian restaurant Pondicherry. Within two months, Samir had brought Prakruti, Meghna, and Aparna to Boston, but within a few months after that, he says, "The lease prematurely expired because of fire at that location, and four months after I started working there, the Pondicherry closed down."

It was at this juncture that Samir and Prakruti showed the grit, willingness to work, and inventiveness that characterize so many newcomers to our shores, each answering in his or her own way my question as to whether at that point they wished to be back in India.

Prakruti: "No, never! I was the one who really wanted to come here. I heard so many good things about this country."

Samir: "If we had a tough time, it wasn't because of this country. We were just in the wrong place at the wrong time, and that must be the only reason. We had to struggle. We really did struggle after the Pondicherry closed down. What to do? Could we go back? Could we stay? If we stay, how do we stay? If you are willing to work hard, it's all possible!"

Writing his own page of the American dream, Samir went back to square one, first flipping burgers at Burger King, then, realizing he needed a structured restaurant in which to work, joined Howard Johnson's, later managing the Ground Round affiliate in Brighton.

Those very American experiences underpinned Samir's later success in joining American technique to the spices of Indian cuisine. Samir says, "It was very enlightening how the restaurants were run in this country compared to how they're run in India. It taught me a lot. One of the things that really amazed me was productivity, the volume of work that was achieved from the employees. It was amazing compared to the work we got out of employees in India!"

The swift upward mobility still pervasive in American society propelled Samir and Prakruti from the Ground Round: "I worked and managed a kitchen in the Brighton Ground Round for a few months, when I realized that the regimented environment was not meant for me. I needed to do my own thing. I told my wife that things were going to be very tough if we didn't do something. And she was all for it, saying, 'Samir, we have to be on our own. Working for others is not going to make it for us.' "

From that point on, not working for others did not exclude working *with* others in opening Indian restaurants, but even that ultimately proved a deterrent to Samir and Prakruti's ultimate goal of operating a distinctive Indian restaurant, different from the plethora of such eateries that now dot the landscape.

At first, scraping together limited resources, the couple opened Barbeques International in Allston, " sort of a Ma-and-Pa operation with two kids in tow," Samir recalls. Branching out from there, mostly with Indian partners, Samir opened Bombay Bistro in 1991, on the present site of Rani Indian Bistro, later opening Rangoli in Allston, Tanjore in Harvard Square, and Bhindi Bazaar in Boston. One might think that Samir and Prakruti had reached the pinnacle, but quantity did not add up to the quality of distinction and difference that this ambitious couple wanted, along with material success. Samir explains:

"Indian restaurants — I wanted to have a distinctive one. Running a full restaurant is very different and very difficult. If you want to have a certain style of food and presentation, it's easy to delegate but very different to supervise. I tried for several years, and have come to the conclusion that it's impossible to run those restaurants the way I wanted to run them. So instead of going in the wrong direction, I decided to sell some of my shares to my junior partners, let them run them and have their own identities. I want to run Rani the way I want to run it. And the first thing we've done is revise each and every recipe. Every curry that used to be made at Bombay Bistro is made very differently. And that, we hope, will make the product stand out for what it is."

Samir and Prakruti, concentrating their combined efforts on Rani Indian Bistro, now provide Brookline and Boston with a truly unique Indian restaurant. Prakruti says, "I practice, practice, practice at home! I enjoy food, so I experimented with many different kinds and styles of cooking, focusing more on Indian food, and came up with different recipes, plus touches from the old style of cooking, which include basically onions, tomatoes, garlic, plus ginger and spices. Now I do a different technique using the same spices but getting different flavors out of them."

Samir adds, "North Indian or Punjabi food is what is served in most Indian restaurants. We have a southern specialty, specializing in the Hyderabad style of cooking, Hyderabad being a region in southern India. The flavors we have in this style include black mustard, curry leaves, coconut, and tamarind, not very commonly used in Indian cooking."

Samir and Prakruti's adherence to the particularly American virtues of doing it for one's self, going it alone, and hard work is now being rewarded not only with unfettered commercial success, but also with recognition for excellence; Rani Indian Bistro received *Boston Magazine's* Best of Boston for Indian food for 2004.

Certainly the American dream includes a place to live as well as a place to work, and why not Brookline? Samir said that while living in Brighton, Sanskruti attended Les Petits Nursery School on Mason Terrace, with its panoramic view of Boston to the east, and "Prakruti and I were thinking, 'Wouldn't it be wonderful to live on a street like this?' And then one day we saw a sign that a house on Mason Terrace was for sale, and we bought it!"

Wanting to know more about Sanskruti's experience growing up in diverse Brookline, I asked Prakruti about her daughter's attendance at Driscoll School: "Sanskruti is really enjoying school and friends," her mother told us. "My older kids didn't have that many friends going to Boston public schools, but I think Brookline is a really close-knit community. There are no other Indian kids in her class, they are mostly Jewish kids, and it seems like every other weekend she goes to a bar mitzvah!" Concerned, Samir added, "I think she's very popular, and sometimes I ask her if she's that popular, is she studying or is she going to some popularity contest every day? But she has very good friends, we've never had any complaints, and as a family we have never run into any racial incidents. I feel I'm blessed that I haven't run into that kind of difficult or unsavory situation. Right now, we're having a lot of fun and enjoying life."

Plainly the experiences of Fred and Lilly and Samir and Prakruti demonstrate that the notion of strength through diversity continues to thrive, improving Brookline and American society, despite those nativistic pockets of resistance in our land that seek to homogenize our population.

DAVID SCHMAHMANN

Novelist and Lawyer from South Africa,
American Citizen

I HAVE WRITTEN ELSEWHERE THAT BROOKLINE is a unique micro-cosm and crucible of the democracy that we call "America." Who better to assess the validity of that notion than David Schmahmann, a Brookline resident who grew up in apartheid South Africa in the embrace of his loving, liberal, and activist Jewish family, emigrated to the United States as a young adult, became a successful lawyer in Boston, achieving a partnership in a legendary law firm where Louis Brandeis practiced before ascending to the Supreme Court, ultimately abandoning that secure path to follow precariously his irresistible compulsion to be a novelist, surviving multiple rejections along the way, finally emerging successfully in his literary career, and now living happily with his family in Brookline.

Brookline Access TV interview, May 6, 2003.

My introduction to David Schmahmann came while reading *The Fruitful Branch,* a book of stories by twenty-one Brookline writers about their library experiences, published in 2002 under the auspices of the Brookline Library Foundation to raise money to complete the funding for the renovation of the main branch.

Because Brookline contains far more than twenty-one talented and published writers, it is hardly surprising that those represented in *The Fruitful Branch* all wrote interesting, lively, and sensitive accounts. David Schmahmann's contribution, entitled "The Healing Power of Dreams," resonated strongly with me, it being a deeply felt account of his struggle through multiple rejections from publishers, weaving together boyhood in South Africa, his family there and here, his experience of the United States, and the private dreamworld that defines the man. On a memorable day soon after I read his story, I had a lively meeting with David in his Beacon Street office and interviewed him later that day.

David's early life in Durban, South Africa, as well as his individual and multidimensional writing style, was perhaps best elucidated when he spoke about his allegorical, if not autobiographical, first published novel, *Empire Settings* (2001):

"*Empire Settings* is a story of a young white South African affluent boy in his late teens who falls in love with the mixed-race daughter of an African domestic servant. That was illegal, and parts of it violated many social conventions that verged on taboo. They were eventually forced to separate.

"The boy, Danny, leaves South Africa and emigrates to Boston, starts his life in Boston, marries a girl to get his green card, is successful in Boston, and is never quite able to forget this girl he left behind.

"When twenty years later a pretext arises for him to go back to South Africa on family business, he accepts, but primarily to find what happened to her. And what he finds, when he finds her, is something that is really beyond anything he could have imagined, and something quite beyond what he expected.

"That's the story of *Empire Settings.* It's told from the perspective of different people: Danny himself, an African domestic servant, Danny's mother, his sister, and the girl. They each see the story somewhat differently, and to some extent, the life of the story exists in the inconsistencies of how each one sees it."

Empire Settings, taking place mostly in South Africa but also in the United States, might also be thought of as a novel showing, objectively, the differences and disparities between South African and American society and, subjectively, the differences and variations in David's identity as he lived his life in each of those countries. As he says, *Empire Settings* had to do with explaining himself in his new country, wanting to become "encapsulated, confirmed, and understood," feeling, when he said those words, as he does now, somewhat of a "foreigner" in his adopted — but much loved — country.

As David says, "When I came here, everything looked the same, people spoke the same language, everything seemed to be the same. It took a lot of time, actually, to realize how very, very different the society and the culture in which I had grown up was from that in America. In presenting Danny's view going back to South Africa, after twenty years in America, as *Empire Settings* does, it does present and describe many of the things I experienced and that I feel."

Noting that serious race problems exist in both the United States and South Africa, I asked David whether he sees those problems differently. The question elicited from David not only a direct answer, but also his deep appreciation of his new country and the town of Brookline, providing us with an acute view of how lucky we are, despite the ongoing rendings of the national fabric. (This is written a little more than seven months prior to the Bush/Kerry presidential election of 2004.)

"I think that there are enormous differences between South Africa and the United States," David said. "I think that in this country, for all of its problems, there was a commitment made a long time ago to try to fix them. In South Africa, the commitment was made in 1948 to segregate the races, and to do it, really, in a way that was unfair and punitive. That got undone in 1994, but there are fifty years of damage to undo in South Africa, and for all the flaws and for all the problems here, this country does not have that kind of damage that it needs to undo. In 1948, which really is a critical year in both countries, the United States decided to desegregate its army, and other steps were taken that led to the desegregation of public education, and a variety of laws were passed and court decisions came on after that, which attempted to ensure a fair society. We live in an imperfect society here, but we have made dramatic progress in remedying past injustice, and in trying to reach a society that is fair.

"In South Africa, the exact opposite happened. There, it was determined to unscramble the egg and create apartheid. I think many Americans take for granted how grand our society is. We're such a big country, with so many different ethnic groups, so many different interests that pull in so many different directions. But we should wake up each day aware of that, because it's not a simple matter to live peacefully. I am really, really happy, really joyful, to live here, and to be an American."

The lawyer in David came out strongly when he added, "Our system does, by and large, work, as ineffective and inefficient as it often is. It does work to keep the peace, to ensure economic justice, to do the things that it's supposed to do. It does most surely ensure our freedom."

David enlarged on those sentiments when he talked about Boston and Brookline: "As far as Brookline goes, when I came to Boston for the first time, I really felt that it was a city that felt like home in a way that was inexplicable, given that I was getting off the airplane for the first time. That feeling has never gone away.

"Brookline is a hometown, and I think that other people who live in this town must feel the same way. Sometimes, when I walk around town with visitors, they get taken aback by how proprietary I feel about it. There are great little parks on every corner, there are places that you don't expect, and all of a sudden, where there should be two or three houses, there's a little discrete park. I love it when new buildings are built, places are fixed up and refurbished, when trees are planted. I do feel very proprietary and very protective about Brookline. I think that it's a unique town, and that it's a great town to live in. I hope that I will be able to live my life here.

"It has a great school system. I have a two-year-old, as I told you. We fully expect at this point to send her through the Brookline public school system. It may be somewhat indiscreet to say this, but when I was a partner in my law firm, I got to interview a lot of young men and women who wanted to be lawyers.

Although I fully understand and appreciate the merits of those very smart private schools and the very smart universities, there was something stronger and something that I really recognized as being an asset in many of the people who came through my office looking for a job who had been to public schools and who had been to the less elegant universities. There is something about public schools and universities that are somewhat less elite that does turn out people who are solid, in my view. So, I really do expect my daughter to go to the Brookline public schools."

Plainly, authoring *Empire Settings* has brought David Schmahmann to a deeper, more precise, and more appreciative sense of freedom and democracy in America, and in Brookline: "I mentioned to you off the air earlier that one of the things that has surprised me was that after I came here, I wanted very much to be an American. I wanted to be American, to feel American. I became an American citizen with a great joy and pride.

"As I become older, the fact that I am a 'South African American,' with the emphasis on the 'South African' in 'South African American,' it has become clear to me that I will never be the sort of American my daughter or my wife is. Because I was a South African through such interesting and formative years — I left when I was seventeen or eighteen — the fact is I am actually as South African, or more South African, in my internal architecture. That has become something that is interesting to me, and it's interesting to write about. In part, that's what drove me to write this novel. When I practiced law, if I really wanted to understand a topic, the best way to understand it was to write and publish an article. That's how I learned about Burmese law, and I practiced law in Burma. With literature it's very much the same thing, except it's an emotional experience, rather than a technical experience."

To me it appears that David Schmahmann's "South African American" is as "American" as any other American, a good argument for the American tradition of inclusiveness.

BOOK IV

DOGS

Puppy Puppy Ruttman at home.

Photo by author.

DEBORAH B. GOLDBERG
AND HER DOG SAWYER

Chair, Brookline Board of Selectmen
Builders of Community

IT WILL COME AS NO SURPRISE to anyone who knows Deborah
Goldberg, the retiring chair of the Brookline Board of Selectmen,
that the words *family* and *community* are on the first page of her
personal lexicon. This was evident early in the interview I did a year
or so ago with Debbie on Brookline Access TV, when she spoke
with equal love about her family — the well-known Goldbergs on
her father's side and the equally well-known Rabbs on her mother's
side — and about her lifelong Brookline community.

Brookline Access TV interview, February 6, 2003. *Brookline Bulletin*, April 29,
2004.

Debbie, because she is a canine lover as well as a people lover, is particularly able in her work as a selectman to make the link between that and the continuing nurturing and building of Brookline community, as demonstrated in the recent institution of the off-leash "Green Dog" pilot program.

Debbie, appearing on the show with her small dog, Sawyer, sitting contentedly on her lap, sees the off-leash program as encouraging for the next generation of citizen involvement in Brookline community. She puts it this way:

"I think we have to find a way where there's an ability to use the parks for everyone in the community. I also think that dogs are very important to people who have them, and that there's a group of people in town, in the twenty-five to thirty-five age group, who don't have children in schools yet, who are, believe it or not, the largest population group in the community. And if you look at who is active in town affairs, that group is sort of an invisible group. And a lot of them have dogs. They are usually condo owners, and they don't really have the backyards to allow dogs to run. And they've developed a social life associated with dog ownership. And they are the group that has come forward with this, people who are informed, caring, highly educated, and interesting.

"I see this issue as a way to bring these folks into town government, and get them more engaged, because we are looking for the next generation who is going to be interested in the town. We've tried all sorts of ways to figure out what would appeal to them, and it is an issue like this that gets people going. I want this group to feel that we can work together to find a solution that will be comfortable for everyone involved."

Loving and appreciating my own magnificent standard poodle, Molly, my response to Debbie's remarks were heartfelt: "When you say that we really ought to have a program like this to bring people together, I agree with you. Dogs are important to people, people are important to people, and the more times you throw people together face to face, you are building community. Less and less do people interact the way they used to, and I see the Green Dog program as related to the idea of community."

In fact, the notion of community has been so central in the course of Debbie's life that it seems almost ordained that she would someday achieve her present position at the pinnacle of Brookline town governance. Her values flow naturally from the warmth, togetherness, and values she inherited from both sides of her family. Debbie reflects and remembers in this way:

"Yes, I don't know any families that weren't close. My grand-parents on the Goldberg side lived a block and a half away, and they were always at my house. My other grandparents [the Rabbs] lived on Commonwealth Avenue. In the summers, we were all at the Cape on the same property. There was no separation of church and state in terms of the business and family. The other business of the family was charitable work, and I thought that was all one big thing. That's what life was: You worked together, you worked for the greater good of the community together, you worked for the greater good of the Jewish people together, and family, family, family. So I come at this from a lot of directions."

It was natural, then, that Debbie worked as the Mascot Child in an early Mike Dukakis campaign for state representative, going in his coffee station wagon from poll to poll, telling how "really pas-sionate" she felt about getting Mike elected. Then her father, Avram, ran for Town Meeting member, getting Debbie to think, as she puts it, "This is life! You have a company that you work for, you work for charitable causes, and you work toward the public good in the political arena. So I always knew that not only would I run for Town Meeting, but that I would run for selectman one day.

I always told everybody, including my husband [Michael Winter], before he became my husband, that whatever happened, I was always going to live in Brookline. This was because I always knew that I would run for public office here. First, I ran for Town Meeting, and then I ran for selectman the following year. It's a desire for continuity. One of the reasons I'm so committed to the community is I want to try and continue what has been my expe-rience and my feelings about Brookline for the next generation. I hope that my kids will live in Brookline and feel as passionately about Brookline as I do."

The question that occurs to all of us who love Brookline is whether the "community" we know can continue against the ravages of the impersonality of the communications revolution. At bottom, Debbie is optimistic on that question:

"I think our core values will stay the same. We're a pretty progressive, liberal community. It has always been that way in Brookline. I think we're a community that is interested in the world. We are a community that is committed and passionate. But we're more of a transient community than we used to be, and we've lost certain things that were evident when I was a kid. Then, I think we had a lower-middle class, a working class of people. People lived in apartments, they were families, they had maybe one car, definitely not two. They took the T to work. Coolidge Corner was the hub of that community, a commuter community.

"With the buying of condos came the problem of parking, particularly for the largest group of people, those twenty-five to thirty-five with no children, who need parking. Their condos have an incredible value, and they pay high taxes. That's the change in the community. I still think we have enough of our core values, our commitment to education. People move here to send their kids to our schools because they are so great, a real value in this community."

Of course, Debbie recognizes that affordable housing is key to the continuity of Brookline community, citing the family history of her associate on the board of selectmen, Robert Allen: "Take Bobby Allen, whose family has lived here for multiple generations. It is becoming harder and harder. I often mention to people, talking about affordable housing, that my own stepdaughter can't afford to live in Brookline, so the affordability of living here is becoming more and more challenging. And that scares me, because I don't want the character of our town to change, and part of it is that continuity, some of which we still have, some of which we have lost. There's something good about that small-town feeling."

As is well known, Debbie's parents, Avram and Carol (Rabb) Goldberg, oversaw Stop & Shop for several years. Her mother's example was key in Debbie's ascent: "I have two fabulous parents! My mother was a very unique woman. She went to work at Stop & Shop in her twenties, and in the long term she became one of the top businesswomen in America. She was a role model for me because she showed me how to maintain your femininity and still be out there achieving things in the world and not letting really anything get in your way, particularly in terms of sex-role stereotypes and glass ceilings.

"My mother did teach me. Women have a lot to add. In that sense, Brookline is unique; we have had women selectmen for a long time. There have been Brookline-Newton women legislators for a long time, and presently. My mother was a pioneer, a mentor to many, and continues to be. I love her very much!"

Indeed, it was a gift to Debbie's mother that enhanced Debbie's love of dogs, family, and community: "I was in the seventh grade at the Runkle school when we got Monty. He was a birthday present to my mother on her thirty-fifth birthday. And I didn't really believe he was ours. I was on an overnight at Debbie Finley's house on Garrison Road, and when I came home, there was this dog, and I was certain that he belonged to friends of my parents. But Monty stayed and they left."

And Debbie stayed too, much to our benefit!

LOIS RUTTMAN AND MOLLY RUTTMAN

The Dog Whisperer and Her Dog,
Brookline Citizens

THE HARMONY OF the voices of Brookline and Brookline community is enhanced by the utterances of our dogs, cats, and other pets, and the people who bond with them. In that regard, for a while now, I have wanted to write about our majestic standard poodle, Molly, whose friendship my wife, Lois, and I have enjoyed since a September day almost seven years ago when we first laid eyes on this astoundingly beautiful animal. Never could I have believed that within a scant six weeks after interviewing Debbie Goldberg and writing the preceding story about her and her dog Sawyer, and how the interaction of dogs and people build Brookline community, I would be taking pen in hand to write about Molly with such a heavy heart.

I heard only a few hours ago from the veterinary surgeon who biopsied Molly's recently discovered diseased liver, speaking to me in sufficiently grave tones about having to wait for the histological results to dim my already weakened hopes for her. I could not imagine, until the last few weeks, that this animal, whom I think to be the finest being I have ever known, combining, as Molly does, an apparently unique array of qualities and attributes, would come to such a pass in the midst of her buoyant life.

Molly's benign yet enthusiastically animal presence has inspired Lois and me to dub her with various nicknames — Mol, Molecule, Big Girl, Goodness, Seabiscuit — but perhaps the most accurate nickname was bestowed by our next-door neighbor Tam Thompson, who, one day walking by Lois, Molly, and me sitting in front of our home on Sumner Road in Brookline, looked warmly at Molly, whom she knew well, and called her The Great Spirit.

Indeed, even in Molly's present extremity, having lost her desire to eat and close to twenty percent of her body weight over these last several weeks, she continues to show her remarkable physical beauty and vitality, to the surprise of the vets charged with her care. Only a few days ago, as I walked her near Brookline High School, a woman called to me from across the street to warmly and enthusiastically praise Molly's appearance and bearing. Thanking her, I briefly described, to her shock and dismay, Molly's present plight, which — at this writing — seems likely to end her life within weeks.

In preparing to write about Molly, I jotted down adjectives and ideas to better describe her, surprised at the profusion of words flowing from my mind and heart to the pen in my hand. Perhaps the best way to convey "The Great Spirit" Molly possesses is to combine these ideas with some of Lois's and my life experiences with her.

Molly is a patient companion as you walk with her close to home. When I stop to talk to a neighbor and become involved in a long conversation, she at first stands ready to continue, then, sensing it will be a while, sits by my side, uttering not a sound and making no move to continue the walk that she dearly loves, acquiescing in her dignified way to my wishes, waiting patiently to walk on when the time comes.

Without fail Molly is kind, gentle, and attentive to many of the elderly and infirm residents of the nearby Hebrew Rehabilitation

Center for the Aged in Roslindale, where Lois almost daily visits her resident mother, and where Lois and Molly volunteer their spirit and services. Christa, a dedicated worker at HRCA, who is always thinking up and leading events like birthday parties and musicales to entertain the residents, would often bring Molly into the party and sing this refrain:

Just Molly and me and baby makes three — we're happy in our blue heaven.

What you have read up to now was written on Friday, March 26, and Saturday, March 27, 2004, mostly in the afternoon following the morning we took Molly in for her exploratory and a little the next day shortly before we were advised we could come pick Molly up around four in the afternoon. Sadly, within hours of returning home to Brookline, Molly became critical, her bounding physicality finally overcome by the insult of the open biopsy. At the veterinary clinic the following afternoon, Lois and I made the painful decision to put Molly to sleep, opting not to undertake heroic measures with a small chance that Molly would survive very long, and the certainty that even if she did, her striking quality of life would be permanently and greatly reduced.

At the last, Molly passed with the dignity and calm that every day marked this noble and majestic animal. Characteristically, Molly uttered a soft and deep sound in her throat as she drew her last breath, audible perhaps only to me as I held my face close to her face, a sound that seemed to me to be Molly's evocation of her lifetime of acceptance, defining her life into a final last acceptance, the acceptance of death.

Some days later, I ventured to Lois that "we did the right thing." Lois, not a person given to hyperbole or sentimentality, although filled with true sentiment and generosity, answered with words of less restraint than I had ever heard from her before: "Yes, we did. We did the noblest thing for the noblest animal."

At this point, I must say that although my own relationship with Molly was deeply and mutually loving, companionable, and special, it remained a bond between a man and his dog, unlike the otherworldly link between Lois and Molly, truly soulmates, so ideally suited to one another that I am convinced Molly viewed Lois as one of her own kind, fully equipped to partner with her in all adventures. Always I admired Lois's fierce protectiveness and self-less loving of Molly (indeed, her respect for all animals), and remain in wonder at Lois's gift of inspiring Molly to view her as a hybrid person/animal, a dog whisperer, so to speak.

It seems to me, however, that the most important quality possessed by Lois that allowed Lois and Molly to inhabit the same animal world, and to inspire Molly to view Lois as one of her own animal family, was Lois's uncanny and rare ability to naturally enter Molly's world on Molly's terms and to enjoy Molly's friends and adventures through Molly's eyes and ears. Once the name of any of Molly's animal friends became known, Lois never forgot that name, invoking that name for Molly and herself whenever that animal appeared.

Largely, their adventures took place in several locales in Brookline in the immediate vicinity of our home on Sumner Road. Lois had created a "run" for Molly on one side of our house between the shrubs and the fence, the better for Molly to go down to the front of the house to commune with her many friends walking up and down Sumner Road, people and dogs both, who would come to visit her regularly. Molly was particularly enamored of the greyhound, Lucky, who would come by almost every day with Dr. Richard Wolff. Molly loved Lucky, so much so that from inside our house she could sense Lucky coming down Sumner Road. She'd go to the dining room window and bark to be let out, then race down the "run" to the front iron gate to get Lucky's attention. Molly was partial to male greyhounds; she also adored Yatzi, whom she met at HRCA. Devi, a male black standard poodle, would also visit Molly at the front gate, and a parade of other people and dogs would often come up the driveway to the gate to socialize with her.

Lois often took Molly on a walk to Brookline High School, a short distance down the hill from our home. Always occupied with the welfare of the wild and stray cats living behind the high school, Lois would bring food for them, putting it down in rows on the sloping cement divider at the rear perimeter of the school. Within seconds the cats would come out and eat voraciously, as Molly and Lois stood back respectfully, looking on with satisfaction. Near the high school live other friends of Molly, Emma, a Portuguese water dog; the black dog Jake, sort of a guard dog, whom Molly befriended; and Ritmo, a male standard poodle.

On the low side, near our home, runs lengthy Clark Road. Molly befriended Maximilian, a white bichon frise who lives in the corner house on Clark opposite our house. Farther down Clark lives Eloise, a brownish terrier, who would run back and forth in the window barking at all the dogs going by, including Molly. Lois tells the story of "the two of us running for our lives" from one of the two cats living across the street from Eloise's house, where Molly had another friend — another Molly, an old golden retriever.

The fact is that as Lois and Molly lived it, the big feature on Clark Road was the abundance of cats there, providing Molly and Lois with continuous adventure. In the second house on Clark Road there are two cats, "a black and a white, and a white and a black," as Lois puts it, the latter easily scared. Molly would play-fully chase her up a tree. The male was fearless, Lois recounting that "he beat us up" one day, chasing "us" away. During these Clark Road adventures, Lois constantly advised Molly person to person — or was it animal to animal — that kitties don't like a lot of noise, you have to be patient, sit and watch them, that kitties like quiet.

One of the best adventures Molly and Lois had was a few streets away on Beaconsfield Road, where there was a kitty hiding behind a fence, thinking he was safe, not knowing his tail was stick-ing out from under the fence onto the sidewalk. Quietly Molly went over to investigate and pawed that tail sticking out. The kitty took immediate flight.

Farther down Sumner Road lives the man who knows all the dogs, Mr. Stuart Dunbar. Lois calls him the "cookie man" — always in one pocket he has dog treats and in the other pocket people treats. Stuart leaves cookies for the dogs at the base of the tree in front of his house.

Lois puts it this way: "We just met a lot of people and dogs and cats." Among them were Selectman Debbie Goldberg's dogs up higher on Fisher Hill. One time when Lois and Molly came by, Debbie opened the front door beckoning all of her dogs to come piling out to greet Molly and Lois, and, good trainer that Debbie is, beckoned them right back in a few moments later.

Talking about Molly's Brookline friends, I must not leave out the peripatetic cat, Ashley, who early in his life lost his uncommonly beautiful tail in an accident, living those years next door to our house with Joanne Caulfield. Ashley now has changed his residence to another house nearby, at least the third residence contiguous to our house he has had in his long and mostly tailless life. Before Molly came to live with us, Ashley, though never living with us, was a constant visitor, becoming almost part of the family, his gentle nature emboldening me to allow him to close his sharp incisors gently upon my hand. However, his natural fearfulness kept Ashley away after Molly came to live with us. On one occasion, Ashley was near our house, and Molly, on her side of the fence, chased him up the driveway on the other side. He interpreted her playfulness as aggression, so these two mild and gentle animals never really met on common ground.

Is it any wonder that at this writing, a few months after Molly's passing, Lois expresses a sense of incompleteness, a sense more akin to an animal's loss of its mate than a human's loss of a pet? For myself, Molly remains a palpable presence, as I know she will be forever.

Molly's unsurpassed quality of acceptance has permeated our separate selves to the center, setting an example, teaching us, changing us, improving us to be better able to express patience, tolerance, indeed love to each other and to others. No one who has unreservedly loved an animal and been loved in return will doubt these words and its metamorphosing power to change one's life. That acceptance was demonstrated further by the fact that Molly was never envious or jealous when Lois or I attended, petted, or held other dogs or cats in her presence; indeed, she would look on with bemusement and approval, seeming to relish our enjoyment of her fellow creatures and express her oneness with all beings.

How wondrously athletic Molly was! Our modest-size backyard consists of an open grassy area around which there is a semicircular hillside covered with bushes and shrubs of various kinds, backed by an enclosing fence which continues down the side yard of the house to the side gate. Many times Molly would run at top speed — upwards of thirty miles per hour — amazing and delighting Lois and me with her ability, day or night, to run up and down, through the bushes, back into the yard, back through the bushes, along the top of the hill at the fence, down the fence to the front of the house at the gate, and back again, over and over, never slackening speed, somehow never injuring or impaling herself on the thousands of branches and boughs seemingly in her path, inspiring in us a sort of reverential awe for her animal spirits, abilities, and senses, and an amazement that we should be living with such a wild creature, otherwise so domesticated, kind, and accepting.

Oh, to be able to live as a human for even one hour gifted with Molly's animal spirits, abilities, and senses, how much more experience and appreciation I would have of the wondrous world in which we live!

In the house, too, Lois and I played with Molly. Her favorite game was kick the soccer ball, and whether at that game or another, she would run fast from room to room, leaping as necessary, yet never in all those years did she damage or break any item of furniture or furnishings, making me believe to a certainty — with wonder — that this must come from some rare combination of physical prowess and intelligent respect for objects around her. Even in the last few days of her life — probably when she didn't feel like playing kick the soccer ball — she accepted my suggestion and played with enthusiasm.

Molly was a quiet dog, easy and relaxing to be with. Days would go by and she would not make a sound. Yet she knew her territory, and if she felt our house was being encroached upon, she would bark, a full-throated, deep bark, one so satisfying to hear, coming, as it did, from her depths. In all the years I lived with Molly, never once did she growl, bare her teeth, or show anger or irritation.

I have spoken of my many walks with Molly. On a deeper level, every time we walked together, we communed. I talked to Molly about many things, and she looked back up at me to show that she was listening. I often stopped to bend down and hug her and whisper in her ear. During one down time in my life, lasting a few months, mostly every day Molly would accompany me on very long walks to the top of Fisher Hill in Brookline and back again, sympathizing and sharing with me.

Friend Ran Blake, the noted pianist and composer, attending a Thanksgiving dinner at our home, described Molly, perhaps presciently, as a "celestial hostess." Ever the humanist, Ran's perspicacious judgment of Molly that she is a "magnificent specimen of humanity" cut to the essence of Molly's being.

Molly was a citizen of Brookline, if one's definition of community embraces people, animals, trees, plants, open space — indeed, all that lies beneath the sky — as I think it should. These ideas were in the air when I interviewed Debbie Goldberg, the chair of the Brookline Board of Selectmen as I write, on my local access TV program recently. Debbie, who knew and appreciated Molly, appeared on that program with her small dog Sawyer sitting on her lap, saying she thought that Brookline's new off-leash Green Dog pilot program would contribute to Brookline community, drawing my agreement.

Certainly Molly expanded Lois's and my community, in ways big and small. We always had cordial relations with our next-door neighbors on Sumner Road, Susan and Gene Briskman, but when Susan's collie Maggie and Molly became fast friends, rough housing daily in our backyard, our friendship blossomed. When neighbor Sandy VonLichtenberg started visiting with Natasha, a pit bull also mollified by Molly, the same thing happened.

Molly's citizenship contributed to other communities as well. At the Hebrew Rehab, resident Ed Landry would ask Lois whenever she appeared without Molly, "Where's Molly?" There, on the very day after Molly's passing, when Lois appeared as she does every Monday to officiate the Monday-afternoon card game for her mother and other residents, she received sympathetic hugs from many of the staff and residents whom Molly had touched. Later, Molly's friends at the Hebrew Rehab sent cards, one saying "We will always love and remember Molly."

Seen this way, "community" — whether of Brookline or of the world — is a seamless interweaving of all of God's creatures. However divinely inspired some humans may be, obviously man has not yet divined the path to peaceful existence, making one wonder what our existence might be like if somehow some of us could combine Molly's "great spirit" with our own powers of reason, logic, and speech.

POSTSCRIPT

Molly's story may not have had a happy ending, but now it does have a new beginning, as I write these words a few days before Labor Day of the year Molly died. Mirabella, an almost pure white standard poodle of gentle, loving, and playful disposition, born, unbeknownst to us until a later time, only a few days after Molly died, came to live with us a little over two weeks ago. Almost immediately she distinguished herself from Molly by stepping into her water bowl with one of her hind legs, spilling its contents. From that moment, I began to think of her as "my funny valentine," and the affecting lyrics of that Frank Sinatra favorite describing how to love one with "a figure less than Greek." Lois and I will never forget Molly, but we hope to live happily for many years with Mirabella, affectionately called Puppy Puppy.

As I write these words, Lois and Mirabella almost daily visit venues like Brookline Avenue Playground, Larz Anderson Park, and Amory Playground, where the off-leash "Green Dog" pilot program prevails, each of them gamboling on the green, as it were, making and enjoying new friends and building the community of which Debbie Goldberg and I spoke.

BOOK V

BROOKLINE
HIGH SCHOOL

Photo courtesy of Brookline High School Library.

*Headmaster Bertram H. Holland with Graduates Judith Louise Norman
and David Boyer (June 1962).*

Photo by author.

From left: Sam and Mari.

MARIANA FOLCO AND SAMANTHA CHENG

Seniors at Brookline High School,
National Honor Society Members

FOR THE MANY OF US WHO GREW UP and attended Brookline schools in the quarter century or so before and after the middle of the twentieth century, it trips off the tongue easily to say that Brookline was a great place in which to grow up, and still is, and that the schools here are the best, then and now. Of course, during that stretch of time, Brookline metamorphosed from lily white to diverse and polyglot, that being most evident at Brookline High School, where many nationalities are represented and many languages spoken. In the process, Brookline has become somewhat elite, with rising home values and rents essentially forcing out the lower middle class, including many of Brookline's own public service employees.

Brookline Access TV interview, November 30, 2004.

Notwithstanding these momentous changes, the best evidence that Brookline retains its essential character as a great place in which to live and go to school comes from the testimony of accomplished and thoughtful teenagers, like Argentinean-born and bilingual Mariana "Mari" Folco and American-born and articulate Samantha "Sam" Cheng, fast friends, and both on track to graduate from BHS with honors in 2005.

Academically and athletically gifted Mari Folco is able to view Brookline from a long perspective: "Brookline is a unique and special place. Being a small town right outside of Boston gives Brookline a nice atmosphere. It's very liberal and very diverse. It's very accepting of everyone, a really nice place to grow up. I've really liked coming back here. [Mari came to Brookline in 1990 at age three, went to Runkle School, then moved back to Mar del Plata in Argentina in 1996. She returned to Brookline in 2001, going to Baker School for three months, then to BHS.] Even though I left, then came back, and lived in different parts of Brookline," she says, "I've always felt at home here because I feel like I know the town well. Just being at the high school, where everyone from different parts of Brookline comes together, you just get the feel of what every part of Brookline is. I've also learned from a lot of your shows [which Mari and Sam have capably transcribed for me] about all the great people that come out of Brookline."

Effervescent and energetic Sam Cheng had a similar take: "I feel like I've lived here for so long. I know a lot of people in my neighborhood. Working with Brookline Recreation, I know some of the town employees and the people who have been here for a long time. It's a really good community to grow up and live in because everyone is so accepting of everyone else, and there are a lot of people who care about you who you don't think would. It's a close community but a big one at the same time. There are always new people you can meet and new aspects you can find, but there are always those people you will always know in the community as well."

Perhaps predictably, both Mari and Sam would choose a public school education in Brookline over a private school, even if money were no issue. Sam focused on diversity in answering that question: "In public schools, you see every sort of person you can see. In private schools you are limited to the people who can afford private schools, which gives you a sort of limited view of the world."

Mari homed in on the quality of Brookline schools: "I would also choose public schools, especially in a town like Brookline, where the public schools are great. There is no need to pay for a private education when you can get one just as fulfilling at Brookline High School."

It is evident looking at and listening to Mari and Sam that each of them is fulfilled, at a time when many teenagers are betwixt and between and worse, impelling one to want to know more about them, their peers, and the schools in which they have been educated.

Sam and Mari's volunteer activities and athletic endeavors, directly growing out of their Brookline school experience, begin to flesh out the portrait. Sam was the organizer and cofounder of the BHS Food Drive in the eleventh and twelfth grades. She spoke about that:

"I organized it last year with my friend Aurelie Cao. We met at hockey, and we decided to organize a food drive for Thanksgiving. We sent out notices to each of the homerooms at the high school, and we had Paul Erelli, the community service coordinator, help us with that. We donated food to the Boston Food Bank. In the end, we got about two hundred donations.

"I like to do volunteer work. Another one is Student Action for Justice in Education [S.A.J.E.]. It was organized a couple of years ago by some people in my grade. Essentially, we're working for human rights and workers' rights. Right now we're working on a living-wage campaign. I actually just joined this year, and what I wanted to do is start a Books Not Bombs campaign. That would be a voter awareness drive, where we would tell voters on their way to the polls information about how the education funds in this country are being misused and being directed toward the building of more prisons, building up the military, and developing nuclear weapons for our country, even though Bush is saying that he wants to stop nuclear proliferation. Unfortunately, it fell through. We didn't have enough time to organize."

Mari Folco, with the advantage of her bilingual ability,

speaking without accent in both English and Spanish, volunteered at Runkle School to work with her own former English as a Second Language teacher to help young Hispanic students there who did not speak much English:

"When I moved back to Argentina," she says, "I stayed in contact with Ms. Guzzi, my first-grade teacher at Runkle, because she was a great teacher. While living in Argentina, we came back to visit a couple of times, and I saw her then. Last year, I decided I wanted to help out at Runkle, but Ms. Guzzi wasn't available because our schedules didn't fit, so I ended up going to my ESL teacher who helped me when I first came here. She has a class of students who have just moved here, whom she helps with Spanish. I went and helped this one boy in the second grade who just moved here from Colombia. I went once a week during a free block, and helped him with reading, writing, and learning basics, like colors and the alphabet. It was a lot of fun!"

I suggested to Mari that she might well have said to that boy, in Spanish, "I want you to learn this stuff because you're going to need it when you go to Brookline High School, because they teach classes in English there!" I asked her to speak those words in Spanish. She did: *"Quiero que aprendas esto porque lo vas a tener que usar en el high school cuando empieces a aprender cosas en ingles,"* an exercise that might represent the diversity and multiculturalism that pervades present-day school and community life in Brookline.

Gentle-spoken Mariana Folco is quick with a thought, quick with a word, quick with a smile, and quick on her feet, Samantha Cheng saying that, "She's a scary runner! I'm scared of her when I'm running! She's so fast! It's like I'm running, and I'm like, 'Bye, Mari!' and half an hour later I come trudging in and there she is."

Mari's burgeoning athletic career at BHS presages great success on those fields, as Mari advances to higher education, leaning now toward "something humanities oriented, maybe social studies." Mari spoke of her multi-athletic activities without needing to take a deep breath: "I started in my freshman year with just crew, and now I'm on the varsity crew team. I've been on it since freshman year. In my sophomore year I added winter track, so I had those two sports. Last year, my junior year, I added on cross-country, so this year I was doing all three, cross-country, track, and crew. I had the last couple of weeks off because it was between seasons, so I just ran on my own."

Up to this point, Mari had not mentioned that she is a captain in all three of those sports, suggesting that some people must think she has leadership qualities. I asked her about that and Mari responded, "I guess so. It's fun!"

It may be that Samantha Cheng comes "trudging in" in Mari's wake on their runs together, but that has not stopped her from participating in lacrosse, ice hockey, and cross-country at BHS, as well as figure skating since she was six years old: "I've been skating since I was six, and I started just recreational skating at Larz Anderson with those double-edged blades that no one in the world has, but for some reason I did. But I just kept falling and falling. Finally, I got the hang of it. Then I went to the Babson Skating School in Wellesley, where one of my friends went. I've been skating there since I was seven. So I've had a group of friends there since then. We're all in the freestyle program, which has three levels, bronze, silver, and gold. We're in silver right now. I doubt by the time I graduate high school I will be in gold. You should see me skating. It's like 'Free Willy' launching myself on the ice," she said, smiling.

Observing the warm friendship between Mari and Sam, each from an entirely different background, I wondered aloud whether such pairings were unusual at Brookline High School, and about the ups and downs of diversity there. Sam offered that cross-cultural friendships are "definitely not unusual," and thoughtfully detailed the elements of diversity at BHS:

"It's like everyone has respect for each other, for all different races and cultures. It's not a discriminating society, but there is a degree of self-segregation at the high school. You do see a lot of people of one race being friends with each other, and only hanging out together, but not necessarily being unfriendly to people of other races — just preferring to hang out with people who are of their own culture. I guess they feel like they have more to relate to. I have a friend who is Jewish in Asian American studies. She is one of the only kids that isn't Asian in the class. There was a discussion one day in which the Asian kids talked about how they felt like they'd rather be friends with people of their own race, because they felt they could connect better to them. It was just interesting, because I've never felt that way even though I'm of the Asian minority. I've always had friends who are different. I mean, Mari's Hispanic, and I have friends who are Jewish, Christian, African-American, Swedish."

Not surprisingly, Mari Folco spoke similarly: "You can see a lot of diversity at the high school, and in a way it does create some cliques, but not necessarily in a bad way. There are so many different clubs, the Latino-American Club, the Asian-American Club. There are all sorts of clubs. In a way, all the Asian people start hanging out together because of their club. In a way, they kind of separate themselves, but at the same time, everyone is there together without a problem. You walk around in the halls where people are eating on the floor, or where they can find a little spot, unless they eat in the cafeteria, and you always see these clusters of people, and you always see all kinds of different-looking people in those groups, so it's not everyone being totally segregated."

Naturally, Sam and Mari have very definite opinions on the quality of instruction they have received in Brookline schools, and how well it has prepared them for higher education and life itself.

Samantha Cheng, whose multiple interests have not yet coalesced into a definite career path, says, "I'm looking into biology, but I'm looking more and more into public health policy, and environmental sciences, probably doing something in a government agency. But that's for now. I might change later to God knows what, like history!"

As Sam continued, speaking with admiration of her teachers, it soon became apparent in this interchange between Sam and Mari that the quality of education at Brookline High School inheres in a synergy between the highly qualified teaching staff and the highly diverse student body.

Samantha: "I think all of my teachers, or most of them, have been amazing teachers! I've learned so much from them, not only in the academic sense. There are some teachers to whom I can talk in a personal way, not just in a student/teacher relationship, but as a person to talk to. It's good that way."

Mari: "I agree. There are all sorts of really great teachers, and also just a lot of good curriculum and good classes. Especially, as a senior, there are a lot of different classes you can choose to take. In earlier years, you have to take a certain English class, standard or honors, or a certain math class, and either U.S. or world history, but as a senior, you can choose what science you want to take, what history you want to take, so there's a lot more different types of classes. For example, I'm taking Good Citizen in the Good Society, which is English and history combined. It is a really interesting class. It's taught by two teachers, one an English teacher, the other a history teacher. We talk about a lot of stuff going on around us today, the media, hunger, problems with identity, which is really great, because we are learning about English and history at the same time, but also talking about the real world. The teachers in my class are Mr. Colburn and Ms. Simon. In the other blocks, the teachers are Ms. Ringwall and Ms. Hanaghan."

Samantha: "I feel like the classes I'm in challenge me a lot, especially since students take classes to their academic potential, so you're always in a class with people who can challenge your ideas. For example, in my history class, Contemporary America, there are kids in my class with very conservative views, very liberal views, and some with more moderate views. During discussions, you can see that people respect each other's opinions, but also everyone is learning from each other, not only from the teacher, but from other students."

Mari: "I pretty much agree with that. In the classes, there are always people who talk more, some who talk less, there's always one person who gets the conversation started, so opinions can clash in the classes. Also, talking about the levels of courses, there is a lot to choose from. There are standard, honors, and advanced-placement classes. So everyone can find a spot for themselves. If you're in honors, if you want to be more challenged, you can move up to AP. You can move up or down, and it gives everyone a lot of choices."

Knowing and listening to Mariana Folco and Samantha Cheng, one can accurately opine that, individually and together, they are moving up, exemplifying the quality and diversity of Brookline life and community on its three hundredth birthday.

Photo by author.

Dr. Robert J. "Dr. Bob" Weintraub

Headmaster of Brookline High School, Educator

THE APPELLATION "DR. BOB" applied to Dr. Robert J. Weintraub by the numerous and diverse student body at Brookline High School may appear, at first hearing, to be an unnatural juxtaposition, tying together, as it does, a term applied to a person of high educational standing with a common nickname. In Bob Weintraub's case, once you get to know this fast-paced, easy-talking, and passionate educator, it seems entirely natural, even though describing himself as "Bob" to his first students threatened the early demise of his present legend in the making upwardly arching career as headmaster of Brookline High School, a school held in the highest esteem both here and elsewhere.

Bob's first run-in with his own nickname came on his first day as a teacher, fresh out of Lehigh University where he earned a bachelor of arts in English/journalism. Bob learned a lesson that day

Brookline Access TV interview, March 6, 2003.

he never forgot: "My first day as a teacher I was working in a white working-class section of a community called Totowa, next to Paterson, New Jersey, teaching English. So what I did to prepare for my first class, I put my name on the board, 'Bob Weintraub.' I sat on my desk, and the kids started to come in for first period. These two kids, I remember it was like thirty-three years ago, and the first two kids came in, one was named Patrick, one was named George. These two kids walked in and they kinda looked at me, and they looked up at the board, and they looked at each other, and said: 'Hey, we got Bob for a teacher.' When all the other kids started piling into the room — there were a lot of kids in those classes, probably close to forty kids in the class — Patrick and George would say: 'Hey, guys, we got Bob, Bob is our teacher, isn't that great? We got Bob!' I said to myself, 'I think I made a mistake!' So my first move as a teacher was a disastrous mistake, and I completely lost that class.

"As soon as that class was over, I immediately erased the 'Bob' part of Weintraub and I wrote 'Mr. Weintraub,' which was pretty uncomfortable for me, but it was an important lesson. The second class went a little bit better than the first class. So you know, I love literature and I love writing, and I felt I could just teach through my love of the discipline, but that was not true, and I had a lot to learn. So I started learning on the job, and my first year was difficult.

"The second year of teaching was much, much more effective," he says, "and I realized I had to be a grown-up and I had to distance myself to some extent from the kids. I totally loved being with the kids, it was fun, and the better you got as a teacher, the more fun you had, so there was real motivation for me to get better and better and better. Then once you feel a little bit confident and comfortable being a teacher, then the distance between the kids can start to shrink a little bit, and you can start to have the kind of relationships that I really, really like to have with kids, and I believe I continue to have as headmaster of Brookline High School."

With that experience imprinted on Bob Weintraub's mind, you'd think he would be the last person to describe himself as Dr. Bob and might also wonder how that term became affixed to him. Indeed, it was in happy circumstances, which continue to this day:

"Dr. Bob actually has an origin," he says, "having to do with when I first got the headmaster job. I was the acting headmaster at the high school in 1992, I believe it was, because the previous headmaster had left late in the school year, and so they sort of needed someone to take it for a year, which I was actually afraid to do, because the job itself appeared to be overwhelming. But I agreed to do that for one year, and the arrangement with the school committee at that time was if you were an acting headmaster, you could not apply for the full-time position. Then a very flattering thing happened. A group of kids actually organized a campaign to change the rules, because they liked me, and that was nice. They thought it was stupid to not at least give you a chance to apply for the job. So the 'Dr. Bob' part came back then, when they created these hats. I think the hats said 'We love Dr. Bob,' and I was very appreciative that they did that, although I had nothing to do with it.

"They organized this campaign, they went to the school committee, got parents involved, just to let me apply for the job. So the school committee changed the rules for me, and allowed me to apply for that job, and then, ultimately, I was selected for the position, and was a little bit surprised."

The name stuck, but this time Dr. Robert J. Weintraub did not let it come between the easy openness that he always maintains with the thousands of students who have passed by under his administration and the more difficult and stricter demands of being headmaster. Bob explains his modus operandi, giving due credit to his fine staff:

"I'm pretty clear about it," he says. "I'm friendly, but I'm not their friend. I mean that's very clear to me, that was clearly the lesson that I learned early on in my teaching career. I think and hope the kids understand that I expect them to work hard, and I expect them to be decent and respectful citizens of our school community. If they are not, there's a consequence. I'm not the disciplinarian, in a sense, for most of the kids at the school. We have a very strong leadership structure at the high school, we have deans and associate deans. And you know, on a day-to-day basis, Deans Gretchen Underwood, Diane Landy, Adrien Mims, Lindsay Murphy, Rosemary Pierson, Jimmy Cradle, and the program people like Ellen Kapovitz, Bill Grady, Owen Minot, and others — these are the folks who really, on a day-to-day basis, monitor the lives of the kids.

"For the most part, I determine the kind of relationships I have with the kids. I actually teach at the high school; I've created a course for myself, which makes me very happy. But mainly I wander around, and I supervise the place in my own way. I do management by walking around, try to get to know a lot of the kids.

"If there is a disciplinary problem that is extremely serious that has something to do with a violation of the most fundamental standards of our community, having to do with drugs or violence, violations like that may end up in my office for very serious disciplinary action, such as expulsion. In those meetings, I am not friendly.

"I am very serious, and I think the kids understand that. I am very happy working with kids, and working with wonderful teachers and secretaries, and custodians, and support staff at the high school. I think people view me as a happy person because I am a happy person. I've never ever gone to work unhappy. I look forward to it, I bounce into the place, go into the cafeteria, get a cup of coffee, interact with kids, interact with adults, and again, I'm a lucky person in that sense."

Plainly, in the sense of becoming a fine educator, the "Bob" of Totowa, New Jersey has moved 180 degrees to the "Dr. Bob" of Brookline, yet has moved not an inch in terms of his ability to relate productively and warmly with every single student he supervises.

Not a prototypical headmaster, it might even be said that Bob Weintraub is *sui generis* in that role, coming to it obliquely, almost by happenstance. It is interesting to trace Bob's peripatetic path from the legendary Bayside High School in Queens to the position he now so humanistically exercises. Born in Massachusetts, but early moving to the Bronx and then to Queens, Bob graduated in a class of 1734 students, an easy place to get lost:

"It was a huge high school," he recalls. "How was it? It was big and impersonal, it created New Yorkers. In order to get any attention, we had to distinguish ourselves in some way, so we had a lot of obnoxious New Yorkers coming out of that place, just because otherwise you go through too anonymously. So I think the big impersonal high schools in New York helped create the character of New Yorkers. I don't know, maybe I'm one of those. I think New Yorkers are more aggressive. We have a lot of successful people coming out of my high school in Queens. It sort of forces you to distinguish yourself."

Certainly that aggressiveness helps Bob to gain his ends, but it is warmed and well tempered by his family experience to this day. Bob speaks of his family with the affection and love that informs his work:

"My mom, who now lives in Maryland, took care of the family, that was her responsibility. My dad, who passed away a couple of years ago, was a businessman at first, and then he went to work for the U.S. Department of Labor, and had a good career there. I have a brother and a sister, both accomplished people. My sister is a lawyer, and just became the chairman of the Federal Election Commission in Washington, D.C. She's mainly done public service law, and the President appointed her as one of the six commissioners. My brother — like my sister and myself — graduated from Bayside High School, and he now is the director of Homeless Services in Boston, work he has been doing for many years now. So I'm very proud of my brother, Rich, and my sister, Ellen. I come from an incredibly loving family, and I think that helped contribute to our success."

It seems that public service runs in Bob's family, backwards and forwards; this became evident as Bob talked about his wife, Judy, and their daughter and son, Sarah and David: "My wife, Judy, makes it possible for me to do this kind of insane job right now, because she's supportive, and she does a lot of stuff beyond her own very responsible job as district manager of the Boston Social Security Office. Women work more now, but I don't think women have given up the other responsibilities they have running the home, and Judy does that.

"Sarah joined the Peace Corps, and has been in Ecuador for the last two and a half years working on a health project. David is a senior at Wesleyan, and perhaps will become a high school teacher. They were both students at BHS while I was headmaster. We survived that. I tried to stay away from them at school. I tried to convince them that one advantage they had with that situation was that they could have access to my bathroom. But they never actually used that opportunity!"

Saying that his going into education was an "accident," Bob talked of joining the Volunteers and Service to America Program (VISTA) immediately following college, going to Birmingham, Alabama, and doing work in social justice and civil rights. From that came the opportunity, described as a "good deal" by Bob, of obtaining a free master's degree in teaching at Montclair State College as part of a program called the New Jersey Urban Education Corps, in return for which he committed to a term of teaching in the inner cities of New Jersey, leading directly to that first "We got Bob!" day as a teacher. He also met Judy through that program.

During those early years, Bob also found time to travel in Europe and Asia, and to do an extended work/study program on Kibbutz Sdot-Yam in Israel. Not long after that, Bob's educational career in the Bay State began when he became a counselor in the Massachusetts Advocacy Program, in Concord and Somerville.

Serendipity and seriousness may not be the definition of any well-accepted dynamic, but somehow the progression of Bob's life created a coalescence of a sort of magic brew that brought to Brookline a headmaster trusting and nurturing of a partnership among the students and the teachers and the parents, geared not to leave any kid out, especially those kids who might not have the natural abilities of some of the more gifted students, a sort of democracy within a democracy within a democracy. Bob spoke of that:

"Did I have dreams of becoming a principal and administrator? Not at all. You know, I went into this business because I love my subject, English, and I love children. That's why I went into this business. So now I'm the headmaster of Brookline High School, and not much has changed really, but it's kind of surprising. I still get up in the morning and look in the mirror and say, 'Oh my goodness. I have this big responsibility!'"

Bob describes that responsibility with eloquence, generosity, commitment, and passion: "It's about every kid. That is the passion that I hope all of us feel. We have some of the most talented and brilliant kids in the world at Brookline High School, but then we also have some of the most disabled and complex kids in the world. The spectrum of kids is extraordinary, from the most

talented to the most wounded. And the most wounded have talents as well, and the most talented have wounds as well. So it's
not as clear-cut as that. But what drives me, and part of why I get
up every day excited to go to work, is that a school's responsibility is to dignify the experience of every one of those kids. So if you
have a brilliant kid, you have to dignify the experience of that brilliant kid by challenging him or her with content, and with an experience at the high school that broadens them and allows them to
grow intellectually, socially and spiritually.

"The same thing has to happen with the kids who really have
a struggle, or the kids who are very disabled, who are just as important as the kids who easily pass MCAS [Massachusetts Comprehen-
sive Assessment System]. And I'm talking about severely disabled
kids right now, who actually attend graduation with their peers who
are seventeen or eighteen years old, and they walk across the stage,
or sometimes they go across the stage in their wheelchair, and they
get the same blue-bound certificate, the package that every other
kid in the school gets, except in their packet there's a Certificate of
Attendance, not a diploma. But then they remain with us, those
disabled kids, the special needs kids, for another four years, because
we are responsible for them until they are twenty-two years old.
Some of the most emotional times that I've had at Brookline High
School are those ceremonies we hold when these kids turn twenty-
two, and then they receive a diploma from Brookline High School.
Then the responsibility that we have is to dignify that experience
— just like for every other kid — to make sure that we help the
special needs or disabled kid go to the next step beyond high
school. So that's what school is about. School is about every kid!"

Bob Weintraub seamlessly relates this democratic spirit that
prevails at Brookline High School to the town itself: "That is part
of the passion that I think the community of Brookline brings to
its children. That's one of the reasons I moved here, it's one of
the reasons many people move here, and it's one of the reasons I'm
so proud to be a citizen of this community, because of that commitment. That's why there is a battle going on between our community and a much more intrusive state government right now
[that is, the MCAS dispute], because they are telling us that they
will tell us what the standard is, and they will tell us who will

graduate from Brookline High School. That has been really difficult for us. I'm offended by a one-test graduation requirement
because it diminishes the accomplishments and the progress of a
few kids. But MCAS is a complicated question. First of all, as
headmaster, I'm responsible for enforcing the law. Beyond that, I
think it's my responsibility to make sure that Brookline High
School, in terms of our reputation, looks as good as it can look.
We are living in an era of distrust and mistrust in the public schools.
The whole idea of "No child left behind," which led to MCAS testing, is all about accountability. We're in the age of accountability,
which in Brookline is less relevant, because we all know in Brookline that the schools are hugely accountable to the community. If
you didn't have good schools in Brookline, the leadership of those
schools would be thrown out, me included.

"The mythology about illiterate kids graduating with diplomas
from high schools has to do with the low socioeconomic centers of
our state and country, like Lawrence, Lynn, Holyoke, Springfield,
Boston, Fall River, Medford. The mythology is that those are the
systems that need to dramatically improve. Money flowed in the
1990s, mainly into those inner-city schools, and now the bottom
line is achievement, and the translation of that bottom line is the
MCAS scores of kids going to urban schools, coming from families that are not so supportive, and may be dysfunctional, having
far fewer economic resources in the homes and in the communities. So those kids don't have as great a chance as the kids in
Brookline, where, hopefully, the families are pretty strong, the
neighbors are certainly strong, the community is strong, and the
schools are excellent.

"I have my own ideas about how to make urban schools
better," he says, "but I'm working in Brookline right now, so my
responsibility is to make Brookline High School the best school it
can be. Today we have a revolutionary paradigm that every kid is
an intellectual. It's never happened before in the history of the
world, and we talk about the Golden Age of Greece, and the foundation of democracy, but do you know how many people voted,
do you know how many people were citizens in those days? We celebrate those great democratic days, but perhaps five percent of the
population were voting citizens. Today one hundred percent of our

kids are viewed as intellectuals, capable of high academic achievement. It's a dramatic shift, it's a wonderful shift, it's an incredibly challenging shift for schools. That's actually what MCAS is about as well; it's part of that philosophy."

With statistics that would make Alex Rodriguez blink, Bob Weintraub has done a lot to make Brookline High School "the best school it can be," perhaps equivalent to a .400 batting average. At BHS there are students from seventy-five nations, speaking forty-seven foreign languages. The average SAT score is 1,167. The student body includes eighteen National Merit Finalists and a one-third membership in the National Honor Society, eighty-six percent of the student body going on to college, with an 0.1 percent dropout rate. The school boasts advanced placement courses, a career in technology educational department, a performing and visual arts department, a school within a school, interscholastic sports teams comprising seventy-four teams in forty different sports, fifty-eight student activities, three student newspapers, five hundred volunteers sent out to the community at large, student constitutional governance, an innovative mediation student-student program — all supported not only by the taxpayer dollar, but also by Brookline's unique 21st Century Fund, now in the process of raising well over ten million dollars in private funds for innovative programs at Brookline High School, for which there are insufficient funds from public sources.

Asking Bob about my former neighbor and the late BHS Headmaster Bert Holland, a man as prototypically traditional as Bob Weintraub is cutting-edge, he generously spoke these words: "Incredible, wonderful man, and brilliant. I actually worked very closely with Bert Holland. He helped us start the Alumni Association. He came to all the alumni events. A caring and great man. Different style from me, much more conservative, but a great headmaster and a great teacher."

The equation of public education and democracy was in Bob Weintraub's mind when I asked him about the importance of public education and the mission of the public school:

"I think that public education launches people in this country," he said. "It always has, and it always will. It's a fundamental democratic institution, and it's one of the reasons that it makes me proud to be part of it. It is the embodiment of democracy, it's one of those institutions that support democracy because it gives everybody a chance, and that's why it is so important to work on those schools that aren't doing so well."

A statement that neatly summarizes the life of Dr. Robert J. "Dr. Bob" Weintraub, headmaster of Brookline High School.

PAUL EPSTEIN

BHS Social Worker, Charismatic Twin of the Charismatic Epstein Family

IN THE VERY FIRST MOMENT that Paul Epstein entered my consciousness, so too did the generosity of spirit that characterizes him. The occasion was a letter written by him to me early in December 2003, on behalf of the Brookline High School Social Work Fund, seeking to raise money to reunite "Elizabeth" with the rest of her family.

Elizabeth was then living in a subsidized apartment in Brookline with four of her ten children, three of them attending Brookline public schools. Elizabeth had arrived in Boston from Rwanda four years previously, at the time leaving behind her husband and all ten children.

When I interviewed Paul Epstein a few days shy of a year after that letter was written, the effort had borne fruit: "That was part

Brookline Access TV interview, December 2, 2004.

154

of the ultimately successful campaign to raise some funds to help that family," he told us. "The family was able to come. Some of them were already over here, some were still in Africa waiting. They had all their clearances to come, and all they needed was their airfare. Now the family is reunited, happy in Brookline!"

Talking one on one with the charismatic Paul Epstein, it is easy to believe that he is a social worker who often makes the crucial difference in an errant kid's life, his commitment to his calling clearly coming through his words:

"I go to work and I never know what is going to come through my door," he said. "I could have any type of kid, any type of student, male, female, and from whatever background, with any type of problem. So it really is a catch-all, and that's what makes my job exciting. The hope always is that you might be able to change the course of a kid's life. I know that there are times when I feel like that hasn't happened, but I absolutely love the job because in what other line of work can you say that it can happen? Not many, not many! Social work is one of them. When I get engaged with a student and form a relationship, of course there is the hope that that relationship will impact that student's life positively. I think some of the time it does."

Paul's enthusiasm for his work made me wonder why he chose his career path. "That is an interesting question," he responded. "I actually know why. It was due to one experience. It happened in college when I was a sophomore at Wesleyan University. I volunteered to become a Big Brother. The thing about that is that the big brother gets as much out of it as the little brother. So I became a Big Brother. I was introduced to a kid from Middletown, twelve years old when we met. I was about nineteen, so we only had a seven-year gap, which seems like nothing now. In January, that kid is about to start graduate school in library science at Simmons College. He will be coming to Boston, and we're going to see each other a lot more frequently. We're still in really good touch. So it's amazing to me that my little brother is in graduate school. And I have a second little brother now, named André, from Hyde Park."

It seems poetically proper that Paul Epstein, himself a twin, from a family famous for twins, should twin with his wife, Saskia

Grinberg (Paul says, and at this point it comes as no surprise, that people say he and Saskia "do look alike") in the social work they both do and previously did together at *The Home for Little Wanderers.*

"My first job out of college was working for *The Home for Little Wanderers,* and doing child care. It's a residential program for children who are temporarily living away from their family for some reason or another. I was part of the child care staff that took them out in the summer for wonderful trips, and was at the residential halls at night tucking them into bed, reading them stories, and waking up with them in the morning. So that was an incredible first job for a young future social worker. I met Saskia on that job. She is also a social worker and still works there. I don't know if I want to say this on air, but I'm going to. I may regret it later! When we met, Saskia was my boss! So there it is, on the record!

"I no longer work there. It was a job I loved, and I don't think I would have left, but I really had to leave. It would have been inappropriate to have a relationship with a coworker, let alone my boss. Maybe I never would have ended up back at Brookline High if Saskia wasn't so beautiful. Saskia actually went to Brookline High too, at the very time that Theo and I did. She was in the same grade, the same year. So during freshman year we were walking the same halls together, not knowing each other, and not knowing that one day we'd be married. She stayed one year and then moved to Lincoln."

As Paul talked more about Saskia, we learned what seems to be a previously unknown fact about twins Paul Epstein and Theo Epstein, which might well serve to further warm the already good relationship between Boston and The Netherlands:

"Saskia was born in Holland. Her mother is Dutch. She was born there, and she came over at a young age. I consider myself Dutch. Theo and I were conceived in Holland, when my father was there for a year on a fellowship. I don't speak Dutch. Theo and I were born in New York [at this point, I refrained from uttering the infamous epithet often heard from the Fenway faithful during Red Sox-Yankee games]."

Whether we are talking twins, East Coast and West Coast, Hollywood and Brooklyn, or Brookline and Holland, there is no question that two is the lucky number beyond belief for the Epstein clan. In their case, perhaps the gambler's plea should be "two come two" rather than "seven come eleven":

"My father [Leslie Epstein, director of creative writing at Boston University, Rhodes Scholar at Oxford, and author of such well-received novels as *San Remo Drive* and *King of the Jews*] came from a Hollywood family, so that side of the family is West Coast, very much Hollywood, almost a Beverly Hills situation [Leslie's father, Philip, and his uncle Julius were twins, famous for pranks and feuding with Jack Warner, and the writers of the classic film *Casablanca*, as well as *The Man Who Came to Dinner* and *Arsenic and Old Lace*]. My sister Anya has returned to the West Coast roots of the family, living in Los Angeles, and has started a family after writing TV shows for a while. My mom [Ilene Gradman, twin sister of Sandy Gradman, who together with Marcie Brawer for many years has run the community-oriented Brookline women's shop, The Studio] is from Brooklyn, New York, not Brookline, Massachusetts. So Mom's got her New York roots, and she was raised there. My mother and father met when my father was teaching English at Queens College, after graduating from Yale, and my mom was taking his course. So again, the inappropriate relationship [he laughs]. It was actually my mom's twin sister who originally had the crush on Professor Epstein, but Mom ended up with him."

The close relationship between twins Ilene and Sandy, having survived the Queens College lists for the affections of Professor Epstein, set the paradigm for the close relationship now existing between brothers Paul and Theo:

"I've learned the lesson of how to be a twin, what it means to be a twin, from my mom and Sandy, who could not be closer. I have to say that Theo and I are also that close. We speak every day, although that wasn't so great when he lived in San Diego and the phone bills were triple digits."

The close friendship of Paul and Theo was forged not only on the playing fields of Brookline, with which we are all familiar, but also at other venues in Brookline that took on that character in the fertile sporting imagination of the twins, in league with their boyhood friends in the Parkman, Powell, and Brown Streets area of Brookline, where in earlier years Bob Kraft had contested, and where earlier still John F. Kennedy and Charles Kickham had competed at the Still Street playground:

"That little neighborhood was, and I think it still is, a very special place to grow up within Brookline. My fondest memories from childhood are Theo and myself, and a friend named Denny Kanarek, of the Powell Street Kanareks, inventing so many games. One in particular stands out, called tenny ball, which is basically baseball with a tennis racket instead of a baseball bat. If you know the corner of Powell and Parkman, there is an open parking lot right on the corner, submerged below the medical building there, the back side of the lot now being The Holiday Inn. The lot used to be covered in blue vinyl, and that was *the blue monster* instead of *the green monster*. If you hit a shot to right center in tenny ball — that is, if you were a right hand hitter, and you hit it the other way — if you were good, you could hit it over *the blue monster*. That was our game! However, if you hit it to left field, you were going to hit a window in that medical building. As I look back on it, I imagine that there were probably doctors meeting there with patients, and, *bam*, a tennis ball comes off the eighteenth-floor window! Later, as we got older, we could actually hit it over the medical building. That was one game.

"Another game, Larry, was gutter ball, which was totally dangerous and inappropriate, now that I look back on it. On the side of Parkman Street closest to Powell, just feet in from Powell, there is a gutter on the side of each sidewalk on the street. We would take the same tennis balls that my dad had left over from playing tennis and play soccer with them. The goal was the gutter, Theo in one gutter, me in the other, and we only scored by hitting it in the other person's gutter, and the ball was gone. The interesting part is that cars were coming around the corner, turning onto Parkman Street. It's a miracle Theo and I are still alive! At the Parkman Street block party, my other good friend, Josh Cummings, who is now a Boston police officer, tackled Theo, who was making a catch of a football in the street. Theo's glasses came off and went down the sewer."

The twins' athletic inventiveness extended from the streets into the Epstein's Parkman Street apartment, where their jousts added to the maelstrom (appropriately, a word of Dutch extraction) of activity, Leslie cloistered, writing and listening to classical music,

Anya in her room listening to pop music — the more decibels, the better — Ilene rushing in from a long day at The Studio, transmogrifying from retailer to restaurateur to the Epstein family, while Theo and Paul were beating the heck out of each other in the apartment hallway, much to the chagrin of the neighbors:

"The Markells didn't like that too much," Paul remembers. "We lived downstairs in a three-story brick building, common in that part of town. We were in the middle apartment. There we had the long hallway, which became the playground for all the different games we played there: baseball, soccer, tackle, football . . . The Markells would take their broomstick and bang on the heating pipe. In an extreme case, they would actually come up to the second floor and demand to see us. At that time, Theo and I were about fifteen years old, freshmen in high school. We should have been a little more mature, but we were still playing games that rattled the light fixtures below. When the Markells came up and banged on the door demanding to see us, we locked ourselves in the bathroom. In turn, my father demanded that we come out. The Markells said to us, 'How old are you guys?' We said, 'fifteen.' They said, 'Fifteen years old, you guys should be out drinking beer and chasing girls!' [Paul laughs.) We did after that!"

There being no mutual exclusion between chasing balls and chasing girls, Paul and Theo have carried their athletic interests forward from that day to this:

"At Brookline High School, Theo and I played soccer together, and then when Theo was playing baseball, I was doing track and field. I continued both of those sports at Wesleyan, and I'm still playing soccer. Sports have been a huge part of my life, and the family's life. We love sports. I believe it has something to do with building character and camaraderie. I'm always thrilled when the students at BHS are taking part in a sports team, or doing something extracurricular."

Meeting and talking closely with the centered and at-ease Paul Epstein, one is easily convinced that indeed he is "thrilled" with helping Brookline High School students who have wandered off the beaten path, and persuaded that the effect of Paul's mesmerizing appearance and open personality on those students must be beneficial.

Photo by author.

MELVIN H. "MEL" WOLF

Musician, Mentor, Family Man and Businessman,
BHS Alumni Association Treasurer

FOR MEL WOLF, THE NEW DEAL was the real deal. President Roosevelt's WPA sounded into Mel's ear the musical note that has reverberated in his life ever since, as he recapitulated, appearing with me on Brookline Access TV to talk and play music.

Mel talked about that, and a little bit of Depression-era Brookline history to boot:

"The WPA was a federal agency that put specialty people to work, all of them being out of work during the Depression. Work was created for them, and they were paid by the government. When I was in the sixth grade at Devotion School, the WPA Orchestra came there to play. It had quite an effect on me to see all these gentlemen," he recalled. "There were all kinds of instruments, and it was a wonderful concert. It had a real effect on me.

Brookline Access TV interview, March 5, 2003.

160

It really pushed me into trying the clarinet. I got on to the Devotion School Orchestra. Both Brookline and Owen Carle [Mel's best friend] have pictures of the All-Grade Grammar School Orchestra. All kids! Little kids! Owen was in it, his sister was in it, lots of kids were in it. At that time, we didn't have any music courses in school, but we did have the forerunner of the Brookline Music School. The teachers there used to come after school, and you would have private lessons with them for fifty cents a lesson."

Mel Wolf spoke warmly of his (and my) principal at Devotion School, Charles H. Taylor, as had Mel's friend, Owen Carle, former Brookline School Committeeman, when he appeared with me. At this writing, after a long hiatus, John Dempsey, the present principal of Devotion School, has given assurances that before very long the auditorium at Devotion School will be rededicated as the Charles H. Taylor Auditorium: "Charles Taylor was a naturally good person and a natural athlete," says Mel. "He really knew how to handle children. In those days, he wore a tie and a separate starched collar, as Herbert Hoover used to wear. He'd come out into the gym all dressed up in his suit with the high collar, and he'd show us how to jump over the horse. He was an awfully good batter, and he had a great memory. In the late forties, when he retired, they threw a great party for him in the main ballroom at the Statler Hotel, now the Park Plaza. After the meal, Mr. Taylor stood up there on the stage. Everybody came up, and he greeted every single person, asking each of them questions. When I talked to him, he asked, 'How is your sister Ruth?' He remembered everybody, and he handled problems with children very well."

Unassuming and low-key in demeanor, it might be said that Mel Wolf is a one-man band, branching out instrumentally from the clarinet to play — at various times, in many venues — saxophone, oboe, piano, and organ, to name a few instruments. Mel's musical talent with society orchestras like those of Ruby Newman and Meyer Davis has taken him to cotillions in Boston and Newport and a Clinton inaugural ball, and he has performed with a galaxy of stars, including Paul McCartney, Liberace, Aretha Franklin, Whitney Houston, Bob Hope, Bert Bachrach, Harry Belafonte, Englebert Humperdinck, and Sammy Davis Jr.

He describes Sammy Davis Jr. as "the most interesting

entertainer I ever worked with. We had an all-day rehearsal the day before. The rehearsal was just with his conductor, who passed out all these charts, and said, 'I don't know what this guy is going to do! When he comes out on stage, he's not even sure what he is going to do, so he might just talk for hours. So we'll start at page one, and be prepared!' Sammy Davis was a fabulous performer."

In fact, it seems that Mel's music informs his whole life, harmonizing its diverse elements. While a student at Harvard, the title of his honors thesis was "A Sociological Study of the Swing Band and Jazz Musician Profession." Mel was awarded an A.B. with honors.

By that time, the war was on, and Mel enlisted in the Navy, serving on a troopship in the Atlantic, then as a communications officer and a senior watch officer in the Pacific. He was present in Tokyo Bay when the Japanese surrendered on September 2, 1945. During all that time, Mel was never without his clarinet, playing for the crew, and also played a portable organ for Catholic and Protestant services. Perhaps predictably, Mel graduated from troopship service to communications officer on the cruiser, USS *Pasadena*: "I was asked if I wanted to play baritone sax in a big band on the USS *Pasadena*. I thought, 'But I'm an officer!' But I was told that this was an unofficial band — there are two officers in it, and one is an Annapolis man! I got duty on that ship as a communications officer. We had this terrific big swing band, and we were sent all over Japan playing USO shows. We played for the Japanese too, and they loved it."

Mel Wolf's swing band experience began at Brookline High School, where he and classmates Bob Rines, Norton Wolf, Roy Friswold, and Jack Cunningham performed for the school. Brookline is where Mel returned from war to stay, married now for almost sixty years to his "lover and best friend," Ruth Feinsilver, BHS 1943. They have four children, all now successful professionals — one a rabbi, reflecting Mel's strong religious beliefs — and thirteen grandchildren, to date.

While continuing his musical career from his Brookline base, Mel was also an executive in men's outerwear and packaging for thirty-five years before taking up yet another career as the treasurer of the Brookline High School Alumni Association.

I asked Mel about Robert "Bob" Rines, with whom Mel played in that BHS swing band. Mel's description of him shows Bob to be one of those amazing people Brookline seems to engender: "Yes, I knew Bob Rines from Devotion School, all the way up. He was a wonderful violinist. He was a nephew of Joe Rines, a very famous bandleader from Portland, Maine, who was nationally known on the radio in the late twenties and early thirties. Bob's father was a patent attorney.

"Bob was also great on piano and flute," Mel recalls, "a good writer, and a wonderful student. After the third year in high school, he disappeared, and turned up at MIT, going there after three years of high school and coming out a physicist. Bob was a radar expert at the time of the beginning of radar. He was sent to Great Britain during the London blitz to help with the radar defenses. Then he went into the Army as an engineering officer. When he came back, he went to Georgetown Law School and became a patent attorney like his dad. Later he founded Franklin Pierce Law School in Concord, New Hampshire. He was very successful as a lawyer, and he still writes music for off-Broadway shows. He had the feeling that the Loch Ness monster was for real, and he organized a group to go there and set up equipment to find the monster. He goes a couple of times a year to monitor the operation. I would say he is an authentic genius."

So would I!

As a fan of the swing band of an earlier era, Mel is naturally a devotee of leaders like Glenn Miller, Benny Goodman, and Artie Shaw, uncasing his clarinet on the show to play Goodman's arrangements of "Don't Be That Way," and "Memories of You," Shaw's "Begin The Beguine," and Miller's "Moonlight Serenade," as well as the melody from one of Mozart's celebrated clarinet compositions, which showed Mel's universality.

That universality finds its concrete form in the continuing and tireless work Mel does as the treasurer of the Brookline High School Alumni Association, work that binds together all of those who have passed through the halls of Brookline High over a span of close to a century:

"The association is an independent, tax-exempt corporation of volunteers. We are not part of the high school. We are not supported by the town or the high school, financially. We raise our own money in the form of annual dues of fifteen dollars. Some people choose not to pay. We have a database of twenty-nine thousand, some deceased, but we do have twenty thousand good addresses, to all of whom we send newsletters twice a year. It costs us a lot to do that. Marcy Kornreich [BHS '74], who was one of our presidents, puts the newsletter together.

Linda Golburgh, Brookline's assistant town clerk, was our third president. Bill Shander [BHS class of '86] owns a Web site company and volunteered to run the association Web site. Bill is as compulsive as I am about doing things right away. If I mention that a change is necessary on our Web site, Bill gets it done immediately. Our Web site is www.brooklinehighalumni.org. We are a resource for alumni. We perform certain services for reunions. We pay bills out of a class's own money. We have tax-exempt status, so sales taxes and meals taxes are saved. We send out lists of addresses and mailing labels, all free for that class. We give a few scholarships to Brookline High students, and Brookline Rotary matches one of our scholarships. We support certain functions at the high school, such as a teachers breakfast once a year and the athletic hall of fame dinner each year. I have been active since the incorporation of the association in 1990."

Long before that, in the summer of 1969, Mel Wolf was mentoring Brookline high students in a way that changed lives. For example, back then Mel was instrumental in getting a summer job for Michael E. Roberts, then going into his junior year at BHS, at S. H. Ansell and Son, where Mel was a manager. Mike Roberts wrote to Mel in November 2002:

"That summer — both working in the warehouse, and riding to and from work with you — changed my life in a very positive and substantial way. I only wish that I had let you know many years ago just how much I truly appreciated the role you played in helping me during that very critical period in my life."

Modestly, Mel expands on the story: "Michael was a nameless kid — a friend of one of my children. He had no background at home. His family didn't know anything about college, and he wasn't going to do anything about going to college. I said, 'You should start thinking about taking your boards and achievement

tests and start looking at colleges.' He went to his guidance counselor at Brookline High and they set him straight. He got into
Cornell. I found out from my second kid, who met with Michael
once in a while, that he became a very successful businessman in
the dot-com field. He lives in Milton now. I guess he has done
very well. I hope I have helped other people too."

Melvin H. "Mel" Wolf is a master of the counterpoint of life,
harmoniously combining the melodies of his own life as a musician,
mentor, family man and businessman, and the keeper of the Brookline High School family, into a rhythmic song of community, giving
back every day of his life.

Photo of portrait at Devotion School by author.

Revered longtime Devotion School Principal Charles H. Taylor.

Photo by author.

DR. ROBERT I. SPERBER

Superintendent of Schools, Educator, Humanist

THERE IS NO QUESTION THAT DR. ROBERT I. SPERBER presided over what might be called "the Golden Age in Brookline education," in his years as superintendent of schools, from 1964 to 1982. He instituted broad and lasting changes under the three headings: modernization of the school system; meeting individual differences among students and teachers; and committing the schools to serve the entire Brookline community. None of this could not have been accomplished without the sharply honed social consciousness that Dr. Sperber brought to Brookline, all of which shone brightly when I interviewed him, his words elucidating how his high level of social consciousness took root:

"In addition to being an American, I'm also of the Jewish faith. I have known prejudice. As a youngster we lived down the street from a parochial school, and periodically I felt the sting of

Brookline Access TV interview, September 19, 2001. *Brookline Tab*, October 11 and October 18, 2001.

anti-Semitism. I remember when I was an adolescent, traveling with my parents in New England, being denied access to hotels and inns because of our religion. Those are shaping events in one's life, and I think it had a profound effect on how I feel about treating other people fairly."

It wasn't long before Dr. Sperber was able to put his beliefs into action. From 1961 to 1964 as the assistant superintendent for personnel in the school system of Pittsburgh, Pennsylvania, under the late Calvin Gross, Bob found whites teaching white students and blacks teaching black students — to his mind, not the right thing in a northern city at the time of the civil rights struggle. So Bob went down and recruited black teachers in the South and made arrangements for these teachers to work with white children and got white teachers to teach in predominantly black schools. He also identified some black principals to take assistant superintendent positions. There had never been any black leadership in Pittsburgh in the central office," he says. "I gave this activity the name of 'conscious preferment.' As a result, my family was subject to hate mail from southern cities and the Klan. We had to cut off our phone because of these attacks. So you begin to get a sense of the amount of hatred that existed in this country then, and, I'm sorry to say, I'm not sure it's changed that much."

Bob Sperber, then as always, was way ahead of the curve. In this case he subjected himself to the criticism of his peers as well as to threats from without.

Obviously, this prime educator was fully formed by the time courageous Viola Pinanski, then the chair of the school committee, spearheaded bringing Bob Sperber to Brookline in 1964, ready to recast Brookline's already fine school system for the benefit of all its students and teachers, as well as the community generally.

In fact, shortly after arriving here, in September 1964, Bob addressed his teachers and administrators for the first time prior to the opening of the new academic year, and his remarks then bear repeating now, prescient as to what Bob was going to accomplish, and insightful of the man and his beliefs:

"First, the general objective of education is to cultivate the excellence that is in each child, gifted, bright, average, retarded or otherwise handicapped, and to relate this nurturing of individual ability to the improvement of our society. If as teachers we cannot implement these aims that underlie the American democratic society — namely the belief in the dignity and beauty of the individual and his development — then our society will begin to decay. As teachers we are in the front lines of the battle to preserve and enhance our civilization. There can be no more important work!"

The first thing Bob did to effect his philosophy was to modernize the school system, creating a professional infrastructure. He replaced Civil Service personnel with professionals in personnel, curriculum and instruction, and business affairs with the approval of the school committee. He appointed the well-remembered Ann McDonald to be the first head of Curriculum and Instruction, making full use of her talents; her duties previously as an assistant superintendent had been general rather than specific.

Then, embarking on a peripatetic course to seek out the right people for Brookline, Bob went to Atlantic City, where the conference of the American Association of School Administrators was being held that year, and brought back two gems, much as Eddie Collins had done back in the 1936, when he went to the West Coast and came back with Ted Williams and Bobby Doerr.

"I recruited two really excellent people," recalls Bob, "Dr. Ferdy Tagle [from New York state] as the finance person and another chap from New Jersey, a man by the name of Bud Sheridan, who took over the Personnel Department. Over the years he chose some really outstanding people both as classroom teachers and as school principals. I remember that Owen Carle and Jacques Dronsick, who were on the school committee at that time, and were businesspeople, interviewed the finalists for finance, and they felt that Tagle would do a good job — and they certainly were right, because he turned out to be excellent."

Yet another example, it seems to me, of that rare cooperation we have between the professionals and the citizen participants here, which makes Brookline the community it is!

Bob also recalls for us the respected BHS principal Bert Holland (my own neighbor for many years on Sumner Road), whom Bob describes as "a wonderful gentleman of the old school, a man really concerned about individual youngsters." Bob tells us of his sit-down with Bert, who readily agreed to Bob's idea to move the directors of instruction in each subject area from the high school to the town hall, and to give them responsibility for developing curriculum and sharing the hiring of teachers and budgeting, from kindergarten to the twelfth grade, rather than concentrating on the high school.

Bob's idea, and Bert Holland's agreement to it, represented "a basic shift in the Brookline schools," Bob says, "because up to that time the elementary principals did curriculum development largely by what I call the snip-and-paste method. You had literally eight different curricula in the eight elementary schools, despite the fact that all the youngsters in Brookline ended up in one high school. So we had to change that. We had to centralize the curriculum and the teacher training. It was through a new budget approach that we discovered that there were four "have" elementary schools and four "have-nots," the "have-nots" being Pierce, Lincoln, Devotion, and Lawrence, all of them receiving less funds than the "haves."

Bob tells a vivid story about this: "One day I remember is my visit to the old Sewall School. I picked up a textbook, and on the inside it said 'Discarded from the Baker School.' That was the system in Brookline prior to 1964. The books that were discarded from the "have" schools were sent to the "have-not" schools. Clearly that was not something that could be allowed to continue. The system did an outstanding job for youngsters going on to college, but for average students, special needs students, and many others, a good education was not available. This represented inequality of opportunity."

Bob's interest in making things equal extended to teachers as well as students, as when he arrived in Brookline, high school teachers were paid more than were seventh- and eighth-grade teachers. Grade 1-5 and kindergarten teachers were paid even less. To remedy that, Bob proposed a single salary schedule for all teachers, and that was adopted, making good educational sense as well, as children's cognitive development is pretty much formed by age eight, as Bob told us.

I was particularly interested in Bob's introduction of cursive writing by grade 4 into the Brookline schools, since my own handwriting is atrocious and my printing not much better. Before he came, Bob explained, "the system had only taught printing, or manuscript writing, on the notion that if you look at a book, the words are printed, and the thought was that children would learn to read more effectively if they only knew manuscript or printing — but the result of that was that they couldn't read letters written to them from their grandparents or even from their cousins." As I replied to Bob on the show, the world has really gone topsy-turvy, since now we have e-mail letters in print, and who gets a hand-written letter anymore?

This ongoing modernization of the school system following Bob's arrival opened the way for his most innovative and extensive changes — in the field of meeting the individual needs of all students in the Brookline schools from K through 12, while accounting for preferences among all teachers.

Bob explains that kids, and teachers too, learn differently, some by abstract symbols (usually the college bound) and some by concrete, hands-on learning, such as would be the case in technical-vocational programs.

When Bob arrived, he found that no technical-vocational programs were available in the Brookline schools, obviously giving short shrift to concrete learners and favoring the abstract symbol learners who traditionally went on to college. Bob also noted the other side of this issue — that is, that teachers prefer teaching to certain groups of students; some feel more comfortable with abstract learners, some enjoy working with students who learn concretely. Taking this as an opportunity rather than a problem, Bob initiated programs for learners of all types, bringing in vocational programs such as food service, child care, and hotel management, at the same time identifying teachers who preferred to work with one group or another, on the theory (as I remarked in response) that it "takes two to tango."

A "concrete" example of this new philosophy — a philosophy that obviously catered to the educational interests of all the students in the Brookline schools — is the automotive program at BHS, which previously consisted of using a 1936 engine on a block, hardly sufficient as a teaching tool. Bob says these students "needed to operate with real automobiles. The grandson of the famous architect H. H. Richardson had a youngster in special needs at that time, so I approached him, asking if there was some way to solve this problem. On a pro bono basis, he proposed opening the building, constructing a folding door and ramp, so that we could bring in automobiles for repair. Bud Sheridan went out and found this wonderful teacher in New Bedford, Jim Doherty, and put him in charge of developing this first-rate automotive program, which Jim did. It's an example of providing equal opportunity. We're not all born the same, but each of us should be given equal opportunity."

Bob applied similar ideas in creating the unified arts program at BHS, joining industrial arts, home economics, and fine arts to take advantage of the common elements among them to create a connected learning experience. Allied to this, under Bob's administration, the fine arts program was expanded in the fields of drama, dance, and instrumental music.

"I had long felt that the arts were a particular magnet for learning for adolescents," he says. "We had individual offerings in industrial arts, home economics, and the fine arts, but there were natural links among these subject areas, like design and color. We found David Baker — he came as director of the new unified arts program — and he developed curriculum that found the common links among those three subjects. We then went about transforming the old manual arts building into what is now the unified arts building, and we began to see that we could mix students in that environment. Up until that time, only students who were not college bound took courses in the old manual arts building, but once we opened up the unified arts program, we had college-bound youngsters taking courses alongside of them, and we really changed the whole environment of that building."

A prime example of Bob Sperber's transformation of the Brookline school system to meet individual differences is in the field of special education:

"When I arrived, there were few services for special needs students. They were an underserved community, and there was no advocacy for them. There were five small programs in the basement of various schools. These were 'youngsters not to be seen.' I determined to increase the services for special needs and emotionally disturbed children. At that time, in a school system having six thousand students, only sixty students, or one percent, were being treated as having special needs. Statistically, in the average school system, twelve percent would be diagnosed with special needs. Clearly we were not doing the job. So I went to visit Burton Blatt at BU, an expert in the field, who came over to Brookline on contract and issued a report that recommended certain steps to drastically increase special needs services in Brookline. We instituted three or four classrooms for the emotionally disturbed at different age levels, retrained teachers, hired new teachers, wrote new curriculum, and hired Jeff Resnick as the first supervisor of special education. This was prior to Chapter 766. I would like to think that the work we did became the basis for Chapter 766 and Federal Public Law 94-142 in the field of special education."

Along similar lines of meeting individual differences was the formation of the "school within a school" program and the notion of student self-selection:

"Again, individual differences is the theme," says Bob. "Some youngsters could not really learn effectively because the school is too large. If you can't reduce the whole number of students, at least break down the school into smaller units. This is a recent finding, but we sort of knew that thirty years ago."

Bob went on to describe how a hundred or so students studied math, history and English together and made their own decisions about many things, including curriculum and selection of teachers, in a program that began in 1969 and still goes on.

Bob Sperber believes that sports and the arts motivate kids to come to school. During his tenure, Bob dramatically expanded varsity athletics.

"I always believed the fine arts and athletics were two very key motivators," he says, "particularly for adolescent youth. When I came there was not a lot of varsity athletics and few sports for girls. I thought expansion was the right thing to do so we drastically expanded to forty to forty five varsity teams, with major emphasis on opportunities for young ladies."

Probably the most fascinating and revealing story that Bob Sperber told was how Brookline's famous Facing History and Ourselves came into being.

"One day, I was at Temple Israel, my synagogue, and had a conversation with the late Dr. Max Laufer, a very fine gentleman, who was a dentist in Brookline, and who was fortunate enough to get a dental scholarship in 1936 and was able to leave Germany, although many people in his family were killed in the Holocaust. Max asked me a very simple but profound question. He said, 'How is it that the public schools, or any school for that matter, do not teach about the Holocaust?' I went back and spoke to Hank Zabierek, our director of social studies, and we decided to do something.

"We put together a community-wide group of people representing the Protestant, Catholic, and Jewish faiths. We also recruited people who were key scholars in the area, and decided to mount a series of conferences. We included scholars like Laurence Langer, who lived in the community and was a professor at Simmons College. We invited social studies teachers in Brookline to attend. Two who attended were Bill Parsons, who taught at the Lincoln School, and Margot Stern Strom, a social studies teacher at Runkle. They attended a conference we held at Bentley College, and they were profoundly impacted by what they had heard, and decided to do something about it.

"They wrote a resource book called *Facing History and Ourselves*, which became the basis for the organization. We gave them some space in the Kennard House [on the site of the old Park School], and the program was launched with the help of other people like Kitty Dukakis, Richard Smith of General Cinema, and Father Robert Bullock. This launched the program, and Margot has continued it. Later, Bill Parsons left, and he has become the second ranking person in the Holocaust Museum in Washington, D.C. Margot has done a remarkable job: Facing History is now an international program, having trained thirteen thousand teachers, and teaching over a million students here and abroad."

Bob then spoke of changing the gifted and talented student program from one class of only twenty-five students to cover all schools, aided by gifted and talented resource teachers:

"The problem was that a whole bunch of gifted and talented students were not selected, and the needs of those students were not being met. So we changed the model, eliminated the single class with the approval of the school committee, and got gifted and talented resource teachers who went around, kindergarten to eighth grade, to provide for the hundreds of gifted and talented kids."

Other changes brought about under Bob's leadership were the introduction of elementary school guidance counselors; pairings with international schools in Japan and Israel, on the theory (as events have lately shown us) that we live in one world; the expansion of the foreign language program to eight at BHS; and the introduction of moral education units into humanities courses, drawing on the ideas of Prof. Lawrence Kohlberg, of Harvard. Kohlberg advanced the notion of melding moral education with the teaching of humanities courses. For example, a teacher could lead a discussion about dropping the first atomic bomb on Japan and the morality of Truman's decision.

In 1968, Bob followed the lead of the school committee and selectmen in converting the town-run libraries in the school system to school libraries, an endeavor close to his heart, as his wife, Edith, for many years was a librarian in the Lincoln public schools.

"We found that the collection in the school libraries did not match the curriculum, the training of a municipal librarian being different from that of a school librarian," he says. Implementing recommendations made in a study by an outside library consultant, Bob says he "went down to the American Library Association meeting in New York and found Priscilla Moulton there, and convinced her to start a school library system in Brookline. She did an excellent job, and so did others who followed."

Though many programs introduced or changed during Bob's administration drove toward his goals of meeting individual differences among students and teachers, and in advancing equality and democracy in the school system, perhaps the advent of Metco in the first year of his administration is the most representative:

"In September 1964, Chairwoman Viola Pinanski of the school committee created a subcommittee, chaired by Leon Trilling, to answer the question, could Brookline help black children in Boston getting a segregated and inferior education to get a better education? As school superintendent, I was on that committee. We met with Ruth Batson and Paul Parks, and from that emerged the idea of an interdistrict busing program. By 1965 we got funding from the federal government and the Carnegie Foundation and launched the Metco program, which is still in existence today, and still strong. Black parents still want their kids to come to the suburbs. It has changed lives for the better for all the youngsters who have come out."

Bob's vision saw that the school system could be extended to serve all citizens in Brookline, then thought to be an advanced concept but now generally accepted, opening the schools to provide hot lunches (under the guidance of Marion Cronan of the home economics department) and medical services for senior citizens; modernizing the adult education program and making it self-supporting, and one of the best programs in the state, under the leadership then and now of Linda Larson; and involving parents (for the first time) and teachers in choosing principals — for example, when Virginia Thompson, beloved principal of Driscoll School, retired, and Irwin Blumer was chosen as her successor.

Another important innovation was the parent-run, school-based, Extended Day Program.

"The school day ended at around two o'clock, and with mothers working, there was a growing need to establish a parent-run after-school program in each of the elementary schools," Bob said. "This has proved to be a valuable contribution for Brookline parents. In fact, one of the first thing parents look for on moving to Brookline is whether a slot is available in the Extended Day Program.

Perhaps the jewel in the crown of Dr. Sperber's ideas about serving the whole community was the establishment of the Brookline Early Education Program, on the theory that a child's most important teacher is his or her parents:

"I had long felt we had an upside-down situation, spending more money at the high school level and less money at the beginning levels of education. So I collaborated with Francis McKenzie, director of Public Personnel Services, and Burton White, of Harvard, to write a grant. We received a five-million-dollar grant from the Robert Wood Johnson Foundation and the Carnegie Foundation and launched the Brookline Early Education Program, the first school-based program for parents and newborns in the country. We selected 285 families, including pregnant mothers, for a birth-to-age-seven program. We selected Don Pierson, then a Weston elementary principal, to be our director. The program provided different levels of support, depending on the needs of the children.

Some of the families were at the Heath Bromley Project whose children were admitted through the Metco program. What we found was that everybody profited, but profiting most were youngsters from the lowest-income families and for mothers who had the lowest levels of education. They received the most intensive levels of help from our doctors, psychologists, and others. Those youngsters really profited the most. The test results of kindergarten and second grade were quite significant."

As could be expected in the long and rich continuum of Brookline history, Bob tells of Brookline's new superintendent of schools, Richard Silverman. "[He was] kind enough to ask me to come in recently, and we chatted for a couple of hours about the challenges ahead in Brookline education, such as the need for closing the gap between majority and minority students; being able to hold talented teachers in the classroom by giving them multiple career roles in and out of the classroom and changing the academic environment so that talented teachers don't leave; and pioneering individual education plans for all youngsters, not just special needs students."

Although Bob left as superintendent of schools in 1982, he and his family came to Brookline to stay. He was recently elected a Town Meeting member, and in yet another example of talented citizens volunteering their services to the town, serves as co-chairman of the Economic Development Advisory Board.

"I have long felt that we needed to expand the commercial tax base of this community," he says. "It is very small, only eighteen percent of total income. So we created the Economic Development Advisory Committee, which later became the board around 1988, and is now under the direction of a wonderful executive director, Amy Schechtman. Our major aim is to raise funds for the schools, public safety, libraries, etcetera."

Obviously, the board has been successful in meeting this need, for it is central to several developments either completed or in the pipeline that are expanding the tax base, such as the Brookline Hospital conversion, the Town Barn project on Cypress Street, the hotel projected on Webster Street, the condos constructed on the former Mary Baker Eddy site at the top of Fisher Hill, and the project at 1010 Commonwealth Avenue.

Bob considers Brookline to be a nurturing community, and believes that there is more tolerance in Brookline for expression of ideas.

"It's a community Edith and I committed ourselves to," he says. "Our three children all went through Brookline schools, and all of them are doing very well. We have seven wonderful grandchildren now. I'm sorry my grandchildren don't live in Brookline. My kids benefited from living here."

So too does each and every one of us continue to benefit from Bob's long residence here in Brookline, both as school superintendent and as a committed citizen of our town.

BOOK VI

POLITICS

Brookline Democratic Town Committee Garden Party (1974).
Shown from Left to Right: Father Robert F. Drinan, William Delahunt,
Michael Dukakis, Joan Hertzmark, and Allan Sidd.

Photo by author.

Sumner Z. Kaplan

The Man Who Changed Brookline from Republican to Democratic

YOU CAN DESCRIBE SUMNER Z. KAPLAN in a lot of ways. You can call him "Honorable" because he was a judge, you can call him "General" because he was a general in the Army, you can call him "Rep" because he was a four-time representative in the state legislature (first Democrat ever from Brookline), you can call him "Selectman" because he was a Brookline selectman for twelve years, you can call him "Minister" because he performed the marriage of Dick Goodwin and Doris Kearns. You can also call him son, husband, father, grandfather, and friend. You can call Sumner a lot of things and they're all good.

Sumner Kaplan — the catalyst who changed Brookline from Republican to Democratic in "that wonderful year" of 1954 and paved the way for Michael Dukakis's later ascent — appeared on

Brookline Access TV interview, February 8, 2002. *Brookline Bulletin*, January 29, 2004.

my program on my birthday and a few days after his own, prompting me to remark that there might be something in the stars, as each of us Aquarians, having known each other for a long time, views the other as looking at life as a series of half-full cups. One thing is for sure: on this hourlong program, Sumner must have been smiling seventy-five percent of the time, as he has been all his life.

So I wondered out loud, How does a guy get to be that way, happy, thinking of others, an "unreconstructed" liberal?

Growing Up In Roxbury

Sumner started off talking about his early years in Roxbury.

"My dad came from Russia and started off here selling shoelaces. My first political experience was through my father, when I was a kid about twelve years old. I campaigned through the streets of Roxbury for Harry Kalus, who later became a judge. That's where I got started.

"We had marvelous times in Roxbury — marvelous people," he said. "We kids played ball in the streets every day, walked to Hebrew school and back every afternoon, went to the YMHA almost every night. We were all in clubs there and had friendships and a fraternal life that one really longs for today."

Obviously *friendship* is an important word in Sumner's lexicon.

"Certainly is — kids I went to grammar school with, we're still friendly, still good friends. My high school classmates from Boston Latin School — we meet together all the time. And certainly my fraternity brothers from Mass. State College [now UMass]. For sixty years now we've been close associates and meet constantly throughout the year. So we've maintained our friendships, and have reunions all the time, as I do with my army buddies from World War II."

Sumner continued, speaking of one of his oldest friends from grammar school, to Latin School, to college, to this day — Alan Silverman (whose parents, Esther and Joe, lived in the next apartment during my youth at 26 Gibbs Street):

"It was a different atmosphere then. Friendship was in the air. It doesn't quite exist anymore. Everybody is too hurried and too harassed and under too much pressure."

An apt comment as the world seems to spin out of community and into cyberspace.

Family and Other Influences

Family lies at the heart of Sumner's liberalism.

"My grandfather compared FDR and Moses, much to the chagrin of his religious mother, who castigated him for comparing anybody to Moses. But I think that's the one thing my father insisted on. He thought FDR was the savior of the world, and felt that FDR's type of liberalism was the same as his, and he became an unreconstructed New Dealer, and made the rest of us unreconstructed New Dealers."

It was from both sides of Sumner's family that he received his strong Jewish identity. He has always been very active in the American Jewish Congress and recently served as president of the New England region of the Congress, focusing on issues of health care, economic justice, welfare reform, human values, and immigrant rights.

"Yes," he says, "my grandfather on my father's side was one of the chief rabbis of Boston. He headed what they called the Beth Din — the Jewish Judgment Court — in Boston, then used often instead of the state courts.

"My grandfather on my mother's side was the second president of the Jewish Home for the Aged, which later became the Jewish Rehabilitation Center [now in Roslindale, one of the top geriatric facilities in the nation], and he had that presidency for many years. Then my uncle Paul Cohen became president. My uncle Jack Rabinovitz became president. So we kept it in the family for a long time. Their pictures are hanging at the Jewish Rehab now."

Naturally, there were some academics who powerfully influenced Sumner along the way, one of whom was Aaron Gordon at Boston Latin School, a man who had a Brookline connection too:

"He was such an inspiring teacher — such a lively mind — that he really sparked my interest in history and political science and politics. It's funny. Later on when I became chairman of the Brookline Board of Selectmen, I got Aaron to be head of the Personnel Board. So I was his boss then, and he was my boss in Latin School."

A strong influence as well was history professor Ted Caldwell at Mass. State.

"He saw something in me that I didn't see in myself," Sumner says. "He saw a political future in me. He really nurtured it. He was willing to talk to me about matters of political science, history, and how governments are run. He certainly was a great influence in my life."

It was at Mass. State that Sumner's rise to the rank of brigadier general later, in the Army Reserves, began. It started with a fall, due to his inability to get on a horse, as was required in ROTC:

"So Sergeant Kronk — the ringmaster or whatever he was — said to me, 'Kaplan, you'll never make a soldier. In fact, I'm not going to let you ride anymore — you just read a book during the period' — and that's what I did. But I fooled him. I did all right in the Army."

Indeed Sumner did, serving in combat in Europe during World War II, building and rebuilding bridges over the Rhine. He was discharged as a captain, and rose to the rank of general later in the Reserves.

Sumner had moved to Brookline around the time of his final year in high school, which meant that his family had to pay for his last year at Boston Latin School. He had married his wife, Ellie, during the war; the couple returned to Brookline, he to Harvard Law School, and took up residence in the new vets project on Egmont Street, numbering among his friends there Alan Barkin (elected with Sumner early on as a Town Meeting member, and active with Sumner in the 1953 fight to keep rent control in Brookline), Arthur Goldstein, Jimmy Esposito (later a well-known constable in Brookline), and Billy Connelly, a fireman who, Sumner tells us, won the lottery and "got out of there fast."

It was around this time, too, that Sumner found a way to transfer his baseball activities from Franklin Field to Braves Field.

"The federal government had a very gracious program where they gave everybody wearing a ruptured duck — that was a sign that you were a veteran; it was a little pin — twenty dollars a week for fifty-two weeks, and where best to spend it but at the ballpark. So there were all of these veterans sitting out there at the ballpark. We enjoyed it very much."

This got Sumner to talking about a Boston Braves pitcher of the thirties, around the time Sumner first moved to Brookline, living on Strathmore Road, his story redolent of a lovely time past when Major Leaguers walked daily in our midst.

"Huck Betts! Huck Betts was a pitcher for the Braves in the thirties, and I was living then on Strathmore Road, and we would go to Cleveland Circle every day to play ball, and Huck Betts was there. We thought it was the greatest thing in the world. He used to throw the ball to us, and pitch to us, and we had a great time with him up there. It was a lot of fun!"

Those Wonderful Years of 1953 and 1954

It was the rent-control issue in 1953 that brought Sumner to the forefront. In order to continue federal rent control in Brookline at that time, a town meeting was required, either called by the selectmen (no chance, all Republicans) or by petition of the citizens. That set the stage.

"People in Brookline were very nervous — widows, retirees, and others couldn't afford what the rents were going to be if rent control went off. Two women started circulating petitions. I was a Town Meeting member from the project. So was Dick Barkin. We joined in the petition.

"By chance I got Dick Goodwin — who was later the speechwriter for JFK and LBJ and later married Doris Kearns, whose marriage I performed — to be the main speaker at Town Meeting, and by a very few votes we put it over. Bunny Solomon [well-known Democratic activist, previously interviewed on my program] and I ran around — after we got Town Meeting called — and got eight thousand people to sign a petition in Brookline to continue rent control, and luckily — mainly because of Dick Goodwin's emotional speech — we were able to get Town Meeting to adopt rent control for Brookline. And as a result of that I decided to run for state representative, and got elected the next year [1954]."

I remarked that this was a rent-control movement that moved into a Democratic Party movement, so I wondered how it was running against Republicans entrenched for so long that they thought they couldn't be displaced.

"Well, it wasn't easy," he told me. "But I decided to use some

Roxbury tactics! I went door to door, and also stood at the street-car stops. And one day one of the leading Republicans, who knew me, Alan Morse, at that time chairman of the board of selectmen, came up to me at the Coolidge Corner stop and said, 'Sumner, we don't do that sort of thing in Brookline,' and I said, 'Well, I do, I'm going to be elected.' Now they all do it all the time. It really started the Democratic movement here in Brookline. It showed a Democrat could get elected, although I must say the Republicans tried everything in the book to defeat me, including not letting me sit up there on the platform with the others when Candidate Nights were available."

Obviously, behind Sumner's ready smile lies a resolute personality, borne out by his accounting of opponent Stanwood Wellington III's invitation to Sumner to have a drink during the campaign:

"Nicest guy you would ever want to meet. He invited me for a drink at the Beaconsfield Hotel [where the Star Market now sits]. He said, 'Let me buy you a drink. I want to find out something.' I couldn't afford to buy him a drink, I can tell you that. He said 'I want to know how you're going to get elected.' 'I'll tell you Stan. I'm going to get more votes than you!' "

And Sumner did, thus changing Brookline forever.

Mike Dukakis gave Sumner a lot of help in South Brookline during that first campaign, but one night the always punctual Mike was late to a planning meeting. Here's why:

"We were going to have a planning meeting at Eddie Novakoff's house on Gardner Road. Mike didn't show up for a little while, and we were all wondering where he was. When he arrived late, he told us that he had entered a redbrick home on Gardner Road and was seated in a large circle of people. He said it felt strange because there was silence, nobody spoke. After a while, Mike was restless and curious. He spoke up, 'Where's the candidate?' The host asked, 'What candidate?' 'Kaplan, I mean,' said Mike. 'Sir,' said the host, 'you must be in the wrong place. We are in mourning here, sitting shiva.' And sure enough, the candidate was next door at Eddie Novakoff's. We never forgot that."

Sumner credits his wife, Ellie, and his mother, Hattie, for his campaign victory:

"I couldn't have been elected without my mother and my wife. No question! My mother certainly knew every Jewish person in Brookline. She was on the phone and sending out Dear Friend cards daily. In fact, we were so poor during this election — we didn't know anything about fund raising — we got a few bucks from members of my family, and when I say a few, I mean a few. One time we stamped about one hundred and fifty letters wrong. We wanted to save the stamps, so we dunked them all in hot water in the bathtub, and when the stamps floated off, we got them back, and then we were able to glue them on the right letters. That's how bad off we were."

It seems to me that Sumner's love of a funny story and open countenance represent his down-to-earth appraisal of where each of us stands in the cosmos. He has a favorite saying, read long ago in the *Saturday Review of Literature*:

"I advise young people who get frustrated, look, remember this saying: 'Never fail to overestimate the unimportance of practically everything, and you'll go through life with a smile.'"

Although Sumner does gives a little advice here and there, it appears that he never wanted to do it on a day-to-day basis, as demonstrated when he talked about the day he married Dick Goodwin and Doris Kearns:

"It was a mixed marriage ceremony along with Father Groden. Dick wanted to have somebody represent the Jewish faith there, he saying, 'I'm insisting you do it as my friend.' And I did it. It turned out to be a lot of fun. The whole Camelot crowd was there, headed by Ted Kennedy, Kevin White, and a lot of other people from the JFK administration. I can remember at the end of it some woman came up to me and said, 'Oh, Rabbi Kaplan, I have a similar problem.' I said, 'Look, lady, I'm no rabbi, and I'm not interested in similar problems.'"

Political Personalities

Sumner's elected service to the town of Brookline, stretching as it did from 1952 when he was first elected to Town Meeting until 1975, which was the last year of his service on the board of selectmen, gave him the opportunity to know all the political personages of the town during that period, Democrat and Republican alike, and he has affectionate, insightful, and sometimes pungent remarks about all of them.

Joan Hertzmark: "I think Joan was the bulwark of the Democratic Town Committee. I think her devotion and her ability to make, literally, two thousand calls during a campaign — and her loyalty to Mike Dukakis — were unbelievable. She was just a firehouse, an unbelievable worker who sought absolutely nothing in return, and did it all so pleasantly."

Ponnie Katz: "Ponnie is an amazing woman, an example, I think, of both women and men in Brookline who early on got involved in one of the beauties and one of the delights of Brookline – participatory politics. She is another person who seeks nothing for herself except the good of the town — dedicated to the issues and studies the issues. She's an example of what I think the quintessential Brookline citizen should be."

Alan Sidd, Michael Dukakis, Haskell Kassler: "Alan Sidd was certainly a knowledgeable and street-smart politician. He died much, much too young. I think had he lived, he could have been helpful to the Dukakis administration and put a little more humanity into its operations.

"Mike worked hard on my campaigns from my very first campaign until my last. In the Democratic primary, when he ran for state representative, it was the first time I ever did it, but I endorsed him for the election. I think he was too process oriented, much too process oriented, and didn't have the street smarts or the approach that Alan Sidd had, and I thought Alan Sidd might have indoctrinated him with that, had he had more time.

"Hakky was a loyalist. He was loyal to me. He was loyal to Mike. Mike put him on the UMass Board of Trustees for a while. I think he deserved more.

"While a lot of other people were talking about going down South during the riots in the sixties and during the marches, Hakky went down and he got bopped in the head! And I remember — I was at Command and General Staff College at Fort Leavenworth at the time — I got called by people in Brookline whether I could get in touch with Tip O'Neill and others to see what could be done about Hakky. But he came back fine. We served together on the board of selectmen. He served honorably and very well on that board, and I think the fact that some people were bitter and big-oted about his standing up to The Country Club on trying to find out why they didn't have black members — I think that hurt him in the next election. Some bigoted people went out to get him. I supported him in that stand. Hakky is a great guy!"

Beryl Cohen: "Yes, I thought Beryl had a future. He certainly became the liberal leader of the State Senate. He was well liked. But then he got turned on by the members of the Senate when he ran for lieutenant governor. I think he ran at the same time that Dukakis ran for lieutenant governor. Beryl thought he had the sup-port of the State Senate. They just dumped him, and that was a bitter blow that was very difficult for him to absorb. It was a blow because he felt that friendship would have carried him through. It didn't. He was very upset after that. I guess he just got out of politics and went back to his law career, where he took on some very esoteric cases in the welfare and human rights field."

Freyda Koplow: "Yes, Freyda and I ran together for state rep. It was a triple district at that time when we first ran. I think it's a shame that they broke it up from the triple district. I think it meant a great deal more to represent a whole town than just a segment of it. But Freyda was one of the boys [are you listening, Freyda?]. She was all right. She was a Republican, a solid Republican, she would use every trick in the book to beat you. But at the same time she never was unfriendly. I used to drive Freyda home every once in a while from the state house. We were always friendly. She became state banking commissioner. She was always friendly with everybody."

Recently Sumner moved from his home of forty-seven years on Russell Street in North Brookline. I asked him to talk about the well-known "Mayor of North Brookline," Ralph Sussman.

"Oh, Ralph Sussman. Ralph Sussman was a codger. I always thought he was eighty years old his whole life. When Sussman wanted something done — he spoke with a heavy Jewish accent — when he wanted something done, he wouldn't let you alone! He was up your house one o'clock in the morning, four o'clock in the afternoon, two o'clock in the afternoon, breakfast time — and he'd say 'You gotta get this done.' When I got elected state rep, he came up to see me — he was a strong Republican. But all he was interested in was his Russell Street area. 'Sumner, we gotta make Russell Street one way.' I said, 'Mr. Sussman, we'll make it one way.' I didn't consult anybody else on the street. Everybody did want it one way, I think, and I asked the town to make it one way, but I didn't discuss with them whether it should be one way coming in from Harvard Street or one way going out. So you can understand once it was made one way, I lost half of Russell Street as supporters. But that was Ralph!

"And then Ralph insisted on getting the lights at the corner of Harvard Street and Fuller Street — and he got them! And then he insisted on the housing project that went up on Pleasant Street for the elderly — it was called the Ralph Sussman House. He was a marvelous guy! His daughter was Harriet Sussman Bremner, who became a member of the Housing Authority. His son-in-law was Herbert Bremner, who was head of the Brookline Mental Health Association, and did a great job — all strict Republicans, by the way."

Sumner Kaplan On Brookline Citizen Participation

After hearing this, I remarked to Sumner that Ralph Sussman was about as good an example as anyone of the unusual if not unique level of citizen participation that has persisted here for so long. Sumner's extended response strikes me as the best statement I've ever heard about this phenomenon:

"There's no question that Town Meeting has done more to keep Brookline honest, non-corrupt, and to cause citizen-participation activity than anything else. It is also a stepping-stone if people want to run for office. It gives you the first chance to go out and greet people, to see how to run for office, to meet other activists, to begin to get up in Town Meeting and make a speech, to get on the Advisory Committee, to get on subcommittees.

"But I gotta tell you a story about Tip O'Neill. When Tip O'Neill was redistricted, and Brookline became part of his district, I was one of the few people he knew in Brookline. So I threw a big party for him, and he got elected. All these people from Brookline would pepper him with questions. He said 'Sumner, these people are really interested in the issues.' I said, 'You bet your life!' Then when he got into office, he called me one day and said, 'Sumner you're costing me money.' I said, 'What do you mean?'

He said, 'I had to hire somebody special just to answer the Brookline mail. I gotta get outta this district.' He did get out of it later, but I think Brookline people had a great influence on Tip's liberalism. They certainly influenced him about the Vietnam War.

"So it is Brookline participation. It's not only Town Meeting — it's people like Ponnie Katz. People get on these committees. You have the Putterham Association. You have the Chestnut Hill Association. You have what they used to call the Brookline Committee, the Citizens Committee, Precinct 1 has a committee, and they're all participating. I mean, they're gadflies, and they can drive you crazy when you're in office. But let me tell you, it keeps the town going. It's a model town.

"We've also been lucky to have special people like Arthur O'Shea, Dick Leary, and now Dick Kelliher, who are great administrators. I think they understand that they have to be great in order to cope with this citizen participation.

"And then you have the school committee. The school committee deals with great issues, and people participate, issues like fluoridation, the handwriting thing [cursive or not?]. Now they've got the big MCAS issue — whether MCAS should be a graduation requirement. And people are participating in that. The Brookline School Committee has taken a strong stand against MCAS — and really, as an example of citizen participation, citizens are on them every day about it.

"So I think Brookline is great town. And I think people are to be congratulated. I think all the citizens are to be congratulated, you're to be congratulated."

Thanking Sumner, I remarked that Tip O'Neill said, "All politics is local," but maybe Tip didn't want it to be *that* local.

The Board Of Selectmen Years

Sumner served on the Brookline Board of Selectmen for twelve years, and talked about some of his compatriots there.

George McNeilly: "Yes, it seems like George was on the board of selectmen forever. George was a perfect gentleman. He had a sense of decency and fairness, and was a marvelous guy to talk with. George was an old Yankee, and thrifty. I think he told me he was wearing the same suit he wore when he was — well he wasn't

Bar Mitzvahed — but he used that analogy. George was a great guy, and a fair-minded guy. He never raised his voice. Some others on the board did, including me. I could raise my voice. Sometimes we had some bitter fights."

Matty "Matthew" Brown and George Brown: "Two different guys. Matty was a very smart, very clever guy — a good Republican politician. He and George both, I think, were on the Republican Town Committee. But Matty was a very bright guy and totally political. I respected him for that. Matty and I debated Republican-Democratic issues many times.

"George was totally local. He liked to take care of his boys — his friends — and do the things they wanted to be done.

"They were all decent guys. Some were very political, and we had some great arguments. Remember, I came to the board of selectmen from the House of Representatives, which was a pretty rough place to be. So the board of selectmen to me was like a piece of cake. I remember after the very first meeting, I made a public statement to the press, and Matty Brown called me in and he blasted me. I said, 'Forget about it I come from a tough training, and if I want to say something — remember, there were four Republicans and me on that Board — I'll say it.' But Matty and I became good friends. Arthur O'Shea called me that night, and said, 'Nobody has ever spoken to Matty Brown that way you did.' "

It seems like poetic justice that Louise Castle and Sumner Kaplan were both elected the same year (1963) to the board of selectmen — Sumner having been the first Democrat elected to anything in Brookline for eons, and Louise, who recently passed away in her early nineties, the first woman ever elected selectperson here.

Louise Castle, Ellie Meyerson, Herb Abrams, Mort Godine: "Louise and I were elected together. Ellie was lovely on the board of selectmen, pleasant and nice to be with. Herb was a scrapper, and he and Hakky Kassler went at it a lot. Herb was an interesting guy on the board. I thought he was one of the most political, and one of the most interested in advancement, of all the members of the board. Mort was a sweetheart! I think he got on because he wanted to give something back to Brookline, and he did. Mort wasn't very issue oriented."

Will Brookline Remain a Community?

Ever young, Sumner had a ready answer when I asked him whether the younger or older citizens of Brookline should be taking the lead in running the town.

"I think there are a lot of young people coming in," he said. "The fact that they had seven hundred people at the Democratic caucus a few weeks ago indicates to me that young people are interested, and we have to foster their interest. If they want to participate, let's make room for them. We can all become elder statesmen, become mentors, go on committees, but let's let the elected offices go to the younger people who have the energy, and who, I think, are looking for and yearning for participation."

Even before 9/11 the world was changing rapidly, so I asked Sumner, "Is Brookline moving from community to some sort of impersonal cyberspace or is Brookline going to remain a community?" Sumner offered an optimistic yet cautious view:

"Well, I hope we remain a community and I think we can remain a community, if, as I say, the younger people are nurtured and brought in, and given their shot. Let's not be too hard on them. Let's not be too hard on our elected officials in this town — because in this town they're elected as a result of participation. I would hope to see a lot more participation than there has been in recent elections."

Sage advice from Sumner Z. Kaplan, arguably the most important political figure in twentieth-century Brookline history.

Photo by author.

MICHAEL "MIKE" DUKAKIS

*Governor of the Commonwealth, Candidate for
President, Professor, Lifelong Brookline Citizen*

THE AFFECTIONATE AND AFFECTING WAY in which Mike Dukakis has
near total recall of his teachers, friends, and political allies as he
grew up and matured in Brookline reflected not only Mike's respect
and recognition of those who brought him along to be the man he
is, but also the quality of Brookline community during all those
years up to the present. From his recounting of those influences,
it is easy to understand why Mike chose the path of service to his
community in politics and public life — as Brookline State Representative and three-term governor of the Commonwealth and now
on the board of Amtrak and teaching and lecturing twelve months
a year at Northeastern, UCLA, and other schools.

Mike's recall goes back a long way. He talks of his kindergarten teacher, Grace Kilbourne, and the much later visit to her

Brookline Access TV interview, December 21, 2000. *Brookline Tab*, February
22, 2001.

in retirement in Rockport that he and his wife, Kitty, made.

Going to grammar school at Baker, Mike describes principal Bob Newbury as "tough — no fooling around with Mr. Newbury — a great guy." Smiling, Mike told of his earliest political experience, running for president in Mrs. Ripley's third-grade class at Baker School.

Mike gives thanks to the Brookline Music School (it then gave lessons in the public schools, having no home of its own; one of its teachers was his future father-in-law, Harry Ellis Dickson), where brother Stelian on clarinet and Mike on trumpet were taught. Mike went on to be the "first chair in the trumpet section at BHS" under another mentor, John Corley, who recently passed away, but who was for many years not only Brookline High School band leader, but also leader of the MIT concert band.

Mike was an honor student at Brookline High School, and played on the basketball, baseball, tennis, and cross-country teams at BHS. He speaks of his basketball coach there, John Grinnell, as "a great influence on me," who was "in the box with my family when I was nominated for president — a great moment — and he was a wonderful guy with strong political views. He hated Joe McCarthy."

Of course, Mike recalls the powerful influence of his mother and father, whose story might be called the American dream collapsed into a very short time frame. Both mother Euterpe and father Panos were born in Greece, came to this country, and quickly learned the language. Mike says Euterpe was perhaps the first Greek American woman ever to go to college in New England, graduating from Bates in 1921 as a Phi Beta Kappa. Panos went to Harvard Medical School and practiced just outside of Brookline across from the Museum of Fine Arts, delivering thousands of children during his more than fifty-year career. Obviously, their sense of hard work, education, and responsibility rubbed off on Mike.

Mike extended his cross-country running at BHS to tackle the Boston Marathon at age seventeen in 1951 while still in high school, certainly a combination of living out his Greek heritage and a Brookline tradition. Let Mike tell how he was able to run the marathon at seventeen when you had to be eighteen. "Despite my

reputation for integrity," he says, "I told a small but important lie
— I just kind of adjusted my age."

Mike and his friend Buzzy Wiseman ran that race under the
colors of the Tracy AC, a mythical organization, which Mike and
Buzzy conjured up from the name of their BHS cross-country
coach, Dick Tracy (believe it or not), whom Mike says he and
Buzzy loved — a great coach, who was wonderful with us, and was
at every check point during the race."

Mike finished the race in a creditable 3:31 (Buzzy beat him),
and tells the hilarious story of his mother waiting for him at the
finish line in Boston screaming "Mike, Mike" and "a big burly
Boston cop" saying to Mike's mother within his hearing that "your
brother is okay lady," to which Euterpe replied with feeling,
"Brother! That's my son!"

But let's retreat a few miles to when Mike entered Brookline
grasping his side in pain, facing dehydration, not having had any
water in the race up to that point, reduced at one stage to walking, having "an awful thirst," and the prospect before him of practically all of Brookline High School waiting for him to pass.
Brookline community to the rescue!

"I'll never forget running down Beacon Street that day," says
Mike. "It was really something with all my buddies running in and
out of drugstores — in those days we had corner drugstores — getting me water. It was a great experience!"

Mike tells a wonderful story about, as he calls her, the "best
teacher I ever had," Kate O'Brien, the head of the modern foreign
languages department at BHS, who taught French to the multilin-
gual Mike. After Mike went into politics, he says, Ms. O'Brien
made a small contribution every time he ran for office, ten or fifteen dollars. Then came 1986, when Mike was running for his
third term against Ed King. Immersed in that campaign, not thinking about running for the presidency, he received a letter enclosing
a check for one thousand dollars left to Mike in Kate O'Brien's will
(she had died earlier that year). The will said it was given "in the
hope that he will run for the presidency." Mike says he "still
chokes up thinking about it," not even thinking then about ever
running for the presidency, and calls this "my first contribution for
my campaign for the presidency."

Both of us recalled taking Latin at BHS from Concetta Vanocor and Jane Perkins "with the snow white hair." Mike said he "never understood English grammar until I took Latin."

Mike recalls with respect and affection some well-known Brookline political personalities who inspired and helped him along the way, most notably Sumner Kaplan and Allan Sidd.

Of Sumner, Mike says, "Sumner was the guy who really was the mentor for all of us — the guy that pulled us together — we sort of coalesced around him." Mike says it was from Sumner that he learned grass-roots politics, and like Sumner, he said, "I rang every blessed doorbell in the town."

Of Allan Sidd, former Brookline Town Treasurer and Democratic pundit, Mike says that unlike many political hangers-on, Allan "never hesitated to tell me when I was doing something wrong or ill advised — and that you need that kind of guy." In a more personal way, Mike says about Allan (which this writer echoes, being lucky enough to have counted Allan as a good friend), "Allan was one of a kind, and I miss him to this very day. He was hard living, funny, had a laugh that you could hear down the street, loved politics, was a gambler, smart as a whip, very liberal politically — an interesting combination — and a guy who would level with you."

Mike also speaks of when he and Elliott Richardson co-chaired Louise Castle's first run for selectman. Mike's advice to her was to meet people at the car stops, and says now, "I'll take a certain amount of credit during that campaign for introducing [former selectman] Hakky Kassler to his wife Mary," introducing the couple, now long married with adult daughters, on the platform at the T stop at Beacon Street and Summit Avenue.

So along with being an athlete, scholar, politician, and teacher, Mike is a matchmaker as well.

Mike's life really has been one of service, certainly sparked initially by his parents, but plainly nurtured by Brookline teachers and the Brookline community generally. Mike also credits Brookline institutions in this path, such as Town Meeting. Of this august institutiton, Mike remarks that Town Meeting "gives an awful lot of people an opportunity to serve — Town Meeting gave me the opportunity to seek elective office and to get involved, to be a part of the town." Perhaps naysayers about the continuance of Town Meeting government in Brookline should attend to that.

Mike credits another Brookline institution with his interest in using public transportation to ameliorate the community-demolishing effects of the automobile, remarking about the old T cars that "those wooden trolley cars were something — the motormen would spin those levers around; I never could figure it out. We grew up with that system and that has a lot to do with my commitment to public transportation."

So Mike Dukakis is Brookline then and now, his memories over the course of his life showing that Brookline "community" makes this town not only a great place to live, but also a great place to mature and grow into a person who respects and enhances community values.

Photo by author.

BERNARD "BUNNY" SOLOMON

American Original, Politico, Legendary Northeastern University Supporter

AS EVERYONE WHO KNOWS HIM KNOWS (and that includes many, many people), Bernard "Bunny" Solomon is truly an American original, a Brookline man who has been there, done that, and knows everyone, great and small, in and out of Brookline, then and now.

Bunny's personal traits and accomplishments as a businessman, volunteer, philanthropist, government official, politician, sportsman, raconteur, husband, son, father, and friend are well known to all, and all of that was warmly and vividly shown on the program when we talked of his life, starting as early as kindergarten.

It was there that Bunny's (now seventy-eight) long and still continuing political career really took root, when Miss McNutt, at recess one day (in a flourish of political incorrectness) asked the thirty or so five-year-olds which candidate each favored in the Al

Brookline Access TV interview, September 22, 2000. *Brookline Tab*, April 26, 2001.

Smith vs. Herbert Hoover campaign for president. Bunny says, "I have a sharp memory that I was the only kid for Al Smith," a result not unexpected in those years when Brookline was a Republican stronghold.

When Bunny returned from his infantry duties in Europe during World War II, he very quickly became embroiled in the political wars, striking up a friendship with JFK, cabbing with him here and there, and often hearing from Jack at the end of the cab ride, "Bunny, you take care of it." Perhaps these were not the easiest words to hear for the fiscally careful Bunny, who was later appointed by Governor Foster Furcolo to be the state purchasing commissioner. His friendship with the Kennedy family continued; "I know Teddy very well today," he says.

Bunny ran Adlai Stevenson's campaign in Brookline in 1952, early showing his political acumen by packing Bowker Auditorium at BHS when FDR Jr. came to speak on Adlai's behalf.

But it is Bunny's friendship with Harry Truman that leads us to the genesis of the name "Bunny," as well as telling us a lot about both Bunny and President Truman. The time is 1948, the scenario is Truman's campaign against Dewey, and the event is his decision to take his legendary campaign train through Massachusetts, west to east. At that time, Bunny was president of the Young Democrats of Massachusetts, and was "thrilled as a young fellow" to be asked to go west to meet and board the train. Bunny's father drove him to the far reaches of the state, where Bunny boarded the train and witnessed several of Truman's speeches from the famous caboose, the people in unison exclaiming, "Give 'em hell, Harry!" On that ride Bunny met President Truman and some of his cohorts, like Averell Harriman and New York Governor Herbert Lehman.

Some years later, after Truman was out of office and coming to Harvard to speak, by which time Bunny was Governor Foster Furcolo's special assistant, Furcolo put Bunny in charge of a luncheon to be given in Truman's honor, saying to Bunny, "I know you love him more than you love me." Bunny met Truman's plane at Logan, not knowing whether the former president would remember him from the campaign train. Truman did, saying, "Oh, I remember you. They call you Bunny. I told you we were going to win that election."

So where did Bernard get the nickname Bunny? Well, when he was born, Aunt Irene came in from Chicago to help out, exclaiming on first seeing the newborn, "What a cute little bunny!" Bunny adds, "I don't remember this, of course," but if you know Bunny, you know that he remembers just about everything else.

Bunny recollects that, "You don't see barbershops anymore — another thing you don't see are drugstores. People used to hang out in drugstores — you could get a Coke or a soda — and you don't see that anymore. Coolidge Corner is entirely different. I can remember when there were vacant lots there."

Bunny has great memories of the Coolidge Corner Theatre, too. "Before it was built," he says, "Brookline kids had to go to the movies at theaters like the Capitol, in Allston, and the Egyptian, just outside of Brookline, for Saturday serials and giveaways. About the time I was in the seventh or eighth grade, I remember the Coolidge was built — the first picture was 'Disraeli' about the Jewish prime minister of England, played by George Arliss."

Around that time a couple of Bunny's friends, as he tells it, "snuck into the Coolidge, but they were caught and ran out onto the fire escape on the back of the theater. They were told to come off the fire escape, and one of them, now a very well-known Boston businessman, still my friend, who shall remain nameless, yelled back, 'If you don't tell my mother, I'll come back; otherwise I'm jumping!' — getting the answer, 'Don't jump, don't jump!' " Thus Bunny's friends got off the hook of both parental and official punishment.

Bunny says parental disapproval was a bigger thing in those days: "I knew my mother was mad when she yelled 'Bernard.' If she yelled 'Bunny,' everything was okay."

It's predictable that an American original like Bunny would like vanilla ice cream. That taste came early too. Bunny says, "I used to like a store called Morgan's on Beacon Street next to the Brookline Trust. You could get a vanilla ice-cream cone for four cents. It was terrific. I can still taste it. I still like vanilla ice cream better because of Morgan's four-cent ice-cream cone."

At BHS (and later Northeastern), Bunny's life became intertwined with that of his good friend Joe Grady, the two of them figuring out that you could win elections at BHS by forming a

Jewish-Irish coalition. Bunny's friendship with Joe Grady went way beyond politics into Bunny's rapidly expanding social life. As he tells it, "Joe's grandfather 'Farty' O'Neil owned a bar and social club on the second floor at the corner of Boylston and High Streets, and Joe and I would sneak in when we were kids. Later, when Farty died, he left Joe six hundred dollars. Joe bought a Dodge for two hundred, and when he found out that I was going to Northeastern, he said he'd go too, using another two hundred for the tuition. Joe picked me up every day in his Dodge, and we would cruise by the Simmons dorms, getting to meet a lot of young women. We had a lot of fun. My social life was in great shape."

Northeastern became a lifelong passion for Bunny, as he is by far NU's biggest fund-raiser ever. His loyalty has been recognized in several ways, including his election to the Northeastern University Corporation and NU's board of overseers and board of trustees. He is also a member of the university's Athletic Hall of Fame, and has received an honorary degree from his alma mater. Very recently, as a result of Bunny's leadership in raising two million dollars to renovate NU's Cabot Physical Education Center, the basketball court there was named in honor of Bunny and his dear recently late wife, Jolane, eminent in her own field — she was Boston College's first-ever tenured female professor.

Bunny's inclusive, warm, and gregarious nature is evident in his more serious remarks on my program concerning the ripening of America and Brookline, in answer to a question about growing up Jewish in Brookline:

"America has matured," he said. "Brookline is a good example of the maturity of this country with regard to religious differences. I still live in Brookline. I love Brookline. It is a great place to live because everyone loves each other. It's good. Viva Brookline!"

Photos by author.

Cameron F. "Cam" Kerry John J. "Jack" Corrigan

CAMERON F. "CAM" KERRY

*Brother of Presidential Candidate John Kerry, Attorney,
Brookline Resident*

JOHN J. "JACK" CORRIGAN

*Commissioner of Brookline Youth Baseball, Kerry Aide,
Attorney*

INTERVIEWING CAM KERRY AND JACK CORRIGAN on April 16, 2004, on Brookline Access TV, shortly after it became clear that Cam's brother John would be the nominee of the Democratic Party for president of the United States in the fall 2004 election, a number of words and names were mentioned or came to mind that might seem to have no connection but in this pivotal year do — such as *grass roots, Brookline, Iowa, Michael Dukakis, Sumner Kaplan, John Kerry, Cam Kerry,* and *Jack Corrigan.*

In fact, as I spent an hour or so talking with these two

Brookline Access TV interview, April 16, 2004.

gentlemen, both active Brookline residents and outstanding professionals in their own field of the law, the phrase *grass roots* was mentioned no less than seven times as Cam and Jack related Brookline, and their respective lives in the town, to Iowa and John Kerry's quest for the presidency.

Grass roots is defined in the Oxford Dictionary of Current English (1998) as "*ordinary people* [emphasis added]; rank and file of an organization, especially a political party."

Certainly, if John Kerry is to succeed to the presidency, he will have to touch "ordinary people," as he obviously did in the Iowa caucuses when he suddenly and surprisingly emerged from a crowded field of aspirants to become the nominee.

Cam Kerry was on the scene in Iowa as his brother connected with the voters: "One of the things that stood out in Iowa was that John's got incredible energy, stamina, and focus, that's what his crewmates saw in Vietnam, that's what they saw in Iowa. He went out and answered every question, and really engaged with voters one on one. Thanks to cable television, C-Span, and the Internet, people across the country were able to watch that. It's just been this extraordinary wave that's built from Iowa across the country to the Super Tuesday primaries and here in Massachusetts. And it's still going. The enthusiasm, the excitement of Democrats across the country is extraordinary. We are still a very divided country, and it's going to be a very tough and difficult race. It's going to take an awful lot of people behind what we're doing, people going out there and doing grass-roots work. I'm just so grateful that we have people like Jack Corrigan aboard to help with that, but it's going to take everybody's participation."

Experienced political operative Jack Corrigan, John Kerry's liaison to the recently concluded Democratic National Convention, echoed Cam: "There's a really tremendous opportunity with the Democratic party this united to go out and organize at a grass-roots level, raise lots of money in small chunks, and get a lot of people involved in the organization at a local level. I think that could make the difference in this election."

As I write, less than a week after John Kerry appeared to make that one-on-one connection in his rousing address to the convention accepting their nomination, and following that with forays on the grass-roots level into territory thought to be Republican, it appears to a certainty that John Kerry's ability to reach that relatively small and as yet undecided coterie of voters will decide this election.

It is at once ironic and fascinating that John Kerry should be taking his cue as the key to winning this election from the Brookline legacy of Michael Dukakis, himself the Democratic candidate for the presidency in 1988, and with whom John Kerry, Cam Kerry, and Jack Corrigan have all enjoyed close personal and political relationships. John Kerry, of course, was lieutenant governor in one of Mike Dukakis's last terms as governor of Massachusetts. Both Cam and Jack spoke of Mike.

Cam: "I have just enormous respect and affection for Mike. When he first came to Brookline after that 1982 campaign, I lived one street over from him. He was my neighbor as well as my governor, and he's always had the ability to be both, and kind of keep in touch with the grass roots. Mike brought some extraordinary people into state government, and we're fortunate that there are a lot of them, like Jack Corrigan, still involved in politics."

Jack Corrigan (who now lives on Rangely Road in the house in which Mike Dukakis grew up): "Mike is one of the most admirable public servants I've ever seen. The most remarkable thing about him, I think, is that he got there by working his way up from the grass roots. He got elected state rep, ran for attorney general, ran for lieutenant governor, ran for governor, once unsuccessfully, once successfully, and then was reelected after that. So he worked his way up to the nomination for president of the United States, doing it with a grass-roots approach all the way."

The rung-by-rung approach Jack described applies as well to now octogenarian Sumner Kaplan, who preceded Mike Dukakis in the grass-roots ring-every-doorbell-and-stand-at-every-T-stop approach, which not only changed Brookline from Republican to Democratic and underpinned Sumner's political prominence, but also established Brookline as an exemplar, even if not the inventor, of the grass-roots approach to elective politics.

Given all these connections and cross currents, it seems reasonable to suggest that what goes around comes around — should John Kerry be elected president, it would hardly be far-fetched to suggest that Brookline people and Brookline values (a word often used during this political season) will have had a significant effect on the outcome. That raises the question of what it is about Brookline that drew Cam Kerry and Jack Corrigan, two estimable men of different backgrounds, to live and take part in Brookline life.

Jack Corrigan grew up tough in Somerville and attended parochial schools, Boston College High, Harvard, and Harvard Law School (where he now supervises and runs seminars for third-year law students who practice as prosecutors in district courts), all along the way, by his own admission, viewing Brookline from without as a "wine-and-cheese" community. That began to change when Jack was assigned to the Brookline Municipal Court as a Norfolk County assistant district attorney, where he came to admire then judge Henry Crowley and later judge Larry Shubow, as well as the quality of Brookline life, especially its public employees: "In that capacity, I worked with some very impressive public servants in Brookline, the police department, the fire department, the town employees. I knew that Brookline schools were great. I got a different idea of Brookline from what I previously had from its political image, and I was very impressed with the town. So when I could, I bought a house here."

Jack was described by Mike Dukakis in the media as "a very smart guy, very savvy, he is a great organizer, has great political instincts, he is a great strategist, superb in the field, he doesn't waste time, he's out there, he's tough, and he pushes people," adding that "he has a wry sense of humor, but he's no Johnny Ha-Ha."

That wry sense of humor showed up early in the interview when I suggested that the house he bought in Brookline is a famous one. Jack said, "Well, the house I live in now has some historical significance, but the house I bought in 1991 is actually across the street. The historical significance was that it was the cheapest house sold in Brookline that year, so I could afford it. The house I live in now is the house that Mike Dukakis grew up in. My wife, Kathleen, has had some fun going around the neighborhood, introducing herself as Mrs. Johnny Ha-Ha, and also telling people that if I don't shape up I'm going to be Johnny Boo-Hoo!"

Although serious and centered, Jack Corrigan's wry sense of humor showed up again when he talked about his and Kathleen's immersion in the Brookline community. His wife's favorite job, apart from raising their three young children, is as a volunteer at the Baker School library, where her twin sons, Matthew and Patrick, are seventh-graders and her daughter is a fifth-grader. Jack, who serves as Brookline's commissioner of Youth Baseball, said, "Well, you know there are two Major League owners who live in Brookline, John Henry from the Red Sox and Frank McCourt, who just bought the Dodgers. So I think if I impress them enough with my job in Brookline Youth Baseball, there's no reason I need to stop there. I'd just rather be commissioner of Major League Baseball." Laughing, Cam and I agreed that we didn't think Jack was kidding.

Joking or not, considering the range of Jack's organizational skills and his political connections, that larger role may yet come to pass. Jack told us that baseball is his favorite sport, and he is enthusiastic about Brookline's youth baseball program:

"We have seven different leagues that we run in the springtime, and we have a summer league and a fall league. We start with first-, second-, and third-graders. We have about six hundred and fifty kids who are involved, boys and girls, all volunteer organizations, all volunteer coaches. I think people have a wonderful time, starting right now in April. Spring evenings, summer evenings, people just watching their kids play baseball. We try not to be too competitive. We are pretty competitive, but we try not to let it get out of hand. It's a nice community activity, and the kids have a lot of fun."

Cam Kerry recalls, "When my brother John was nominated as Mike Dukakis' lieutenant governor, and Jack was the field director in that campaign, I got to know Brookline, and it's actually when I first got to know Jack himself."

It appears that apart from the political wars, Cam and Jack meet most often on the soccer and baseball fields of Brookline. Cam tells us, "We run into each other around town in various places. One of those is at the soccer field. Jack's sons play soccer. I've seen them out on the field. For a number of years I have been involved in Brookline Youth Soccer because both of my daughters have played on youth soccer teams. It's been wonderful to be able to be one of the soccer coaches, one of the greatest pleasures of my life. The traveling teams go to other towns, representing

Brookline against other town teams, traveling for games sometimes close to Rhode Island."

Jack adds, "Actually, I'm going from this show to pick up my daughter from a soccer field. My kids know a lot more about the game than I do. When I was a kid, people didn't play soccer, so the rules elude me a little. I know you're not supposed to use your hands unless you're a goalie, and you can hit it with your head, and you can kick it, and you go toward the net, and violence is discouraged."

Cam Kerry, relating the education of his younger daughter, Laura, to the attractions of Brookline that led him and his wife, Kathy Weinman, a highly respected Boston criminal defense counsel, to settle in Brookline, says, "Laura is actually a veteran of Brookline Access Television. On another program, she's been here a few times to talk about books that she's read. My older daughter is about to graduate from Milton Academy. Laura goes to the Park School here in Brookline. Brookline is a wonderful community, and that's really what brought us to the Park School. Brookline is quite fortunate to have such wonderful schools, both public and private. We had wonderful choices. I didn't grow up here. I grew up around Brookline. I went to college at Harvard, then to Boston College Law School. I had Brookline surrounded. I got to know Brookline very well after coming back to Boston from Washington, D.C., where I was lucky to meet my wife, to run my brother's 1982 campaign for lieutenant governor."

In a sense, although Cam has lived in Brookline more than twenty years, he still has Brookline surrounded through his long association with Temple Israel, which is an integral part of the Brookline "community" although it lies a few feet beyond Brookline's border with Boston:

"I converted to Judaism when Kathy and I married," he said. "I was really looking ahead, and to being able to participate in raising my daughters as Jews, and to be able to stand up at their bat mitzvahs as a full participant, a very proud moment. They both had them, wonderful occasions. Temple Israel is another wonderful community. Part of what made my conversion come about was the wonderful and warm welcome from the clergy there. They have been a part of our lives for many years."

One can hardly gainsay that a sense of humor is more than handy to any man or woman whether in a light or serious time. When telecommunications attorney Cam Kerry's cell phone rang during our TV show, the sense of humor of Cam, Jack, and John Kerry came to the fore, I remarking, "Well, we told you folks that Cam Kerry is a telecommunications lawyer, and he is an expert in that field. Now, wouldn't he have with him a telephone that would make noises?" Cam laughed and said, "You would think he would know how to shut it off." Jack remarked, "That doesn't make him an expert on shutting it off." Kiddingly saying to Cam that he must have been the guy whose phone rang during a concert at the Boston Symphony Orchestra, I asked him about John Kerry's sense of humor, his answer perhaps shedding some light on a man often criticized for having a mien too serious: "Well, he's got more of a silly, playful sense of humor" (Jack interposing that "He's not as silly as me"), all of us laughing as Cam continued, "Absolutely. With his daughters and in other situations too John can be pretty goofy," adding, as a rejoinder to my following remark that John and Teresa seem to have a great relationship, "Yes, Teresa's got a great sense of humor, and any candidate for president needs that around him."

Of course, Cam answered some questions in the interview about other, better-known aspects of John's personality and experience, observed over their lifetime together, but in these dangerous times his revelation about John Kerry's humor and goofiness, and the humor of the men and women closest to him, provided no small measure of comfort to this hopeful auditor as the fall election approaches town and country.

BOOK VII

CITIZEN
PARTICIPATION

Drawing courtesy of Brookline Public Library.

Old Town Hall (Demolished 1963).

Photo by author.

CHOBEE HOY, VOLUNTEER

A Woman's Story for Our Time

THAT THE BROOKLINE COMMISSION FOR WOMEN is honoring Chobee Hoy for her personal achievements and contributions to Brookline at its eleventh Annual "The Woman I Most Admire" award ceremony on Thursday, March 29, 2001, comes as no surprise to anyone who knows anything about Chobee. The fact that this award will be given at Brookline High School, and in the Martin Luther King Room, is replete with significance, mostly shown by Chobee's own words when I interviewed her earlier, in March.

Chobee's remarkable story may well be a paradigm for our time, perhaps least of all for her well-known success in business (although that too is part of the paradigm), as that success is the natural result of Chobee's upbringing in a southern family that valued volunteerism and giving back to the community as a high

Brookline Access TV interview, March 14, 2001. *Brookline Tab*, April 5, 2001.

ideal; Chobee described her mother as a volunteer "of the highest order."

What makes Chobee's story even more interesting is that her volunteerism is lifelong, preceding as it does her success in business, a reversal of the usual path taken by many of those who do give back. It is as though Chobee and Brookline (where volunteerism is highly valued) were on a collision course all the way, and how fascinating it is to trace how Chobee got from there to here, both geographically and spiritually, as it were.

Chobee's unique and unforgettable name goes back to those southern roots. Her family repaired from her native West Virginia to Florida during the winters of her youth due to her mother's illness, resulting in her nickname "Chobee" after Lake Okeechobee in central Florida. (Later, Hoy replaced her maiden name of Kyle; Chobee is of Scotch descent.)

Hearing about Chobee's parents and family demystifies her combination of business acumen, artistic interest, and community spirit. Her dad, son of a West Virginia coal miner, himself having only a second-grade education, began his own successful wholesale furniture distributor business, still finding time to read voraciously. Chobee describes her dad as "the brightest man I ever knew," and a man who "never forgot where he came from," jokingly but seriously describing himself as having come from "horse thieves and coal miners."

On the distaff side, Chobee tells us, her mother was an accomplished pianist, and one of her aunts was a professional opera singer who sang with the Chicago Opera and later, in her eighties, at Chobee's wedding, at which she, formerly a cheerleader at St. Petersburg High, married (who else?) the captain of the football team.

Chobee's peripatetic course took her north, finishing junior college in Montpelier, Vermont, where she first started thinking about living in Boston, though never believing she would. But when her husband's career path took him to Boston University to teach around 1960, the couple chose Brookline "because of its school system," and soon after moved into a Victorian house on Osborne Road, where their three children, Gil, Deacon, and Tracy, grew up, and where Chobee still lives. Gil, of course, is a selectperson (to use Chobee's word) here in Brookline. Deacon is an actor and real estate agent in

New York City, and Tracy, a professional singer now giving most of her time to family, lives here in Brookline.

All of Chobee's children went through Brookline schools (Heath, Devotion, BHS), and all became accomplished musicians through the Brookline Music School. Tracy plays the piano and sings, Deacon is a fine clarinetist, and Gil is an accomplished enough flautist to have been able to go in that direction had he wanted to. Chobee tells the great story that when Gil was a kid, he played the boy David in Leonard Bernstein's "Chichester Psalms." After the performance, he was picked up and hugged by the demonstrative Bernstein — a Brookline native.

Even in those early years in Brookline, Chobee was able to balance being a mother and housewife with volunteer work at Boston State Hospital (for the mentally ill), saying of that and other volunteer work that she always "tried to treat it as a job I was hired to do." In fact, when Boston State received a grant a few years later, Chobee (despite her lack of a degree in social work) was asked to take a salaried position there as the director of volunteers, an obvious recognition of the commitment and quality of her volunteerism. Chobee held that position until Boston State was deinstititionalized and the care of the mentally ill shifted to the municipalities.

It appears that the Boston State experience set a pattern in Chobee's life, wherein the quality of her volunteer and other work impelled organizations to desire her services on a full-time basis. That and her family's needs ultimately (and seamlessly) led to her present business success, Chobee never giving up — in fact, increasing — her volunteer activities along the way, so that now she probably gives equally of her time and effort to each.

Asked how she is able to do it all, Chobee expresses herself this way: "You take and you give, and the giving is the volunteerism. It's a very important part of my life, a very rich part of my life, and also a very important part of Brookline, more so than any place I've ever been. My story is family, business, and volunteer work — a lot of what I do is because of the family."

Even more illuminating, Chobee says she sees her life "as a circle — I really can't tell you where one thing begins and the other ends. Where does volunteerism or work or family or friends start and end? I don't know, it's like a circle, a lot of it blends in and a career in real estate allows me to live that way. Basically it's a blessing. It's perfect for me and I'm so grateful."

After Boston State Hospital closed, Chobee saw a caterer's ad in the Tab looking for "someone to teach our cooks how to cook." Chobee (accomplished in the kitchen; what else is new?) answered the ad, did the job, and predictably was asked to join the catering staff. But another opportunity came along, again in predictable fashion, when the Girl Scouts of America hired Chobee to be a director despite the job description calling for a college degree, which Chobee didn't have. Chobee happily stayed there four and a half years, despite the irony that this very independent woman did not like the regimented atmosphere of Scouting as a kid.

But when Gil came to her and said he wanted to go to graduate school, Chobee (by then a single mom) knew that nonprofits were not going to work, and she needed to make more money to support her son's education. Indeed, friends had been encouraging her for years that she was the perfect fit for real estate work. Around 1980 she got her license, worked for a while for Lyn Medoff (whom Chobee credits with teaching her a lot), then formed a partnership known as Hoy, Kosloff and Rothstein, and finally, in her desire to be independent, started Chobee Hoy Associates in 1990.

Over and above the financial independence that running a successful business provides, Chobee has fun in real estate, saying, "I do like houses. I like shapes, sizes, structures, and decoration, so for me it's a lot of fun to go to houses — it's like a house and garden tour. It's the people aspect that I like the most, and also the problem solving. The real estate business is much more than merely taking orders. You need negotiating skills, and I love that part of the business because those skills make all the difference in the quality of the work a person does. After all, all of us are nest builders. The nest becomes an extension of self, and this is a part of the job I like."

The personal interests Chobee brings to the circle of life that she describes extend from real estate to her volunteer work and back again every day of her life. Among her interests is the Coolidge Corner Theatre Foundation, to which she was introduced by its former director, David Kleiler, and with whose present director, Joe Zina, she now works, describing him as "wonderful, doing a great job." Chobee feels that saving the Coolidge Corner Theatre has been a tough job, but she believes it is "healthy now," and expresses her interest in the preservation of the building (a church in its original incarnation), and talks of the new forty-five-person screening room there as "cozy and wonderful." She sees the Coolidge Corner Theatre as "diverse," like Brookline, running the gamut from personal appearances by famous people like Claire Bloom to the sex sellout each year when Grand Opening shows what Brookline citizenry can really do.

Chobee is also active in the Brookline Arts Center, in the old fire station on Monmouth Street, describing it as "a little jewel," as well as in the annual Artists Open Studios, hosting a party at her house on the last day of that event. "Artists are part of our soul," Chobee says.

Chobee's deep sense of social responsibility is demonstrated in her work at the West End House in Allston, efforts on behalf of the Brookline High School 21st Century Fund, and her views on the lack of affordable housing in Brookline.

Chobee, along with other interested Brookline people sees the West End House (in Allston for the last thirty years, following its storied past in Boston's long since razed West End) as a "sanctuary" for the underserved Black, Hispanic, and Asian populations of Allston, where youngsters can find sanctuary and interests in "that time between" the end of school hours and the return of their parents from work. Along with Brookline folks like Ira Jackson, Sandy Bakalar, Martha Weinberg, and Barbara Gray, Chobee is engaged in a capital campaign to repair the building, which is in dire need, saying it's "like a religion" to provide this place where these kids can come to do their homework, and then use the gym, swimming pool, and other facilities there. Chobee sees this as an endeavor similar to Boston's After School for All Partnership, reported by the Globe recently to have raised twenty-three million dollars to be spent over the next five years, and other such after-school programs that excite kids "about their own and the world's potential," certainly a better answer than allowing elementary and middle school children to have time on their hands to assemble arsenals.

As Chobee says, "If we don't take care of these underserved communities, I don't see how we can look at ourselves in the mirror."

In the same vein lies Chobee's interest in the Brookline High School 21st Century Fund. Chobee says BHS remains a great school, but since Proposition 2½ cut deeply into school funds, it requires an infusion of outside funding, not only to do its core job of teaching better, but also to take a leadership role in serving its diverse and underserved population. Chobee says Headmaster Bob Weintraub has taken the leadership role in the effort to raise a ten-million-dollar endowment for BHS for these purposes. One and a half million has been raised so far — Mike Wallace and others have been generous with contributions, and the ubiquitous Ira Jackson, among others, has been generous with time.

Chobee affectingly expresses herself on this effort: "African Americans have been underachievers only because of what [has not] been available to them. I see this as an opportunity to create a program for catchup time. It would be wonderful if BHS could be a role model. That is part of this dream. I am convinced that public education is the foundation of our country. It is the great equalizer."

Chobee sees this endowment as being used in part to fund an Afro-American scholars program at Brookline High School, as well as a teachers-mentoring-teachers program. The endowment might also be used to bring the Facing History and Ourselves program (a nationally known program emanating out of its Hurd Street, Brookline, headquarters) to BHS as well, so that man's inhumanity to man (i.e., the Holocaust and other such genocidal events) can be taught to the diverse BHS community in the hope of bettering the social condition.

Chobee sees all these as good ideas that need to go forward, and "quite frankly need money" to do so.

Chobee's opinions on affordable housing are pungent; she sees the lack of affordable housing in Brookline as a threat to the community we have always known, saying, "I do see that lack as a threat, a serious problem not only for people without money but for the middle class too. It would be a real loss if Brookline became a town only for the very rich and the poor. The middle class serves a real purpose — probably a majority of the volunteers are middle class. It is important that people who don't have a lot of money can stay in Brookline, and that we find a way to have affordable housing. I don't think the way is rent control. Rent control is inherently unfair; only the owner pays the bill. We must all share, and figure out a way, through tax breaks, federal funding, whatever. Otherwise, Brookline will change. It's the diversity that makes it beautiful. I see that diversity at BHS. That's America!"

So, too, Chobee is America, in any way you care to name, and in everything she says and does. Others may disagree (it's a free country), but to this writer Chobee represents the ideal to which Americans ought to aspire and the values all of us should be pursuing.

Photo by author.

*Monmouth Street Firehouse (1883), now the home of the
Brookline Arts Center.*

Photo courtesy of Arlene Stern.

From left: Arlene, Roger, and Sadie Stern.

ROGER STERN
Developer and Philanthropist

ARLENE STERN
Director, Brookline Council on Aging

THE ART OF RESPECT FOR YOUR ELDERS

WE ARE LIVING IN A SOCIETY that puts a much higher premium on youth than age, one in which the old saying "Respect your elders" is more often breached than observed. Perhaps this is less true in Brookline, where we now have the new and thriving senior center, brought about in large part by the efforts of the late Roger Stern and his wife, Arlene Stern, a couple whose combined and individual reputations will doubtless become legendary in Brookline history.

Brookline Access TV interview at the home of Roger Stern and Arlene Stern, February 25, 2002. *Brookline Bulletin*, February 19, 2004. Roger Stern passed away on September 22, 2002.

A more unlikely couple would be difficult to find, he a lifelong Republican and real estate developer who grew up in Brookline and she an unreconstructed liberal Democrat social worker from Brooklyn. Somehow, to the benefit of all of us, Roger and Arlene pooled their disparate backgrounds into a successful and fun-loving marriage and a public alliance based on their mutual love and respect for the elderly that has brought about the Brookline Senior Center and the innovative programs now ensconced there.

Roger and Arlene's first date must be the funniest on record. By that time, Roger was already the owner of three elderly housing buildings in Brookline, the two on Center Street and 1550 Beacon Street, and Arlene had recently begun her twenty-two-year career as director of the Brookline Council on Aging. Dorothy Singer, then the chair of the council, was the matchmaker; having already appointed Roger to the council, she apparently felt (presciently) that Roger and Arlene had something in common to talk about. Arlene spoke about that first date in her hilarious style when I had the good fortune to interview both of them at their home a few years ago, shortly after the establishment of the senior center and Arlene's retirement from the council.

"Our first date was memorable! I don't like to mix my personal and professional lives, so I spoke to Roger, and said, 'Roger, we can't be seen together in Brookline, no matter what. So you'll have to pick me up after all the staff leaves, and we can't hang around Brookline.' So Roger said, 'Well, let's go out to dinner in Salem.' Okay, that's far enough away, and we started on our way. We had a lovely evening talking and eating, and perhaps one or two glasses of wine, and sooner or later we get back to where my car is, right in front of my office, and son of a gun, my car is not there! And Roger says, 'Are you sure you left your car here?' And I said, 'Yes, this is my office, I always park my car here.' 'Okay, we'll have to go to the police station, it must have been towed,' Roger said. So off we go to the police station.

"I wouldn't let Roger come in with me. I didn't want to be seen with him; it could besmirch my professional reputation. So I went in, and yes indeed, the car had been towed, the officer telling me, 'Lady, you have to pick it up tomorrow,' and I had to beg, saying 'Oh, I'm a town worker, I have to get home, I have no way of getting home.' So sooner or later they did give me the name of the tow place, and we did go over there, but the tow place wanted cash for me to redeem my car.

"Well, I went back out and told Roger about it, and that I didn't have any cash on me. So he peeled off the money. I said, 'You can't come in with me, because I can't be seen with you, no matter what.' And I did get my car back. It was a very long first date. Indeed, it was a very long and funny first date!"

Not that that sealed the deal. First, Arlene had to run the gamut of Roger's formidable mother, Sadie Stern, an encounter for which Arlene was prepared by others who, as Arlene tells it, "kept saying, 'Oh, wait till you meet Sadie, she's really gonna eat you up and spit you out.'" And, indeed Sadie tried to do just that when Roger introduced Arlene to his mother as she stepped off a plane at Logan bearing her back from Florida, saying, "Oh, is this the dame from Brooklyn?"

Arlene proved to be indigestible, replying, without missing a beat, "How did you get so short with such a big nose?" "And then after that they were friends forever," put in Roger. And indeed they were, "because we both liked the verbal duels, and had a lot of fun doing that with each other," Arlene said, demonstrating the same outspoken, unorthodox, and good-humored style in cementing a good relationship with her mother-in-law as she did many times thereafter when forging the multiple relationships that brought fruition to the dream of the Brookline Senior Center.

Long before Roger and Arlene met, Roger, the scion of a real estate family, embarked on the course that would ultimately lead to donating the land on Winchester Street on which the senior center now stands. Not long after Roger returned from service in the Korean War, he and his family built the beautiful apartment building (now all condos) that stands at 131 Sewall Avenue. A few years later Roger – then living in a bachelor apartment at the Brook House – was educating himself about affordable housing, he says, by "taking the books from the newly formed Massachusetts Housing Finance Agency, leaving them by the pool, and between swims I was reading them, gathering up my information, getting ready. That's the start of 100 Centre Street."

Roger went on to talk about how he found the Centre Street

site: "Well, one day, a Saturday, I was driving from Brookline to Harvard Stadium, to see one of their football games, and I happened to stop at a light on Centre Street, and I looked at this great big lot of land that was filled with tires and junk, more junk than you can imagine, and I said 'Oh, that's a nice piece of land.' From that point on I just inquired who owned it, went to see the owner, and sure enough the land was for sale, so we took an option and we were the first ones in the door at the Massachusetts Housing Finance Agency [MHFA]. We made applications, went through the routine, got the money, and by golly, we built the place, everything went as smooth as silk on that building. We had people at market rent, at middle-income rent, and at low-income rent." The rest, as they say, is history. Roger developed two more buildings along the same lines, at 1550 Beacon Street, and 112 Centre Street, all sold, shortly before Roger's passing, to The highly regarded Hebrew Rehabilitation Center for the Aged, despite the fact that Roger probably could have reaped a few million more by selling the package to an interested Chicago real estate investment trust. Asking him why he did that, Roger replied, "Yes, I probably could have gotten more money, but I thought it was the right thing to do, to have Hebrew Rehab run it. They run things carefully and closely, and I like the idea of having them be the successors."

Then came that moment when the parallel paths of Roger and Arlene and Brookline geriatric history converged and merged to change the Brookline Senior Center from a dream in the sky to a reality on the ground. In the late eighties, Arlene had been fighting through feasibility study after feasibility study and thickets of citizen opposition to the idea of a senior center. Well into that struggle, a momentous moment in Brookline history arrived when Arlene and Roger were attending separate meetings in the same building.

Arlene tells the story: "Actually, it was a quite momentous moment because we had just sat there and figured why doing a senior center was not feasible. At that point Gordon Horowitz wrote me a note, he having done some work professionally with Roger, in which he said, 'What about that piece of vacant land that Roger owns on Winchester Street?' And I said, 'I don't know much about it, you know more than I do.' Then, at the end of this meeting, we're starting to adjourn, and Gordon says, 'Hey, what about that land of Roger's, could the town lease it or rent it, do you think that's a possibility for a senior center?' And Roger (who by that time had come into the meeting) looks around and says, 'Lease? I'll give the land to the town.' Okay, that was an interesting proposition, and that changed the direction that we were headed in. Roger's offer of a gift of land didn't present the opposition with a whole lot of new ammunition for why we shouldn't do the senior center."

Sure, there were good business and tax reasons for Roger to donate the open land, appraised at more than one million dollars, but Roger's love of his wife and love of elders were strongly in the mix. He said he was "fed up with the opposition, Arlene was getting a lot of undeserved publicity, and I thought it was a beautiful location, one to which seniors could go on foot. I think seniors are great, based on my experience with them — you know, thirty-two years with them, and you get to know them."

Arlene puts Roger's contribution to the elderly in more expansive terms: "I think the elderly love him, and indeed that shows, and I think that his reputation in geriatric circles is right up there. I don't want to ruin Roger's mean and lean reputation, but he's the last of the good guys, and I think that's how a lot of people remember him. He was the kind of guy who would come home and say, 'Arlene, I would love to help the elderly, who ultimately need to leave my building after living there for twenty years and go to a nursing home. How can I help them?' I said, 'Well, if you did more services, that would help. If you got a social worker, that would help too.' Roger would do it! It was great; there wasn't a whole lot of bureaucracy. Roger experimented, and indeed, his is the only elderly building in Brookline that does meals."

In fact, one of Arlene's claims to fame is her achievement of hiring and utilizing professional social workers at the Brookline Council on Aging, and then at the Brookline Senior Center, advocating and appreciating their unique skills, whether they serve as board members, employees, or volunteers. The Council on Aging gained a statewide reputation for its dedicated, high-achieving staff of professional social workers. Accordingly, Roger described his wife as "inventive; she came up with programs that no other city or town has, all of them in place and functioning." Arlene adds, "Social workers do it better, and I admit my prejudice. I thought that social workers could go out into the community and see elderly who might be in trouble, who might need some help, help in the house, and be a facilitator of getting these services."

Other innovative services for the elderly instituted by Arlene and her cohorts are the BLAB (Brookline Legal Assistance Bureau) program, in which volunteer lawyers advise the elderly on a pro bono basis; the BETS cab discount program; and classes for the elderly in computers and other subjects. As Arlene says, "There's a whole group of folks that the town has not served adequately, and these folks are now coming, and feel very comfortable coming to the senior center. That's exciting!"

When you think about it, Roger and Arlene have joined forces not only to create the senior center, but also to empower the elderly in an era when it seems the elderly get less respect than they deserve.

Arlene put it this way: "In Brookline, people want to know what's going on, and are very involved. I think that in Brookline, when I first came, people were nice to the elderly, but they said, 'You know, we need them when it's time for a vote, but otherwise we don't need the elderly too much.' The elderly get enough in this town was what I heard frequently. So it was good that the elderly began speaking and advocating for themselves. Lots of elderly have lived in Brookline a very long time, and as soon as they got together as a group there was no stopping them. They enjoyed going to Town Meeting, they enjoyed advocating for the senior center. And hopefully, other people in town see them a little differently now, and have a lot of respect when the Council on Aging or the senior center wants or needs something."

From this vantage point, it does appear that respect for the elderly, both as a political constituency and as individuals, is on the rise in Brookline, due in no small part to the lifelong efforts and commitment of Arlene Stern and Roger Stern.

Photo by author.

OWEN CARLE

American Original, Longtime School Committeeman, Brookline Folklorist

SO FAR IN MY BRIEF (and fascinating) career as a TV host and journalist, unlike the late estimable Charles Kuralt, student and seeker of American originals and Americana, I have not had far to go to find American originals. The borders of Brookline have been far enough. A few weeks ago it was Harry Ellis Dickson, a few months ago it was Bernard "Bunny" Solomon, and this week it is the colorful Owen Carle, former groundbreaking Brookline School Committeeman for fourteen years.

On the program, Owen speaks mostly of his early and teen years, growing up in modest circumstances on Verndale and Amory Streets. His memories tell us a lot about Brookline in the 1920s and thirties, and sharply remind us of the comments of Chobee Hoy. Chobee said that the present lack of affordable housing in

---

Brookline Access TV interview, April 20, 2001. *Brookline Tab*, May 17, 2001.

Brookline threatens to change the diverse character of "community" in Brookline by excluding the middle class. "The middle class serves a real purpose," she said. "Probably a majority of the volunteers are middle class."

The inspiring story of Owen Carle's rise to prominence here underlines this precipice on which we now totter, hopefully to be remedied by the recently passed Community Preservation Act (and other measures that might be taken), allowing communities to impose a one to three percent tax on real estate for the preservation of open space and historic buildings and to provide affordable housing, triggering (at least for a while) matching funds from the state. As Owen relates his workaday youth, it is plain that if he were growing up today, it would have to be in some less expensive town.

In fact, one of Owen's earliest jobs had a heavier component of love than money, when he used to run messages from Irving Weiss, of Irving's Toy and Card Shop on Harvard Street, to Irving's wife, Ethel, when they were living on Brainerd Road in Allston. As Owen says, "I used to like, and still do, Hershey's Kisses — silver bells — I would be given three silver bells as my pay." Owen agreed with my rejoinder that "kisses are better than money." Indeed they were, as Owen became a fast friend for life of both Irving and Ethel Weiss, going to Braves games with Irving before his early death, and serving Ethel to this day as her friend and accountant.

Owen speaks with admiration of his principal at Devotion School, the legendary "Mr. Chips" of Brookline education, Charles Taylor. Owen told a story that demonstrates not only Mr. Taylor's love of athletics and competition, but also the unfortunate loss of music from Brookline grammar school curriculum, and the alterations at Devotion School that did away with its marvelous auditorium (akin to the inexplicable ripping down of Boston's Opera House, and the destruction over the years of other public spaces in Brookline). Let Owen tell it:

"We used to have music classes under William Burbank, who as director of music at Brookline public schools went around from school to school in the years just after radio had come in. When he came, we would assemble in the auditorium at Devotion School. Mr. Burbank would put either an Atwater Kent or a Philco in the front of the Devotion auditorium, which I regret we don't have today. In those days we had three or four classes per grade, thirty-eight or forty people in the class, and we would all assemble, and Mr. Burbank would turn on Walter Damrosch from New York directing symphonic or classical music, which was the main thrust of the music program."

Owen goes on: "Mr. Taylor came in during one of Mr. Burbank's lectures and in the middle of the broadcast, saying, 'Excuse me, Mr. Burbank, I'd like a few minutes of your class,' so the radio was turned off and Mr. Taylor spoke to us, saying, 'I understand we played a baseball game yesterday and lost,' and said to me because I was the captain of the baseball team, 'Owen, why did we lose? Can't we see to it in the future that we do better?' Mr. Taylor was dedicated to winning, but not at all costs. He thanked Mr. Burbank, who was probably not happy with the interruption, but then again, the principal is the principal."

Owen talks about his regret that music and other grammar school programs have gone by the boards. "Grammar schools had music in those days," he remembers. "We had an all-town grammar school orchestra, and students from all the grammar schools would come to meet at the Devotion auditorium to practice. We would compete on radio programs against schools from other towns, had two or three concerts a year in Boston over major radio stations; we accompanied assemblies and participated on a town-wide basis. I'm sorry that today grammar schools don't have these programs in music, track, basketball, baseball, and dramatics. I believe with 2½ they were cut back, but I think mistakenly so."

Owen's summing up of this loss is pungent: "Sometimes you learn more through music, dramatics and sports participation than you learn in the structured classroom. As a supplement to the classroom, with these programs you can approach many students you couldn't approach otherwise."

Owen's violin and piano playing, which came naturally from his gifted mother, Florence Owen Mills, a New England Conservatory graduate and winner there of the Fritz Kreisler Award, gave way around age twelve to work, school, and sports. Indeed, Owen's mother introduced him to baseball and sports generally;

having lived in Canada from age six to sixteen, and seeing women there playing ice hockey, she said to Owen early on, "Why aren't you skating — girls play ice hockey in Canada." Owen's mother took him down to Amory playground to get him started.

She also took Owen on Ladies' Day every week to see the Braves, where the rotund Eddie O'Brien would announce the lineup by megaphone three times, clockwise from first to third. Owen demonstrated on my program, cupping his hands to his mouth, announcing in stentorian tones, "NOW BATTING FOR THE BOSTON BRAVES, AL SPORER," reminding us that this was the name of a Braves catcher in the early thirties.

Owen's major source of income as a teenager during the Depression was selling newspapers. Many can still recall him at Coolidge Corner, with his money changer strapped around his waist, hawking all the Boston papers in hot competition at that time — such as the *Globe, Post, Herald, Transcript, Christian Science Monitor, Record/ American* — working out of Johnny King's Coolidge Corner News on Harvard Street.

Owen recalls that he and other newsboys would at times shout nonsense to relieve their boredom during slow periods, phrases like "Big shipwreck in subway" and "Two babies die in a milk bottle."

Owen says, "Most of us worked and I regret youngsters today don't have a chance to have a job like that." Indeed it was a job, ten miles a day and seven days a week. Owen's route and routine as a newsboy was onerous; nonetheless, he found time to take the difficult science course in school and play on the baseball, football, and hockey teams. That routine got Owen out of bed at 5:30 A.M., to be at the Coolidge Corner News at 6:30 six days a week, walking from his home on Verndale Street to the Coolidge Corner News, back to Brighton to do his regular paper route, finishing in time to return home for breakfast, then walking to Brookline High School for classes, to Tech Field for athletic practice, then reversing this procedure to do his evening route. On Sunday Owen would work from eight A.M. to one P.M. pushing around a big wheelbarrow with the Sunday papers. Saturday was no picnic either, going out to collect twenty-two cents from each customer for the papers for that week, saying "I couldn't believe it" when some customers would tell him to come back next week if he didn't have the three pennies change for a quarter, telling us that "we would have to make up that money."

Owen recalls that "in addition, when the Phinney family started the *Brookline Citizen* in 1935, copies had to be delivered held by an elastic on every doorknob between five A.M. and eight A.M. every Friday morning, after which we had to go to the *Citizen* office in the Arcade to get the pay of one dollar." Owen says, "We hated Roosevelt then," because when Social Security came in, a penny was deducted, leaving the pay at ninety-nine cents. So Owen earned $4.50 a week (more or less) for his everyday all-route efforts to help the family — and learned a lot about life and people along the way.

When Owen worked his paper route in Brookline Village on cold winter nights, from time to time Frank O'Hearn, of Sagamore Liquors, would let him come in back to warm up, saying, "Don't tell anybody, I'm not supposed to have minors here." Owen says, "I got warm in there or at the old White Tower on Boylston Street."

Delivering the old *Boston Record* at night, Owen tells of going to Lally's Funeral Home. "I won't mention names," he says, "but when I went into the back room, some of my school teachers and the owners were playing poker sitting on the caskets in the back of the funeral home."

Naturally, Owen got hungry out there and speaks of Barney Sheff's, which "came into Brookline from the West End with the label 'King of Delicatessens' and it was good. I used to like the old pickles in a barrel, which I think today are outlawed by the Health Department. When my newspaper job on Saturday nights at Coolidge Corner from nine P.M. to one A.M. was finished, I used to walk home. At that hour Barney Sheff's was still open, and I would spend a nickel of my hard-earned dollar for a kosher pickle, and literally would live on it for a day, sucking that salty brine. My mother said, 'Get that old pickle out of your room,' and I suppose the counterman at Barney Sheff's didn't like to see a bedraggled schoolboy fourteen or fifteen years old in the store at one in the morning spending five cents on a pickle. Certainly they did not live on that."

Showing his intellectual prowess early, Owen was on all sides of the newspaper game, delivering the *Citizen* on Friday and writing for it at the same time in his column "Brookline and the Sports World," delivered in Neal O'Hara — staccato style. He coupled that with his regular sports column in the same paper, getting the lead several times, especially around Thanksgiving time with pre- and post-Newton-Brookline football stories.

Significantly, Owen's early Brookline life prepared him for his adult roles as public accountant and fourteen-year school commit- tee member, serving there with such notables as Sylvia Burack, Viola Pinanaski, and Florence Peabody. These were devoted people, Owen said, "not using the office as a stepping-stone to another office, and who brought the town along against conservative ele- ments into the twentieth century in curriculum, teacher personnel, and building modernization." Owen also talks of how this group — at a time when the highly respected Robert Sperber was the school superintendent — applied a missing "morality" and equity to the school system, so that each grammar school in town was at the same level in curriculum and length of school day.

Perhaps the monologue that Owen delivered on my program concerning his work as a public accountant best sums up the fruition of his Brookline upbringing, and the value of being your own man:

"In public accounting, especially tax preparation, you learn more about a person in a one-hour sitting than you might ever learn if you were a wife or a husband or a close friend, because money touches everything. You learn their living conditions, whether they wash the dishes, clean the floor, keep the house well, have a well-landscaped lawn, how many children they have, what religion, what race, their philosophy, political and social, whether they are for NAFTA or against it, their attitudes toward society, their position on any issue you can talk about, whether they like books or not, whether they get along with their children — there is nothing you don't learn! Do the children play baseball, piano, does the family go to church or temple, where do they go, you name it, there is not a single thing you don't know about a family, are they rich or poor, apt to lose their temper, polite, courteous, or sarcastic, tend to bend things when they shouldn't, are they over- sensitive, I can go on and on. When you do this work for years — and you have to keep it confidential, of course — you learn a lot about society, about life, and it has been a big help to me, you meet all kinds of people.

"It is not like working for a company for a long time and getting a gold watch when you retire. That is limited. I consider public accounting like being on the school committee, a place where you learn about life. I had a psychiatrist as a client, and he used to say to me, 'Owen, I should ask you to review some of my patients' tax returns and have you interpret them for me. I would learn an awful lot in a short time and start off in a higher level of understanding in assisting them as a psychiatrist.' "

These memories of Owen Carle's early life raise a serious issue for Brookline, whether changes in the demographics and diversity of the town's population will forever alter its character, resulting in a loss of community and citizen participation. A vital factor relating to that issue is affordable housing.

In any event, looked at in a less weighty way, we can all celebrate Owen Carle's life as one example among many of youngsters growing up, learning, and forming their character in Brookline, and later giving back to Brookline in equal measure.

Photo by author.

ETHEL WEISS

Guardian Angel

ONE MIGHT ASK WHY, at age eighty-five, Ethel Weiss continues to run her tiny shop full time. Indeed, when that question was put to her as she worked there recently, her answer came readily, in a simple and powerful way: "I love being with people, and talking and being useful, and that's basically it. I listen to good advice, and I give advice if they want it."

In fact, that advice is mostly given to the children from the nearby Devotion School (grades 1-8), and Kehillath Israel Synagogue, these youngsters every day crowding into Ethel's little store, where there is not much money to be made from the trinkets, toys, cards, and candy she sells for pennies, but where Ethel's advice, freely given, helps the children grow into adults who value community, family, and the spirit of giving.

Tape recorded interview at Irving's Toy and Card Shop, February 22, 2000. *Brookline Tab*, December 21, 2000.

Ethel has a wisdom all of us might wish to emulate. It may be that Ethel Weiss — by daily living her life the way she does — tells us all what it is to be ripe in a modern world that seems to be spinning from the community of the twentieth century into the surreal chatroom cyberspace of the twenty-first.

Perhaps it is no accident that Ethel's shop is only steps from JFK Crossing at the corner of Harvard Street and Beals Street, a little way down from the unassuming wooden house where John Fitzgerald Kennedy was born, now administered by the National Park Service, and visited by thousands annually. Perhaps it is no accident, too, that Ethel's store sits side by side with the more-than a-century-old Edward Devotion School, where so many of Brookline's sons and daughters, some now famous, have been educated, and directly across the street from the long established Kehillath Israel Synagogue, a center for Brookline's large Jewish community. These places reflect the community and family values still flourishing in this famous town of nearly sixty thousand, surrounded on three sides by the city of Boston, founded in 1636, not long after the Pilgrims landed at Plymouth, and incorporated in 1705.

Ethel wears a badge in the shop that reads *I LOVE MY CUS-TOMERS* and echoes that: "I do love my customers," especially the many children from Edward Devotion School and Kehillath Israel that troop through the shop daily. Ethel acts as sort of a guardian angel for these children, trying to inculcate values of community, caring, and charity, not to mention honesty. "The children respond very well," she says. "I work on them, I compliment them when I can, and they respond to my trying to teach them the correct things. Some kids try to steal a little bit, . . . so I just watch them and try to teach them the correct thing. And I have these signs here in the store that say DO UNTO OTHERS AS YOU WOULD HAVE THEM DO UNTO YOU and also STEALING IS NOT COOL. I am trying to teach these children better values."

To use the vernacular, Ethel puts her money where her mouth is: "I have established awards at Devotion School that I give to the kids. I have an endowment there. There are five awards. These are to be given to the boys and girls who are judged to show warmth, love, caring, and understanding to all, and who generate goodwill and good behavior to their peers."

Of course, the Brookline of today is far different from the Brookline of Revolutionary times, when William Dawes rode out from the Edward Devotion House on the same day as did Paul Revere from Boston to warn the residents of other towns that "the English are coming, the English are coming!" Likewise, Brookline today is very different from the nineteenth-century town that was the home of Frederick Law Olmsted, America's most famous landscape architect, who designed (among many other parks) Central Park in New York City and the park that fronts the Capitol in Washington, D.C.; and H. H. Richardson, the architect of Trinity Church in Boston.

It might be said that it was not until the twentieth century, an era during which Brookline was both the birthplace of John Fitzgerald Kennedy and the home of 1988 presidential candidate Michael Dukakis, that the town reinvented itself from a farming community and summer retreat of Boston's wealthy to a community of immigrant Irish (like the Kennedys), Jews, and other Europeans, and their children, who had gained a footing in the land of opportunity. That community, like Ethel and her late husband, Irving, found in family-oriented Brookline a place close to the city to rear and educate their children, where the voice of every citizen could be heard in the governance of the town in its representative Town Meeting, and a tradition of broad citizen participation in the multiple functions of its municipal government.

So it may be accurately stated that the values of the Kennedys in a grand way and of the Ethel Weisses in an ordinary way are both represented in the mix of professionals, academics, youthful dot.com and other entrepreneurs, municipal and regular employees, and elders, some working and some retired, of all races and religions, including newcomer Russians and Asians, that now make up Brookline's diverse population. Many of those, like Ethel now and the Kennedys then, sought out the stable community environment that happily still persists in Brookline, but which in many places elsewhere in the land seems to be threatened by outbreaks of violence across the whole spectrum of American society, where a steady decline in community and family values seems to be increasingly supplanted by reliance on, if not idolatry of, money and material wealth in the new impersonality of cyberspace.

Perhaps it can be said that Ethel Weiss stands as a symbol for all those values, including hard work and persistence, that make Brookline a great place to live.

In August 2004 Ethel Weiss turned ninety, and is still flying around her shop as a guardian angel, with no plans to alight.

Congregation Kehillath Israel.

Photo courtesy of Martha Jackson.

IRA A. JACKSON

Communicator, Catalyst, Connector, and Convener
Delivering Profits with Principles

As I SIT DOWN TO WRITE ABOUT IRA A. JACKSON exactly one week after the presidential election of 2004, an election in which some pundits ascribe President Bush's election to the ascendancy of Red State "moral values" over Blue State "permissive liberalism," I am struck that "liberal" values, and their practical effects, passed on by Ira's parents to him growing up in Brookline, may bode for a better balance in our society between corporate profits and community interests.

Perhaps the paradigm enunciated by Ira Jackson and coauthor Jane Nelson in *Profits with Principles: Seven Strategies for Delivering Value with Values* (2004) expresses a far more valid moral mode for the interaction of business with society at large than the Halliburton model. If so, academician, public servant,

Brookline Access TV interview, February 27, 2002.

and businessman Ira Jackson's long history as a bridge builder working at the intersection of business, government, academia, civil society, and the community would point to Brookline and Blue as the true moral center of gravity.

Being related to Ira on his father's side, and sharing his experiences growing up in Brookline, added resonance as he spoke of his parents:

"My dad [Philip Jackson] was a tall, strong, quiet, dignified lawyer. My mom [Anne Jackson], thank goodness, is still going strong in her nineties, painting up a storm. My mom picked up a paintbrush for the first time when she was in her seventies, not knowing that she had that magnificent talent. So she's Grandma Jackson, Grandma Moses, and very eclectic, very creative, very uninhibited. My parents were opposites, but opposites attract, an excellent combination, yin and yang. They were a very attractive set of parents and people for a young man to have as the formative influences in his life, growing up in Brookline. My mom was very energetic and very political. My dad, who passed away in the late eighties, was low-key, dignified, had a great sense of humor, was a big sports fan, a big Red Sox fan.

"Both of them served in Brookline Town Meeting together for about thirty years [Ira following his parents' example, became one of the youngest — if not the youngest — Town Meeting member in Brookline history, being elected at age eighteen on an anti-Vietnam War ticket as a Harvard undergraduate]. My mom was the firebrand, the one who would go to march in Washington and carry the antiwar placards. My dad was on the Advisory Committee and did the unheralded work that makes a community strong, what my colleague Bob Putnam [author of *Bowling Alone*] at the Kennedy School would call 'social capital.' Both of them paid their dues, investing a lot of social, not financial, capital, a lot of human capital in strengthening Brookline and helping the development of new skills and aptitudes here. I think they were really wonderful citizens! I continue to hope I can emulate them. I can recall that Mike Dukakis announced his candidacy for State Rep in 1962 in my parents' living room. I didn't invent my activism or engagement. I grew up in a family that showed me the way."

Philip and Anne Jackson, in showing Ira the way, undertook

a journey to Brookline taken by thousands of others, then and now, illuminating the town's richly diverse demographic, and unique character. Ira shed some light on that, humorously telling of the connection between the Lowells of Harvard and the Jacksons of Brookline, by way of Dorchester and Chelsea:

"My dad took the streetcar from Dorchester to Harvard every day," Ira recalls. His dad was a janitor at the Upham's Corner Strand Theater. To work off his tuition payments, Dad chopped wood at the house of President Lowell of Harvard. On the days he chopped wood, he'd have to wear a tie, for the privilege of chopping. One day in the middle of winter, Mrs. Lowell asked the boys in for tea, after they had chopped the wood. She went around the room asking, 'Where are you from young man? What's your name?' My dad answered, 'Philip Jackson, I'm from Boston' and Mrs. Lowell said, 'Jackson — we have distant relatives in New Hampshire named Jackson — perhaps we're related.' Dad said, 'I don't think so, I think I'm from a different branch of the Jackson family.'

"My mom's family came from Lithuania, my dad's family from Russia. Wonderful pilgrimage! It's the traditional immigrant migration from Chelsea, where I was born, and where my mom used to teach at the Williams School. I remember vividly the day we moved from Chelsea to Brookline. It was a big event in our lives. I was only four years old. We're still here!

"I grew up on Griggs Road, where our door was always open. My mom would have an open table for neighbors. It was just wonderful! For them and many others, Brookline was viewed as Mecca. It was a way to enter the mainstream of a society. I think it was a pilgrimage many immigrants made, not limited to Jews. I'm Jewish, and to go from Chelsea or Dorchester to Brookline in the early fifties meant that you had arrived. Brookline was a town that took its public services seriously. It was an honest community and most important, it valued education. That has always been the meal ticket to achieving the American dream. I think it was paradise for my parents to live in a lovely home in Brookline set against a public park within walking distance of the Michael Driscoll school, and to be able to be active in liberal Democratic town politics.

My dad took the T to work. We could buy bleacher tickets for the Red Sox games. What is wrong with this picture? It had everything! It had urban existence, with all the attributes and benefits of suburban America, and a more homogenized culture, which, at that time, was what many middle-class-aspiring professional families wanted. I think Brookline today has retained many of those same strengths, but it's a much more interesting place now than the Brookline we moved to then."

Ira Jackson is certainly qualified to discuss just how interesting a place Brookline has become, and whether, indeed, it is unique, his life having taken him many places, the road always leading back to Brookline. Early on, Ira was administrative assistant to Mayor Kenneth Gibson of Newark, New Jersey, and then to Mayor Kevin White of Boston. He followed that with several stints in high posts at the John F. Kennedy School of Government (where he now is), serving in between as the Massachusetts Commissioner of Revenue (1983-1987), and executive vice president and director of External Affairs with BankBoston, now Bank of America, from 1987 to 1999. Recently Ira served as the president of the Arthur M. Blank Family Foundation in Atlanta (2002-2003), overseeing grant making to organizations serving at-risk youth, preserving green space, and having an impact on civic and community causes. After that short hiatus, Ira and his family have once again taken up residence in Brookline, only a few yards from his alma mater, Brookline High School, positioning him geographically and spiritually to affirm the words he had spoken about Brookline in a global as well as culinary sense when I interviewed him prior to his stay in Atlanta.

"You can't find better Chinese restaurants and bagel places in closer proximity anywhere in America," he told us then. "The principal attraction for us in Brookline is its diversity. Brookline High School is a case in point. I think seventy different nationalities are represented at Brookline High, speaking thirty-five different native languages. One third of those kids come from families where English is not their first language. Yet Brookline has never had higher SAT scores, and has never enjoyed more success. Today Brookline does better in terms of all of its kids. The majority are going off to college.

"I view Brookline as a metaphor for America's future. Certainly there are problems, some racial tension, some violence, some poverty. But we have harnessed diversity and made it an advantage. I think Brookline is emblematic of the America we want to become.

"Going back to Bob Putnam's *Bowling Alone,* he writes that with the advent of television and the consumer culture, we've become couch potatoes, and we 'bowl alone.' I think that in Brookline, *au contraire,* there is more citizen participation, there is more initiative, there is more social innovation than ever before. Maybe not enough, maybe too many of us still don't know our neighbors, and it's not Camelot."

That little disclaimer aside, Ira continued to rhapsodize from his well-connected vantage point, his allusions from time to time of a musical nature:

"For example, take my neighbor down the street, Malcolm Lowe, the concertmaster of the Boston Symphony Orchestra, a world-class musician. He's a parent, he's engaged in the community, he does fundraising for the PTO, his kid is a hockey star. Brookline has that diversity which my wife, Martha, and I seek. We wouldn't be happy in a homogeneous gated community. Brookline is real, and we've preserved a lot of our culture — the Coolidge Corner Theatre coming back, the Brookline Music School being renovated beautifully, the Brookline Foundation, the first of its kind, where citizens give philanthropically to support teachers and give them grants so they can do things during the summer that nurture their soul and their mind. *Facing History and Ourselves,* founded years ago by one of our public school teachers, Margot Strom, is now doing work around the world. Now a bunch of us have come along and created the 21st Century Fund at Brookline High School. We're crazy! We are trying to raise a ten-million-dollar endowment to support innovation and excellence at Brookline High School, so that Brookline High, even though it's a public school, can have an endowment to do innovative and creative things, just like Phillips Andover Academy. Why not? It's a special town!"

Wondering aloud whether there is another community like Brookline, Ira expanded on his observations:

"I'm sure there are other communities like Brookline, but Brookline is unique. First of all, we're surrounded on three sides by Boston. That makes us unusual. I live closer to downtown than anybody who lives in West Roxbury and Hyde Park, and that's probably why we live where we do. We're not an island, we have the attributes of a suburb, but we're almost part of Boston. Although most people don't view us as a Yankee town, Brookline is basically a Yankee town with old Yankee values. It was a street-car suburb where some Yankees with good values set down some markers, and we've been smart enough to preserve them.

"Now some new arrivals are reinvesting, and bringing their own ideas, but not throwing out the baby with the bathwater. I live a couple of hundred yards from where Frederick Law Olmsted lived and came up with the idea for the Emerald Necklace. Olmsted was a Brookline boy, as was his friend H. H. Richardson, the architect of Trinity Church. Elliott Richardson, who defied Nixon, was a Brookline boy too. Why do we have such a great public school system? Because those earlier generations of Brookline residents cared about the quality of public education and the quality of our library. Bob Kraft and others are leading an effort to obtain private funds to improve the library. Of course, President John F. Kennedy and Mike Dukakis are Brookline boys. I think it's pretty unusual that one town produced two Democratic candidates for president of the United States in a thirty-year span. I think we're the largest town in America. We certainly must be the largest community that is still governed by a town meeting."

Whether or not Brookline is unique, it certainly seems that Ira himself is *sui generis.* I jokingly suggested to him, "I know you're doing great things, but *what is it* exactly you do?" reminding him that I had heard him described in alliterative terms as a catalyst, a communicator, a connector, a convener. Ira spoke generally about the work he does at the intersection of business, government, and civil society, and then applied that specifically to the founding of City Year.

"America is clearly an economy that has been robust, and has benefited. It has created a lot of opportunities and wealth because of the efficiency of our markets and our free-enterprise system. This is a remarkable achievement. Capitalism and democracy took on all the other isms that you and I were haunted by when we were growing up — fascism, totalitarianism, socialism, communism — and won hands down. But the market, and efficiency, is not enough. We also care about treating citizens with social equity and fairness in this complicated globalized society where government hasn't had adequate resources, and where the private sector doesn't represent the public interest, and where there are so many other voices trying to be heard. There is a crisis of legitimacy and trust.

"What we work on is to try to figure out that sweet spot where we can find a space in our society, locally, nationally, globally, where we can align the efficiency of markets, at the same time achieving an equitable outcome in a collaborative and effective way to have both economic progress and social justice, whether of what used to be called Third World nations, like Vietnam, or in our own backyard. My life work and passion has been focusing on those centers."

Ira Jackson's role as a founding board member of the socially-conscious City Year program, while serving in the seemingly incongruous position of an executive vice president at BankBoston, elucidates perfectly what it is that Ira does. He had pithily summed up his work when he quipped that "for capitalism to remain on a roll, capitalism needs to gain a soul," a message he conveyed as Brookline High School's graduation keynote speaker to the class of 2000. Ira then spoke of City Year:

"A couple of Harvard students came to see me when I was first at BankBoston with an idea they called City Year. I asked them what their business plan was, and they said, 'We don't have one,' but I was convinced that these kids had the right stuff, they had good values, and they had this terrific idea. The idea was that they wanted to start a privately funded urban "peace corps" that would bring together black, white, Hispanic, rich, poor, and middle-income kids in a way that you can't do through government programs. These kids would give back to the community, and in the process they would be a vanguard across racial and class lines in our society to make the inner city a better place. It was a crazy idea, but I thought it was a great idea. I gave them the bank's money. I saw no reason why we shouldn't invest in these kids. All we could lose was money! Bankers make lots of loans that don't get repaid. If we succeeded, it could really make a difference for society.

"It's paying back dividends a million times over! That twenty-five-thousand-dollar grant to City Year at the beginning has led to

City Year having three thousand kids go through the program in ten communities around America. We brought Governor Clinton by to see it in 1992, when he was running for president. He fell in love with the concept, and modeled Americorps on City Year. Americorps has now had twice as many participants as JFK's Peace Corps, and is now going to go to South Africa. It's an idea that is helping to change the world.

"I've been privileged to be there at the creation of City Year and other initiatives, including the New England Holocaust Memorial. Brookline, Boston, this region, is a place where a guy or a gal like myself who has had the luxury of being exposed to government, business, academia, and the nonprofit world can come in contact with people in institutions, and can, at the margin, maybe make a difference, add some value."

As Ira A. Jackson continues in his life work of attempting to graft onto capitalism the spiritual and moral components of soul, guided by the lessons taught to him by his mother and father, Anne Jackson and Philip Jackson, it may well be, ironically, that the preferred prototype for delivering values into the American social stream is the one practiced by Ira A. Jackson, from Brookline, Massachusetts, New England, USA.

BOOK VIII

PUBLIC SERVICES

Fire Station, Brookline Village, Looking West (circa 1915).

Photo by author.

ROBERT T. "BOBBY" LYNCH

Brookline Recreation Department Director, Enhancer
and Critic of the Quality of Brookline Community

IT MAY BE THAT ROBERT T. "BOBBY" LYNCH, currently director of
the Brookline Recreation Department, whose own family history
cuts deeply into the history of Brookline community, is uniquely
qualified to judge the quality of that community, then and now.

In our interview, Bobby spoke with affection and humor
about family and friends in Brookline, calling them almost inter-
changeably by their given names and their nicknames.

Bobby comes by his interest in recreation naturally, following
in the footsteps of his legendary father, James J. "Tiger" Lynch,
who was for twenty-eight years the director of the Brookline Recreation Department, and for whom the (former) James J. Lynch
Recreation Center on Brookline Avenue was named.

But why was James J. Lynch Jr. called "Tiger"? Bobby

Brookline Access TV interview, April 17, 2002. *Brookline Bulletin*, April 8,
2004.

explained: "The 'Tiger' was from his pro wrestling days. He wrestled for Brown University, and then went on to be a professional wrestler. And that's where it came from, Tiger Lynch. He wrestled at the old Boston Arena, in Canada, and all over the New England area. It was quite a story. This was when he first started out in the Brookline Recreation Department."

Apparently, wrestling with other wrestlers and wrestling with recreational and community problems over the years come naturally in the Lynch family, which consisted of dad Tiger, mom Mary, Bobby, and his nine siblings, six other boys and three girls, all growing up in the staff house on the Larz Anderson estate, which provided them with a sixty-four acre backyard.

Brother Billy, following the Lynch family traditions of wrestling, nicknames, community, and recreation, was from time to time known as the Masked Marvel and Billy the Kid. Bobby talked about that:

"My brother Billy was six feet five, and he'd wear the boots with the heels, so he'd be six feet six. One night a week, he would go down to the Boston Arena and be Billy the Kid, with the ten-gallon hat and two six-guns, and the next night he'd be the Masked Marvel. And we, I mean me and a couple of my brothers, would go down to watch him. And we'd sit up in the back and boo him, because he was the bad guy. We did that for four or five years. The promoters asked him not to take his mask off until he got back in his car. So that was kind of weird, coming out of the Boston Arena with a guy with a mask on. But that's what they asked him to do."

Talking about his mother, Mary, who went to the Pierce School and graduated from BHS, living in the long gone "farm" section of Brookline (where the Brook House now stands), moved Bobby to speak about the removal of that piece in the jigsaw of Brookline community and his philosophy of recreation:

"They took a lot of the old tenements down and displaced a lot of people. They put up the Brook House and a lot of small developments. I see a lot of differences in the town. I feel like when I was younger, I knew more people — actually, that I knew everybody! I knew the policeman, I knew the fireman, and I knew all the schoolteachers. Unfortunately, I don't think that exists anymore. I always try to get people together by having activities that bring on socialization. I coached Pop Warner football in Brookline for eight years. My wife [nickname Peppy] was involved, and all my three kids played. I think those were the greatest eight years. I don't even know how many people I met, adults and kids alike. We didn't win all the time, but that wasn't the big item. The big item was that we all had a good time together each year, and met a lot of people.

"One of the great things about recreation is not only the sport, but being able to socialize with other people, to be able to meet new people. Many of the activities we have are a good way to stay physically active and healthy, like the swimming pool, or youth or adult sports. It could be one of the most important things in a community, especially a community like Brookline, which is so diverse and changing all the time. It's a top priority."

Speaking of the swimming pool at BHS, Bobby recalled that during his dad's term as director of Brookline Recreation, a famous fire that lit the night sky destroyed the gym at that site: "You had the main floor, which was the gymnasium, and then you had the running track up above. And below that, there was the boxing room, where [Brookline-born world middleweight champion] Paul Pender trained, coached by Bobby Varnum, who worked for the Recreation Department for many years. I have a lot of memories of the old gym.

"I remember there was a big banquet one year there, and the keynote speaker was Johnny Kelly, the famous marathon runner. People were looking at their watches and saying, 'Where's Johnny Kelly? He was supposed to be speaking five minutes ago!' Everybody is looking for a car, and then there's Johnny Kelly, running down Tappan Street in his suit and sneakers. He ran from his house in Watertown, which for him was like running across the street. And he ran up on the stage, gave his speech, and ran home. I thought that was pretty good!"

As we all know, kids' sports in America today often leads to mayhem. My interview with Bobby took place shortly after the incident in a nearby community in which one hockey dad killed another after a kids hockey game. So I asked Bobby whether he saw that as a threat in Brookline. His answer, based on his long history in the town, perhaps demonstrates Brookline's uniqueness, but certainly shows us that the enhancing elements of competitive sports in Brookline have remained constant over the years:

"I don't see that now as a large problem in Brookline. We couldn't run a lot of the recreational teams without the support of the parents and volunteers, who are actually out there doing the work for these youth sports. And in Brookline we're fortunate that we haven't run into that problem. I just think the organization of youth sports in Brookline does a good job of counseling. I think the people of Brookline already had a good attitude to start out. I think it's a problem nationwide more than a problem in this community.

"I grew up on the Larz Anderson estate, and I used to walk down to Cypress playground to play on the Cypress baseball diamond. I don't remember the scores, I just remember playing. The most important thing I learned was confidence in myself, and that I could play. I remember Mr. Burns. He taught kids not only how to play baseball, but how to have fun. Everybody played. At that time I was about eleven or twelve, and I was a roly-poly kid, kind of overweight, and not very athletic. But Mr. Burns had a way of convincing you that you could do it, whatever it was. Play second, be a catcher, which I ended up being. What a tough job! I don't think I would have ever done it if he hadn't encouraged me. That's true recreation! Real good recreation can supply a child with a lot of fun, and adults too."

Bobby's progress from there stands as an example for boys and girls now growing up in the Brookline schools. He went on to be a catcher on the baseball team and goalie on the hockey team, despite not considering himself much of an athlete, and capped it all by playing first-string center on the BHS football team, guided and coached by the legendary Ed Schluntz, for whom the BHS gym is now named. Not that Coach Schluntz's rigorous guidance didn't cause Bobby some stressful moments:

"I learned a lot from him about 'Don't give up, and you can do it,' that sort of thing. You can carry it with you all your life, which I have. He used to be a tough taskmaster. On Friday nights, before the game, he used to play tapes of past games. He'd have a camera with slow motion, and would run the stills, back and forth. People around me would say, 'What's the big deal?' but back in the 1960s, that was a big deal. And we'd sit there and he'd say things like, 'Watch Lynch now,' and we'd just keep watching it and watching it. I used to have a little box of pencils, and I'd snap a pencil every time he talked about me. But that was good — I was the kind of kid who needed that. I was getting kind of lazy, like I was getting too comfortable. So when he would say, 'Who wants to play center instead of Lynch? He's not hitting anybody,' of course I'd get out there and do the job like I was supposed to!"

Perhaps it is the color, affection, and gentleness of nicknames that contribute to the lack of violence in Brookline recreation. Bobby told me, "A lot of the Brookline kids had nicknames. There was Nozzle, Twiggy, Vroom Vroom. I don't know where half of these came from. Fats, you can figure out what that comes from. Lumpy. Wedgie. Spider. A lot of the kids had nicknames. I knew Nozzle all my life, and it wasn't until I was an adult did I know his real name was Robert."

I was interested to know why Nozzle was Nozzle. "I think when he was a kid," Bobby enlightened me, "he used to play around with a hose, and the name just stuck."

Recalling that some firsts in Brookline recreation were firsts in the nation, Bobby cited "the Tank" as the nickname for the first public indoor swimming facility in America, more officially known as the Natatorium, gone from its site at BHS, much as the study of Latin has disappeared from the curriculum. Bobby went on, "Brookline Avenue playground and Cypress playground were the first public playgrounds in America. And I think Brookline also had the first park commission."

Of course, people like Bobby and his family who work in Brookline public service are the glue that holds Brookline together over the long haul. Bobby spoke of some of these dedicated people, not only in the recreation field, but in other town services too.

After the completion of Bobby's father's service as director of recreation, that post was taken over by Evelyn Kirrane, a famous name in Brookline history, for whom the indoor pool at BHS was named the Evelyn Kirrane Aquatic Center in May 2003.

"Evelyn Kirrane was a great person," Bobby remembers. "She was a pioneer in recreation. She was one of the first people to do a lot in recreation for special needs individuals. Back then, we had a really extensive program for the mentally retarded in Brookline.

She also did a lot for senior citizens with the Golden Age Club. She was just a wonderful person, and a great recreation director. And, of course, she came from a terrific family. Her brothers, Bill, Jack, and Eddie, were all athletes. Bill became recreation director for Quincy, and he refereed for our Senior Hockey League at Larz Anderson. Jack and Eddie were on the U.S. Olympic hockey team that beat the Russians in the sixties. That was quite a story! Jack was the captain. Terrific Brookline family! They lived down on Clyde Street near The Country Club."

Bobby's vision of recreational services covers a person's lifetime; he believes that such services should be provided by the town to all citizens at any age at nominal cost. So naturally his path intersected with that of Arlene Stern, recently retired as the director of the Brookline Council on Aging, who was key in the building and establishment of the new Brookline Senior Center. Bobby spoke with affection of the colorful Arlene:

"Terrific, she's a wonderful lady. When I first started at the Recreation Department, she was very helpful to me. She's a real straight shooter and she'll tell you how it is. And to watch your rear end! She would always say to me, 'No matter what I say, watch yourself.' I miss her already. Roger is terrific too [Roger Stern, Arlene Stern's late husband, who donated to Brookline the land on which the senior center now stands]."

Not only has "the Farm" disappeared, but so has (Whiskey) Point, where Bobby lived in the veterans housing project on Hyde Street. Bobby speaks of this loss, much as people in Boston mourn the loss of the West End:

"It's been a big change. My wife, Peppy, and I think those years were some of the best years of our life, because everyone knew each other. You knew all the neighbors, you knew all the kids in the area and the kids knew you. It was terrific! There was a lot of socialization. You'd sit out and shoot the breeze, and the kids would play. Over the years, I don't see that happening anymore. I know things change, people move out, new people come in. I just don't think the new people have that support system. It's been lost over the years. Years ago, you would have within close proximity a grandmother, a grandfather, a couple of aunts, uncles, and cousins. That just doesn't seem to be happening anymore. I don't know what it is. I think I'm very lucky to have what I had when I was younger. I think it helped me a lot. I feel bad in a way that it's breaking down. Brookline has lost some of the things that I used to really enjoy. I don't see any way to put it back."

Like many of the people in Brookline town services, Bobby has had to move out of town, and although he thinks Brookline is still a great place to live, he believes that, as he puts it, "it's changed so much."

"A lot of times, I'm in Brookline in the evenings for meetings. My wife and I will sit in the window of a restaurant down in Brookline Village. And say we are there for an hour and a half, not one person walks by the window that I know. And that just wouldn't have happened fifteen years ago."

As recreation director, Bobby infuses his good ideas for better Brookline community, such as the first overnight camping program for children ages seven through nineteen: "We went down to Miles Standish State Park in Plymouth with a hundred and forty kids and all the stuff. We got tents for three days and we had a ball. It was pitch dark and there wasn't a light for three miles, but it was good, and you learned a lot. We got all the kids hamburgers, hot dogs, and corn on the cob. And you don't buy corn on the cob for kids on a camping trip because it rolls right off the plate! But it was a great trip and everyone had a wonderful time. All the Brookline businesses donated food."

Bobby's good ideas keep coming. Presently, he is working on a new recreation master plan, recognizing present needs such as an outdoor pool, an indoor hockey rink, a recreation community center, and new playing fields. One new playing field will soon be coming into existence with the capping of the landfill on Newton Street in Chestnut Hill, and another will likely follow upon Brookline's purchase of the old Fisher Reservoir (empty since 1952) on Fisher Hill near Newbury College.

Bobby may well be right that there has been some diminution of Brookline community. But, that trend will be lessened or halted altogether as long as we are lucky enough to have people of Bobby's caliber serving in key Brookline posts.

Photo by author.

DANIEL C. O'LEARY

*Brookline's Own Friendly, Calm, Studious, and Prepared
Chief of Police*

IN THIS UNSETTLED TIME FOR AMERICA, it is reassuring that here in
Brookline our first line of defense is headed by homegrown Dan
O'Leary, whose accessible yet professional qualities were plain to see
when I interviewed him.

In speaking to Dan, it soon became apparent that he was always
becoming the man he is now is. He grew up on Somerset Road with
his parents, two brothers, and three sisters, playing baseball mostly at
the Cypress and Pierce playgrounds, attending St. Mary's through
the eighth grade and then Brookline High School (1972).

"I had a real good time growing up in Brookline," the chief
recalls. "Brookline is great for kids, and still is great. My memories of growing up really revolved around the playgrounds and
parks. My memories then go back to playing baseball every single

Brookline Access TV interview, October 26, 2001. *Brookline Tab*, November 8,
2001.

day. I started hanging around down at Pierce. We had rivalries, us against other parks. The recreational leaders used to throw you in the backseat of a wagon and drive you around and drop you off, and you would have games all summer long. It was great! Sometimes I would bike around with my baseball glove hanging off the handlebars. You don't see that now."

"We were fortunate, too, in having Fenway Park so close. When we were growing up, we used to hop on the trolley and go down to Fenway, and go in there and watch the night games.

"I remember one summer in particular. It's a story I like to tell my thirteen-year-old son. That summer, on the street right near the left field wall at Fenway, around the second inning of every night game, you would have twenty or thirty kids just standing there, and there would always be a Boston police officer watching that gate. Without fail, around the second inning, he would say, 'Boys, I'm going to the bathroom,' and he'd walk away. We would open the gate, and thirty kids would be running in to find seats. For one whole summer, that was a nightly occurrence. That was a lot of fun!

"I was in Little League, and finally made the 'majors'. I remember getting up that first morning in the majors and putting my uniform on. It was the first time I had a uniform. I probably put it on around seven in the morning, even though the game wasn't until sometime in the afternoon. In the first two or three games I played, I think I struck out every time up. Finally, we had a night game at the Robinson playground. I got a double. I was very excited. I got to second base, and as soon as the pitcher got the ball back and went into his stretch, I took a lead. The next thing I knew, the umpire was running out from behind home plate shouting, 'You're out!' I didn't know what to do. I went and sat down on the bench, and the manager, Harry Greenberg, had to come up to me and say, 'You can't lead off in this league.' So welcome to baseball. That was my first hit, and I was called out right away. Those memories stick with you!"

Well, they certainly stuck with Dan O'Leary, forming in him his lifelong love of learning, which has prepared and continues to make him an ideal chief of police for this community of close to sixty thousand people, leading one hundred and forty sworn officers, forty-one civilian personnel, operating on a budget of approximately eight point five million dollars.

That might have been the last time Dan O'Leary was caught off second base. Not long after that, a BHS English teacher, known to Dan then as Coach Robinson, an all-American lacrosse player at Princeton, offered to teach kids at the high school how to play that sport on his own time. Dan says, "I took him up on it. I was up there every day that he was there. A lot of days I got one-on-one instruction. I'll always appreciate what he did. He didn't have to do that. I still play. My son plays, and I coach lacrosse now. Next year will be my third year."

I mentioned to Dan that when former school committeeman Owen Carle appeared on my program, he talked about sports being the highest form of morality. Dan agreed:

"It teaches sportsmanship to kids, especially in a sport like lacrosse, in which there is a lot of hitting. And I think the coach can be a big influence when these kids are age thirteen or fourteen, and they are at a point where you have to give them guidance. And at that age, their minds are wide open, and they'll listen. So you try to get them to assume a leadership role by having the eighth-graders come up and say a few words to the sixth- and seventh-graders. That is a way to get a kid to feel good about himself or herself, an opportunity to show that they can influence others' lives. We were losing the last game of one season at halftime. The eighth-graders spoke, and we went out and won the game. It was a great example that those eighth-graders set for the sixth- and seventh-graders."

So it comes as no surprise that Dan O'Leary, the learner who became a coach and a teacher (now an instructor in several police academies under the auspices of the Massachusetts Criminal Justice Training Council), remembers well those who taught him along the way. These mentors include Ed Schluntz and Ron DiVincenzo, his football coaches at BHS; Tom Conroy, his baseball coach there; and math teacher Meade Reynolds.

"Meade Reynolds was the teacher who broke the ice on a lot of things. He joked around, but he would hold you to task, kind of give you a hard time, but you were learning at the same time. He had a way of doing that. He made learning fun! To this day I still see him on a regular basis. We are both on the board of directors of the Brookline Credit Union."

At BHS, Dan wanted to take more courses and fewer study halls, so he approached the always nattily dressed headmaster John Passalacqua to be allowed to do so.

"He called me in and asked me why I wanted to do it," Dan recalls. "I explained why, and he said to me, 'We'll experiment. We'll try it!' He did it for me. That was a favor!" Thus it seems Dan opted out of study halls and into study.

Upon graduation from BHS, Dan asked himself the inevitable question: "What do I want to do?" Dan chose the highly regarded criminal justice course at Northeastern University.

"I took everything I could in criminal justice," he says. "I enjoyed it because I was learning the law, and how to enforce the law. My constitutional law professor there was Hakky Kassler [former Brookline Selectman]. In my junior year, for practice, I took the police civil service exam, at that point never thinking it would lead to anything, but I did well on it, and what started out as practice ended up as a good move, because I was hired by the Brookline PD a few months after my graduation in June 1977."

Not surprisingly, considering his already established study habits, doing well on tests and advancing rapidly became the order of the day for Dan O'Leary.

"The first time I was eligible to take a test," he says, "was the sergeant's test. My wife worked days and I worked nights, so I used to drive her to work, then I'd come home and I'd study and read. So I ended up doing very well on the test, and I got promoted to sergeant in 1982, within five years of being appointed to the force. I think I was the youngest sergeant that Brookline has ever had, making it on my first try."

This pattern continued. Dan won the post of lieutenant in 1985 and captain in 1992. Then, in 1995, the position of chief of police of Brookline opened up. Dan aspired to it but had scant hopes because of his youth (he was forty at the time), relative inexperience, and the nationwide search that was undertaken for the position.

"As I've studied and become interested in police work, I've always wanted the position of chief," he said. "I think a lot of people aspire to the next position, and that is something I've done.

In 1995, it was the first time that the chief's position was out of
civil service, and Brookline developed a new process of choice
under Rich Kelliher, the town administrator. It was opened up to
a nationwide search. There were one hundred and nine applicants.
A professional firm was brought in and the field was narrowed to
eleven, who had to go through a ten-person oral panel consisting
of Selectmen Tom Hennessey and Ronny Sydney; some leading residents of the town; sitting police chiefs; and an academic from the
JFK School. It was a formidable group of people," he says.

"Fortunately, I survived the oral panel, and they narrowed the
field to three. I got called back in for a second interview. That
interview was described by one of the people interviewing as a 'root
canal.' The panel was Rich Kelliher, Tom Hennessey, and Jerry
Hayes, Brookline's personnel director. We went into Rich Kelliher's office, and I was in there for more than two and a half hours.
That was when I was on the hot seat. I left that meeting and said
to my wife, 'Well, I'm not going to get that job.' I truly believed
that. I got to work the next day, and was called to go over to speak
to Mr. Kelliher. The rest is history: I got offered the position.

"I think the way the selectmen and Rich Kelliher ran that
competition was very good — an open process — and I think it
speaks well for Brookline. Those of us on the Brookline force
applying for the position were assured that even though the search
was nationwide, we would not be boxed out."

These good feelings and easy relationships between the town
fathers and the police department (mirrored in the wide citizen participation we have in town government here) serve us well in these
difficult times. In this regard, Dan O'Leary speaks of the town's
willingness to match grants for police needs:

"Beyond matching grants, every time we've asked for something, and we've been able to justify it, the selectmen and Rich Kelliher, and his people, have been very supportive and try to ensure
that we've obtained what we wanted. I don't think that I've ever
been flat-out denied by them for any request for public safety needs
and the needs of the PD, in training, equipment, or technology.
The best example is the new building [now being constructed on
Washington Street].

"We designed it," Dan says. "The town, meaning the Building

Commission, the citizen input group, Rich Kelliher, and the board of selectmen, basically said, "You're responsible for what happens inside that building. You make sure you design a building that you'll be able to live with. This goes for the fire department too. It will be one public safety building. When we open our doors, people will be impressed by it because it was designed to meet our needs. It has great security, a good layout, the cell blocks are more secure from the offices, with little risk of escape, and combined dispatch to provide better delivery of police, fire, and ambulance services."

Similarly, Dan sees the interaction between the citizens of the town and town officials as a force for good:

"Brookline is a great town and always has been, improving all the time. It has a very active citizenry, and I appreciate that. That's the way it should be. When you have citizens who know what they're doing and get themselves involved, you have a better community. The citizens may not know it, but they make us work a little bit harder. I think everybody is better off because of that. I think that the citizens in taking the role they do by calling when they do, and wanting answers to which they are entitled, make us be on our toes. It makes for a better relationship and a better town. It's a great place to work!"

As might be expected, the Brookline PD was preparing for September 11 long before it happened. Dan O'Leary believes that the unknown can lead to fear, and his response now is to get out information to make people more comfortable and to make sure that we are prepared, as well as cooperating with outside agencies:

"The other night, eighteen high-ranking Israeli police officers were in Brookline, and we had a closed-door meeting with them. The police officer in charge of Tel Aviv advised the value of intelligence and cooperation. Right along these lines, Brookline has been very fortunate, and we've been a member of the Federal Joint Terrorism Task Force since its inception some years ago. We cooperated with them when the Ryder Cup was played here in 1999. Now we have to take that to another level. We're staying on top of this, doing exactly what the Israeli commander, who is living this, told us to do. We were already trained on anthrax back in 1998-99, and the entire PD took re-training on anthrax in recent days. We are also consulting with bioterrorist experts."

Dan O'Leary is fortified in these hard times by his mentors past and present, and by his hands-on experiences in the field. For years he looked up to his boss at the Brookline Police Department, the late Frank Hayes, and he still gets good advice from his father-in-law, George Simard, a former Brookline chief of police.

"He was the chief for eleven years, has lots of experience, and was well respected, and I value his opinion," says Dan.

Among Dan's many experiences in the field, probably the most significant is the fateful day a few years ago when John Salvi struck clinics on Beacon Street. Arriving at 1842 Beacon, Dan discovered, as he tells it, that "this guy left on the floor a bag containing weapons, ammunition, and ID."

Immediately taking the initiative, Dan recounts, "We traced John Salvi down from what he had left behind. Within a matter of two or three hours we were at this guy's house in New Hampshire, and he was arrested the next day."

Among the many programs that the Brookline Police Department runs in partnership with the citizens of the town, Dan particularly spoke of racial profiling and Citizen Police Academies.

"On racial profiling, Brookline did not have to do anything when the new law was passed in April 2000, requiring documentation on people being stopped," he said. "We've been doing that since 1997 on a voluntary basis, keeping more statistics than what the law calls for. That's kind of an example of how I like to run the Brookline Police Department, and how I think the town of Brookline wants to see the PD run — that is that you are ahead of the curve, being proactive rather than constantly reacting.

"With the police academies, the citizens get to interact with the officers. They go out on ride-alongs, and they see what we do. We have academies for adults, high schoolers, and seniors."

That brought this response: "I think I qualify as a senior citizen," I said. "Can I have a date with you to go on a ride in one of those academies?"

"Sure," said Dan, "but you have to sign a waiver and wear a vest."

"I'll go!" I said quickly, feeling, after a couple of hours in Dan's company, that I would be in very good hands indeed!

Photo by author.

HERBERT N. GOODWIN

Lawyer, Judge, Activist, Nice Guy

THE GOOD NATURE AND MISCHIEVOUS yet gentle sense of humor that characterize Herb Goodwin, recently retired after ten years as the presiding justice of Brookline District Court, were apparent when he appeared as my guest on Brookline Access TV.

Those and other qualities showed themselves early, as Herb recalled family, friends, school, and baseball, growing up on Thatcher Street and in the Egmont Street project.

"We played a game called baseball against the stairs. My apartment house on Thatcher Street was right across from the Dexter School, which is now Dexter Park Apartments — John F. Kennedy went to Dexter School — and every once in a while one of our balls would go over the fence into Dexter School. We'd have to fight to get them to throw it back to us. Or a football of theirs would come flying out, and they would yell at us to throw it back. But we got

Brookline Access TV interview, November 29, 2001. *Brookline Tab*, December 13, 2001.

along pretty well with them. I had my own policy about throwing
their footballs back. The policy varied depending on who got hold
of the ball. I always threw it back, as befitting a judge. But no, I
really did! We would argue on that, but eventually the ball would
come into my hands, and it would go back."

But young "judge" Herb could not resist the "strategic advantage," as he terms it, offered to him by the apartment house in
which he lived when it came to snowballing the Dexterites.

"I could climb up on the roof," he recalls, "and I could throw
snowballs down on them. They never did reach me up there."
Well, I suppose it also befits a judge to look with advantage on
those below from his high perch.

Like so many others who have appeared on my program, Herb
has indelible, and sometimes hilarious baseball memories growing
up in Brookline, especially since he lived so close to Braves Field.

"When I first came to Brookline," he says, "the summer
before I went into the sixth grade at Devotion School, I became
enamored of the Boston Braves right away. The park was a few
minutes from where my house was. I used to go over there on a
regular basis, turning stiles for ten or fifteen minutes to earn my
way in, which they let you do in those days. I used to go in to
almost every game. I got to know all the ballplayers pretty well
after a while.

"My favorite Braves ballplayer during the forties was Johnny
Sain [Spahn, Sain, and pray for rain]. One summer he lived at
Pelham Hall, and he used to walk down Pleasant Street to go to
the ballpark, and every now and then I'd see him from my window.
Once or twice I came out to follow him to the park. He'd go in
one way and I'd go in the other way to turn stiles. I wasn't trying
to catch him; I wouldn't have known what to say to him.

"In those days, after the game was over, all the kids would pile
out on the field and run and leap on their favorite ballplayer. So I
wanted to get to Tommy Holmes [then holder of the National
League record for hitting in consecutive games — thirty seven], like
every other kid. I was there when he broke the record. I just want
you to know that. But I could never get to him on time, because
every kid would get there ahead of me. I couldn't get near Tommy
Holmes.

"So at some point I decided I was going to pick out my own guy who nobody else was going to jump on. I picked out a centerfielder named Carden Gillenwater. I saw how he would come in and run exactly across second base. So the time came I'd run out and meet him exactly at that spot at second base and leap up on him. After a lot of games, I would leap up on Carden Gillenwater.

"After that, oftentimes I would walk around to the back where the Braves players came out, and get autographs. Of course, I would get Carden Gillenwater's. I remember one time toward the end of the summer. Finally, after having jumped on Mr. Gillenwater God knows how many times, and gotten dozens of autographs from him, he finally recognized me, and said to me, 'Son, didn't I give you my autograph once before?' and I said, 'Well, yes, you did Mr. Gillenwater, but I traded it.' Then he asked, 'Who did you trade my autograph for?' I said, 'Stan Musial.' A big grin crossed his face. I still remember it. I looked it up. He was only about twenty-three then. I didn't know that at that time. Then he said with delight, 'You traded my autograph for a Stan Musial?' and I said, 'Yes I did,' and he said, 'Well, here's another one.' He gave it to me."

Herb's memory of turning stiles to get into Braves Field rang familiar, as that was a device I employed during those years, along with other tricks of that trade, all recounted by Bunny Solomon, Charles Kickham, and Owen Carle on previous programs, but Herb Goodwin came up with one I hadn't heard before:

"My friend, John Jacobson — whom I still see — lived over on Pleasant Street, where his parents had a house right near Commonwealth Ave. Occasionally we would park cars at the house, filling the driveway with just enough cars at the then going rate to buy us tickets to the game. But one day John's father came home early and was very upset because he couldn't get his car in the driveway. So that ended that!"

Herb's first year at Devotion School was just about legendary principal Charles Taylor's last, but Herb recalls a "go-to" with Mr. Taylor: "We disagreed about something — I don't remember exactly what, except [Herb smiling broadly, but with that twinkle in his eye] that he was wrong, absolutely wrong!"

After Herb's dad, Joseph, passed away young, his mother,

Belle, for economic reasons, moved the family (Herb and his brother, Richard) to the then new Egmont Street project, where Herb found lots of people he liked. Herb recalls the competitive world of boys high school clubs in Brookline around mid-century, such as the Royals, Spartans, Trojans, Ruliviks, and Herb's own Egmont Dukes.

"I did like living in the Egmont Street area," he says. "In fact, myself and some others formed a group called the Egmont Dukes, a club we had that we thought was a little bit better than most of the other clubs around — like the Spartans, the Washington Square AC (Senator Beryl Cohen was in that), the Tappan Terriers, and the other mainstream rival clubs that were formed. But the Egmont Dukes sort of reigned. The original Egmont Dukes still meet — in fact, today I was trying to set up a dinner meeting for next week some time. It was a prestige thing. I can't recall what we really did except talk about ourselves. We still do! When I meet guys now from high school, they all remember the Egmont Street Dukes."

Asking Herb whether he had to keep his dukes up, he said, "We didn't have to keep our dukes up — nobody would mess with the Dukes!"

Before his sophomore year at BHS, Herb took up tennis, and soon achieved local notoriety at the game:

"I went out for the tennis team, and the tennis coach was a guy named Monty Wells, who had been an Olympic hurdler and was a very nice guy. He taught physics at the high school. I did become captain of the tennis team in my senior year — I was number one in that year, and the number one in the previous year had been Mike Dukakis."

But if that was the upside of Herb's BHS years, his perennial lateness might have been the downside. The subject makes a great story, though:

"I used to come late occasionally to school. It was a long walk from where I lived. David Meyers was the assistant headmaster. Miss Katherine Ginty was the headmistress. Mr. Meyers kept me after school for being late. He had various disciplinary chores. Nothing seemed to work, in his view. So finally, this time, he asked, 'Why were you late?' and I said, 'I didn't know what time it was.' There happened to be a song out about that time by that title, 'I

Didn't Know What Time It Was,' so he said I would have to learn the words and sing the song to him and Miss Ginty, and others too, in her office. I did do that. It was embarrassing. I don't have a very good voice.

"As a matter of fact, when I was in Devotion School, the music teacher divided the room into blackbirds, robins, and bluebirds. I was a blackbird, and I remember once the blackbirds were coming in to sing, and the teacher came over to me and said, 'Why don't you just mouth the words.' A teacher could never get away with that now. My voice is better now."

Obviously, Herb Goodwin is not afraid to tell a story on himself. He tells another one having to do with his habit of lateness, extending into recent years, just before he became a judge, when he was taking an adult education course here in Brookline:

"I stopped in an empty classroom trying quickly to finish the reading assignment before class. Here I am sitting by myself in this room, and all of a sudden I just burst out laughing, because here it was — how many years later — and I was doing the same thing I did at BHS. Running in the last minute, and trying to finish my assignment."

Well, Herb has finished all his assignments very well, including ten years as presiding judge of Brookline District Court, from which he retired only a month or so ago. Following his retirement, he was feted by some three hundred people at the Veterans Hall on Washington Street at an affectionate party planned and hosted by people like Bob Gray and Suzie Hall, who worked with him at the court.

Prior to becoming a judge, Herb conducted a private practice for many years here in Brookline. He has also served in the Tax Division of the Department of Justice under RFK in Washington, D.C., as an assistant U.S. attorney here in Boston, as chief of the Consumer Products Division of the State Attorney General's Office, and as chairman of the Alcoholic Beverage Control Commission, having been appointed (as he was later, to be a judge) by then governor Michael Dukakis.

The qualities of Herb the man, Herb the lawyer, and Herb the Brookline citizen coalesced to make him the citizen activist he has been.

In his work as chairman of the North Brookline Neighborhood Association, he was notably effective in drafting, and getting passed by Town Meeting, zoning legislation to downsize density in the North Brookline area.

"In my view," he said, "I don't know of any other town or city where ordinary citizens like you and me can actually affect the way in which we live. People can affect the way they live here in a very dramatic way through the use of Town Meeting, which is a legislative body. I think it's unique."

Herb proved the point in his work on the divisive rent-control issue as a member of the Brookline Tenants Council, resulting in the passing of rent control, obviously needed then to preserve the community character of certain areas of Brookline, most especially North Brookline.

In fact, Herb's zealousness on that issue, in his work as a Town Meeting member, resulted in what I called a "run-in" with then moderator Ben Trustman.

"I don't know that it was a run-in — a run-in implies two people colliding," said Herb. "I was just run over. Yes, it was my first year in Town Meeting. Rent control was the issue. I sort of walked around Town Meeting talking, lobbying. Mr. Trustman heard me. He stopped the whole town meeting and pointed at me and told me to sit down. For years I was kidded about that. I stopped, and I sat down!"

The story moved me to ask, with a smile, whether Herb, in his work as a judge, has had occasion to ask somebody to sit down. "It's happened, yes it's happened," he said.

But as all who have appeared in Judge Herbert Goodwin's court know, he has been a judge (unlike many others) who treats lawyers, litigants, and citizens appearing in his courtroom with respect.

As a Brookline School Committeeman, Herb cast the deciding vote in establishing certain academic requirements for graduation at BHS, over and above the minimum (if not minimal) state-mandated requirements in phys ed, American history, and English.

Herb Goodwin sees changes in Brookline community, but continuity as well. Noting that despite the fact that the demographics of the town have changed, Herb says that "it has always struck me that about thirty percent of the citizens of the town are very active in this town — and that thirty percent still exists. I think the schools have benefited from that, and the general administration of the town too. The community has stuck together pretty well. I think that is primarily because of the educational status of the people who live here. I think they take an interest in the kids' education and in the community. They have the time, the energy, and they know how to do it. There are a lot of special programs at BHS that I don't know that any other schools have for kids with problems, to help them get through. I think it's unique. It has been a gradual process over several years to come to the point they are at now."

Herb went on to say that as presiding judge of the Brookline District Court, he became familiar with all of these programs at BHS, and worked with the people there to "effect the best result for the student involved."

As a lawyer, I know of Herb Goodwin's work in making his court and its departments responsive to the needs of the Brookline community. In this regard, I would cite the work of the Probation Department at the court working with the police and the schools in diversionary programs for juveniles to keep them out of further trouble. I know also of Herb's successful work in fighting to keep Juvenile Court for Brookline youngsters here in Brookline, rather than being moved to Dedham, as has been the case with most other district courts in Norfolk County. The fact is that the Brookline District Court is one of the few district courts that serve only one town, and Herb Goodwin has correctly viewed the court, despite it being part of the state judicial system, as part of the Brookline community, and tried, during his tenure, to make it work that way.

Herb has lived on Manchester Road for more than thirty years with his wife, Rhoda (a practicing psychologist here in Brookline), and that is where they brought up their three daughters, Joanne, Lauren, and Carolyn, all of whom attended Devotion School.

"When I moved back to Brookline, my brother [Richard Goodwin, who achieved early fame as JFK's primary speechwriter] commented that I bought a house halfway between Devotion School and my mother, which is precisely where Manchester Road is. And one thing I'll say about the continuity of this town — I have to admit this, it surprises me — when my daughter was old enough to go to the Devotion School, we went to the candy store next door — Irving's — and I couldn't believe it! The same woman was there. I recognized her immediately — she was there when I was a kid!"

Of course, Herb is referring to Ethel Weiss, who was there when I was a kid too, and represents as much as anybody, as Herb says, the continuity that characterizes Brookline.

I told Herb that when I was a kid, I used to buy three candy hats for a penny at Irving's. He replied, with that mischievous sense of humor, "I didn't buy hats. I had a full head of hair then."

Herb reminded us that his brother, Dick, had attended BHS, and was the editor of the *Murivian* there.

Speaking of his famous sister-in-law, Doris Kearns Goodwin, Herb confirmed to us from the inside something we had all known from the outside.

"She is a very, very nice person — a wonderful person! As a baseball fan, she is as big a fan now as I was then, which is more than I am now. She is a real baseball fan. In one tough Red Sox game, she would walk out of the room, because she couldn't bear to watch what was happening, and somebody would have to go to tell her what was happening."

Herb spoke admiringly of such Brookline personalities as Sumner Kaplan, Mike Dukakis, and Jack Backman:

"Over the years I thought Jack Backman was a very important senator. He was in the forefront of a lot of liberal issues and causes. He got them discussed. He brought issues out that other people weren't going to do, and a lot of that became legislation. He didn't back down from a fight. He had courage!"

As an old friend of Jack Backman, I heartily second that motion.

Herb tells of attending a summertime meeting at Jack Backman's house with his then law associate Mike Cutler, who still lives in Brookline:

"It was very hot and humid that night. At some point Mike and I left and drove to Walden Pond. We went swimming."

Pursuing the point, I asked, "In what state?" Herb replied,

"In Massachusetts. That's the only one I know. I can't recall precisely."

Pressing the point further, somehow having the idea that there was more to it, I said, "I thought you told me it was a skinny-dipping adventure!"

Herb put a lawyerlike spin on his reply: "I think you were presuming," he said. "You were putting yourself in my place."

Well, whether or not Herb and Mike swam au naturel that night, he's right about one thing. I love skinny-dipping, and told Herb that, "I bet Thoreau skinny-dipped when he spent all those months out there."

It seemed to me fitting that my time with Herb should end on a light note, as a vein of humor and kindness seems to have run through all that Herb has done across these many years, gracing all of us here in Brookline.

Photo courtesy of Boston Braves Historical Association.

Fans storm Braves Field Gaffney Street Gate prior to sixth game of World Series (1948).

Photo by author.

JAMES C. "CHUCK" FLAHERTY

Town Librarian for All Seasons,
Brookline Public Library System

JUST AS THE NEARLY ONE-HUNDRED-YEAR OLD main branch of the Brookline Public Library on Washington Street was a work in progress over the last century, until it reopened after renovations a year or so ago, so was Chuck Flaherty a work in progress before he emerged in Brookline fully formed about ten years ago, when he was appointed — after an intense competition — town librarian of the Brookline library system. Chuck spoke about all of that when I interviewed him some months prior to the reopening of the main branch.

Chuck, who combines an easy-to-take intensity with an almost encyclopedic knowledge of library science — and the Brookline library system, which he oversees — grew up in Dedham, lives now in Billerica (where his wife, Barbara, is the head librarian), went on

Brookline Access TV interview, August 22, 2002. *Brookline Bulletin*, March 11, 2004.

to Northeastern, and earned his degree in library science at Simmons, then honing his skills in Framingham from 1974 to 1993.

But it was at Northeastern, while working with the renowned Massachusetts Historical Society on a work-study program, that Chuck not only discovered that his destiny was to be a librarian, but also developed the interpersonal and logistical skills required for that role. Chuck tells us, "It was a great, great experience for three years. The society embarked on a renovation program that lasted about two years. So I had a lot of firsthand experience about what needed to be moved, and all the difficulties in terms of renovating an older building. What was really most important to me working there were the people who came to me, who took an interest in me, and were willing to give me some key advice along the way, and served as mentors for me. Truly, it was working at the society that got me working in libraries."

Predictably, at Simmons, Chuck became the president of the Graduate Students Association, and further developed the personal and political acumen with which he operates today. Chuck tells us, "That association was a student government association, and during my time there I got to represent the students when we wanted to get a coin-operated photocopier on the third-floor student library. I got to deal with the dean in terms of could we or couldn't we have a coin-vended soda machine in the corner of that library. I got to deal a lot with the faculty, and a lot with students. It was working with people, planning a program on how to prepare a résumé, getting the speaker, and publicizing the program. It was really that experience that convinced me I really didn't want to go into a career that would have me working in a historical society, that I really should be working in a public library."

The fruits of Chuck's experience were fully on view to the more than five hundred people who attended the Library Gala at the main library this past February 8. Everyone was greeted personally by Chuck and efficiently and pleasantly whisked off to registration and to check their coats, and soon all the guests were mingling. Truly, that is a metaphor for how Chuck runs the Brookline Library System, consisting of the main library and the heavily used branches in Coolidge Corner and South Brookline.

Chuck Flaherty is not one of those librarians who hide in their office. He says kiddingly, "A moving target is harder to hit," affirming that he loves to work with people. He says that in a public library, "you are working with all kinds of people. You're working with senior citizens, children, parents of children, people looking for career guidance, people looking for recreational reading. How we handle our patrons is the single most important thing we do. I think it's much more important, frankly, than the quality of our book collection. Now, not every librarian or patron will agree with that. But people come to the library for all kinds of reasons. Some of them are simply looking for recreational reading; others might have a medical or health issue they're dealing with at home and they're looking for guidance. They find that their spouse has been diagnosed with a disease or has been given a new medication, and they want to know what the side effects are. How helpful you try to be is what the patrons are going to remember most. It's important that we realize that people really do appreciate what we do. On this issue, we have guidelines for staff, and we have done some training."

Chuck's flexibility and economy are reflected in his ability to give the patrons what they want while getting the biggest bang for the buck. He puts it this way: "I really think if a librarian is not careful, he can build a collection and develop a plan for library service that is how he thinks it should be, and not necessarily what the community is looking for. We did a survey, and really tried to find out what the patrons want, and children's services came out number one. So we've increased the portion of the budget that goes to children's services from about ten percent to about fifteen percent over a period of a few years, and we are trying to maintain a constantly improved collection as we move ahead. I've tried to stretch every dollar that I can in a way that is best for our library patrons and users."

Who better to ask than Chuck Flaherty whether books are on the way out in the face of the computer revolution? "No," he answered, "books are here to stay. There's no question about that. I think people will be lying down with a bright light late at night to read a book for many, many years in the future. As far ahead as I can see, people are going to be using books. It doesn't mean technologies aren't going to change how libraries operate, and how people live their lives. It's already happening, and technology is bringing lots of changes to the library. I think having all that information on computers makes a whole lot of sense, but for the recreational reader I think it is going to have a fairly limited application, so I believe the book is here to stay. The new technology is available so people can gain access to new information. But for the recreational reader, I think technology has a fairly limited application.

"One of the beautiful things about working in a library is that we're here for everyone. You can come in and read Thoreau or the funny papers. People are important to me, and both [types of] people have an equal right to come to the library and get any information they are looking for, whether in a book or on a computer, whatever works."

There is no question that Chuck Flaherty is well placed by virtue of his personal, educational and professional experience to judge whether Brookline is, indeed, a unique community:

"I think Brookline is unique in many ways. The educational level of the people who live in Brookline is far above the national standards. There are thirty or forty foreign languages that are the first languages spoken in the homes of Brookline High students. So, there are lots of different populations to be served, and the types of information people are looking for is wide ranging. People in Brookline can be very demanding. They are well-educated people, many of whom, over their lifetime, have had things their way, and they come to the library expecting to find what they are looking for. We have significant collections in Chinese and Russian. We also have a very large English as a second language collection. We also have a very large books-on-tape collection. It's popular with people who are learning English. People come in to borrow the book and the book on tape, and they'll go home and read the book while listening to the book on tape to help develop their English-language skills. Brookline truly is a unique community."

It may be true that Brookline folks are demanding, but it is likewise true that Brookline folks will put their money where their mouth is to get what they want, and to see that it is done right — most recently with respect to the renovation of the main branch,

at a cost of thirteen million dollars. When the town was first
approached about this project, the need was acknowledged, but the
answer came back that there wasn't enough money. Chuck tells the
story from there:

"We just started to scratch our heads and try to think of what
we could do to make this dream a reality. We got working on a
grant application, and we were told that eventually we would qualify for three point six million dollars in state money, but that still
wasn't enough money to get the town to commit. Then we pulled
together a group of people to help. Gabriela Romanow [a library
trustee and president of the Brookline Library Foundation] was the
primary moving force in raising four million dollars in private funds.
So we got three point six million from the state, four million privately, and the balance came from the town of Brookline. It was a
real partnership!"

In the same vein of citizen volunteerism exhibited by the
Brookline Library Foundation, Chuck spoke of the Friends of the
Library, who raise substantial funds each year with their annual
book sale, and the Brookline Library Music Association, which
presents six concerts for our enjoyment each year. Chuck also
noted the committed and energetic ongoing work of the library
staff and elected trustees of the public library.

At the time I interviewed Chuck Flaherty, the renovation of
the main library was still in progress, but now that it has reopened
everyone can see that Chuck's promise of a boldly reconfigured
library with eighteen thousand more square feet of public space
with many innovations on the same footprint has become an
astounding reality. Chuck predicted all of this.

"We'll double the size of the Children's Room and make the
building fully accessible for the handicapped," he said. "We'll inte-
grate new information technologies, and totally replace the electrical wiring, data wiring, and the HVAC system. We have added a
floor at the back of the building, raised a part of the roof, moved
the administrative offices to the rear of the building, all key in getting that extra eighteen thousand square feet of space for our
patrons. Before the renovation, the only public space in the lower
level of the building was the old Childrens' Room, small and
fragmented. We're creating a new Children's Room downstairs on

the opposite side, with full-height windows. Also on the lower level will be our periodical section, young adult collection, and fiction collection, with a little café as well.

"On the main level we will really open up the space, reinstating the original two entrances, which will be on either side of the front terrace. The circulation desk will be in front when you enter, with an egg-shaped desk so patrons can come in on either side, return their books, and then either exit the building or they can go left or right if they wish to continue in. We are creating a new grand staircase leading from the main level downstairs. The restoration of that main lobby area is something I'm very proud of. The original 1909 building contained a lot of marble from Italy, and I think the architect has done a remarkable job finding marble and other materials that are complementary to what was there originally. We are trying to recapture some of the architectural beauty of the building that was disguised when the building was renovated in 1970. I think the main library is going to be an important building in town, "the people's palace, maybe."

A maybe when Chuck spoke it, but a reality now!

As anyone who has looked around the renovated main branch knows, a great feature is the roundly elegant new Brookline Room, where Brookline's local history is housed, albeit with appropriate levels of security. Chuck spoke of the Brookline Room: "We've created a new Brookline Room on the main level, with four basic areas of security. You don't want to make the Brookline Room overly accessible because we are really the curators of Brookline's local history, and, in many instances, we have only one copy, and you can't just leave it out for anyone to pick up because, unfortunately, it might just disappear. In the Brookline Room we'll have open shelves so people can help themselves, and other shelves will be locked behind glass doors so people will be able to see the material but will have to ask to get it. We'll also have three lockable rooms — closets if you will — where materials that are valuable, but not tremendously valuable, will be stored. Then, too, we'll have a preservation vault in the basement, where we'll keep extremely valuable materials." One might observe that this strikes a nice balance between accessibility and the sensible protection of Brookline's valuable legacy.

As digitally enhanced as the renovated library may be, Chuck Flaherty still sees our libraries as gathering places for the community, similar to our schools and churches:

"We'll have two public meeting rooms in the building," he says. "Historically, the library has been a place where community groups and nonprofit groups have come together to hold meetings. In addition, we will establish a training space in the building, to train our patrons in how to utilize information technologies, and we'll provide classes for that. We also invite all the sixth-grade classes in Brookline schools to come to the library and spend the morning touring the building, understanding what electronic sources we have available, and giving them a quick little lesson on how to use them. In spite of these technological advances, I think that people will continue to come to the library in greater and greater numbers. With the coming of the Internet, I've had people say to me, 'What do you need libraries for anymore?' Well, people keep coming. People keep borrowing materials, and I think we're going to see that continue for many years to come."

James C. "Chuck" Flaherty is a town librarian who looks ahead while not forgetting the past, a man well able to carry forward the traditions we have always associated with our libraries into the cyberspace of the present and future for the betterment of the Brookline libraries and the benefit of all Brookline citizens.

Photo by author.

Brookline Public Library (1909).

RICHARD LEARY

Town Administrator — The Evolution of Brookline Governance

RICHARD LEARY, BY VIRTUE OF HIS long experience as Brookline's executive secretary from 1969 to 1985 and town administrator from 1985 to 1994 (not to mention his continued residence in Brookline), has had a singular vantage point from which to view the peaceful evolution of town government through the combined efforts of professionals like himself and citizen volunteers, which characterizes Brookline as different from all of the other 350 towns and cities in the Commonwealth. This significant story was told in a most absorbing fashion when Dick Leary appeared as my guest on TV. He combined that most interesting history with his view of the people (both professional and citizen participants) key to the continuation of Brookline's stable town governance in the face of

Brookline Access TV interview, May 14, 2001. *Brookline Tab*, July 12, 2001.

its considerably more complex government, with increasingly higher budgets.

Dick Leary came to Brookline in 1960 as the administrative assistant to Brookline's legendary executive secretary, Arthur O'Shea. Although O'Shea favored Leary among many applicants for the position, Dick Leary's first experience with Brookline citizen participants was to run the gauntlet of an interview before the selectmen in the Hearing Room of the old police station, which Dick describes as an "imposing scenario to be interviewed in that chamber" by then selectmen Alan Morse, Gene Carver, Tom Noonan, Matthew Brown, and George Brown (George Brown was then in the midst of his record eighteen years as a selectman).

"Mr. O'Shea recommended me, and I got it," Dick says. Lucky for us!

From his perch, Dick Leary has been able to look backward and forward over a span well in excess of fifty years to tell us how Brookline town government has evolved from fairly simple to very complex without ever succumbing to a town manager form of government, a form that has been the plague of many other communities, and more significantly, without ever giving up the high level of citizen participation from talented residents of the town, not to mention without any of the corruption and dislocations that occur frequently elsewhere in Massachusetts.

As Dick himself puts it, "It is a history of gradual, as needed, continuing study, adaptation, and implementation, as required, unlike other communities, which made changes suddenly, resulting in chaos." Leary says with admiration that Arthur O'Shea was "uniquely the right person at the right time in the right place" when the selectmen were looking for their first chief administrative officer (then called the executive secretary) in 1942.

That was a watershed year in Brookline history; from that time on, not only the selectmen, but also the executive secretary (since 1985 called the town administrator) gathered and centralized increasing power, resulting ultimately in most of Brookline's executive power lying with the selectmen, rather than diffused among the several previously elected heads of the various departments. This streamlined Brookline government, as needs to happen in an era of higher budgets and complexity in the running of a town.

Before 1942, the major change in Brookline's town government since the town's inception in 1705 (indeed, the tercentenary is upon us!) was the adoption in 1915 of a representative town meeting. Moreover, as indicated above, many positions were elective, which resulted in fragmentation of effort and responsibility. Even though the selectmen's duties were more limited then, their time, essentially given as volunteers, was limited. There was no professional in place full time to put into effect on a day-to-day basis the board's decisions and policies.

Things started to change when in 1940, the Public Administration Service of Chicago was commissioned to do a survey of town government. As a result of its study, the recommendation was for the then popular town manager form of government for Brookline. This idea was rejected, mainly because of the fear of Brookline citizens that they would lose control of their own government.

However, also as a result of that study, the first executive secretary was appointed in 1942 in the person of Arthur O'Shea, although he was given no actual authority and had at his disposal only his power of persuasion to carry out his duties. That was enough for Mr. O'Shea in his dealings with the many elected boards and officials. As Dick Leary says, "Arthur had to get people to work with him and for him and to do what he wanted by persuasion, since he had no actual powers — he was effective in getting people to cooperate and to accomplish things through persuasion, being subtle, having a great sense of humor, dignified, and having the respect of department heads and the community — so he was the perfect individual to launch this new system of town administration, and wonderful for me to work under. He groomed me as his potential successor."

As Dick tells it, an executive secretary with no real power sufficed for a while, but in the late 1950s it became apparent that the professional who was there all the time needed some power, and the old bugaboo of whether we should have a town manager came up again. This resulted in the appointment of a blue-ribbon Moderator's Committee, generally known as "the Committee Appointed to Study the Question of the Town Manager Form of Government." Staffed by citizen participants, perhaps predictably the town manager form was not adopted, but on the committee's recommendations, the annual Town Meeting in 1959 unanimously voted to substantially broaden the powers of the executive secretary, still Mr. O'Shea, joined the following year by Dick Leary as his assistant.

Of course, Dick has known all of the key citizen players during his long service here. Several of them stick out in his mind, such as Louise Castle, who served on that Moderator's Committee and became a three-term selectman of the town of Brookline starting in 1960, the first woman ever to serve in that capacity. Dick has great admiration for Louise, and everybody who has ever met her knows what a fine person and citizen participant she was.

As Dick says, "Louise had been president of the Brookline League of Women Voters, a real force then in the community, and that is why she was asked to serve on the Moderator's Committee. She had also been on the Advisory Committee and a Town Meeting member. Louise was elected as selectman in 1960, and it wasn't until she became a selectperson that really substantive changes took place as far as centralizing town government under the selectmen took place, such as the board of assessors being appointed by the selectmen, as well as the appointment of the town's first full-time assessor in 1965, appointment of the members of the Conservation Commission immediately upon its establishment in 1966, and so on, centralizing government under the board of selectmen. Louise was a driving force in that movement. She was a very effective selectman, and I respect her a great deal, and still do. She was a key figure in the move to a more centralized and streamlined system of town government."

That trend really picked up steam in 1963 when the General Court approved the creation of Brookline's Department of Public Works and consolidated the Park and Recreation Commissions. In 1992 Dick Leary and the retiring town treasurer, Shirley Sidd, appeared before Town Meeting to urge consolidation of five separate departments into the now smoothly functioning Department of Finance. That proposal was adopted overwhelmingly, putting the assessors, comptroller, Purchasing Department, Collections Department, and Information Services Department and their forty or so employees under one roof.

Dick goes on, "Everything was happening in tandem in that

period — the boards were changing from elected to appointed — and the duties and responsibilities of the executive secretary became stronger. This was an evolution."

As Dick puts it, "Brookline had the benefit of administrators who had lived in Brookline for many years, and so were familiar with Brookline and the key officials, rather than someone who came in from outside with no backing in the community. This was helpful in the continuity and stability for which Brookline is noted." Dick points out that Mr. O'Shea served for twenty-six years and he for twenty-five years, which gave Brookline fifty-plus years of such (dedicated) service. "I don't think there is any other community in Massachusetts that can make that claim," he says.

Obviously, as the town boards were being coalesced under the control of the board of selectmen from the 1960s through the 1990s, the necessity of more actual power in the hands of the executive secretary became apparent, especially when Proposition 2½ came into effect, which required the husbanding, balancing, and proper allocation of the town's budget in order to give citizens the full use of the money being spent.

Things came to a head around 1985. Here was another chance for Brookline to adopt the town manager form of government. Would Brookline go for it? To help determine the issue, the selectmen appointed the Committee on Town Organization and Structure (CTO), chaired by citizen activist Ruth Dorfman. Not now (perhaps not ever) was the answer! In a finely tuned adaptation to change (as Mr. Leary has remarked above), Brookline chose to give its executive secretary, thenceforward to be known as the town administrator, actual powers in the day-to-day management of the town, but carefully refused to cede the ultimate control of town government away from the board of selectmen and Town Meeting, for fear of losing the citizen participation (probably not too drastic a statement) that makes Brookline famous.

The result was Chapter 270 of the Acts of 1985 (these extensive changes required the imprimatur of the General Court, after Town Meeting's near unanimous ninety to four approval). This was a milestone in Brookline government. It established the position of town administrator, and, as Dick says, " was signed into law by Governor Dukakis, a Brookline resident, and one of our most prominent." Dick displayed an original copy of the Administrator Act on my program, signed in Mike Dukakis's flowing hand. This act was amended two years later, to reorganize and consolidate many of Brookline's departments into the bailiwick of the board of selectmen and the town administrator.

That act gives the town administrator powers over the daily administration of the town, including recruitment and recommendations for town heads, supervision of department heads, and, perhaps most important, formulation of the annual financial plan, as well as other powers and duties.

Perhaps Dick was being extravagant in stating on the program that, "with a few minor exceptions, I think you could say that the town administrator in Brookline is essentially the same as a town manager — not quite — we almost made it but we still don't call it a town manager."

If that statement is extravagant, it is certainly an overstatement we can appreciate, given Dick Leary's loyal and highly competent service to the town. For my part, as one of those citizen participants and being town manager-averse, I took some issue with Dick on his statement, remarking that the selectmen might disagree with what he said. He replied, "Citizen participation has been our tradition for a long time — that the elected officials should have the final say — that's where our system differs from other communities that have gone the town manager route, and that's why we still have Town Meeting, I think. I have not detected any strong sentiment for change to a city manager form of government. That is largely because of the tradition of citizen participation and involvement in Town Meeting, and in the twenty-five or thirty boards and committees that comprise the citizens' role in the town. People have always come forward to serve in Brookline. That is what distinguishes Brookline from other places. I don't know another community in Massachusetts with the same structure."

Dick went on, "The selectmen have the last word, and they should. I have noticed that when there is any accomplishment, the selectmen are the ones who take the credit, and rightly so."

It seems to me that this slight backtracking by Dick Leary regarding the limits on the powers of the town administrator and who has the final say elucidates a truth about Brookline, making this town unique in its government: that the evolution of Brook-line's government provides for a town administrator (as Dick sees it) with enough day-to-day power to run the government efficiently (thus ensuring that Brookline will be able to draw the very best people to serve in that position) while reserving the final say for the highly skilled and unpaid citizen participants in town government, including most notably the board of selectmen (paid only a nomi-nal amount). Obviously, this is a delicate balance achieved slowly, carefully, and thoughtfully over the years, making our town a model to other municipalities in providing smoothly running government for sixty thousand strong.

So what makes Brookline different? Is it in the air? I asked Dick Leary that question, and his answer was no surprise. "Here there are always new people coming forward," he said. "We are living out a tradition begun in 1705." Perhaps surprisingly, Dick does not see that a lessening of the middle class because of how expensive it is to live in Brookline is any threat to citizen participa-tion. "Lots of people move to Brookline because they know of its heritage and tradition of citizen participation," he says.

Dick appreciates Ruth Dorfman (CTO's chairman at the time of the 1985 Town Administrator Act) as a symbol. "She epitomizes the citizen activist in Brookline," he said. "She was a longtime Town Meeting member, president of the Town Meeting Members Association, a member of the Preservation Commission, and chair-man of the CTO. She has been one of the more active citizens in Brookline, and wrote an article that appeared in the *Brookline Tab* in 1999 called "Try a Town Committee, I Guarantee You'll Like It," which encourages people to become involved in town govern-ment. It's people like Ruth who really make the town function the way it does."

At the end of the program, I asked Dick about the strangely named case of *Brookline vs. Dukakis*, which appeared on his résumé under "Professional Experience":

Dick, smiling broadly, told us all about it: "That was a land-mark litigation. As you can understand, we were not anxious to bring it, but we felt strongly that Governor Dukakis had over-stepped his authority in withholding local aid from cities and towns in those dire economic times in the late eighties. So Brookline led the challenge to the governor's action in withholding $210 million in local aid — ultimately the case went to the Supreme Judicial Court, a decision came down in Brookline's favor, and in that case we were joined by one hundred and forty other cities and towns. The case has become well known in municipal government. That victory got Brookline two million dollars, and other communities benefited to the extent of $210 million. That was a good one!"

So, too, was it a good one that Brookline had the great and good fortune to have Dick Leary steering Brookline in the crucial years from 1960 to 1992.

BOOK IX

PRESERVATION

Devotion House, Harvard Street.

Photo by author.

CATHLEEN CAVELL

Reopening the Carlton Street Footbridge into the Emerald Necklace, Associate Town Counsel, Concerned Citizen

INTERVIEWING CATHLEEN CAVELL in June 2003, shortly after the favorable vote of Town Meeting on reopening the Carlton Street Footbridge, into nineteenth-century Brookline resident Frederick Law Olmsted's Emerald Necklace, brought sharply into focus not only that issue and its significance with regard to continuing civility in Brookline "community," but also Cathleen's fascinating personal and family history.

Cathleen herself, migrating here from New York City to attend Harvard College, followed graduation from BU Law School with long stints as Brookline Associate Town Counsel and assistant bar counsel at the Massachusetts Board of Bar Overseers, and now serves as an adjunct professor at Boston College Law School, a

Brookline Access TV interview, June 3, 2003. *Brookline Bulletin*, June 3, 2004.

member of the Supreme Judicial Court's Advisory Committee on Ethics for Government Lawyers, and a practicing lawyer.

In Brookline, she has been a longtime Town Meeting member, a member of the Democratic Town Committee, and an elected delegate to the Massachusetts Democratic Convention. And the credits don't stop there in this amazing family. Cathleen's husband, Stanley Cavell, professor emeritus of philosophy at Harvard University, has published more than fourteen books about such diverse subjects as Shakespeare, Freud, Emerson, Thoreau, and the cinema. Not surprisingly, growing up in this happily academic household, whose walls are lined top to bottom with fiction and videos, Cathleen's twenty-six-year-old son, Benjamin, recently published a book of short stories entitled *Rumble, Young Man, Rumble,* very favorably reviewed in *The New York Times.* Can there be any question that younger son David, soon to be a sophomore at Tufts at the time of the interview, about whom Cathleen says, "his soul is right there, right behind his eyes," will follow in achieving some form of distinction?

Although Cathleen's work as associate town counsel and assistant bar counsel often involved tough issues, such as special education cases in which the parents of a special needs child disputed the educational plan the town had presented to them, and disciplining errant lawyers, Cathleen's openness and generosity were evident in discussing that work.

Regarding special education cases, Cathleen said, "Those are difficult cases. One reason was that my clients, my witnesses, were the school people. And most people don't become special ed teachers because they're harsh, narrow-minded, mean-spirited people. They become special needs teachers and counselors to others because they want to help people and they want to spend their lives making things work better for people, who very often have all sorts of significant learning and other disabilities. And for these people to be on the stand to testify is very hard for them. They hated it. Often, in these cases, the parents of a special needs child disputed the educational plan the town had presented to them. It was also hard for me, because I was a mother, and I could identify with those parents. And very often in these cases, one feels that it is human difficulties, even tragedies, arrayed against money.

And it's not easy to advocate for saving money in a circumstance in which what you see on the other side is people dealing courageously with disappointments and difficulties."

Cathleen was associate town counsel from 1977 to 1989, during which time she served under David Turner, still Brookline's town counsel, of whom she spoke with unabashed admiration:

"One of the most charming aspects of David Turner," she said, "is that he's a feminist, something he might not recognize about himself. He's very welcoming and supportive of women, and, perhaps not by accident, he has a whole group of talented women who started their careers with him, and who continued their legal and paralegal careers with him. He's a wonderful mentor and terrific fellow. I'm very fond of David. He's a terrific lawyer as well. I think he probably is the best municipal lawyer in Massachusetts. And I don't mean to just confine it to municipal law, but that's an area that he knows very well. He's very good at it!"

Turning to Cathleen's work as bar counsel, I remarked that Brookline has an abundance of lawyers living within its borders, and expressed my feeling as a lawyer observing lawyers that most lawyers are high-minded types who traditionally have been the guardians of liberty. Cathleen, having worked more than ten years cracking down on the bad apples, could have a jaundiced view. Not so.

"It's a really tiny fraction of lawyers who are unethical," she said, "or who behave in a way that is a serious infraction of the ethical rules. And there's usually some cause like substance abuse, real personality disorders, or terrible tragedies or traumas going on in their lives. For example, a partner becomes ill, and, all of a sudden, a lawyer is taking over much more work than she or he can handle. These aren't casual infractions. And the vast majority of lawyers are not only ethical, but seek to be ethical, and to practice ethically. Often the rules are hard to interpret and vague, and it's sometimes difficult for a lawyer to know what's right and what's wrong in a given circumstance. We got calls all the time from lawyers trying to do the right thing, but the right thing wasn't so clear. Lawyers assume enormous responsibilities and burdens because they are taking on the responsibility for the welfare of their clients, and in return, lawyers have a very high threshold, a very high standard of conduct that they are expected to adhere to. A very high percentage of lawyers, I think, do adhere to that."

Of course, it was the issue of the reopening of the Carlton Street Footbridge into the Emerald Necklace, a *cause célèbre* in Brookline for several years before the recent town meeting vote to do it, that brought Cathleen and me together. That issue is pivotal in Brookline's past, present, and future — the past because the bridge goes back to the creation of the Emerald Necklace, the present because the controversy about its reopening brought to the fore the divisions and fissures in Brookline community, and the future because of the impact the reopening will have on green spaces in the Brookline park system.

This historically significant story starts, of course, with Frederick Law Olmsted's conception of the Emerald Necklace late in the nineteenth century. Olmsted, one of Brookline's most famous residents ever, is remembered as the father of landscape architecture. His last workshop was located at his residence, Fairsted, on Warren Street, now administered by the National Park Service. Fairsted lies very near the home of Olmsted's close friend, the architect H. H. Richardson, the builder of Trinity Church in Copley Square and the man responsible for Olmsted coming to live and work in Brookline in his later years.

The Emerald Necklace circuitously wends its way from Boston's Public Garden, through the Back Bay Fens, and for miles along the border between Brookline and Boston, thence to Jamaica Pond and on through the world-famous Arnold Arboretum (founded and administered for fifty years by another famous nineteenth century Brookline resident, Charles Sprague Sargent), and culminates in the vast reaches of Franklin Park. It was beautiful at its inception, and still is, despite having fallen into disrepair in certain sections, such as in the Carlton Street/Longwood area of Brookline, where the footbridge is located.

The notion of reopening the footbridge was a surprising catalyst for the fierce opposition the proposal aroused in some Brookline residents living close to the bridge, especially since the ninety-two-million-dollar cost of the restoration of the Emerald Necklace is to be borne nearly completely by the state and federal governments. That opposition was based mostly on the contention that open access from contiguous Boston neighborhoods would spark increased crime and create a place in a residential neighborhood where people from outside would congregate, and that, historically, the bridge was not a pivotal part of Olmsted's vision for this particular area. This is an incorrect view, according to Olmsted scholar and American University Professor Charles E. Beveridge, editor of the Olmsted Papers for the Library of Congress.

Cathleen spoke of Olmsted's vision for the Emerald Necklace: "Olmsted's conception was of an oasis in the city, a place for city dwellers to find respite, to be literally restored by the sight of green space, by inhaling greenery, and open air and open space. The response that Olmsted was looking for when you entered one of his planned landscapes was 'Ahhh!' It was that feeling you have when you see a magnificent rosebush and inhale it at the same time. It forms a sculpted vista, like the planned landscape you see as you enter other Olmsted creations, such as Central Park, Prospect Park in Brooklyn, and the grounds of the Capitol in Washington, D.C."

As further evidence that this historic and rare steel-truss footbridge — a style of bridge construction no longer in use — was part of Olmsted's vision for his Emerald Necklace, Cathleen says, "The first Brookline Town Engineer, Alexis French, designed this bridge. French worked with Olmsted, and collaborated with him on this bridge and other bridges in the Riverway Park, which lies between Boston's Riverway and Brookline in the Longwood section of the town. Alexis French was Olmsted's engineer. He drew the plans for this part of the Emerald Necklace, including the Carlton Street Footbridge." This is the so-called valley stream area, where Olmsted turned running raw sewage into a scenic stream coursing around man-made islands, which are important in flood control.

Cathleen spoke about that: "Yes, we've had two 'hundred-year floods' with the Muddy River overflowing its banks within about five years. Those floods caused lots and lots of damage to private homes in the Longwood area of town, and to the museums and the hospitals too, lots of flooding in the Fenway. Already, the Army Corps of Engineers has begun working on that. In fact, Riverway Park is the next park in the Emerald Necklace that will be restored. The restoration will follow the landscaping plans that Olmsted drew, restoring much of the original landscape, resurfacing the paths, putting in new benches, the whole park refreshed and restored, so that the footbridge will be a bridge into a newly remarkable refurbished park, similar to the refurbishing of the Olmsted Park section of the Emerald Necklace bordering the Brook House on Pond Avenue near Brookline Village. So reopening the footbridge will make Olmsted's 'pleasure ground' available again to the Longwood neighborhood of Brookline."

There can be no question that the issue of the reopening of the Carlton Street Footbridge, lying in Longwood, the earliest developed part of Brookline, was divisive and bitter, even nasty, raising questions about the normally civilized nature of public disputes in Brookline. In light of the divisions between liberals and conservatives, left and right, new and old, citizen and citizen, in these few blocks of the town, I asked Cathleen whether the long dispute bodes well or ill for Brookline "community." Did it perhaps signal some disintegration of that quality of Brookline life? After some hesitation, Cathleen answered:

"I think it's all about community, and the larger community of Brookline, even Boston. One of the things I found so hard to accept about the controversy was the idea of some that it was a neighborhood issue. It really isn't. It's about the larger community. For one thing, it certainly is about the whole town, because the whole town paid for the bridge. Something like twenty-four hundred dollars, I think, in 1894, and the whole town will pay for the town's share now, to the extent that the town pays, no matter what we do. But beyond that, I have a problem with the idea that in a democracy, the abutters to an amenity could have veto power over whether the amenity survives or not. For one thing, I think we have a responsibility to our children and our grandchildren, and beyond, to be responsible stewards of their history and their future."

Cathleen's remarks about community and democracy brought to mind the perennial question of whether Town Meeting is an anachronism that might be dispensed with.

Cathleen's response was that Town Meeting was instrumental in getting the restoration approved. "I like the town meeting form of government," she said. "I think the town meeting works. It's a democracy! Perhaps things would have worked out the same way in a city form of government, but as matters worked themselves out, I think the position of Town Meeting in favor of restoration of the bridge was a very significant one. And I think the majority brought others along with them."

Cathleen Cavell, committed as she is to the values of family, public service, and citizen participation in the building of community, stands as an example of what we hope for in a "citizen."

Photo courtesy of Timothy Sullivan.

Early view of the Emerald Necklace and Sears Memorial Chapel in the Longwood section of Brookline.

Photo by author.

DR. JOHN B. "JACK" LITTLE

Preservationist and President Elect of the Brookline Historical Society

DR. JOHN B. "JACK" LITTLE OF BROOKLINE is known around the world in his field of radiation research. He presently serves as the James Stevens Simmons Professor of Radiobiology and chair of the Department of Cancer Cell Biology at the Harvard School of Public Health, but preservation and historical issues were on his mind when I interviewed him.

Jack Little is well qualified to discuss these topics, as he is the president elect of the Brookline Historical Society, and comes from a Brookline family dedicated to the preservation of Brookline and New England antiquities. Jack's mother was Nina Fletcher Little, author of the well-known 1949 volume *Some Old Brookline Houses*, published by the Brookline Historical Society. His father was Bertram Kimball Little, for many years the director of the Society for

Brookline Access TV interview, August 15, 2001. *Brookline Tab*, September 20, 2001.

the Preservation of New England Antiquities. Jack himself lives in one of those "old Brookline houses," at 305-307 Warren Street, as did his mother and dad before him, Jack growing up in that house.

Jack Little early on followed in his parents' footsteps. He built radios and collected antique cars, filling up the yard with those cars and drawing his mother's mild rebuke, "Why don't you just keep collecting stamps?"

But Jack kept collecting antique cars, all of which he still has in various locations, including vintage Model Ts, an old Citroën (which he drove through Europe during his Army service), a Maxwell (of Jack Benny fame), his dad's old Nash Rambler, a mint 1931 Packard, and a "comfortable" 1982 Caddy for everyday use. In fact, Jack drives all of them around Brookline from time to time, and if one of these days you are confronted with a vintage car moving slowly in front of you, that could be Jack!

Jack tells a great story about how he saw the country in one of those vintage cars, a 1926 Model T Ford, which he bought at age eighteen with a friend:

"My friend and I fixed up the Model T and drove it from June to September around the country, twelve thousand miles in all. My dad gave me a hundred dollars, and I brought back that hundred dollars. We worked all the way, camping out, cooking, picking plums, working in the wheat harvest. Our best job was when we worked in a pea cannery in Mt. Vernon, Washington, at $1.12 an hour, with half time over nine hours and double time over twelve hours. We worked about fifteen hours a day. So when we came back, we were able to give each of our parents back one hundred dollars. We really saw the country."

Jack's love of old things (he has deep historical and preservationist instincts) was not limited to antique cars, but extended to old radios and the building of TV sets before there was TV.

"I used to collect radios when I was a kid," he said, "not only collected them, but I built them. I started when I was about seven or eight years old, I think, culminating in the TV set I built when I was in high school. I designed it myself and I built it, and I got it all ready to go, but there were no TV stations on the air in Boston. I had to wait for a year for the first stations to come on the air. I didn't want to spend the money to buy the picture tube if there wasn't going to be any TV. At first WBZ came on with a test pattern, and then with the same travelogue over and over. So I turned on my TV, and the sound worked. I rushed down to Radio Shack, bought a picture tube, plugged it in, and it worked!"

Jack's mother and father were very active in the Brookline Historical Society, and did work on the preservation of the Devotion House, Putterham School, and the Widow Harris House. As the incoming president of the Brookline Historical Society, Jack discussed issues presently in the news concerning those properties.

"The town, of course, owns the buildings. The Brookline Historical Society has sort of been responsible for the stewardship of the buildings, and we've always had a curator who lives in the Edward Devotion House.

"There has been sort of an unfortunate occurrence in the Widow Harris House recently. The town has apparently made the decision that they want to renovate these buildings for rental, to bring in additional revenue for the town, and they've charged their building commissioner to take responsibility for this. So he has decided to go ahead with these renovations, which would not include the Putterham School, but would include the Widow Harris House and the Edward Devotion House.

"Unknown to any of us, either on the Preservation Commission or in the Historical Society," he continued, "the workers got into the Widow Harris House and destroyed a lot of the original fabric of the house — tore out ceilings, walls, put holes through the floor. It's a very unusual house. I think it's the only house extant in Brookline that is what we call a vernacular house, which means a house that ordinary people lived in [as opposed to the grand houses later built in Brookline], simple farmhouses that most of the people lived in. The Widow Harris House was probably built 225 to 250 years ago, and is part of Brookline's legacy. These houses don't really exist anymore because they were long since taken down.

"The other thing that is unusual about the Widow Harris House is that it has never been renovated. It's practically in its original condition. It has been very sad, I think, that the town workmen have gotten in there and started to make these renovations, which have destroyed part of the house.

"It's ironic. The Brookline Historical Society is right in the midst of a quite expensive historic structures survey. This involved an architectural firm and an architectural historian who go through each of the houses with a fine-tooth comb. Not only do they carry out a detailed architectural survey of each building, but they also look back and collect all the history of the houses, who lived in them, and then they are able to tell us just what changes have been made in the houses over the years, and also will tell us what should be done to preserve the houses.

"So now we are trying to keep workmen out of the Edward Devotion House. The architectural historian has found that part of that house dates probably back to the 1600s. As to the Widow Harris House, we are going over there next week with the architectural historian hoping to find out how we should support the ceiling that has been taken out, and how best to restore what has been done to it.

"So far the Edward Devotion House has not been touched. I feel as if we should keep someone at the door. I hope that house is not going to be in danger. I think it is not realistic — in my opinion — to think that those houses can be rented out at market rents. They should have curatorial kind of people living in them who know what they are looking at. It's a wonderful house!"

As Yogi said, "It's déjà vu all over again," as Jack recollected similar threats to Brookline's legacy of very old structures.

"We almost lost the Widow Harris House back in the 1950s," he said, "when Mrs. Larz Anderson died and left the property to the town. Members of the community, led by the Brookline Historical Society, worked to retain the Widow Harris House, and also to effect the moving of the Putterham School from Newton Street to put it on the Larz Anderson estate, in a similar setting to where it was. Both structures still stand there."

As I remarked to Jack, one of the themes of my program *From Community to Cyberspace* is the importance of preserving what our community has been, not only in the sense of people, but regarding historic structures as well, so Brookline citizens of the future will know what the town was like in the past, to better understand their present and future.

Certainly that was in Nina Fletcher Little's mind when she

wrote *Some Old Brookline Houses,* under the auspices of the Brookline Historical Society. Jack has memories of that.

"As a kid, I said to my mother, 'Why did you call it *Some Old Brookline Houses?*' Why didn't you just call it *Old Brookline Houses?*' My mother responded, 'Well, after I have written it, surely someone is going to turn up an old house that's not in there.'

"A lot of those old houses are still standing," Jack says. "My mother had fun doing it, and I used to go around with her at times. I may have taken one or two of the pictures in the book."

Jack's mother was president of the Brookline Friendly Society (and its arm, the Visiting Nurses Association) for many years. That was a volunteer society helping Brookline people who had come on hard times, including many families living on what was known as the Farm, where the Brook House now stands. As a youngster, Jack helped too: "I used to collect radios, but also I would go and buy radios that didn't work, fix them up, and several of these I gave to my mother at the Friendly Society, and she would give them out to families who didn't have a radio or couldn't afford a radio."

In fact, the headquarters of the Friendly Society was at the Farm, right where the waterfall in front of the Brook House is now.

"It was a wonderful building, sort of an early or mid-nineteenth century farmhouse, and sat there hidden by other buildings at the Farm, but in later years, before the Brook House was built, they tore down those buildings in front of it, and it sat there looking out on that intersection. I always felt that when they built the Brook House, rather than having that sort of funny waterfall that is right where the house was, they should have left the house there, and could have had it as their administrative office, but that didn't happen."

Jack's family are among the many Brookline people who give freely of themselves, not only to Brookline, creating what might be called the ongoing story of Brookline as part of the wider world. In Jack's mother's case, not only did she write about old Brookline houses and do important historical work in Brookline, but she was also the author of the classic work *American Decorative Wall Painting, 1700-1850.* Nina Fletcher Little also was a major force in the preservation of the Abbey Aldrich Rockefeller Folk Art Collection at Colonial Williamsburg.

"When that folk art collection was given to Williamsburg,"

Jack said, "they wanted to build a museum to house it, and they hired my mother for two or three years to help them with the design of the museum, doing all the research on the paintings and the folk art. There had been no scholarship on who were the people who painted these pictures and where they came from. It turned out that many of them were itinerant painters who went from town to town and house to house, and said that if you will give me room and board for a couple of months, I'll paint paintings of all your family. My mother was able to identify some of these artists, find out who they were, and then to find their paintings and ascribe certain paintings to them."

Jack's parents both passed away in 1993. Wendell Garrett, editor-at-large of the magazine *Antiques* and senior vice president at Sotheby's, wrote a tribute to them for the Brookline Historical Society, which to my mind explains why it is so important to preserve our past. He described Bert Little as a "man for all seasons" and said of Nina Fletcher Little that she "wrote to vivify our sense of our past, and collected to keep our traditions alive. The world around her was changing beyond recognition, and this may be one of the reasons why she gathered around her with the acquisitiveness of a New England collector all vestiges of an engaging and vanishing past."

As a child, Nina Fletcher Little lived at the Maimonides School. Well, not quite, but she did live on the site of the present Maimonides School on Philbrick Road, which during Nina's childhood was the Fletcher family home, evidence of which still exists in the red-tiled wall surrounding that large property.

"It was quite a grand house — full of Victorian furniture," Jack says. "Despite its size, it was really a very warm place for all of us."

I asked Jack about the well-known "yacht room" in the house. "That was a great big room in which my grandfather collected models of historic ships — it was really a wonderful room," he said.

"It's funny, because my grandfather always said, even when I was quite young, 'Y'know, when I die, nobody is going to want this house, a big house like this, they'll tear it down and build a school here,' which is exactly what happened!"

In fact, it appears at that site that the past and present merge seamlessly. The 1978 fall meeting of the Brookline Historical

Society was held at the Maimonides School on Sunday, October 8, at which time Bert Little presented a paper prepared by his wife, entitled "Reminiscences about the Philbrick Road Neighborhood and the Site of the Fletcher Family Home," illustrated with slides. That meeting came to a close with a talk by Rabbi David Shapiro, then principal of the Maimonides School, about the programs and goals of the school.

In her paper, Mrs. Little spoke of one of her vivid memories as a small child: ". . . looking over the wall from an upper-story window and seeing the horse-drawn fire apparatus plunging at top speed with bells ringing up Boylston Street hill — an unforgettable scene!"

Jack himself remembers his mother telling him of another, more poignant Boylston Street memory:

"Oh, that was my mother's little dog, when she was a kid. She was walking down Sumner Road towards Boylston Street. There were streetcars on Boylston Street at that time. The dog ran on ahead, and the car drew up and stopped. The door opened, and the dog jumped on, and the door closed, and the streetcar took off, and she was left standing there. The dog reappeared in Wellesley a day or two later. It had a tag on! The streetcars on Boylston Street ran all the way to Worcester. As a very small child, I remember the tracks, and the station in the middle of the street at Brookline Village."

The difference between Brookline then and now — and perhaps the world then and now — is elucidated by Jack's account of his youthful expedition through the woods to Hammond Pond from Boylston Street.

"Oh, going through the woods," he recalled, "that was a great excitement, a long expedition through the woods to find this mysterious pond people talked about, and ah, my gosh, we found it. Isn't this amazing! It seemed like it had been a real expedition, and now that they built a big shopping center there, it's just around the corner in the parking lot."

On that note of old-time mystery, Jack and I concluded our walk through a past more than a little of which we hope will somehow be preserved.

BOOK X

TOWN MEETING AND GOVERNANCE

Photo courtesy of Brookline Public Library.

Town Meeting in Old Town Hall (1935).

Photo courtesy of Edward N. Gadsby.

Sandy Gadsby

Photo by author.

Jerry Wyner

A Discussion with
Edward N. "Sandy" Gadsby Jr. and
Justin L. "Jerry" Wyner

Present and Past Moderators of Brookline Town Meeting

JUST AS THE FRENCHMAN ALEXIS DE TOCQUEVILLE had a bird's-eye view of America when he wrote his nineteenth-century classic, *Democracy in America*, so, too, do the present and former moderators of the Town Meeting of Brookline, Massachusetts, Edward N. "Sandy" Gadsby Jr. and Justin "Jerry" Wyner have a bird's-eye view from their podium of the workings of democracy in Brookline, and whether, indeed, Brookline is a microcosm of democracy. It is from that vantage point that Sandy and Jerry over the course of many years have had the opportunity to judge the truth of de Tocqueville's words:

> The town then exists in all nations, whatever their laws
> and customs may be. It is man who makes monarchies

Brookline Access TV interview, May 14, 2002.

and establishes republics, but the township seems to come directly from the hand of God. Town meeting and primary schools are the science, they bring it within the people's reach. They teach man how to use and how to enjoy it.

Of course, to "bring it within the people's reach" is what we would all hope for not only in our local legislature — that is, Town Meeting — but also in Congress and the state legislatures, for the most part frustrated by the ferocious contentiousness and harsh invective heard daily in those forums. Yet in Brookline, a town larger than most cities, with a population approaching sixty thousand, such divisiveness is notable by its absence, as has always been, for the most part, the case.

In fact, this quality has always drawn a diverse, discerning, educated and participating group of citizens to reside within Brookline's borders. They believe the town, if not unique, is a very special place where citizens are able to reach those who execute the government of the town in order to have a voice in its governance, mostly through its representative elected Town Meeting, but also in other direct contacts with those charged with town governance, giving life and force to freedom and democracy in Brookline.

With these ideas in mind, I interviewed Sandy Gadsby and Jerry Wyner on Brookline Access TV in May 2002. My intention was to test these ideas from their viewpoint, asking such questions as whether Town Meeting is the one organ that lies at the center of Brookline's identity or whether — as some people think — Town Meeting is an anachronism, and that even now Brookline is run by the pros and should change to a city form of government; whether, indeed, Town Meeting is central to the interests of the citizens of the town, the idea of Brookline "community", and keeping the town on a democratic course. What developed out of the ensuing discussion was a picture of the totality and interconnectedness of Brookline governance that strongly suggests that Brookline might well serve as a model to other governances, municipal, state, and federal, of the "science" of Town Meeting and the public schools of which de Tocqueville speaks, the organs that bring freedom to the people.

Simply listening to Jerry and Sandy tell how they came to run for moderator of Town Meeting sheds light on the broad citizen participation that is key to giving Brookline its special character.

Sandy's path to Brookline, after his college years, is not uncommon. After growing up in western Massachusetts, Sandy graduated from Amherst College and Harvard Law School. Currently he is a partner in the Boston law firm of Foley, Hoag & Eliot, specializing in acquisitions, e-commerce, venture capital, and intellectual property. Following de Tocqueville's dictum that primary schools, along with Town Meeting, "are the science," Sandy moved to Brookline "to take advantage of the schools here" for his children, and became interested in politics "through the perturbations and the battles over the Lincoln School," as he puts it. "I was first elected to the town meeting in 1980, and Carl Sapers [moderator at that time] appointed me to the Advisory Committee, where I served for fourteen years. When Jerry decided to step down, I decided to step in."

Jerry, on the other hand, moved to Brookline when he was two years old, attended Brookline schools for the most part, as did his children after him, first ran for Town Meeting when he was twenty-one, and was elected two years later, in 1948. "I ran," he says, "because it seemed to me that if you lived in a community and you wanted to be part of it, you should give to it what you could, and Town Meeting was a wonderful way to become involved."

Jerry graduated from Tufts and Harvard Graduate School of Business, and has served for a long time as chairman of the board and CEO of R. H. Wyner Associates, Inc., including the Shawmut Mills Division. Jerry continues to be active in a panoply of local, national, and international activities, many of them having to do with Jewish affairs. Perhaps as an example of the relative lack of divisiveness between Republicans and Democrats in Brookline politics was the position Jerry held in 1968 as the national chairman of Republicans for Eugene McCarthy for President.

Since Jerry Wyner was first elected moderator in 1970, Town Meeting has expanded its role in the governance of the town, as well as attempting to exert its influence on local, national, and international affairs. Early in Jerry's tenure, Town Meeting expressed a desire to vote on whether or not to send an expression of opinion to the president of the United States to bring our soldiers home from Vietnam. Jerry, relying on the historical fact that long ago the town had expressed its opinion on the Boston Tea Party, allowed, after a full debate, the first recorded vote of any town meeting to go forward on the Vietnam issue.

Around that time, the local issue of whether to establish rent control came up. The town counsel advised Jerry that a vote on the issue would be unconstitutional, as not within the scope of Town Meeting. Jerry responded, "As an official, I should not be the one who prevented Town Meeting from expressing itself. We debated rent control, we passed rent control, it was appealed, and it was found to be constitutional. It seemed to me that the town was healthier when it could express its opinion, and when it wasn't frustrated."

Sandy Gadsby has carried forward Jerry's innovations to expand the role of Brookline Town Meeting. "The Vietnam War resolution established a tradition of this Town Meeting trying to exert an influence beyond its borders," he said, "[a tradition] that a lot of town meetings and a lot of town moderators simply won't permit. Jerry helped establish that tradition in the Brookline Town Meeting, and we do it to this day. Town Meeting approved the banning of cell phones in moving vehicles in Brookline, but that was declared illegal by the attorney general because of the existing state law. But it's a good example of a citizen petition, and it was a good example of a citizen with an idea, getting support from fellow Town Meeting members."

Squarely in the center of this tradition was the vote of Brookline Town Meeting more than a decade ago to banish smoking from all restaurants and bars. Following Brookline's lead, one hundred and three cities and towns in Massachusetts adopted similar bans, and finally at one minute after midnight on July 6, 2004, Brookline's rule became the law of the land in Massachusetts, demonstrating yet again the aptness of de Tocqueville's notion that Town Meeting brings freedom within the people's reach.

Early on, in the nineteenth century, Brookline demonstrated the persistent resistance that allowed it to remain a town, against the encroachments and annexations of the city of Boston's outlying districts into the city itself, now leaving Brookline surrounded on three sides by Boston and within three miles of the center of

Boston. Jerry detailed how that resistance exhibited itself again early in the twentieth century, when Brookline's demographic was fast multiplying and diversifying.

"Up until 1915," he said, "every town that reached a population of fifteen thousand became a city by law, the theory being that the town was then too big to bring people together [in a town meeting]. When Brookline got to that stage, it didn't want to become a city. Special legislation was created in 1915 so that Brookline could have a representative town meeting, retaining final authority for Brookline's citizens as a whole. What it meant in the days that I started running for Town Meeting was that if you wanted to be elected to Town Meeting, you had to ring at least five hundred doorbells and maybe run in two successive campaigns before you won a position, and if you went to somebody's home, you had to tell them what the issues were and why you thought it was important for you to become a Town Meeting member. So there was always a situation where no matter whether residents were interested or not in the town government of Brookline, there were always several people who would personally ring their bell and tell them what was going on in the town, and [ask] if they had any problems. The result was that everybody in town knew at least one Town Meeting member. That made the town meeting very special. After Brookline set that example, there was special legislation that permitted any town whose population became greater than fifteen thousand to remain a town. After going around to many other towns, I think Brookline's Town Meeting is something very special."

Sandy amplified on that: "I think what's important to understand is that Brookline is a highly activist community. It's highly diversified. It is a town surrounded on three sides by Boston, and holding its own as a town. Historically, it's been a very active political community. We have had people run for state and national office from Brookline, like Mike Dukakis, who did both. You can always count on Brookline for a lot of political support. That translates itself into the desire of a lot of residents of Brookline to participate in the political process, and Town Meeting is a perfect forum for that to be possible. There are 240 elected Town Meeting members, and there are some ex officio members like the moderator, selectmen, and the town clerk. So the total is around

246, and there are 246 people, most of whom take a very active interest in their role in the town. Among those 246 are some very vocal and very active political beings. It is part of the moderator's job, of course, to make the process work, notwithstanding the desire of some of these people to monopolize it."

At this point Jerry (in a mild expression of the somewhat tumultuous process of democracy) interrupted Sandy to broaden the discussion: "I always said that a good moderator is like a good waiter; if he does a good job, you don't notice him at all. The objective that I think we have, and I think that's been true of the moderators we've had within my memory, is that Town Meeting works best when no one feels that they were frustrated by not having their side of the issue heard. Whether or not somebody won or lost on the issue in which they had interest, if they felt that their fellow townspeople had heard their pain as to what might happen, and had made their decisions with that in mind, then they could leave with no doubts; and then you can get some very, very difficult kinds of things passed without any ill feelings.

"It is when people suspect that the moderator himself has an agenda," he went on, "and is concerned not with the process, but with the ultimate outcome — I myself am sometimes surprised with the outcome — then they begin to say, 'Well, you didn't recognize that person on my side, and you orchestrated it so that it seemed like it was all one-sided.' The health of our Town Meeting is in the debate itself, and encouraging the largest number of people to participate, particularly when you have contentious issues, and then, no matter what side comes out, people have had their day in court. I think some people in other towns, where I see problems, just lose sight of that. What does the majority want to have happen after they've heard the concerns of the minority? That's what makes for a great legislature."

Sandy's response was predictably consonant: "Well, I'm a disciple. The most important thing a moderator can add to the town meeting process is to make sure that an issue gets fairly aired on both sides, and people feel that they've had a chance to get their point across, and represent their point of view."

Jerry expanded on the difficulty of moderating such a seemingly simple notion: "But in order to do this skillfully you do have to be aware of all of the sides of the issue. There may be four sides of an issue. The worst thing that could happen to you is to have a really healthy debate for two hours, which would be unusual, but could happen with a very important subject, and then have a little old lady who raises her hand and comes forward at the last minute and presents a fact, or what appears to be a fact, that is so disruptive that you can never really get a closure unless you let everybody else come back. So it's important that, to some extent, you have been helpful to get out on the table all of the positions and issues on the subject being debated early enough in the game so that people are discussing everything and it's not just a bunch of fixed speeches."

Obviously, a representative town meeting government can be cumbersome and time consuming, so the question arises on a fairly regular basis whether a city form of government should be adopted, or Town Meeting reduced to an advisory capacity by use of the so-called Australian ballot, a proposal that actually came to vote and was defeated awhile back in Concord. Both Sandy and Jerry see Town Meeting blending with the other organs of town government to result in an efficiently run town where many citizens participate in the democratic process.

Sandy Gadsby: "The more frequent trend in Massachusetts these days is to impose a city type of government. Some towns had been living with a board of selectmen, and the change to a city form happened in recent years in Weymouth and Greenfield; there was a strong movement in Plymouth, which lost the other day. I would have difficulty visualizing a strong movement within Brookline for a city type of government. The town meeting is very deeply entrenched in Brookline, many people get the opportunity to participate, and it is a well-loved system. In my view, and the view of many others, the town is administered extremely well. The town administrator [Richard Kelliher presently, preceded by Richard Leary and before that by the legendary Arthur O'Shea, covering a period of more than fifty years] has surrounded himself with department heads that are pros, and it's an extremely well-run town. So we manage to get around any anachronism there might be in the town meeting/selectmen form of government because of the activism of the citizens in Town Meeting, the professionalism of the people who run the town, and the School Department and the School Committee.

"You have to understand the process," he continued. "Town Meeting is the town legislature. Town Meeting meets to deal with a longer list of issues that are legislative issues than those that have to do merely with appropriations and funding. But before Town Meeting convenes to pass on these, there's a very long and arduous process, in which the Finance Committee [that is, the so-called Advisory Committee], which the moderator appoints, and the Board of Selectmen, elected by the people, each independently considers these issues, hammers them out, adopts a position, and very often has a discourse with each other to try to arrive at a common position. Town Meeting is not a good place to write laws; it's a better place to have a proposal presented, then debated, and then voted on. So essentially, when Town Meeting convenes, the process that's taken place is embodied in a booklet of these combined reports. This booklet has some one hundred and eighty pages or so of commentary by the Advisory Committee, the Board of Selectmen, and others, on the issues before Town Meeting. The booklet goes out two weeks before Town Meeting, so it appears that Town Meeting is very well educated on the issues before they are going to be decided."

Jerry Wyner: "Well, actually it goes one step beyond there, because when Town Meeting members are interested in a particular issue that's coming up, the Advisory Committee posts its meeting and the meetings of subcommittees that are studying and considering that issue. At those meetings, citizens and Town Meeting members can put in their input early on, and that can, in the end, help to have some compromise reached. It's a wonderful process."

That "wonderful process" was sorely tested in 2004, only two years after my talk with Sandy and Jerry, when the proposal to rezone 2 Brookline Place near Brookline Village to accommodate a possible 125-foot-tall lab or office building at the site of the former Skipjack's restaurant was first narrowly defeated at Town Meeting on May 4, then reconsidered and passed in June following some modifications to the original proposal, amid a cacophony between officialdom virtually united in support and a dissenting majority (in March) of Town Meeting members. Without doubt, this latest test of whether Town Meeting is an anachronism raised that question with renewed vigor; the dust has not yet settled at this writing, although many impatient and annoyed supporters of the project who are keen observers of the Brookline scene, were they gamblers, would likely take book that Town Meeting will survive handily.

Certainly, it was surprising in March that this communal effort to promote redevelopment, endorsed by practically all town officials, including the Board of Selectmen, the Planning Board, and Town Meeting's own Advisory Committee (twenty out of twenty-two members endorsed it), local businesses, and even the former governor of Massachusetts, would go down at the hands of Town Meeting to initial defeat, amid charges that the Board of Selectmen had acted with inappropriate zeal and secrecy in promoting the project for reasons of revenue, and that the zoning changes would be a liability that would leave the town open to changes beyond the Town Meeting members' control.

In fact, the process worked to Brookline's advantage, as cooler heads prevailed. Town Administrator Richard Kelliher, speaking with foresight shortly after the March vote, made an informed comment that summarized in its simplicity the beauty of democratic Town Meeting government: "For the moment, Town Meeting has spoken, we're moving along. This can be a difficult business."

Likewise, opponents spoke reasonably and presciently, expressing the hope that there would be development at 2 Brookline Place to benefit the neighborhood and the town. By June, that "wonderful process" had come full circle to give Brookline what it wanted in this instance, confirming in the larger sense the ultimate control that all citizens of Brookline have through its town meeting over the ongoing process of Brookline's governance.

Of course, Jerry, Sandy, and I had no idea that in less than two years, Brookline governance would be subjected to such a severe test. At this point, our discussion took on a tripartite character, as I had been a Town Meeting member for ten years. Thrice, with slight variations, I put the question to Sandy and Jerry as to what it is that lies at the center of Brookline's governance to make it the special place it is, the microcosm of democracy to which I had previously alluded.

Jerry's first attempt at an answer was a little wistful: "I lived my whole life in Brookline up until four years ago, when my wife and I moved to Boston. I was a part of the community, and now I'm just sort of lost. If I were in Brookline, and I had a concern about Brookline's "Big Dig," you know there would be a half a dozen Town Meeting members that resided on either side of me who would know a lot more than I did. If they didn't already, they would get pretty excited about it. I have somebody who is a Boston city councilman whom I might be able to get to meet, but that would be it. In Brookline, when you have a problem where a tree has died on the street, you have many people you can call if you don't get the wonderful response that you would probably get by calling the department administrator himself. It's just a whole different flavor. If you get upset enough, the kind of controversies that occur from time to time is what brings health and a new influx of people to Town Meeting. People run for Town Meeting, and after they have run, they find that there are a whole bunch of other issues on which they can offer their comments."

Not being satisfied that we had answered where the center is, I asked the question another way, remarking that Jerry pointed out that Town Meeting does not lend itself to making certain decisions just like that — things have to be studied. "But where is the essential power?" I asked. "Does it lie in the people through Town Meeting or are we really being run by the pros? Is it a combination of the two? Where is the center?"

Jerry Wyner picked it up at that point: "Well, from my point of view, I think you also have to think that it takes a special type of town administrator to hold that position in Brookline, because he doesn't run it like a czar, like he might in some other places. He has two hundred and forty active people, plus all the rest of the citizens who are coming to him and raising issues. Town Meeting may not be running the town, but certainly there are a lot of things that the town administrator would like Town Meeting to support regarding his budgets and plans for the future. So the town administrator has to be responsive in a whole different way, and so do all the people who work in the Town of Brookline have to be responsive, as opposed to a city run by a mayor and city council. Here, we care about the people, all the way from the top."

Trying to bring us closer to the answer, Sandy Gadsby shifted our attention to the role of the five-person elected Board of Selectmen. "Let's not forget the Board of Selectmen. The Board of Selectmen in this town is the executive, it plays the role of the mayor, the role of the president, the role of the executive. The town administrator in fact answers to the Board of Selectmen, which works much harder than the moderator, and much harder than Town Meeting members, except for those members whom we manage to cajole onto the Advisory Committee. The town is, in fact, run on a week-to-week basis by the Board of Selectmen, delegating their authority to the town administrator. They have a point of view, and that point of view is expressed in the legislature [Town Meeting] through those reports, through their presentations before Town Meeting sitting as the legislature. Sometimes the Board of Selectmen win and sometimes they lose, when there is a contentious issue. But in terms of running the town, it would be foolhardy to take the position that Town Meeting does."

Jerry Wyner brought us closer to the answer with his view that the effect of Town Meeting can be subtle and oblique, as well as direct. "On the other hand, Town Meeting is a buffer," he observed. "It's interesting how people sometimes come on to the Board of Selectmen, and they have had almost no experience. But after a couple of years of working, and being in some cases totally rebuffed by Town Meeting for some of their advances, they mature. I haven't really had any complaints with the selectmen we've had over the last several years, whether I totally agree with them or not. They do a great deal; furthermore, they do some things that the legislature can't do. There's a whole bunch of decisions in terms of granting permits that if made the wrong way could destroy rather than build community. The selectmen take a lot of hard knocks in the hearings they run every week, and in providing leadership to the town. The crux is that one can't work without the other. If the selectmen get off track, if there's a sudden change of balance on the Board of Selectmen, it won't get by Town Meeting. That's what gives us a reasonably steady course of progress. For instance, once in a while we'll fall behind and not build a school at the right time, but we have a commitment to great education in Brookline, and no matter what anybody does we're not going to lose that."

Feeling that we were closing in on the answer, I put the question for a third time: "What if Town Meeting disappeared, if it wasn't there, would the town's character change?"

The refusal of both Sandy and Jerry to adopt the premise of that question typifies Brookline's pride in its democratic form of government, and its resolve to keep it that way.

Sandy Gadsby: "Well, in the first place, there are at least two hundred and forty people in Brookline who are not going to permit that to happen, so the concept of Brookline running as a town without Town Meeting is interesting to think about, but it won't happen. It goes to what I was talking about in the first segment of this show, that Brookline is full of political activists, who in a city like Boston have to be content in merely assisting in the nominating process. In Brookline, we pass laws, and our two hundred and forty-five legislators pass those laws that govern this town, and they are proud of that role, and take it very seriously."

Jerry Wyner: "There are a lot of very accomplished people who could be spending their time doing a lot of other things, but find this a very satisfying extra activity, to be a Town Meeting member, and to make the town as good as they think it can be made."

Hearing this, I suggested to Sandy and Jerry that the answer as to what lies at the center of Brookline's governance and its democratic character appears to be "that the amalgam of constituent parts of our government is what makes the town unique, and makes it survive as an unusual and a very lovely place to live."

When I ventured that I might be overstating the case, Sandy and Jerry each answered that the case was not overstated from his point of view, views important and persuasive, since the moderator at Town Meeting sees arrayed before him all those constituent parts, including the Board of Selectmen; the Advisory Committee; Town Meeting itself, and, by extension, all the citizens of the town; town counsel; other elected officials; the chairs (and in many cases, the members) of all the various boards, committees, and subcommittees; as well as citizens of the town, and others, attending Town Meeting.

One thing is for sure. No matter how the question was put, Moderators Sandy Gadsby and Justin Wyner, keen and experienced both, see Brookline democracy and freedom extending outwards concentrically from Brookline Town Meeting to encircle all its citizens, continuing indefinitely into the future, lending credence to de Tocqueville's notion that the "township" is a divine inspiration, and that "Town Meeting and primary schools . . . bring it within the people's reach."

Plaque at Walnut and Warren Streets opposite First Parish.

Photos by author.

Bobby Allen   *David Turner*

ROBERT L. "BOBBY" ALLEN
Chair, Board of Selectmen

DAVID L. TURNER, ESQUIRE
Longtime Town Counsel

Town Meeting: A Microcosm of Democracy from the Hand of God or an Anachronism?

A COPY OF BROOKLINE'S GRANT, November 13, 1705, reads, in part, as follows:

> At a Great and General Court or Assembly for her Maj Province of the Massachusetts Bay in New England begun and held at Boston . . . and continued . . . and then mett Tuesday, Nov. 13, 1705 — . . . Ordered, That the Prayer of the Petition be Granted, and the Powers and Privileges of a Township be given to the Inhabitants

---

Brookline Access TV interview, August 19, 2004.

of the Land commonly known by the Name of Muddy River, the Town to be called Brookline, who are hereby enjoyned to build a meeting-house, and Obtain an Able Orthodox Minister according to the Direction of the Law to be Settled amongst them . . ."

Indeed, a "meeting-house" was built, and a minister obtained, and from that day to this there has been "settled amongst them" (i.e., us) in Town Meeting duly assembled, all those issues required to bring (freedom) within the people's reach, in accordance with the dictum later laid down by Alexis de Tocqueville, in his classic nineteenth century view of American society, *Democracy in America* wherein he wrote that "the township seems to come directly from the hand of God."

Convening in August 2004, with Bobby Allen, chairman of the Brookline board of selectmen, and David Turner, for the past twenty-eight years Brookline's town counsel, in the frothy wake of the 2 Brookline Place squabble alluded to in the preceding story on Moderators Sandy Gadsby and Justin Wyner, and within months of Brookline's tercentenary year, the discussion on Brookline Access TV gravitated to weighty issues of whether Brookline's Town Meeting form of government is an anachronism, and the relationship of that to democracy and freedom.

Addressing those points, Bobby and David, working smoothly together in Brookline town governance, separated by more than a generation in age, proved to be friendly but firm adversaries.

At thirty-eight, Bob Allen's career has yet to reach its apogee. A lifelong resident of Brookline, educated at Baker School, BHS (1984), Northeastern, and New England School of Law, Bob quickly gained success in his Brookline law practice. At the same time, he took forward the public service tradition of his family (his father retired from the Brookline Police Department, and his brother and brother-in-law presently serve there), first as Town Meeting member and serving on the Park and Recreation Commission, then being elected to the Board of Selectmen, ascending to its chair. From that pinnacle, and with that experience, Bob is more than qualified to assess the viability of Town Meeting, fresh from the convulsions of the 2 Brookline Place controversy. He spoke in a respectful, measured manner to that question:

"That March [2004] decision [voting down the zoning changes required to erect 2 Brookline Place] shows that every now and then Town Meeting can be wrong! It's very hard to get people to understand zoning. Town Meeting has a very short attention span when you get into the technical aspects of zoning, and opponents can throw out certain scenarios that aren't appropriate, and people can buy into it, because it's simple. It was important during that period to meet with as many Town Meeting members as we could. I thought we did a good job, and spent a lot of time advocating for the zoning changes. We need managed growth. Without it we would be a stagnant community. So the board was devastated and frustrated by the down vote in March. Frankly, I was beat! But a couple of citizens restarted the process, and Town Meeting looked at the issue again in June, and this time it passed. So the process worked!

"But town government versus city government is something I could argue from both sides. At times, it is difficult being a selectman, and being held accountable, especially doing it on a volunteer basis and devoting as much time as I possibly can, but not having the power a mayor would have. Recently, I sat down with the mayor of Somerville, who has a lot of policies he believes in, and the ability to effectuate them is much more rapid than the Board of Selectmen's ability to effectuate change in Brookline."

It can be said that David Turner, embarking at age seventy-three upon his twenty-ninth and final year as Brookline town counsel, is as much a citizen of Brookline as any other man, despite never having lived here. A committed public servant, David for a long time has lived in Norwell, where he served as moderator of its town meeting for nine years, town counsel for eight years, counsel to the Norwell Housing Authority, trustee of the James Library, and on the Building, By-Laws, and Wetlands Study Committees. Educated at Babson College and BU School of Law, David was an assistant attorney general in the administration of Edward Brooke, town counsel for not only Norwell, but also Duxbury, Rockport, and Sudbury, and special town counsel for more than 150 Massachusetts cities and towns. Early in his legal career he gave up a more lucrative tax and corporate practice to pursue his municipal interests.

Why did he do that? David's memory of a crucial moment in

his youth provides not only the answer to that question, but also a strong hint as to his answer later to the question at hand:

"I grew up in a family that, during the 1930s, took in people who were fleeing Europe and other places. Those people would come and stay in our grandparents' home or our home, and then we would find them another place to stay or another job, and they would move on. In that process," he said, "they would tell us about what was going on in China, what was going on in Europe. They were not pleasant stories. We knew that the systems in those places were in great distress. We knew of the atrocities taking place. On a Sunday afternoon in 1939, I sat in my grandfather's leather chair and listened to a speech by Adolf Hitler, and when it was over, I remarked to my father and grandfather, 'What an evil man!' Of course, as a young person I had heard stories of how evil he was. They said to me, 'What drew you to that conclusion?' I said, 'His voice.' He had an awful voice. We discussed that for a little while. I remember asking, "What's going on there couldn't happen here, could it?' My father said to me, 'When you are older, you will find that in every society, there are people who are capable of that.'

"That experience has stayed with me through the years, and is probably the reason why I became involved in town government and things political. When I was offered the chance to work as an assistant attorney general, I did it. When I was asked to volunteer for the Navy in the Korean War, I did it. When I came out of the service, there was a town meeting, and as a result of a speech I gave at that town meeting, I was put on the Building Committee. Since then I have been town counsel in Norwell and other communities. I see that experience as a defining moment in my life. I have decided that government service is important to ensuring the stability of government and the protection of people's civil rights. That is why I gave up a lucrative tax and corporate practice for public service."

Robert Allen, lately emerging from the divisive 2 Brookline Place struggle at Town Meeting, and every day making slow progress in the hurly-burly of Brookline politics, understandably has not yet come down on one side or the other on the question of whether Town Meeting is an anachronism:

"I can think of very few decisions Town Meeting has made where I said, 'You'll regret that.' There have been a few, but not a lot. I'm fearful that there will come a time that an expedited form of government will serve Brookline better. I think Town Meeting works for the time being, but I reserve the right to look at it in the future. The town of Weymouth changed to a city form of government, and it works well for them. The town meeting form was not working well, they were not effecting change quickly enough, and although they remained a town, they changed to a city form of government."

David Turner supports how Brookline achieves strength out of diversity through Town Meeting:

"The key to the town government of Brookline is the people. Brookline is a wonderful town because of its diversity. The fact is that here diversity is strength. In the rest of the world, diversity breeds war, upheaval, and conflict. That comes from the people of this town, and the wonderful and diverse traditions that flourish here. It works because of the public school system, the people here, and the nature of government itself, which gets people to work together. In Town Meeting, you have John Hall getting up and bantering with Linda Dean. They come from different places. But you can tell that they have respect for each other. When I first came to Brookline, I walked into Town Meeting and I saw Justin Wyner. I had known Justin for years, but I never knew he was the moderator of Brookline's Town Meeting. I saw all these people, and it was almost like a family gathering of people I'd known for years, and here they are trying to make this town work, debating issues. I said, 'This is wonderful!'

"The longer I've been in Brookline, the more I appreciate its diversity and what goes on here. The strength of this town is really in the people, the traditions, the diversity, and the fact that the government brings them together. The schools are where students learn to live with one another. Town Meeting and town government is where they learn to exercise democracy together. I think it's a wonderful thing. I think volunteer government, and getting people of such diverse backgrounds together to work together, and even become friends, is great. They may not socialize every day of the week, but at Town Meeting, it is like a family reunion. That's where the center of it is. Town Meeting is where the people come and do their thing. And it goes from there to the selectmen who select the policy, and the citizen committees that review it."

Seasoned, skeptical, and sympathetic Town Counsel David Turner eloquently expressed his view that Town Meeting comes from the hand of God and is not an anachronism:

"I think you have to look at the function of government. If the function of government is efficiency, and making it easy for those who supposedly lead it, to make decisions and implement their policies, the city form is far more convenient because it's far more remote from the people. If the function of government is really to foster an interest in community and to bring people together, to get people to understand the democratic process and to protect human rights, the town meeting form works best. The protection of human rights is first and foremost in my mind because of the childhood experience I just related. I think it's very easy for society to slip into a mode where human rights are sort of pushed aside.

"We're seeing a little bit of that now nationally, and that disturbs me," he said. "I think Town Meeting gets people involved, and they learn to work together. It is not always convenient, and there are times when it is maddening and frustrating. But it does work. My experience with Town Meeting began in 1955, after coming out of serving in the Navy during the Korean War, and I found myself embroiled in a town meeting dispute. I've been at it ever since. As a moderator of Town Meeting, there have been times when I thought the town meeting had made a mistake, but five or six years later, I took a look back, and saw that Town Meeting was right! I think there is a purity and a wonderful element of community in Town Meeting. You don't get that in the city; I'm really in favor of the town meeting form. I hope Brookline does not change that. I hope Brookline continues with what it has, because I think it is meaningful, and is a beacon to the world, a beacon that shows how diversity can work in a positive way. God knows, the world needs that beacon, that example. Hopefully, the world can someday follow Brookline's example."

David Turner, invoking God, as did the Great and General Court at Brookline's birth in 1705, and as de Tocqueville did in the nineteenth century in opining the divine source of the township, had, out of his long experience, spontaneously stated the imprimatur of Brookline's town meeting form of government.

BOOK XI

9/11

Brookline High School Destroyed by Fire (1936).

Portrait by Bachrach.

Roland Hayes, American Tenor, Longtime Brookline Resident.

A NEW BIRTH OF FREEDOM

IT IS HARD TO FIND A SILVER LINING in the cataclysmic events of September 11, but from day one the suggestion of one came into my mind, and has since rapidly grown. It is the rebirth of what might be called a sense of community across the whole spectrum of American society, an aspect of our culture that, it has seemed to

---

With slight changes, this appeared as an op ed piece in the *Brookline Tab* on October 4, 2001.

me, for several years now has been diminishing, signaling a society that had already reached its apogee and was on the way down. Many have commented on this, most recently Professor Robert D. Putnam, of Harvard, in his critically acclaimed book *Bowling Alone* (2000).

Putnam directs his attention specifically to the loss of community in America over the last thirty years or so, caused by such factors as pressures of time and money (such as two-career families); suburbanization, commuting, and sprawl; the effect of electronic entertainment, especially TV; and, most important, generational change from the baby-boomers onward.

To my mind, the problem is even broader, and for want of a better expression, I call it the "trivialization of America."

Before September 11, despite still thrilling to the sight of the flag and singing the national anthem in unison with my fellow citizens, which reminds me ever and again of the personal freedom, freedom of expression (writing this piece is an example of that), and our right to "life, liberty, and the pursuit of happiness" that we enjoy, that trivialization was before my eyes, all day, every day.

Examples were rife: the tawdriness of the Clinton impeachment proceedings by both the politicians and the press (whatever one thinks of Clinton); the press pandering on the Gary Condit flap; the incivility between Republicans and Democrats in Washington; the incivility generally between and among the citizens in our land; the elevation beyond all seemliness of material values and the casino approach of millions of Americans to Wall Street; Hollywood's appeal to America's lowest common denominator, selling worthless movies about inconsiderable people or containing computer-generated special effects that we won't see for a while now; the infection of the American mind by network TV with the gross infusion of infotainment, further diluting the ability of the citizenry to know what is happening in America and the world and to critically appraise it; the glut on TV of mind-numbing sitcoms and demeaning shows like *Survivor*; the debasing and/or lack of support for the educational system, which had been and should be the jewel of our society, resulting in most high schoolers (and many college-educated people) at a loss to tell you where Afghanistan is located in the world or where Paul Revere fits in history, ill equipped to figure out who they are and where they come from, and feeling comfortable only tapping on a keyboard, fingering a mouse, and being hypnotized by a screen, unmindful of the distinction between the computer's control over them and their control of the computer.

In fact, in retrospect, I suppose that thoughts like these made it occur to me a year or more ago to propose to Brookline Access TV my program called *From Community to Cyberspace*, seeking to preserve a record of Brookline's wonderful community values as they have existed since the town was incorporated in 1705, and certainly strongly persisting during the advent of diversity in Brookline in the twentieth century. This sense of community has characterized Brookline specifically, and America generally, at least until recent years, when those values began draining away with increasing and alarming velocity.

How mesmerized we were until the very instant the first plane hit the first tower! Our representatives in Washington continued to be at one another's throat every day, and we were so sure of our future, despite the natural uncertainties of every person's life in any country, that we had already legislated tax cuts in our naïve belief in guaranteed major surpluses for a decade or more to come. True denial!

But not long after the second tower crashed down on the heads of its occupants into a mountain of dust and rubble (certainly a metaphor for what might yet be the crashing down of a hyper-materialistic and self-absorbed society), a hope rose with the rising dust and smoke when we heard of the two hundred or more firemen and policemen who rushed toward the towers to help the victims, much as people already in the towers stopped their egress to help slower victims in their attempts to escape. But then they too were killed, just like the passengers on the flight heading toward D.C., who resisted and heroically died with the attackers, thus averting yet another disaster, probably at the Capitol itself, whose dome, had it fallen, would have crushed our spirit and resolve even further.

One might have predicted different reactions on that horrific day, and in the days immediately following. Instead, the kernel of the best of America has, at least for now, taken root and grown, as shown in myriad ways, such as near unanimous support for the president; the muting of political infighting to support the national effort; people gathering to mourn the dead and to bind themselves together for a new kind of life; the desire to stay close to family, friends, home, and community; a renewed civility for our fellow citizens, strangers or not (offset by some of the incivilities shown to Arab Americans in our midst).

So have the terrorists done us a favor of sorts amid the chaos? Perhaps they have, by forcing us to come together as a people needing each other, and not "bowling alone," in addition to the obvious favor of teaching us in the most forceful way imaginable that we are not alone, it is not we and they, it is one world, and that every person in the world is our neighbor, in the face of horrors that can be unleashed upon any of us at any time.

But will this new sense of community last? Well, maybe it will for a long time, considering that the threat will be out there for a long time, perhaps for the rest of our lives. If the Hollywood hawkers are afraid to give us special effects with buildings falling down, then, it seems to me, there is hope that the litany of questionable values that I cited above may fall away, at least to some extent, bringing a rebirth of more solid and tolerant values in the many threads that make up the fabric of our society in politics, education, business, entertainment, communications, and elsewhere.

Should that happen, it would not be the first time in our country's history. Out of the ashes of the Civil War, the Union held and the slaves were freed, enriching America by liberating millions who have since contributed heavily to its success, including Brookline's Roland Hayes, himself the son of former slaves. Out of the ashes of the Trade Center, we can hope that it will hold again. As Lincoln said, "Let there be a new birth of freedom."

Unhappily, after a short hiatus, the values of community of which I spoke in this piece have continued "draining away with increasing and alarming velocity," even in Brookline, although to a much lesser extent here.

Undefeated Devotion School Baseball Team (1935)
From left, front row: Dexter Kohn, West Woodbridge, Edwin Riley,
Robert Jacobs, Robert Mason. Back row: Richard Chmielinski, Ned Pohler,
Owen Carle, Walter Halatyn, Alvin Goldsmith.

GIULIANI, BASEBALL,
AND BROOKLINE

RUDY GIULIANI, AMERICA'S UNLIKELY FIERCE, loving, and loyal knight, said it best when interviewed in his box seat during the first Yankee-Oakland playoff game: "Baseball has an amazing grip on people. It is a unifying force." He was talking about rescue workers at the World Trade Center who went forward with their grim work while listening on radios to Roger Clemens's quest for his twentieth victory a few days after the horrific felling of the twin towers.

A testament to the truth of these words was seen on national TV, when kindly and calm Yankee manager Joe Torre went to Giuliani's box seconds after the end of the Yankees' remarkable comeback win over Oakland in the fifth playoff game and, affectionately

---

This story first appeared with slight changes in the *Brookline Tab* October 4, 2001 under the title, "Giuliani, Baseball and Our Hometown." Quotes are drawn from Bookline Access TV interviews in 2000-2001.

hugging Giuliani, led him across the field to celebrate flesh on flesh with the Yankee players before sixty thousand ecstatic fans.

In the third game, in one fell, decisive, and seamless swoop, elegant and impassioned Yankee shortstop, Derek Jeter, flashing into our vision out of place and out of time to conjure up a play never before seen, demonstrated particularly American virtues of inventiveness, perseverance, and courage, at once turning the series around, lifting the spirits of New York City and every Hometown, USA, firming our resolve at this crucial hour in our history.

These scenes leave no doubt — as Mayor Giuliani says — that baseball does have an amazing grip on people and "is a unifying force," underscoring an America now showing its resilience and the character to come back from the events of September 11.

One might ask why, but the question is not easy to answer, lying as it does in mystical regions, like music, that reach into the soul, where words are insufficient symbols to explain a phenomenon we know to be true. Surely we know that baseball's power has something to do with family, friends, values, country, and community, whether that community is one of the Yankee players, New York City, Brookline, or any Hometown, USA.

We know, too, that many an American writer has tried to analyze why it is that this kids' game occupies such a big place in our thoughts and feelings.

Perhaps the only way we can truly understand is through the telling and retelling, like folk tales passed from generation to generation, of Americans' personal baseball experiences, which seem always to be related to their fellow human beings in the vast weave of American life.

These experiences are myriad, coming as they do from all people, everywhere in our society, of all ages, beliefs, and persuasions, but taken together, they give us some understanding of the power of "the national game."

Of course, baseball is played in every city, town, and village in America, so every community has its stories. Brookline's may be a bit more varied, as I have discovered interviewing people like Bunny Solomon, Mike Dukakis, Charles Kickham, Harry Ellis Dickson, Bob Sperber, and Owen Carle on *From Community to Cypberspace* on Brookline Access TV, mostly because Braves Field (before the Braves left in 1952) and Fenway Park lie just over the border.

It seems that all of these stories relate to what we think of as particularly American qualities and characteristics, reinforcing the notion of baseball's centrality in the American psyche.

American original Bernard "Bunny" Solomon's memories bring the Brookline of his childhood and early years colorfully alive in the framework of warm family life and his passion for baseball. Bunny puts it this way: "Oh yes, I'm a tremendous baseball fan and I come by it honestly. My father came to America from Kiev around 1895, lived in the South End, and fell in love with baseball, starting to go to games when he was around eleven. He saw the Sox at the old Huntington Avenue grounds and the Braves at the Camden Street yards, both on the Northeastern campus now. He was a real fan, and when I was a kid he would take me along to Braves Field every Saturday and Sunday when the Braves were in town. At that time, the Braves let kids coming with their dad in free."

That got the ubiquitous and well-connected Bunny to thinking about weekday games, which started at three o'clock (no night ball then), after school had ended. Bunny, showing early his ingenuity and resourcefulness, says, "I figured it out that if I said 'please take me in, mister,' somebody would always say yes — and that way I went to every game, and saw a lot of baseball. Later I was heartbroken when the Braves left town."

At that time grammar schools in Brookline had baseball teams for each grade, and Bunny recalls that when he made the sixth-grade team at Lawrence School, "I was so proud, because the team had uniforms." Bunny's father rewarded him by taking him to Sears for a pair of spikes to complete the uniform. Bunny says he quickly "put the spikes on with my uniform. I was so taken with myself that I walked with my spikes on from my house on Stearns Road all the way to Harvard Street to Charlie Drago's barbershop near Coolidge Corner so everybody could see me in my uniform. That was a proud moment for me."

Bunny tells of an even prouder moment that came a little bit later during that sixth-grade baseball season, when catcher "Wiggy" Wiggins, as he recalls, "fell out of a tree at Lawrence playground and broke his wrist the day before a game. Coach [and manual training teacher] Fred Woodlock said to the team, "We gotta find a catcher. Who's gonna catch?" Brave Bunny volunteered and Coach Woodlock accepted, advising him: "Don't worry about the batter. Don't even look at him. Just look at the ball!" Bunny did as he was told, but during the game sneaked a look over his shoulder and spied his dad standing behind the screen, home from work early to watch Bunny catch. Again, "a proud moment for me," says Bunny.

It kind of reminds me of my own adventures pitching on the sixth-grade team at Devotion School. During practice one day, the legendary hands-on principal Charles Taylor came out, asked if he could take a few swings, hit a line drive, and knocked me on my rear end. Until then I thought I was unhittable! A good lesson.

Mike Dukakis recalls the powerful influence of his mother, who wanted him to know things American at a very young age. As Mike tells it, "My mother, God love her, who didn't know a baseball bat from a broom handle, was nice enough to take my brother and me to Fenway Park in 1938 when my brother was eight and I was four and a half. Mike recalls that Lefty Grove was pitching and Jimmy Foxx was playing first base. Foxx hit a ball "like a rifle shot — you could hear the *smack* as the ball hit against the left field wall."

I have my own Fenway Park memories, which include my father, Jimmy Foxx, and Ted Williams.

How clearly I recall my dad (the late Morris Ruttman) taking me to my first baseball game at Fenway Park in 1936 when I was five. We stood behind the ropes strung across the outfield to watch the mighty New York Yankees. I can vividly recall the big number 4 on Lou Gehrig's broad back and how I drove my father nuts asking to go to the bathroom all afternoon.

My patient and generous dad, having recuperated, took me to Fenway again in 1940 to a doubleheader with the Chisox. I seemed to recall as I grew older that the second game ended with a Ted Williams single and a Jimmy Foxx walk-off homer out by the flagpole, but I wasn't sure whether it actually happened or was a figment of my imagination. When I got to UMass Amherst, I went to the library, took some old copies of *The New York Times* out of the stacks, and found the account of that day. Sure enough, it had happened, and I was there!

Speaking of Ted Williams, he played a big part in most kids'

Photo by Alan Lee, Brookline.

Doris and Morris "Moe" Ruttman at Lois and Larry's Wedding. (1963).

lives growing up in Boston during those years. Anybody who knew me then knows that I carried things to fetish proportions. Taking a hundred phantom swings in the mirror every day, my friends started to call me "Ted," not without edge, as my hitting abilities were pedestrian at best.

My decorative late mother (Doris Ruttman), beautiful until her passing a few months ago at ninety-six, must have taken pity on me when my adulation of Ted carried well into my late teens. One day my mother was having lunch with a woman friend at the old Meadows in Framingham, when along came Ted and his business manager at that time, Fred Corcoran. Of course, my mother then was a real stunner, and Ted, either not noticing or not caring about the ten or more years' difference in age between them, was bold enough to suggest that they all have lunch together. My mother declined the invitation (she did tell me and my father that she thought Ted was very handsome), but requested and obtained from him a "To Larry" autograph!

Charles Kickham's baseball memories linked JFK and the development of the wiles and skills that made him the fine lawyer he is. Charles and JFK knew each other well as boys, marching in processionals at St. Aidan's Church, wearing the de rigueur dress of the day, "a Buster Brown collar and tie," he says, and playing baseball together at Still Street playground. Asked who was the better ballplayer, Charles says, "Give him the edge. He was the president."

Charles, in an early demonstration of lifetime resourcefulness, took advantage of the strategic location of his family residence, on Crowninshield Road on the other side of Commonwealth Avenue from Braves Field, to get in as often and in any way he could. "We all found ways to get into Braves Field," he said, "sneaking over the fence on Gaffney Street, getting in free with an adult kind enough to take us along, turning stiles, even paying as a member of the Knothole Gang to get into the right-field bleachers, known [colloquially] as the Jury Box."

Charles tells a great story combining baseball then and his later years as an attorney here in Brookline: "When I was a kid, the Braves were owned by Judge Emil Fuchs, who lived over on Babcock Street. Bob Quinn lived on Babcock too. He sold the Red Sox to Tom Yawkey in 1932. One time on April vacation from school, I walked over to Braves Field by myself. It was nine in the morning, and not a soul was around, so I 'strolled' right through the open gate, and there was Judge Fuchs alone in his office. He said to me, 'What can I do for you young man?' I replied, 'I wonder if I can have a baseball.' Judge Fuchs said, 'I don't have one, but come back tomorrow and I'll give you one.' I did come back, and he gave me two baseballs.

"Turn the clock ahead to the time I am an attorney in Coolidge Corner, around 1950. I got a call from Judge Fuchs, saying he had a minor problem with the town of Brookline, perhaps you can help me. We had a meeting, and I told Judge Fuchs I knew him from years gone by, telling him about the baseballs he gave me."

But getting those baseballs didn't stop Charles from "strolling" into the 1936 All-Star Game at Braves field free, thereby making his own small contribution to the demise of the saga of the Braves in Boston.

It seems like every kid living in Brookline during the Braves years up to 1952 found ways to get into the games as often as possible. Living on Crowninshield Road, Charles was a stone's throw away, and where I lived on Gibbs Street was not much farther. Slick-fielding and light-hitting Marty Saklad (then a member of the Gibbs Street gang, later a dentist in Newton) and I went down to Braves Field during the war years to watch Casey Stengel's Braves lose yet again. Marty, ever the baseball strategist, was miffed that Casey didn't order a sacrifice bunt in a certain situation, so he insisted that we wait after the game so Marty could confront Casey when he came limping out (he had a broken leg at that time) with his opinion.

Of course Casey gave Marty an obfuscatory answer with his loquacious and latent locution, a form of the English language that came to be famously known as "Stengelese" in later years, when Casey skippered the Yankees to several world championships.

Mike Dukakis's father-in-law, convivial Boston Pops legend Harry Ellis Dickson, tells of his friendship with Danny Kaye, with whom he shared passions for music, baseball, and life. The two of them would attend Red Sox games for free in the press box and eat hot dogs.

What Harry doesn't know is that long before he sat in the press box at Fenway, I sat in the press box at Braves Field at age thirteen in the middle of World War II. How did I do that? I guess even then I was a One-Eyed Connolly, somehow "strolling" Charles Kickham-style, unnoticed, into the press box during a Braves-Cardinals game in 1944, taking a seat amid the assembled sports writers. One of them kept asking, "Who is this kid?" Maybe sportswriters are a bit larcenous themselves, because after hearing my story of who I was and how I got there, one of them promptly got me a ham-and-cheese sandwich, and they allowed me to sit there, loving every minute, for the rest of the game.

Considering the vast number of reforms and changes that Robert I. (Bob) Sperber made in the Brookline school system in his years as superintendent of schools, you might think he had no time for baseball. Wrong! Baseball always played a big part in Bob's life. He formed the first baseball team at the Bronx High School of Science, remarking now that he wasn't a very good player, although plainly his organizational abilities were in evidence even then.

Arriving in Boston, he became an avid Red Sox fan, and his staff gave him a "fifty is nifty" surprise birthday party when he reached that milestone.

"The theme was that there were all these fun gifts associated with the Red Sox – a blown-up Boston Red Sox doll and a bat, various songs. They did that because they knew that I'm a fanatic Red Sox fan [he smiled broadly]. It was easy coming to Boston to become a Red Sox fan, because when I was in New York, I was a New York Giant fan, not a Yankee fan. I hated the Yankees, and I still do. It is so easy to be a Red Sox fan. You have to have faith."-

You certainly do. I remember one of the many times that my faith in the Red Sox went unrewarded. That was when the flame-throwing blonde Yale Altman (who once lived in Brookline and was an all-scholastic third baseman for English High School) and I played hookey to go to one of the 1946 World Series games (still no night games), between the Red Sox and the Cardinals. Alas, the bleachers were sold out, but larcenous Larry, noticing that bleacher tickets that day were yellow, like the Chinese laundry ticket that I had in my pocket, contrived a plan in my mind that landed Yale and me in two nice bleacher seats in straightaway center field, a great vantage point to witness the Cards trounce the Sox 12-3. Three of the Cards got four hits each, including the slim and youthful Joe Garagiola.

This year, as might be discerned from my remarks above, I have temporarily become an avid Yankee fan, for reasons that go way beyond baseball and my disenchantment with the presently dysfunctional Red Sox to something that falls under the broad heading of patriotism. At this writing, I am fervently hoping that the Yankees win the pennant and the World Series; it seems that this would be poetic and satisfying justice, considering the travail that New York in particular has so recently experienced.

Perhaps the most poignant baseball memories are those of Owen Carle, longtime Brookline citizen, school committee member, and resident folklorist, drawn mostly from his youth, and showing baseball's cohering affect on community life, the "amazing grip" of which Rudy Giuliani speaks.

Owen found time for everything in those years — school, work, baseball, and music. As he says, "Baseball was king in those days.

Many of us would play morning, noon and night at Columbia, Devotion, Lawrence, and Cypress playgrounds, and Irving's Toy and Card Shop, near Devotion School was the point of congregating." Owen says that in those days, "everybody in town had corners on which to meet before playing, and we would meet at Irving's."

Owen is affecting when he talks of his principal at Devotion School, the renowned Charles Taylor, whom he describes as one of the great influences on his life (my principal at Devotion too, an educator who sticks forever in the mind). Both of us recalled how Mr. Taylor, at sixty-five, would come out to play baseball or high jump with his boys at recess or after school. Owen remarks that Mr. Taylor "taught us morals and honesty indirectly — one day, he hit one over the fence and broke a window across Stedman Street in Assessor Scott McNeilly's house. He immediately ran around the fence to Scott's house, offering to pay for the window."

That reminds me of my own stickball adventures at dusty Devotion playground, where during all of our teen years, my Gibbs Street buddy Marty Saklad and I spent endless hours playing stickball one on one, using the high wall that then separated the upper and lower playgrounds at Devotion as a backstop and the fence of which Owen speaks bordering Stedman Street as home-run territory. Indeed, I think I hit Mr. McNeilly's house a few times, but broke no windows with the tennis ball we used. Arriving home from these sessions very dirty and very late drove my poor mother to the edge of distraction!

By far the most compelling story about Mr. Taylor's genius for the formation of good character in children is the one about Owen's poor performance in French, despite the fact that he was in the "A" division for gifted students, a form of discrimination that has since been reversed, in part through Owen's efforts in his later service as school committeeman. As Owen says: "I think this is a touching story showing Mr. Taylor's passion for both learning and sports, and illustrates both his psychological and intellectual ability, and his deep understanding of how to handle children."

Owen, his face flushing as he relived the moment, recalled: "I got a C, maybe a D in French, and one day came a note from my teacher Miss Gray that Mr. Taylor wanted to see me in his office, where I went shaking. Mr. Taylor's secretary said, 'Owen, Mr.

Taylor will see you.' The door was open and Mr. Taylor said, 'Come on in Owen' — he knew every kid and their parents by name — 'would you sit down, please.' I was terrified and almost paralyzed, and had an optical illusion that Mr. Taylor was far away and close to me at the same time. And do you know what Mr. Taylor said? [Owen's disbelief shows on his face as he tells of this event of seventy years ago.] 'Owen, I understand we won a baseball game yesterday, and that you were the winning pitcher.' I thought to myself, My God, I thought he was going to criticize me about my French! Mr. Taylor said, 'You know I spoke to Mr. Weygant [Owen's baseball coach at Devotion] and got a baseball from the game, and he pulled out the top drawer of his desk and took out a shiny baseball and said, 'Owen, I'd like you to have this. You may leave now.' I got to the door of his office and Mr. Taylor called to me and then said, 'Owen, how are you doing in French?' "

Owen then asks a question that answers itself: "Can you imagine a better way to get the message over? I was really in there about my marks in French. Ann McDonald, former superintendent of schools, and headmistress of Devotion School for years, loved this story as illustrating how an educator should handle children."

A little later at Brookline High School, Owen encountered another person he cites as a big influence, coach Harry Downes, whom he describes as "fair, knew the game, created loyalty, taught hard work and sweat." Owen thinks of Harry Downes as a moral influence on his life too, and quotes the famed French philosopher Albert Camus, who said, "The highest form of morality is athletics," which certainly goes part of the way in explaining the powerful and long influence athletics has had on Owen's life, playing competitive hockey (amazingly) until a few years ago into his midseventies.

Stern Harry Downes certainly played a part in my own athletic life, inculcating morality at the same time. I am thinking of the time I made the junior varsity team at BHS and hit a double with the bases loaded that Harry Downes thought should have been a triple (he was right, I was gazing at the well-struck ball), and promptly removed me from the game. Embarrassing, but Coach Downes got the point across, just as Mr. Taylor had done with Owen Carle.

Like Owen's good friend and tennis partner Mike Dukakis, it was Owen's mother, the gifted violinist Florence Owen Mills, who introduced him to baseball and to sports generally. In those days, Owen tell us, the Boston Braves "had Ladies' Day once a week, and the ladies got in free, and boys with their mother for twenty-five cents, so my mother would take me every week to see the Braves."

Of course those were the Depression years. Owen's family had to struggle to make ends meet, and Owen had to find ways to make money. One time he combined that need with his love for baseball. The occasion was the 1936 All-Star Game at Braves Field, which Owen attended with Al Rubin, "the senior son of the owners of Rubin's Kosher Delicatessen at its original site on Harvard Street," said Owen. "The bottle law was in effect then, so after the game Al and I picked up one hundred and fifty or two hundred discarded tonic bottles on which deposit had been put, put them in paper bags, and carried them back to Harvard Street to redeem at two cents a bottle at Rubin's. But Mr. Rubin didn't want them all, saying, 'I'll take a dozen,' so we had to go peddle them down the street, and I believe we ended up with a dollar or two each. I think Al is now a successful rabbi in the Midwest."

My own Braves Field memory at the same age is less kosher than Owen's. At that time, in the field behind the left-field pavilion, there were many large tractors parked. My red-headed, literate, and daring Devotion School pal, Steve Zoll, dared me to go down there to seek cover (playing hookey from Hebrew school) to indulge our new-found habit of smoking. (Well, maybe it was good to get it out of my system early on, as I stopped smoking not too long after that.)

Owen tells a story that parallels the Yankee comeback this year, and defines American resourcefulness as well as anything could:

"Brookline had a team called the Mustangs. In 1936, when I was fifteen years old, on Memorial Day we went up to Manchester, New Hampshire, to play a baseball game with the Manchester Young Men's Polish Association. We only took nine players. I was playing left field. In the eighth inning we were leading 10-3, and the Polish Association loaded the bases. The batter hit a low line drive into left center. I went running for it full speed. So did the center fielder, and we collided, my outstretched hand hitting him so hard in the mouth that it knocked out one of his teeth, which stuck in my hand. I still have a scar there! That was Billy Maynard, an artist and a baseball player. The ball went through for a home run, and now the score was 10-7. Billy couldn't continue. He was groggy on the bench, but they took the tooth out of my hand and stuck it in his gum, and it stayed in! He had that tooth for the rest of his life. What could we do? We continued with eight players, just me and the right fielder playing the outfield, and we won the game playing with just eight guys!"

Etched in my own mind are lots of baseball memories, then and now, most of them involving parents, friends, Brookline, and the passage of time, all having something to do with the way my character developed and my life unfolded. In fact, it seems that baseball memories mark the seasons of my life, as it seems to have done for those others whose memories I have related.

It is my belief that no abstract analysis, no matter how keen, of why baseball has such an "amazing grip" and is such "a unifying force" in American life can explain that phenomenon better than these shared experiences, whether told by Rudy Giuliani from New York City or Michael Dukakis from Brookline, Massachusetts, or countless others from every village and hamlet.

For sure, that grip and that force are being felt all across America every day and every night in these baseball days following the trauma of September 11, somehow diverting us, helping to heal the wound, and making us yet again feel whole as a people.

Photo by author.

BROOKLINE FIRE CHIEF JOHN E. SPILLANE

Firefighter and Fire Historian

THE HORRIFIC EVENTS OF SEPTEMBER 11, 2001 have reminded us all of the heroic and selfless work that our firefighters do on our behalf. This vital contribution was emphasized again when I interviewed newly appointed Brookline fire chief John E. Spillane, who took over from the respected retiring chief Robert English on August 1, 2000. Not only did John reassure us as to our firefighters' skills and the qualities they bring to their work in perilous times, but also, as a skilled historian of the Brookline Fire Department, he was able to tell us its proud history during the twentieth century, especially concerning several architectural gems among our fire stations here and notorious Brookline fires over the last century.

Brookline Access TV interview, January 24, 2002. *Brookline Tab*, February 21 and February 28, 2002.

Family and School Growing Up in Brookline

Before coming up through the ranks of the Brookline Fire Department and twice along the way winning the Firefighter of the Year Award from the Elks, John Spillane grew up right here in Brookline on Stedman Street:

"I moved onto Stedman Street as an infant," he says. "I almost ended up growing up in the Kennedy house. My father [Jack Spillane, my own classmate, BHS '48] was looking to buy a house in the early fifties, and two houses were available. One was on Beals Street, one on Stedman Street. We chose the one on Stedman Street because it had a bigger yard. It turns out that the one on Beals Street was the birthplace of President Kennedy. So we probably would have had to move at some point after the assassination."

Like John, I attended Devotion School (I grew up on Gibbs Street, right around the corner from Stedman Street), and his good memories evoked my own.

"I have very fond memories of Devotion School," he said. "I can remember most of my teachers. My kindergarten teacher was Miss Chenery; first grade was Miss [Helen] McIntosh; second grade was Miss Chrisley; third grade was Miss Allen. Dr. [Donald] Lytle was the principal [having replaced the legendary principal Charles Taylor, from my own years]. I remember Mr. [Richard] Hoyt. In those days it was unusual to see a man as a teacher. Mr. Lechten was the phys. ed. teacher. Miss Moreau was the fifth-grade teacher. Mrs. Mellus was a math teacher. I think a lot of people remember her. She was a very strict teacher. But you learned math with her.

"It was a fun school to go to. I can close my eyes and I can still remember the floors creaking in the old building on the Stedman Street side. Brookline is a great town to grow up in; there was always stuff for kids to do."

I wondered whether John had learned anything about diversity attending Devotion.

"Devotion at the time was predominantly Jewish," he said. "But you grew up with people who were from all over. There were very few black families in that part of town at the time, but a lot of Asian and Chinese families. Two of the three kids I hung around with growing up were Chinese. It was a great environment."

John's third buddy at Devotion was Jackie Kickham, son of the late John Kickham, whose older brother, Charles Kickham, still practices law in Coolidge Corner at eighty-four years of age.

John's experience at BHS was less collegial. He described his time there as "different and challenging. Vietnam was going on, and BHS had gone from years of strict dress code and behavior to an open campus — a lot was happening."

But it was at BHS that John's interest in history was sparked by a special teacher: "I had a social studies teacher — Mr. [James] Genden — I don't know what it was, just something he did. Because of him I really got into and appreciated history, wanting to read and do more on my own. I really love it! We learn from our mistakes." Certainly a valuable asset for us to have in a fire chief here in Brookline.

From BHS John also remembers his math teacher (now assistant headmaster) Stephen Barrasso, as well as Paul Beauchemin, from the industrial arts department.

Like the Kennedys and the Kickhams, the Spillanes attended St. Aidan's: "St. Aidan's was within walking distance of the house," John said. "At that time it was a bustling place — a very active parish. It had its own parochial school."

John's historical and preservationist instincts came out when I said I would not put him on the spot about the present St. Aidan's controversy.

"It's a beautiful building," he said. "If you look at what they did with St. Mark's down on Park Street, where they were able to save the building while creating a new use for it — that may be one option for St. Aidan's."

Both sides of John's family have a long history in Brookline: "My dad grew up on Roberts Street down at the Point. He went to Lincoln School and graduated BHS '48. My mother grew up on Station Street and graduated BHS '48 too."

So how did it go when John and his father served together for a while in the Brookline Fire Department?

"I came on the force in 1977," John says, "and my dad didn't retire for another eight or nine years. It was an interesting situation. When I came on, he was the training officer. There was no slack. Anybody who knew him would tell you that you wouldn't get any break from him! My uncle Bill was also in the fire department."

"On my mother's side, I traced them back to the 1870s. They were affiliated with the old volunteer fire department — one family member was associated with that, and a few years later one of the first fire alarm operators was my grandfather's brother. That was around 1912, a gentleman named Wallace."

Obviously John comes by his profession naturally. One wonders whether any of John's three boys, now seven, ten, and twelve, will join the family tradition.

"I started out chasing fires with my father," John says. "We call him Sparky, as well. I would go off with him, not only in Brookline. We used to go to Boston or Somerville, or wherever. I saw a lot of fires as a kid, learned a lot, too, from what Dad saw and told me." This led to John's membership in the Boston Sparks Association. Shades of Arthur Fiedler!

How Firefighters Feel about the Work They Do

Always cognizant of the dangerous and indispensable work that firefighters do, and wondering what firefighters thought about their own work, I reminded John of a quote of his in a recent *Brookline Tab* article, in which he said, "It's a job that you can come home from and feel like you've done something worthwhile."

John added, "As a firefighter, people aren't calling you because things are going well. People are calling you because something is wrong or somebody is hurt, or there has been an accident. You are going there to help them. I think you can't be in a better profession than that — to go and help people. I always found it very satisfying and I think most of the people in my profession do. If you can save somebody's life, fine. But even sometimes just to assist in something that to some person is a big problem, that's what we do a lot. We help people."

At that point, I suggested to John that prize-winning oral historian Studs Terkel, in his landmark 1972 book, *WORKING: People Talk about What They Do All Day and How They Feel about What They Do*, was prescient in ending that long book with an eloquent verbatim statement in the vernacular by New York fire-fighter Tom Patrick concerning his personal feelings about his profession. I read it to John, and quoted it on the program, and asked for his reaction.

> Last month there was a second alarm. I was off duty. I ran over there. I'm a bystander. I see these firemen on the roof, with the smoke pouring out around them, and the flames, and they go in. It fascinated me. Jesus Christ, that's what I do! I was fascinated by the people's faces. You could see the pride that they were seein'. The fuckin' world's so fucked up, the country's fucked up. But the firemen, you actually see them produce. You see them put out a fire. You see them come out with babies in their hands. You see them give mouth-to-mouth when a guy's dying. You can't get around that shit. That's real. To me, that's what I want to be. I worked in a bank. You know, it's just paper. It's not real. Nine to five and it's shit. You're lookin' at numbers. But I can look back and say, "I helped put out a fire. I helped save somebody." It shows something I did on this earth.

John's reaction: "It doesn't get any better than that. To be able to express it that way. I think if we think back to 9/11, almost three hundred and fifty firefighters got killed. Then you go back another year to Worcester, where six firefighters were killed. They went into a building they knew was derelict and vacant and really had no value, looking for two homeless people who might have been in there, and that's what we do. It's the whole purpose of our being. To help people. And it doesn't make any difference whether you're a homeless person or a rich man. That's what we do. We try to help people. I think, in this world, it's hard sometimes for people to accept that people get a lot of satisfaction out of doing that in their work. You know you've done something that's made a difference in somebody's life."

If ever it was true that it is hard for people to accept that firefighters get a lot of satisfaction out of that work, John Spillane's remarks go far to dispel that notion forever.

From Hand Tubs to the Modern Fire Department

So how did the Brookline volunteers evolve into the modern department that we have now? Chief Spillane told us about two seminal figures in its history, George Johnson and Selden Allen:

"George Johnson was a fire chief in Brookline for well over fifty years. He started in the 1870s. He was a volunteer. He belonged to what they call a hand tub — a hand-drawn pumper, as shown in the old Currier and Ives drawings of 'The Life of a Fireman.' You had to pull these things, and pump them by hand. He was a carpenter by trade and became chief of the volunteer department in the late 1870s. When he retired in 1923, after becoming a paid fire chief in 1896, the department had gone not only from hand drawn — it had gone through the horse-drawn era, and was a completely motorized department that was one of the top-rated ones in the country. He was a man whose experience saw a complete change, not only in the community but also in the department he was running. He also ran a successful contracting business. He was a builder by trade. He actually designed the fire station that was on Devotion Street. He was quite a character. He was in his seventies when he finally retired in 1923.

"Selden Allen was a very forceful individual. He wasn't a big guy. He knew firefighting and was the person who brought the fire department to the forefront of the community. He was always speaking. He gave lectures on the history of the fire department on occasion. He was actually eligible to retire during World War II, but because of the shortage of manpower, they held him beyond his retirement age until 1946.

"Between those two fire chiefs it was well over half a century — they brought the fire department into the modern era."

I asked John generally about the new combined police and fire facility now under renovation and construction on Washington Street, due to open around April 2002, and specifically about the combined dispatch to be housed there.

"For years we always had separate dispatching facilities," he says, "and what's going to happen now is that everything will be combined in one location. There will be a dispatcher handling fire department incidents, a dispatcher handling police department incidents, and there will be people receiving nine-one-one calls. Obviously, it will cut down on the time it takes to get the apparatus and equipment to the scene. So we will have a complete new group of specially trained [at the Massachusetts State Police Academy] public safety dispatchers. We have always had a very good response. This should make it even better. Hopefully, we will be doing medical dispatches as well. We have always had to call the private ambulance company on land line and have them do the dispatch. Now we will be taking over the direct dispatch of the ambulance."

Certainly reassuring in these troubled times!

Recalling with admiration the efficiency and courtesy with which the fire department EMS personnel had always treated my father-in-law, Jacob Raverby, on the occasions when he needed their help, I asked John about Brookline EMS: "We've been doing it for many, many years," he said. "Firefighters were trained in first aid even before CPR. So we've always been available. It's always something firefighters have done." John adds that even before 9/11, firefighters were cognizant of threats, and for a long time have been preparing civil defenses against chemical, biological, and terrorist attacks.

Community Recognition of Firefighters

Respecting his profession as he does, and being the historian he is, John has had a hand in making sure that due recognition was finally given to firefighters killed or injured in the line of duty long after the fact.

"In the seventies, a little thin book came out about the history of the Brookline Fire Department. I looked through it and noticed there was no mention of a fella named Bob McGregor, who worked at this little firehouse on Devotion Street. As a kid — going into the fire station to get a coke — I knew him for years, and of course he knew me because my father was a firefighter as well. He was killed fighting a fire on Longwood Avenue. And I found it interesting that there was nothing in this little book about him. So I started doing some research, and found a number of other people who had died under similar circumstances, and never anything remembering these people. So in the late eighties we started a project with the Firefighters Union and the Relief Association. We came up with a number of people who had been killed in the line of duty. And we put plaques on all the fire stations honoring them. The McGregor plaque is on the Babcock Street station. Ironically, included in the recruit class we just hired is Mr. McGregor's grandson, his namesake. It was nice to see! I knew the recruit's father from the playgrounds as a kid — he was a few years older than me — he works for the town too, at the Highway Department.

"We had another firefighter, Billy Mahan. His grandfather was killed on the way to a fire, and doing research I found out that back in the teens when that happened, if you got killed on the way to (but not actually fighting) a fire, you got no pension. You didn't get anything. There was a lot of money raised by the firefighters themselves that went to that family!"

Obviously, since then, there has been some honing of the community's appreciation of what firefighters do, brought to a cutting edge by the events of 9/11.

Magnificent Firehouses, Then and Now

As though traveling and seeing the sights, any Brookline citizen could spend an interesting day or two looking at and studying some old Brookline firehouses. John Spillane, historian, told us something about these architectural wonders:

"Station 1 in Brookline Village is probably the best example. That was built in 1908. It was the product of a competition held by the town to replace an existing fire station that had been built in 1870. To look at some of the work that has been put into the tower, the ironwork, and the stonework — it's just magnificent, and as you come into Brookline from the Roxbury area, you see this building. That was the gateway into Brookline. This is what you see as public architecture greeting you to the town. It was, and still is, a magnificent piece of architecture."

John and I reminisced about the now gone Devotion firehouse, which stood on what was then Devotion Street, running from Stedman to Babcock, shown in a picture John brought to the program.

"Yes, that firehouse has long since been closed and torn down," he says. "It was built in 1893, and was in service until about 1965. The only change that really took place was the magnificent brick arches that are shown in this picture around the door were taken out, and big overhead square doors were put in for the modern apparatus to fit in there. [The price of progress, I thought to myself.] But it was a place to remember. As a kid, I played ball in Devotion Field, right next to the Devotion firehouse, and in the back hall of the firehouse there was a Coke machine. You'd go in, put a dime in, get a Coke. You knew all the firemen who worked there, and you'd hop in and out through the hole in the fence. It was a great place, and I think a lot of the guys were sad to see it closed when the new station on Babcock Street opened."

We also talked about another closed firehouse, which still stands but as the Brookline Arts Center on Monmouth Street, on the Boston-Brookline line.

"Right — that was built in 1883. That was built to house what they call the Chemical Company, which was a giant soda acid fire extinguisher, and it was in that station down there on Monmouth and was used as a quick attack piece for a lot of the houses down there. It wasn't an area that had either the water supply or enough property value to require a full fire company. So it had this extinguisher wagon. It was a great station. A lot of those people who worked there loved it, and they were sorry to see it closed around 1965 or so."

John then showed a picture of the Washington Square station.

"That building was built in 1899," he said, "and in the picture you see steam engine No. 2, which was a magnificent piece of machinery. It was purchased from the Amoskeag Company, and it actually won a gold medal at the Columbian World Exposition in Chicago in 1893, and Brookline bought it a few years later. We must have got a good deal. If you look at the photo, you can see how ornate it was. It was chromed, polished, and nickel plated."

"The Washington Square station, of course, is a very distinguished building itself. It's got a different type of architecture, sort of a stepped front on it. If you stand back, you see the steep peaked roof on it, and a hose tower with a big bell in the top."

John told of the oldest extant firehouse in Brookline, the one on Washington Street where the new combined police/fire headquarters will be:

"That was built in 1872. Actually it was built on the site of two other side-by-side wooden firehouses that were built back in 1840. When it was built, it looked like one building, but inside it was divided right down the middle with a wall, so you actually walked into either the hand engine side or the ladder company side. When the renovations of the new building are done, that part of the building which is that old firehouse is actually going to look as it did when it was constructed in 1872, although it won't be a firehouse any more."

How well known is it that two of our firehouses are actually twins, the ones on Boylston and Hammond Streets?

"Yes, they are very similar, the floor plan and layout are almost identical," said John. "Station 4 on Route 9 at Reservoir Road was built in 1930 — a colonial-style structure. It doesn't have a hose tower, unlike many of our older stations.

"One thing I should mention is that the old hose towers also held big bells. You can still see them at Station 7 [Washington Square] and Station 1 [Brookline Village], and those bells were used to call off-duty firefighters, or, in the early days, the so-called call men, who filled out the assignments on the apparatus. The call men only got paid for their time. When the bells hit, then they responded, something like substitute teachers. That is, when they call you, you go to work. In those days, when the fire alarms came in, they would strike them over the bells. If you were off-duty, or out on your meal hour, you would have to respond. Call men would have to come in. They would also send out the no-school signal on the bells, so the kids would know they didn't have to go to school during a snowstorm."

"The fire station on Devotion Street also had a tower bell, so there were bells everywhere in those years. There were bells as well at the old highway garage, the old town hall. Yes, there were bells everywhere!"

To this listener, John's mention of the bells was redolent of the Brookline of my youth, where a few Civil War veterans still marched and "haunted" barns were here and there to draw youngsters into scary adventures.

A Century of Brookline Fires

Techniques of fire suppression have become sophisticated in recent years, so the spectacular fires that Brookline witnessed in the nineteenth and twentieth centuries are becoming (thankfully) fewer and far between. But most of those fires taught valuable lessons, as Chief John E. Spillane explained.

The first one John told us about occurred on December 14, 1896, when a general-alarm fire destroyed Holm Lea, the famous estate of longtime Arnold Arboretum Curator Charles Sprague Sargent, off Warren Street.

"There was this magnificent mansion — Holm Lea — that was basically destroyed. The problem was that the fire department got there, and there was no water. The closest water supply was over two thousand feet away," John recalls. "After that, all the big estates had to do something, and a lot of them began to put in hydrants on their property, water tanks in the attic with hose and pipe attached to them, to be able to attack fires on their own. They also bought extinguisher wagons. We still see today the changes that came because of that fire. Nobody then gave a second thought, until it was too late. The changes that came out of that fire are very significant.

"The fire on December 24, 1897, at 140 Naples Road, only wiped out a house, but it showed that with the way the town was growing, we couldn't rely on the call men anymore. In that fire it took them a long time to get the help there they needed. They ended up having to call Brighton for assistance. So starting after that fire, there was such a public outcry about the lack of paid help that they started to be geared to hiring more paid men and relying less on the call men."

John told an ironic story about Bertram Neal, who was the first fire commissioner, appointed in 1899, a man who had been a call firefighter in Brookline for many years and sat on the Brookline Board of Engineers.

"He was also a very successful contractor and builder," John remembers, "and had his own lumberyard and shop at 140 Boylston Street, but in a case of man bites dog, his factory burned right to the ground one night in a huge fire. He stayed in business and came back, but I'm sure it was rather embarrassing for him."

There have been two spectacular fires, many years apart, where the Korean church now stands at the corner of Harvard and Pierce Streets. The first was on May 24, 1908; at the time, it was the Baptist church.

"The original Baptist church was there, a big wooden church. It was a severe fire in 1908, and again Boston had to be called in. The steeple was very heavily damaged. Two Brookline firefighters, Assistant Chief John Allen and Firefighter Eugene Sullivan, were almost killed. What happened was that part of the building collapsed, and they fell the height of the tower.

"Then many years later, on New Year's Eve 1961, on the same site, the Presbyterian church burned down and was completely destroyed. I can remember as a child going to see that site the following day with my father. My aunt lived next door on Holden Street, and they had to evacuate her house because they thought the steeple was going to go over and crash into her house. So that was a major, major fire. A lot of people still remember that one."

Some among us remember the ferocious 1931 fire at the Congregational church at the corner of Marion and Harvard that blew off the roof. Certainly many people remember the fire that consumed St. Paul's Church at the corner of St. Paul and Aspinwall on January 6, 1976:

"I happened to be home from college," John recalls. "I can remember going down with my dad. As we came around the corner, there was a huge rose window that was at the altar end of the building, and the fire was just blowing right out of it — it took the roof right off the place! However, they were able to rebuild. People were wondering whether it was an arson fire, but I don't think they ever were able to come up with a cause for that fire."

Recalling long-ago Brookline fires frames a Brookline now gone, where, believe it or not, heavy industry existed, as told not only by Chief Spillane, but also in *Images of America — Brookline,* by Greer Hardwicke and Roger Reed, of the Brookline Preservation Commission. On page twenty-one of that book, the imposing edifice that was the Holtzer-Cabot Company factory on Station Street is shown, where the largest fire loss in the town's history to that point occurred on October 6, 1911.

"That was an interesting fire," says John, "because that was one of the few buildings that had an automatic alarm system [ironically, that company made alarm systems] connected directly to the fire department, probably the only one at that time. The automatic alarm came on as it was supposed to do, but by the time the Fire Department got there, the building was well involved. It was a huge fire. Help had to be brought in from out of town. They did rebuild and reopen, but it's part of Brookline's little-known industrial past. There were areas we had for manufacturing then. That was one of them. People forget there were freight yards down around the corner."

John talked about a conflagration at the very end of World War I that accounted for the biggest loss of life in a fire in Brookline's history, on April 26, 1918, at 250 Winchester Street, the so-called Blewett Bakery fire:

"Yes, there was a bakery there, behind what is now a house. It was about two hundred feet long, one and a half stories high, almost at the Boston line. A truck was backing in and backfired, igniting a tank of gasoline. The building was fully occupied. A couple of dozen people were working in there, and the explosion killed five workers. The interesting thing about it was that many of the people working there were interned seamen from ships that had been detained in Boston because of World War I. They were working here because they couldn't go home. It was a long time before they could identify some of them."

Of the several fires at Brookline High School, probably the most famous was on September 25, 1936, when the main building was destroyed.

"The big one that everybody remembers was in 1936," says John, "when the big building that was facing Greenough Street caught fire. School was in session at the time. It lit the sky! It was a huge fire. There are some old clippings taken by news photographers in biplanes circling over the building, which was completely wiped out. It was a very distinctive building. It had this big tower in the middle. That was a big one.

"There were a couple of fires at BHS during the sixties, when I was going there. One was the huge fire that wiped out the library [probably Brookline's only book-burning experience]. A lot of the books went with the library. Being a student there at the time, I remember that it was a question whether the fire was related to the protests going on — whether it was arson. I don't know if they ever found the cause for the library fire. But it was a major fire, a major loss to the town." John also recalled when the BHS gymnasium burned, on Christmas Day, 1962.

Obviously, fire is no respecter of the lines that demarcate any society, attacking rich and poor, public and private, great building and lowly shack. Witness the fire on February 5, 1946, at The Country Club: "Apparently they had a big curling rink before the one they have there now, and at one point that caught fire, and three alarms later it was gone."

Another example of fire's lack of discrimination was the leveling of stately pillared Brandon Hall on Beacon Street near Marion on April 26, 1946, where a pedestrian apartment house now stands.

"It was a magnificent building," John remembers. "The Coast Guard had used it as a barracks for the women personnel [the SPARS] during World War II. The war was over, and mysteriously, the night before the Coast Guard was to turn Brandon Hall back over to the building owner, the Coast Guard people who were on patrol at the building found the door open and a fire burning inside. By the time the fire was out, Griggs Park was under several feet of water. We had probably the most amount of out-of-town help ever into Brookline to fight that fire, until sometime in the 1980s. There was nothing but a shell left, not enough to find the origin of that fire. People who have been around Brookline for a while still remember that one."

On May 27, 1958, when the Waldorf Cafeteria, at 1314 Beacon Street, caught fire, twenty-eight firefighters were overcome with smoke, fifteen of whom were hospitalized.

John describes that one: "It wasn't a very big fire as fires go, but a large number of firefighters got hurt. It was just a very smoky, nasty fire, and it was back in the era when there was really nothing in the way of breathing apparatus. You went in there and did what you could on your belly and tried to get what fresh air you could. A couple of firefighters went out from work after that fire and never came back."

Chief Spillane told of the Tots Toggerie fire at the corner of Harvard and Green Streets on September 27, 1968, a fire that sticks in my own memory, as my office was across the street in the S. S. Pierce Building. John recalled that this fire occurred when the block had such well-remembered businesses as Jack & Marion's, Brigham's, and Dorothy Muriel's:

"It was late in the day that a fire broke out. I am told that Mr. Aronson, the owner of Tots Toggerie, actually could have got out, but he went back in to get the woman who worked for him — and the two of them died in that fire. I remember that as a kid."

Even more people recall the spectacular gas explosion and fire on January 15, 1984, at 149 Beaconsfield Road, in which two residents were killed:

"That was a seven-alarm fire, one of the biggest we've ever had. It's the coldest I've ever been in a fire," says John. "I believe it was determined that the fire was caused by a crack in the gas main out on the street. Probably the gas followed a water pipe, and was ignited by an oil burner in the basement. But we were very fortunate we didn't lose any more people than the two who were killed. It looked like a dollhouse from the back. The building was sliced right down the middle. The whole back of the building fell right down. The Beaconsfield Road side was burning, and actually got into the Dean Road address, as well, right through the back windows."

The Beaconsfield area has had its share of big fires. The classic Beaconsfield Hotel on Beacon Street near Tappan, with its ornate arched entrance, burned in 1966. A less than ordinary condo building is there now. A recent fire in that area occurred on New Year's Day 2001, at distinctive Beaconsfield Terraces on Tappan Street, developed around the turn of the century by well-known Brookline developer Eugene Knapp.

What happened when the Brookline Fire Department was called upon to fight two major fires at one time? That happened on June 15, 1990, when an arsonist set practically simultaneous fires on picturesque but congested White Place in the village and on nearby Park Vale. Those fires actually created a situation that threatened to take down a good portion of the town in the manner of the great fires that from time to time have decimated large portions of congested cities like Boston and Chicago:

"There was a vacant building under renovation on White Place," John recalls. "It was determined to be arson by the state investigators, but nobody was ever caught. It was believed that the arsonist ignited the vacant building because it was empty and under construction. The fire immediately took off and spread, because of the congestion down there, to two or three other buildings — barns and garages. We were very alarmed that the whole neighborhood was going to go up.

"It was thought that the arsonist also lit the fire at Park Vale, which actually resulted in a fatality. We had a five-alarm fire going in one place, and a four-alarm fire at the other. Again, we had a huge response from out-of-town companies. That actually saved the town."

The old structures in Brookline Village continue to pose a fire threat. There have been several fires in the Colonnade block at the corner of Washington and Station Streets., the most recent one a few years ago that knocked the post office there out of commission for a while.

Looking to the Future

Better fire-suppression techniques mean fewer fires, but also less on-the-job training, as it were. How does Fire Chief John Spillane protect against this?

"Training is going to have to be a key to this," he said. "A lot of the older firemen are retiring, you won't have the mentoring to fill in for experience. And because there are fewer fires, the new guys are not going to get as much experience. What we're going to have to do is to see that our training is kept up to date, kept current, kept constant, so that the new people coming on have the tools, training, and skills to do the job. There's a sign in New York that says 'Let no man say my training let me down,' and I think that's a good motto."

John Spillane's allusion to New York is certainly appropriate in these nervous days following September 11. I closed my time with Chief John Spillane by quipping in a serious vein: "In a metaphorical sense, you'll be lighting a fire under them to get them ready."

BOOK XII

BUSINESS

Harvard Street Looking South to Coolidge Corner (1936).

Photo courtesy of Robert K. Kraft.

ROBERT K. KRAFT

New England Patriots Owner, Philanthropist, Modern Odysseus

THE OXFORD DICTIONARY OF CURRENT ENGLISH tells us that the word *odyssey* describes a long adventurous journey, the word taken from Homer's epic poem on the adventures of Odysseus. That same volume defines a poem as an *elevated* metrical composition concerned with *feeling*. Combining those meanings with the fact that Robert K. "Bob" Kraft was president of his class at Brookline High School (1959), running cross-country there, and that he has every day shown the heart and endurance of a long-distance runner, it seems fair to describe his life's journey with the word *odyssey*.

Bob Kraft's odyssey, which has already taken him to many distant places, began in Brookline rooted in family and community, and always returns here, no matter where his adventurous life takes him. Bob spoke of the early years:

"Growing up in Brookline was a great treat. We lived near Devotion School, at 131 Fuller Street, second floor. I was blessed

---

Brookline Access TV interview at Gillette Stadium, September 24, 2004.

with two wonderful and loving parents. My dad was a guy about whom I've never heard anyone say a bad word in my entire life. [Harry Kraft was for many years a beloved teacher and mentor at Kehillath Israel, where an emotional memorial to him was given a few years ago.] He gave me sound advice. One of his dictums was that when you feel proud, go out to the ocean and see how vast it is, and then look down at the sand, and understand that each of us is just like a grain of sand on the beach in that vastness. He would say to me, 'Try to make sure that when you go to bed every night, the people who have touched you that day are richer for having known you.' Of course, he didn't mean that in a financial sense, because Dad was not a man of financial means. He was the greatest person in my life, and the greatest influence, along with my mother, Sarah, who was very strong and gave me a lot of love.

"Growing up, I thought I was a combination of Paul Newman and Robert Redford, except when I walked down the street, no heads turned. I figured out that I felt that way because my mother gave me so much support and love and told me how terrific she thought I was. But she was also a great disciplinarian. Do it her way or you'd get a little kick in the bum. She was tiny, sort of like my wife, Myra, short, sweet but strong. My mother taught me that hard work, perseverance, how you handle adversity, and charity are the main things in life. Altogether it was a very loving household — a typical middle-class family that had the privilege of growing up in a town like Brookline."

Listening to Bob Kraft wax poetic about Brookline and family, it is easy to understand why and how he invested three hundred and twenty-five million dollars of his own money to build fan-friendly Gillette Stadium, fielding there a team successfully submerging ego to camaraderie, and carrying forth the Kraft family tradition of philanthropy personally and through the Patriots:

"In the early years, I went to Devotion School, across the street to Kehillath Israel. I made a lot of friends at those places. I played ball at the playgrounds of Devotion. We played hockey there too," he says, "freezing the other side of the street. Later I played at the Amory Street playground. We didn't have a car in our family, so when I went to Brookline High School, I'd hitch a ride or walk. BHS was a great place and a great community. I was disappointed that I didn't get to play football at BHS because my family observed the sabbath.

"If you love your family and you love your community, it's sort of part of the reason for turning down the big check to sell the Patriots. It's about family, it's about community, it's about roots, and it's about the values your parents give you. If you love your family, if you love your community, you want everyone in your community to do well, you want them to feel a sense of joy and passion about the things they do. That's where the Patriots come in now, where our family is able to share that success with the entire community. We look first at Brookline but then to the entire New England region as being part of us in that endeavor. I guess those values all got instilled starting back on Fuller Street in Brookline with my folks."

It is a maxim of life that everything that goes around comes around, and indeed that proved to be the case when Bob Kraft's love of community reflected back on him as the recipient recently of the Fourth Annual Distinguished Alumni Award of the Brookline High School 21st Century Fund. The gala event was held in a tent constructed on Cypress Field to accommodate close to five hundred attendees. The event itself raised more than $400,000 in private money for the innovative and educational programs for BHS students and faculty sponsored by the 21st Century Fund, a kind of investment in research unique among public and private high schools. Bob Kraft himself donated more than one million dollars to the fund since the previous year's gala, and, upon receiving the award, said, "We all understand that this isn't about honoring me. This is about honoring the school we all came from. This campaign is a model to the country."

Bob spoke with *feeling* about marriage, children, and community: "The best decision I think I made in my life was a partnership with my wife, Myra. Our first home was in Newton, and then we moved back to Brookline in 1972. We got married right out of school in 1963. You know, we were privileged to have four great sons. Jonathan lives in Brookline, and helped build the paper mill we have down in Connecticut connected to the family paper and packaging companies [Rand-Whitney Group Inc. and International Forest Products]. Jonathan has been a driving force here in helping to build Gillette Stadium and doing the things we have been able to do with the Patriots.

Danny lives in Newton and runs International Forest Products. We're pretty proud of that. Josh live in Newton too, and works in Chelsea, where he started a young person's club from nothing in the poorest community in the state. He was able to raise eleven million dollars on his own. David lives in Boston, and works with us in the Kraft Group, a holding company for my family's varied business interests. He's gone off on his own, done some things in technology, and now is trying to take advantage of some cyberspace opportunities. They're all within a five-to-ten-minute drive, so we're pretty lucky to have them around. Myra and I have eight terrific grandchildren, all of them also in the area.

"It's important that we as a family do everything we can to make this community vibrant, so that everyone can do well, that it be a good place for people to live for the long term. Life is long distance, handling the things that come your way. You have to have a vision for what you want. I dreamt about a lot of things beginning in those days at Devotion and BHS, and then you keep layering that on as you go, if you're ambitious."

Continuing, Bob Kraft *elevatedly* soliloquized on Brookline, community, and family: "I think Brookline is a good community because most of us here grew up living in families where folks stayed together. It wasn't a fifty-percent divorce rate. All of us had a view to work hard, dream your dreams, and seek your visions out, and do for yourself what was right. We had a great sense of community. I'm not sure today that there is the camaraderie that was there then. Part of that is that I think technology has now taken hold, and what we used to do, just getting together in groups and chitchatting, just a kind of social interaction, doesn't happen anymore. Computers have taken on a new life. Today, I think the influence of going online, and television, changes kids. They don't interact the same way we did before.

"Family is the foundation of all good things, and one of the great shames is how the breakdown of the family happens all too often. I think there is a selfishness on the part of many adults, and that causes problems for kids. Just think of the holidays, whether it's Thanksgiving, or Hanukkah, or Christmas, — where do people go? We happen to be sitting here on the eve of Yom Kippur, and you have Rosh Hashanah too, and families get together. If you have split families, it puts pressure on kids, toughens up kids. I think the kids lose something by that. The commitment to marriage is not an easy one, but I think when you agree to do it, I think there are responsibilities that come with it, like staying together through tough times, and we all go through tough times. So there are highs and lows, but you're building a foundation at the core, and then the kids leverage that, and then they get to do the same thing. I don't mean to be holier than thou; people do make mistakes. But I can't believe it's at the rate of fifty percent. I can understand that certain people make an error, but once there are children involved, there is a great responsibility. That comes back to our roots in Brookline. I don't remember any families in our era where that happened. We were together! The kids were more close-knit. I still have friends from Devotion School, like Steve Comen, Dickie Sherman, Lewis Moss, and Alan Rachins. We just had our forty-fifth Brookline High School reunion."

Before Bob Kraft came along, the values of family, community, and philanthropy would very likely not have been linked in one's mind with the rough-and-tumble, often violent world of professional football. Long before my meeting with Bob, springing from his concept of the role the New England Patriots should play in New England community, that link had been made, sharply underlined by the team's reaction to a football hazing incident in Barnstable a few days before our meeting, in which the unlucky young victim lost his spleen. Bob Kraft spoke about that:

"We try to keep up my dad's philosophy by giving away significant amounts to different needy. Speaking to the hazing incident," he said, "part of the privilege of owning this team is touching communities in ways that are not about me and not about the players. It's about what those communities represent and what people think we represent. We had one of our players call that unfortunate young man. The next day I called and invited him to come to my office and go to a game. I explained to him that football was all about teamwork, camaraderie, and working together against difficult odds, exactly the opposite of what happened to him. I was hoping that his experience could be built upon.

"I have a philosophy that every crisis is an opportunity. We feel an obligation where the team can touch people, and go around New England to make a difference. Football is not just a sport. It brings together people of all backgrounds, black, white, Asian, Hispanic, male, female, rich, poor. Everyone comes together. It is a concept of family and community, so when you see people having joy over the Patriots winning a championship, hopefully that goodwill can be transmitted to people having tough times. People who really understand football know that it is bringing together people of a certain personality who can work together, subjugating ego, checking it at the door, for the common good. That is what it's all about, and what I hope our family and our organization is all about. Sure, we're trying to win, trying to have a solid financial business, but it's all about trying to make a difference that touches people, going back to what my dad taught me."

The long odyssey of Bob Kraft continues on, and one wonders what further adventures that journey will yet unfold. As startling, surprising, or successful as those will be, history and experience tell us that they will contain copious draughts of the elixir of family and community.

Joe Zina   *Harold Brown*

JOE ZINA
Executive Director

HAROLD BROWN
Landlord

Combining to Preserve the Landmark
Coolidge Corner Theatre

JOE ZINA, JACK-OF-ALL-TRADES AND MASTER OF SOME, came along at exactly the right moment, on the eve of the millennium, to apply his many skills to save the Coolidge Corner Theatre, whose demise had been predicted by the pundits until the very moment Joe applied lifesaving CPR.

    Growing up in modestly sized Ludlow in western Massachusetts, Joe emerged from there steeped in the same small-town values on which we pride ourselves in Brookline. He burnished those by

---

Brookline Access TV interview at the Coolidge Corner Theatre, October 8, 2002.

rubbing up against a multitude of influences in the greater world and became the cosmopolitan and resourceful man he is now, whose acumen was key in saving the Coolidge Corner Theatre. Joe told of the peripatetic course that led him to Brookline:

"I've done a little bit of everything," he said. "I've been very fortunate. I started off as a painter. I did ceramics for a while. I was an art educator. I taught in public schools. I taught a year of college. Then, while I was teaching at Salem State College, I left because I wanted to fulfill one other passion that I had. That was for dancing. I had no idea where that came from, and it was just something I felt I wanted to do. So I moved to New York City, left teaching, and became a janitor while I studied modern dance. I did that professionally and toured all over the world with the Nikolais Dance Theatre. It was a wonderful time in my life — to travel internationally and perform! And when I turned thirty, it was, unfortunately, time to retire from dancing.

"I moved back to Boston because I felt that of all the places I had traveled and lived, Boston was my kind of town because you can do everything and go everywhere in Boston. I can have a car, unlike New York, where you really are a victim of the city. In Boston, you can be your own person. After my dance career, I did exercise programs, worked in fitness clubs, and did art residencies. Trying to be a choreographer in Boston is a very expensive venture. I thought I was compromising artistically doing professional dance and designing choreography here, not having the right materials to work with, as I would have had in New York. I felt that I wasn't doing the best work that I could. I lay on the couch for three months and tried to figure out what I was going to do.

"I then went back to the idea of craft and art, and art making," he continued. "I started a handmade papermaking studio in Allston, which eventually moved to Somerville, called Rugg Road Papers and Prints. It was a learning thing and it was very exciting. I worked there for eighteen years, working with many famous artists and producing a new genre of artwork in handmade papermaking. It was very exciting. Then that changed. I got tired of that, and someone asked me to be on the board of directors of the Coolidge Corner Theatre."

The right man had come to the right place at the right time, working first at the Coolidge Corner Theatre as a volunteer, a role familiar in Brookline community. Joe talked of that:

"We started doing some kids' programs, showing classical films to develop something for children to do in Brookline. I was also very fascinated with the building, which was in a state of disrepair. There was lots of tension because the Coolidge was financially strapped. None of the money was going into fixing it up. It was just going to pay the big debt that was in our lap. So I just figured, 'Well, I'll just grab a paintbrush and fix it up myself!' On Saturdays I would come in, and eventually volunteers came forward because they saw me fixing it up. They said, 'Well, how can I help?' It became a great time because a lot of people came in and participated in rejuvenating the theater. That motivated me to keep doing it. A vacancy occurred, which was the executive director. Because I was on the board, and also in sort of another career change wondering what I was going to do next, I stepped in and became the executive director for what was going to be six months and has now become three years [at this writing, five years]. It's been very good. It's been a wonderful period of time. There has been a lot of community support. Things have been going very well for the Coolidge."

Joe Zina's passion for saving the Coolidge Corner Theatre grew naturally out of his small-town upbringing, and mirrors the experience of many Brookline citizens growing up and attending Saturday matinees at the Coolidge: "I think part of my passion for keeping the Coolidge alive is that I also grew up in a small town," he said. "We had our theater, and it was called the Burr Theater, and I went there every Saturday and Sunday all day for twenty-five cents. That's how old I am. I loved it! It was incredible, but it was turned into a lumberyard. Then I went on to college in Salem, and there they knocked down this incredible building called the Paramount Theater. That makes me think of how people are not aware of how treasured these buildings really are, with all their memories. We should be aware of the architecture. The Coolidge is a historic building. They don't build them like this anymore. It's a beautiful building — the detail here is great, and you don't want to lose this. I mean, something has to be preserved so people know what the real movie experience is, and the Coolidge does represent that."

Prior to the time that Joe Zina from the small town of Ludlow met Harold Brown, the reputedly hardheaded and hard-to-deal with landlord of the Coolidge Corner Theatre from the "small town" of Brookline, over chicken soup in Zaftigs Delicatessen, no betting man would have placed book on these two men meeting in that venue, let alone settling the seemingly fatal financial problems besetting the Coolidge. That day, as he has quietly done on many other days, the mysterious Harold Brown demonstrated his loyalty and love for his hometown of Brookline, giving the lie yet again to his undeserved bad press. Joe Zina tells that story:

"Harold Brown is the landlord of the building. For a long time I had heard all these bad things about Harold Brown and how he was killing the Coolidge. In fact, I think it was just the opposite. After being the executive director for a few weeks, I realized there was this tremendous amount of money that the Coolidge had not honored with regard to rent and loans from Harold Brown. So I went to Harold Brown with the keys. I set them on the table and I said, 'Harold, you know I just don't think it is going to work. There is no way we are going to be able to pay you back this huge debt. There is no way I can move forward with the Coolidge. We need money to fix it up, and the only way to get money is to apply for grants, and you can't apply for grants if you have debt, because everyone assumes you will take the money to pay off the debt.'

"Harold looked at those keys, and he said, 'I see the problem, and we should do something. What can we do?' I said, 'I have no idea how I can repay you $330,000 of debt.' He said, 'What if we just start renegotiating that ninety-nine-year lease?' He was very cooperative. It was a wonderful day! Harold said, 'If I change the lease to fifty years, and if we get rid of all the debt, and I set a rent, and you pay it on time every month, I will forgive all the debt!' For me that meant, okay, I know what my goals are, and if I can just come up with that rent, then the Coolidge can move forward. Harold honored that, so I applied for grants right away. Bay State Federal was the first to come in with a twenty-five-thousand-dollar grant. We were able to immediately put that towards cleaning up the theater — putting in new carpeting, buying paint, doing other stuff, and this whole new period of renaissance began.

"I really do think that was Harold's vision. He's from

Brookline, he was raised here, he came to this theater as a kid, he has fond memories of it, and I think he has tremendous belief in the community. He's a very generous person — I know that there is a controversy about that, and people tell of other experiences — but my own experiences with Mr. Harold Brown have always been great. He is one of my biggest supporters. He actually helps us find other money in the community to put into the theater. Realistically, the Coolidge Corner Theatre is going to be here long after Harold Brown and myself. I think that is his concern, that it be well run, and that it will continue to be part of the Brookline community."

Joe Zina observes that Harold Brown's concern is the concern of the Brookline community at large, as funds continue to roll in to restore the Coolidge Corner Theatre to its former glory with state-of-the-art technology: "Brookline people are very educated," he says. "They're very smart people, they're very civic-minded, they're community oriented. So they believe in the theater, and they're going to preserve it, and they're going to choose to go to the movies here before they go downtown. Yes, I believe in the Brookline community, and I believe they will support this theater."

It is ironic indeed that the Coolidge Corner Theatre should have come into the world with such difficulty. As far back as the days of silent movies people wanted to establish a movie theater in Brookline, but their efforts were frustrated by the town and its citizens, who put up zoning and financial obstacles. During the Roaring Twenties, protests against establishing a movie house in Brookline were adamant, claiming that, "a movie house would not only lead to the disintegration of family life but arrest the mental development and weaken the moral fibre of children."

The long struggle ended in 1933, when the Beacon Universalist Church, standing on the theater site, leased its property to the Harvard Amusement Company, which opened the Coolidge Corner Theatre on December 30, 1933, a slightly belated Christmas present to Brookline, displaying an interior design notable then and being restored now.

Brookline activist and journalist Ruth Dorfman vividly described the transporting scene that met the eye on that first day: "The interior was completely renovated in art deco style, and still visible are the classical bas-relief figures, the Egyptian mummy sconces, the Saturn and Mayan pyramid light fixtures, and the painted ceiling with bird and floral stenciling and abstract geometrical patterns in red, green, blue, with gold and silver highlights and the two exceptional radiating sunburst designs."

How different that magical experience at the Coolidge Corner Theatre then and now is from the multiplex mania of today, with their garish and sterile atmosphere, small screens, and assaulting sound systems amid chaotic crowds, precarious seating, and treacherous popcorn, an experience decidedly nontheatrical. Joe spoke of the contrast:

"When sound movies came, and so many theaters opened up during the thirties, there was a philosophy behind building a movie theater. When you first came off the street, there was a ticket booth outside. After you bought the ticket, you went into a lobby and that was the very beginning of a transition from the outside to the inside. Then you went through an inner lobby, where the decorations became a little more exciting and different. Then you finally went into the main theater, and that was supposed to transport you into another environment, which was something you hadn't experienced before. The Coolidge does that for you, letting you escape to an interior of historical significance, whether Mayan, Aztec, or Egyptian, creating a sense of magic."

Magic reminds us of children, and children remind us of community, and people like Joe Zina and his associates Connie White and Clinton McClung on the managerial end and contributors like Phyllis and Paul Fireman (the Reebok/Curt Schilling connection) on the contributor end are busy expanding the concept of the Coolidge Corner Theatre from movies and magic to live performance and beyond.

Joe Zina spoke of that vision: "The Firemans were interested in giving us money to transform the upstairs small movie house so we could have live children's performances there with some of the kids participating. The Firemans gave us a one-hundred-and-ten-thousand-dollar gift, with which we were able to build the stage, improve the sound system, get all new seats, install theatrical lighting and wheelchair accessibility, and restore some of the murals that had been painted over. So the question is: Why are we doing these live performances? Why are we changing our format here at the Coolidge? Isn't it a movie theater?

Well, my thought on that is yes, it's definitely a movie theater. We show the best of independent and foreign films, have many different kinds of film festivals [the Boston Jewish Film Festival, the New England Film and Video Festival, and many others] that Connie White and Clinton McClung do so well, but there are a lot of hours during which the theater is not used. One of my goals over and above profitability is to make the Coolidge increasingly more interesting by providing services and opportunities for the theater as a venue for happenings of all kinds, a community resource. It's the largest assembly space in Brookline, one of the nicest places in Brookline. If we can find more ways for it to be utilized, I'm in favor of that. This requires updating to state of the art, and we've been doing that slowly but steadily."

Joe sees this in terms of outreach to the larger community: "Nonprofits are using the Coolidge space, such as PALS, the Performing Arts of Lincoln Schools. There is a lot of talent in Brookline, and I would like to see Brookline's talent move out and forward to collaborate with other communities, having their talent come to our kids' variety shows at the Coolidge. We've been doing things with Ballet Rox from Roxbury, mixing the talent from that community with our local talent. The Coolidge has become a melting pot, and it's very exciting to see this take wing."

In speaking about the Coolidge Corner Theatre Foundation's drive to raise one point seven million dollars for the improvement of the Coolidge, Joe Zina touched not only on two new facets of the jewel that is the Coolidge, but also on the community support giving the Coolidge a new life:

"All this money so many people have been contributing is going toward improving the theater, not to people's salaries. We've been able to change our office space into a video screening room, allowing us to show local filmmakers and experimental film. It's a very small assembly space for forty-five people. Very small meetings can happen there, and we've done things there with seniors, as well. We were able to build the neon art deco marquee designed by Mark Favermann, who lives in Brookline — an amazing opportunity for the Coolidge to have a professional involved. Town governance was very supportive of the erection of the marquee, taking a broad approach to the allowance of the building of a small structure with neon flashing lights on an already existing building. I believe the town was persuaded by the notion that the Coolidge Corner Theatre is a center point of the community, that you have only one theater in town, and that you may as well go over the top to get it done. The town was wonderful to work with, just as every person I've met has been so supportive of the theater. Everybody who grew up in Brookline has his life invested in the theater."

If, indeed, the world at large is moving away from the Saturday-afternoon matinees that punctuated our youthful days to a vacant cyberspace of tomorrow where one "bowls" alone, it is fortunate that there still remain among us folks like Joe Zina from Ludlow and Harold Brown from Brookline who recall the last picture show with sufficient clarity and love to preserve it in the joined lives of all of us.

MARSHALL SMITH

*Paperback Booksmith, Catalyst of the Paperback
Revolution, Dedicated to the Fine Art of Browsing*

MARSHALL SMITH BURST UPON THE LITERARY WORLD when he
opened his first Paperback Booksmith in 1961 in Boston, at a time
when it might be stated with some hyperbole that most of the rest
of Marshall's classmates from Brookline High School not many
years before, including myself, were still wet enough behind the ears
to wonder what to do with the rest of their lives. Marshall's pre-
cociousness signaled the paperback revolution, which forever
changed the reading habits of America.

   Not long before that, the uncommon Marshall was following
a common career path as a securities analyst on Wall Street.
Disaffection set in, Marshall saying that, "The part of Wall Street
that I was in was taking more money to make more money, and I
didn't feel that that was productive. So I looked around for

Brookline Access TV interview, October 13, 2004.

something where I could feel more a part of the social world. That was the book business."

Worlds apart but only a few feet from Wall Street lies Greenwich Village, where, in those years, existed a store called Paperbook Gallery, into which Marshall Smith ventured. I suggested that perhaps it was there that his ideas for Paperback Booksmith coalesced:

"That's exactly it," he told me. "Paperbook Gallery was one of the first paperback book stores in the country. Paperback books were nonexistent up until the late 1950s, with the exception of the so-called mass market — that is, murder mysteries, westerns, nurse stories, and Penguin Books, which had about two hundred titles. At that time, if you were looking for a book that had been around for a while, you'd have to go to the library. Bookstores sold only recently released hardcovers and some basic fundamentals. What bookstores basically did was to rent books. There were two stores in Coolidge Corner that rented hardcover books for five cents a day. Paperbacks changed that world, and brought literature, nonfiction, history, political science, and science to the broad public for the first time."

Marshall Smith's "social world" is spelled with a big S, which was apparent when he responded as I quoted his observation "paperback books could become a foundation for the spread of knowledge and education throughout the country."

"Once I got involved in the book business," he said, "that became kind of my business goal or mission. I think a democracy is really founded on a knowledgeable citizenry, and making books accessible to the broad general public is very much a part of that. When I started the first bookstore, Paperback Booksmith, in downtown Boston, there was a book compiling all paperback books in print. At that time there were thirty-three hundred titles available in paperback. They stopped doing that as a separate edition about twenty years ago, and by that time there were over thirty thousand paperback books in print. Paperbacks totally changed the book industry and people's awareness of books. I think the demand for reading came from the GI Bill of Rights, passed by Congress following World War II. I don't think Congress had any idea of what the bill would do. It allowed all of the veterans coming out of the Army and Navy to go to college. For the first time, we had a broad, general, and educated public interested in reading books. Paperback books satisfied that market. The two things came together."

As the originator of Paperback Booksmith, as well as Video-smith, Learningsmith, and Cybersmith, Marshall has obviously been a successful retailer and businessman, but his career takes him well beyond that, and shows him to be a catalyst, innovator, and a social scientist, sans degree, of a high order. Speaking of his early years in Brookline, Marshall provided some clues to his life's path:

"I was born in Lynn, where my mother was born, spent several years growing up in Roxbury, then went back to Lynn for a few years, and my parents moved to Brookline at the time of my sophomore year at Brookline High School, where they stayed for the rest of their lives. My father was a very bright and interesting man, a remodeler of houses.

"I think Brookline High School was a big influence on me," he continues. "It was a high-level school academically, and there I became interested in books and reading. Every once in a while, I'll come across an author and say to myself, 'Gee, I guess I read this book in high school.' One author I can think of is John Steinbeck, who wrote about twenty books, and I probably read eighteen of the twenty in high school, not thinking I was reading anything. I fell in love with and majored in history, specializing in European history. Later, I became a member of the Brookline Democratic Town Committee on the slate organized by Mike Dukakis. I was a Town Meeting member for three terms. Brookline Town Meeting probably had more accomplished lawyers than the U.S. Congress. The debates there were on an extraordinarily high level. I got the sense then, as a historian, that in Brookline the democratic process worked well at the very local level."

Considering Marshall's intellectual and business propensities, it is hardly surprising that his children, Lani, Gregory, and Jed have gone in similar directions. Marshall spoke of his children: "All of them worked at the bookstores over the years. Lani still is in the book world. She is a librarian at the Watertown Public Library, recently getting her master's degree in library science at Simmons College, working during the day and getting her degree at night. Every sense I have is that she loves it. Gregory is working for

Cisco, and has been in the computer electronic world since his college days. Jed is still in that world. He invests in start-up companies in the high-tech area."

Marshall's family was also instrumental in the invention of the name Paperback Booksmith: "The family was sitting around, five or six of us, thinking of a name for the store. In New York, there was the Paperbook Gallery. *Paperback* was much different from now, a tongue-twisting word to say. It was my mother-in-law, Marge Alper, who verbalized it, saying, 'How about Booksmith, Booksmith — *Paperback Booksmith*.' It was a lot of syllables, but it worked."

Marshall himself created the subtitle to the Paperback Booksmith name, "Dedicated to the Fine Art of Browsing." Suggesting to Marshall that the phrase itself appears to illuminate Marshall's philosophy of selling books drew a response revealing his groundbreaking and independent persona: "That phrase was mine. I loved the phrase, I've always been fond of it. I like putting catchphrases under the name of the store that say what the store is. The germ of that idea came to me when I talked to people in the book business about opening up a paperback bookstore. A couple of people had told me that someone had opened a paperback bookstore in downtown Boston and it had failed. I started to look into it. It turned out that the owner had previously run a news and magazine shop. His philosophy was that when you came into the store, you couldn't pick up a book and browse through it. If you touch it, you own it. But that's not a way to run a bookstore. Luckily, that idea kept everybody out of the paperback business. The main wholesaler at that time said to me, 'Don't do it — it won't work.'

"But we opened up our first store, and our philosophy was that if you could browse through a book, you'd get interested and would want to own it. Paperbacks were relatively inexpensive in those days, fifty cents to ninety-five cents. They were easy to take home and build your library. Even today, if you go into the Brookline Booksmith, especially in the early evening or Saturday afternoon, there is a hum in the store. There are people there. They're more than just in a bookstore, they're relating to each other. There's quiet conversation, there's a little classical music in the background. I love browsing in my own bookstore. When I opened the first store in Brookline, a few doors down from where the store is now, a mother came in and said, 'I'm so glad you're here! My kids used to hang out at the pizza parlor around the corner. Now they hang out in the bookstore!"

The hum of which Marshall speaks, beginning in Boston, Cambridge, and Brookline more than forty years ago, continues at the Brookline Booksmith, where Dana Brigham presides: "Dana became the manager in Brookline over twenty years ago. She has brought the store into the community in her own special way. She has brought her personality to the store, made it a family with the employees and a community center within the town. She's done a fabulous job. She fought hard to have readings by authors, and that has developed a following. Readings are very successful and very interesting. One of the things that people comment about the most is bringing authors to Coolidge Corner, especially local authors."

Ever the innovator, it was Marshall Smith himself who brought author readings to the Paperback Booksmith in Harvard Square in the tumultuous sixties. Marshall smiled as he recalled the scene: "Having a bookstore in Harvard Square was exciting. It was different and challenging. I think my favorite event there was having Kurt Vonnegut. After his first four or five books, he became sort of a college cult writer. He hadn't yet broken into the main-stream. I don't know where I got the idea to invite him, because he never gave author appearances. He never went to bookstores. But I wrote him a letter saying I have this idea. What if we have your appearance at our store in Harvard Square at midnight on a Friday night? He wrote back, saying, 'I never do appearances, but this one sounds like fun!' He came over to our house for dinner, and we went to the bookstore at midnight on a Friday. We stopped traffic completely in Harvard Square. It was a mob scene, and Von-negut was great!"

It might be said that from that day to this, Marshall Smith has been great, stopping traffic and creating mob scenes, both inside Brookline and out.

KIM AIRS

Retailer, Sexuality Boutique Grand Opening, Chamber of Commerce Vice President

NOT ONLY DOES SEX LIVE IN BROOKLINE, but so, too, does retail, and Kim Airs is an exemplar of both, and lots more, which will be no surprise to anyone who knows this liberated and fascinating woman, but may be, to some who don't, entirely appropriate considering that I interviewed Kim on April Fool's Day, 2004, on Brookline Access TV.

It might be expected that a multitalented woman of discernment and intelligence like Kim would be wise enough to choose Brookline as the home of her sexuality boutique, in the Arcade Building near Coolidge Corner, but some might not have expected those at all levels of Brookline life to have accepted Kim so wholeheartedly. This reciprocity has been to the great benefit of both Brookline and Kim for these past ten years or so. Her boutique

Brookline Access TV interview, April 1, 2004.

378

has become commercially successful and nationally known, drawing many customers into Brookline's retro retail environment (no shopping centers or strip malls yet in Brookline, a refuge in a country obese with them, and obeisant to them, but still with plenty of small retailers in our several diverse shopping areas in Coolidge Corner, Brookline Village, Washington Square, North Brookline, Putterham, Saint Mary's, Cleveland Circle, and scattered elsewhere). Kim herself has ably served as vice president of the Brookline Chamber of Commerce.

At first blush, the trajectory of Kim's life seems contradictory, but the more one gets to know her, the more the diverse strands of her life interweave to make perfect sense. Quotable Kim says things like, "I love sex and I love retail," seemingly a non sequitur, but out of which Kim, in relating her family background and broad range of interests, makes sense (not to mention cents). Kim tells us about her family:

"My mom is French. She was a war bride. She married an American G.I., so I have a pretty strong European streak in me," she said. "I spend as much time in Europe as I can. I have half my family there, up by Calais and down by Cannes, also in Marseilles. Most of my lineage is actually Swiss. My seven times greatgrandfather invented the string balance for watches. He's considered the father of modern chronology in Switzerland. So that is right in my blood, a neat factoid. I'm able to work really small. I used to macramé! I guess I still can.

"My father owned his own furniture store. We lived on top of it. His father was a troubleshooter for Montgomery Ward during the Depression, which could not have been an easy job, and his father was a retailer. My grandfather on my mom's side was an entrepreneur artist. He supported himself through painting, jewelry making, and watch making. I have an older sister and a younger sister. All the girls are in retail management, one sister in sales for Escada, my other sister at Godiva Chocolate. And yours truly started her own business. I just couldn't avoid retail!"

That explains the retail, but how about the sex? After all, Kim Airs is a woman who can do just about anything, and has: She's been a building superintendent, catering supervisor, waitress, house cleaner, seller of fine jewelry, and an administrative assistant at

Harvard University, and her avocations are inboard hydroplaning racing, motorcycling, and serving as chairman of the U.S. Fencing Association. To top off her eclectic résumé, Kim found time to take a turn as a call girl for a couple of years in Boston!

Perhaps the reason Kim went in the direction she did is revealed in another of her quotable quotes: "I want all people to love sex as much as I do. That's all I want. When you're happy with your sex, boy, does that translate to other parts of your life!"

While working at Harvard in late 1992, having earlier spent an apprenticeship at a sex boutique called Good Vibrations in San Francisco, Kim hatched the idea to open Grand Opening. She rejected downtown Boston as a location because of its high expenses and searched first in the so-called liberal "people's republic" of Cambridge, where one might think she'd have found ready acceptance. Not so! Kim tells that story:

"My primary concern was safety. I was looking for a location where it would be safe for a single woman to go at night and buy a toy for herself. So safety was the main thing. Cambridge made sense, somewhere between Harvard Square and Porter Square. I can tell you something about every building in that area," she said. "But things just weren't happening, nothing was materializing. There was a beautiful little shop, and the guy who owned the building said, 'I'm an elected official. How would a store like yours in my building reflect on me?' So I went to another location in Cambridge, and the gentleman there and I were talking, and he said, 'I have a wife and daughter.' So there was this resistance. And it kind of petered out . . ." (pun intended?).

It was at this point that the frustrated Kim heard a serendipitous suggestion from one of her coworkers at Harvard as to whether she had thought about Brookline. Kim thought to herself, "You don't hear anything bad about Brookline. There are no bad sections of Brookline. There are bad sections of Boston and Cambridge."

Significantly, Kim's ready acceptance of Brookline was successively met on its own ground at all levels of Brookline life, first by Brookline governance, then by Earl Leeder, the landlord of the Arcade Building, then by the chamber of commerce, community leaders, the Coolidge Corner Theatre (where her annual sex show, *You Oughta*

Be in Pictures, of which more later, is shown), other retailers, and the buying and residing public at large. Kim tells that story:

"My coworker was a sixty-two-year-old woman living in Brookline, and I thought her idea was a good idea. I remember the day like it was yesterday. I went from her office to my office, and called the office of the Brookline town counsel. I said, 'Hello, my name is Kim Airs . . .' I very clearly said what I was planning to do, that I wanted to open a sexuality boutique. I'm not going to bamboozle anyone, especially in government. I said everything. I wanted to check the legal restrictions in the town. He said he'd check it out and call me back. The very next day he did call back, and said, 'I have to tell you that there is no law as to what you can and cannot sell in the town of Brookline, except relating to food.' He told me to get a lawyer to make sure I did everything correctly, and there you go! And I was like, 'Oh, my God! That was an okay!' because so many communities have that NIMBY attitude of 'We don't want a store like that,' because of the perception of what an adult store is like. And Grand Opening is the furthest thing from what that kind of store is like. We have nice silk flowers and music. We have white mini-blinds in the windows. There's nothing dirty or shameful about the place at all. We have a really nice woman-orientated staff. It's the antithesis of a porno store. That's my business model."

Searching in Brookline, Kim stepped into hardheaded but hardly illiberal Earl Leeder's Arcade: "At the Arcade, Earl Leeder said, 'I don't care what you sell as long as it's what nobody else in the building is selling.' I gave him a lot of credit for that because I had had such a knee-jerk response to what this kind of store is like. It's really been a great success. It's been nationally recognized. It's the first of its kind on the East Coast."

Having passed these first two tests, the question was, Would the Brookline business community at large accept Kim as well? Indeed it would! Barely three months after Kim opened Grand Opening she approached Director Helen Walter of the chamber: "I went very sheepishly to see Helen at the chamber's office on the second floor of the S. S. Pierce Building. That was a beehive of activity. I said I own Grand Opening, and I'd be interested in joining the chamber. I heard there was a bit of, 'Oh, my goodness, my goodness, can we let a company like this in?' But I never heard anything personally about not allowing me. I was allowed to join the chamber in February 1994. I've been a member for about ten years, on the board of directors for five years, and became a vice president of the chamber."

Brookline's acceptance of Kim is reflected in the words of other business leaders. Polly Cornblath, executive director of the chamber, says, "Kim has generously contributed her energy and enthusiasm and business acumen to many committees. She is the type of businessperson who contributes to the business community, and to the community at large."

These words were echoed by realtor and community activist Chobee Hoy, at this writing president of the chamber, who says, "Kim is a good marketer, and she's also discreet, although running a business that could be quite controversial."

In this dynamic of action and reaction, Kim gratefully gives back to Brookline every day: "So many communities wouldn't allow a business like mine to open because of its nature. They also wouldn't support it because of the kind of business it is. Every step of the way, Brookline's been supportive, because they realize that Grand Opening is a destination store. I get calls from Connecticut, New Hampshire and Maine about how to get to the store. When they arrive, they're tired and hungry, so I send them to Zaftigs, the Coolidge Corner Clubhouse, Rami's, Zathmary's — anywhere they want to eat. Grand Opening truly is a destination, and we support other businesses in Coolidge Corner. The business community here has realized since day one that I wanted to give back to Brookline. For example, we give a ten percent discount to Coolidge Corner Theatre members because they've been so supportive."

Indeed, the Brookline landmark and nationally known Coolidge Corner Theatre and its executive director, Joe Zina, have been supportive and accepting, renting, no questions asked, the main auditorium of the theater to Kim every year since 2000 for her annual sellout amateur adult film show, *You Oughta Be in Pictures*. In fact, my interview with Kim earned me a couple of complimentary tickets to the fifth annual show, a few days later, on April 5. Kim talks about the show, a one-of-a-kind in America:

You Oughta Be in Pictures is a night of locally made amateur adult film. Most of it is very artistic, not what you normally see. Quite a few customers had said to me, 'You know, it's always been my fantasy to see myself having sex on the big screen!' I'm a firm believer that if you have a fantasy, and it's consensual, then try it. See if you like it. Life is too short. So I put a call out for videos. We have such a high level of confidentiality with our customers that they know I'm not going to be copying and selling it on eBay. So I compile and edit the videos, sometimes putting my own stuff in because I think it's hypocritical for me to show my customers, when I like to do that too."

Asking Kim about her happy experience over the years in producing *You Oughta Be in Pictures* brought out her inherent *joie de vivre*: "What is really important to know is that the adult genre of films is like any other genre of films. The fact that it has to do with sex causes a knee-jerk response that all sex films are evil. I can tell you about countless people who have said to me, 'Watching your film has changed my life! It has made me realize that I'm normal.' And people don't realize that. That's how loaded this topic is. When someone admits to his or her interest in sex, all these negative terms fall away and that person is perfectly healthy and happy! A lot of people won't admit that they like sex, men and women both. Why? Because it's so loaded. I always say, 'I care what you think about, but I don't care what you think about me.' I'm happy saying, 'I love sex.' I'm happy I feel that way. I want to share that joy.

"The people who go to *You Oughta Be in Pictures* and my classes are normal people. Some of the people who are up there on the screen are down there in the audience. You look up, and suddenly you say, 'That's me!' It's a pretty amazing thing. People in the videos don't know when they'll be coming up, and the people in the audience don't know who is in the videos. It's a game I play. After the show is over, I offer the people who have been in it to stand up, because without those people, there wouldn't be a show. For those of you who have been in this, now is the time to stand up and get the applause you deserve. Every year, everyone stands up. It's up to them, and they stand up. And the audience goes crazy. It's a sellout every year!" Obviously, Kim has hit a responsive chord among ordinary folks.

The classes of which Kim speaks run the gamut from the very sexy to the very serious, perhaps marking her as the teacher in our midst who explores life most broadly. Only recently Kim did a presentation to the business community at Brookline Rotary called "What's a Nice Girl Like Me Doing in a Business Like This: Challenges Facing a Creative Entrepreneur in Nontraditional Industries," which certainly falls into the category of the very serious. That subject is unlikely to be confused with classes in the very sexy, carrying such course titles as "Basic Flogging for Urbanites," "Take it Off with Kim Airs," "Oh, Oh, Onanism!," "Ifs, Ands and Butts!," "The World Series: Sex Tips For Guys!," "You Go, Girl! Sex Tips for Gals!," "Let's Talk About Sex, Baby!," and "Sexy Mama: Women Can Still Be Sexy When They're Pregnant." Obviously some of those titles suggest a certain backsliding from the very sexy to the very serious, it being a fact that a main thrust of Kim's teaching goes to the core of human sexuality problems, and brings her into contact with the medical community. Kim, a certified sex educator for the Planned Parenthood League of Massachusetts, talked about that:

"Planned Parenthood has an excellent program. You learn a lot about the mechanics of sexuality, gender, and safe sex practices. I'm also part of two medical associations, the American Association of Sex Educators, Counselors and Therapists, and also the International Society for the Study of Women's Sexual Health (ISSWSH). I was invited by Dr. Irwin Goldstein of the BU Medical Center to join ISSWSH as a charter member, to represent those in the trenches of sexuality, at a much different level from doctors. I actually teach doctors things about sexuality that aren't taught in medical school. I also teach them about products that are commercially available — sex toy products — that they might not be aware of in the medical setting.

"ISSWSH is a multidisciplinary group of gynecologists, sex therapists, midwives, doctors, all sorts of people," she explains. "It has proved to be a great challenge. What we have found out is that for women, sexuality is in the mind — that it is much more physically centered for men, while for women it's more emotionally based. So ISSWSH has really morphed into an amazing organization that studies the effects of sexuality, and how it's affected by childbirth, menopause, rape and incest, gender identity, upbringing, and religious upbringing. I learned so much there, and I train my staff with this information, and have the information available to be shown to patients who are sent in by doctors, or to customers who come in with a question. I'm fascinated by the connection between medicine and sexuality, and I'm a smart retailer. That's the combination we have at Grand Opening."

Impressed that Kim could so easily find the nexus between sex and medicine, I ventured an opinion that had formed in my mind since I shed the last vestiges of male chauvinism (I hope!) endemic to my generation: "Women somehow are really smarter, or have more wisdom, when it comes to sex than men do." This drew a thoughtful response from Kim: "You know why? We're responsible for reproduction. Men are too, but we carry the baby for nine months, we're the ones who have to go through the menstrual cycle. There's an inherent wisdom that women have around sex because that's what makes life. And we have to procreate during ovulation, so there's a specific window where we're able to do that. There's an inherent internal, maternal thought process, and that thought process goes with being a woman."

Reading about the open and accepting Kim beforehand, and then being in her company for the hourlong interview only a few days after the decision of the Massachusetts Supreme Judicial Court on same-sex marriage, her unbuttoned response to that decision was predictable: "I'm very proud of the fact that the court realized the law was discriminatory, and that every one should be able to get married. I'm going to start some advertising — Grand Opening supports marriage, cohabitation, and self-love. Any questions? If it works for you, go ahead and get married, no matter who you are!"

Another Kim Airs quotable quote covering the continuum from sexy and playful to serious and thoughtful, reminding us what a grand opening it was for Brookline when Kim stepped into the Arcade.

BOOK XIII

MUSICIANS

Photo courtesy of Brookline Music School.

*Vintage Photograph of Kennard House, Present Site of
Brookline Music School.*

*Harry Ellis Dickson Conducting in Duo with His Daughter
Kitty Dukakis (1983).*

HARRY ELLIS DICKSON

Boston Pops Maestro, Boston Symphony Violinist, Raconteur, and Friend

LONGTIME BROOKLINE RESIDENT, ninety-two-year-old Pops legend Harry Ellis Dickson showed that the double entendre title of his latest book *Beating Time,* written only a few years ago, applies as much today as it did then. It is obvious talking with and looking at him that Harry still is beating time on and off the podium. He tells us he is still thinking of conducting some more and writing another book on the five famed conductors for whom he played during his forty-nine years as a Boston Symphony Orchestra violinist, from Koussevitsky and Leinsdorf (both Brookline residents) through Seiji Ozawa.

Brookline Access TV interview at the home of Mr. Dickson, February 22, 2001. *Brookline Tab,* March 22, 2001. Harris Ellis Dickson passed away on March 29, 2003, at age ninety-four.

This despite one of Harry's pungent opinions delivered on the program: "We don't really need conductors — they are a necessary evil."

Harry, in his forthright way, spoke of many Brookline personalities stretching back to the 1930s. Foremost among them, of course, was Arthur Fiedler, whom Harry described as a "curmudgeon, he didn't trust anybody. But I liked him," he said, "and I was as close to him as anybody, and that's not too close . . . Arthur made fun of audiences and everybody."

Harry tells this story about Arthur. During an interview on NBC radio, the host suggested that he understood Arthur did not like children and dogs, to which Fiedler replied, "I like dogs."

But Harry slays the dragon that Arthur Fielder was not a serious musician: "Arthur was a first-class musician — he knew how to conduct the orchestra and a new piece."

Harry, well known as a raconteur, told a wonderful story combining Fiedler, legendary BSO conductor Serge Koussevitsky, Frank Sinatra, and a foreign-born first-chair oboist of the BSO. As Harry tells it, many thought Fiedler should be given a shot at conducting the BSO, but Koussevitsky — ever the classicist — would have none of it, especially after seeing a Pops concert advertised on a poster displayed outside Symphony Hall that featured Fiedler and Sinatra. The oboist came to him and said, "Who is this Sonata?" Harry replied, "No — that's Frank Sinatra," to which the oboist responded, "I know the [Cesar] Franck sonata," Harry now having to be more explicit, saying, "No, the Franck sonata is a piece, Frank Sinatra is a man!"

Well, perhaps these stories show the gulf between classical and pop music, a gulf that Harry Ellis Dickson surely has bridged.

Harry is justly famous for the establishment of the Boston Symphony Orchestra Youth Concerts, and told of the struggle to get them under way. BSO management did not initially respond to the idea, and Harry says that with his late wife's help, and private backing from people like Brookline's Irving Rabb, the youth concerts got started. In fact, they became so successful that the BSO saw the light, took them over, and now they are a mainstay, having inspired some young listeners to become musicians and even advance into the ranks of the BSO.

So one is not surprised that Harry spoke of being "upset" about the withdrawal of music from public school curriculums, as he believes that music has a place in the formation of character in young people. In a broader sense, Harry says, "I don't know how anybody could live without music," even though, he says, "some of the worst people in the world become great composers," citing Richard Wagner, the "great anti-Semite."

In his self-deprecating way, Harry expressed his distaste for rock and roll: "I try to listen, but I'm disgusted with it. I think it plays on the lowest character traits," but he adds, knowing of its many fans, "there must be something wrong with me."

Harry's talent, diligence, and gregariousness have combined to make a wonderful life. He is friendly with many famous people, musicians and not, and has traveled the world.

When in his early twenties, Harry was one of the first violin teachers at the Brookline Music School. One of his students was ten- or twelve-year-old Mike Wallace. Harry told Mike in later years, "You were my worst pupil, but the most famous." Harry says Mike never practiced. He would come to lessons and talk his head off. Harry remonstrated that "we have to play," but Mike wanted to talk. At Harry's invitation, Mike later conducted Pops by the Sea in Hyannis, where Harry recalls another guest, Julia Child, conducting with a soup spoon.

Of Leonard Bernstein, another Brookline native, Harry notes his great talents as composer and conductor, but, in a mixed metaphor, pointedly talks of Bernstein "smoking like a fish" and never taking care of himself. In fact, shortly before his death, Bernstein was rehearsing Beethoven's 7th Symphony at Tanglewood, and sick and exhausted, retired to his dressing room for medical aid. Harry visited him there. As Bernstein lay on the table being administered to by medics, he said, "Harry I think this is my last concert." Although Bernstein did manage to give the concert a day or two later, in fact that concert turned out to be his last.

Harry spoke, too, of longtime Brookline resident and BSO concertmaster, Richard Burgin, describing him as a "wonderful human being — brilliant and philosophical," but "the most forgetful man I've ever known. He arrived at a concert to play solo and found that he had forgotten his bow." Harry says a violinist is never without his mutes either, but Burgin always forgot them. Ever the jokester, Harry once made a gift of a hundred or so mutes to Burgin at a party, but when Burgin came to rehearsal the next day, no mutes.

With warmth, Harry described Sherman Walt, for many years a world-class bassoonist of the BSO — and a Brookline resident, who died prematurely, struck down by a car in Chestnut Hill. Sherm was "charming, had a great sense of humor, and so great on the bassoon that Seiji Ozawa would take him along to Japan after the season to play bassoon there."

Harry remembers with admiration Boris Goldovsky, late of Brookline in the last few months, famed the world over for his "passion for opera, a man who changed the way opera is performed, all of that starting at Tanglewood when Goldovsky brought the then lesser known Mozart operas *Idomeneo* and *La Clemenza di Tito* to the stage in the opera theater at Tanglewood, those operas now being done all the time."

Harry speaks affectionately of daughters Jinny and Kitty, and calls son-in-law Mike Dukakis a "born miser," but Harry has a little of that in him too: Mike "gives me my haircuts," he says, "and I've never paid him."

Everybody who is anybody turned out at the Ohabei Shalom on Beacon Street in Brookline when Harry received the 1969 Man of the Year award, but his mother, then in her eighties, was not surprised when Harry told her, "Mama, they are making this evening just for me," to which Harry's mother shot back, "Why not?" What other response would you expect from a Jewish mother?

Of all Harry's friendships, probably the most famous was with Danny Kaye. Harry tells of the hilarious first occasion on which Danny Kaye conducted the Boston Symphony Orchestra (he left the podium while the orchestra was playing and went into the audience). Apparently Danny was a conductor not only of orchestras but also of planes — he once took the controls between Rome and Tel Aviv, where Harry and Danny were going to give some concerts. The pilot took over from Danny as they taxied to the terminal in Tel Aviv, saying, it would "look funny taxiing in with you in the pilot's seat."

That typifies Harry Ellis Dickson and his good friend Danny Kaye, always in the pilot's seat, living life to the fullest and giving the rest of us pleasure all the way.

Courtesy of Boston Symphony Orchestra Archives.

Brookline's "curmudgeonly" Boston Pops Conductor Arthur Fiedler.

Photo by author.

Brookline native composer/conductor Leonard Bernstein in concert at Symphony Hall (circa 1980).

Photo by author.

OSVALDO GOLIJOV

Composer of His Generation, Studio in Brookline

ONE HARDLY THINKS OF BROOKLINE as a mecca for world-class composers in the same sense as Vienna, whose musical environment drew Mozart, Haydn, and Bruckner from other cities in Austria; Brahms and Beethoven from Germany; and Mahler from Bohemia, among many others. It is true that Leonard Bernstein, arguably America's greatest gift to classical composing, conducting, and playing, hailed from Brookline, but didn't he go off to the Big Apple to live, spending quality time in Vienna too? But there has been a reverse trend at work as well. Arnold Schoenberg, a turn-of-the-century Viennese master of similar stature to contemporaries Gustav Mahler and Richard Strauss, sought refuge from the Nazis, first taking up residence in America at Pelham Hall on Beacon Street. And the man whom some say is America's greatest living composer, Gunther Schuller, for many years regularly attended musical *soirées*

Brookline Access TV interview, June 10, 2004.

at Dorothy Wallace's home on Chestnut Place, along with other musical greats, including Ran Blake, a renowned pianist, composer, and professor at the New England Conservatory, who still lives and works here in Brookline.

Thus, it is not really surprising that Osvaldo Golijov, hailed by *Globe* critic Richard Dyer, and others, as the leading classical composer of his generation, chose Brookline as a place to live with his family for a while, and to locate here for good the studio where he keeps the blank music paper filled by his lively and creative imagination, adding yet another personage to Brookline's richly diverse panoply.

In fact, listening to Osvaldo talk about what it is he loves about Brookline, when he appeared as a guest recently on Brookline Access TV, one realizes that some of the inspiration for his music, which has reached around the globe, comes from scenes familiar to all of us:

"My wife, Sylvia, and I lived in Philadelphia until 1990, doing graduate studies," he told us. "I was accepted then as a student at Tanglewood, and we loved it there. We discovered Russian relatives living in Allston and Brighton, and decided to come to Boston. Walking on Harvard Street in summer felt great. It was wonderful then, and still feels wonderful! When you leave your home country to live in a different country, you try to re-create what you love about your original surroundings. I love the T; it reminds me of when I was a kid. We had a similar trolley in my town, La Plata, in Argentina. I like the Booksmith, and the Coolidge Corner Theatre. I love all the little restaurants, and also that you can walk two blocks from Coolidge Corner and be in a quiet place, at peace. So it's a wonderful combination. Plus, there was that Copy Cop on Beacon Street, so I could go there from my studio at midnight to make copies and send them overnight. So it was beautiful, and I still feel wonderful every morning when I arrive in Brookline. We lived for a year on Mason Terrace. We loved it, but at that time we could only afford to live in Newton. So now we are living in Newton, and my kids — Talia, Yoni, and Anna — are growing up in Newton. But I don't hang out there. I hang out here in Brookline."

Hanging out here in Brookline, Osvaldo Golijov composed the passionate work that propelled him to the forefront of the classical music world, *La Pasion Segun San Marcos* ("The Passion According to St. Mark"), which premiered in September 2000 in Stuttgart, and here in Boston by the Boston Symphony Orchestra in February 2001, in both places to tumultuous applause, foot-stomping, bravos, shouts, and weeping, a reception rarely given to avant-garde works. One newspaper there went the distance: "Forget new music. Forget old music. Forget Europe's music tradition, Osvaldo Golijov's 'Pasion' is incomparably unique." Drawing upon the influences of his Argentinean youth, Osvaldo's score, in the words of the *Globe*'s critic Richard Dyer, "mingles indigenous South American and African rhythms and forms — flamenco, bossa nova, rumba, mambo, tango — with dance and other theatrical elements, all filtered through Golijov's own cosmopolitan musical personality. The music is colorful, passionate, and barrier-breaking; it crosses between cultures to deliver a universal message of immediate emotional impact."

Perhaps music is the most mysterious of all the arts, the one we could least do without, and listening to Mozart or Osvaldo Golijov, or any of the great composers who reach to the center of our souls, we want to know the unknowable: How do people of such talent come into our midst to thrill and touch us with their creativity? Talking with Osvaldo Golijov gives us some clues, but no answer.

"I did not grow up in Buenos Aires," he says. "I grew up forty miles south in La Plata, which had about a thousand Jewish families. It is also much more isolated. The symphony orchestra in La Plata was not so good. The opera house there burned down when I was a teenager. Before that I went a lot, and then not at all. Another influence was Jewish liturgical music. I started at an early age to sing in the choir in the synagogue, and even before my bar mitzvah, I sang on holidays and at parties and celebrations. Also, there was chamber classical music at home. My mother was a really good pianist, became a piano teacher, and was practicing at home all the time. I loved the new tango of Astor Piazzolla, and now that I'm getting older, I love the old tango as well. In one way it was a very provincial upbringing, but in another way it was open to everything happening around me."

Carrying the Mozart analogy a bit further elicited from Osvaldo the story of his youthful start as a composer, as well as the

*Mozart at the pianoforte, 1789–90, unfinished painting by his
brother-in-law, Joseph Lange.*

gentleness and modesty that overlie the passionate quality of his
hybrid Latino Jewish temperament: "I always loved music. I
started to compose very early. I knew early on that I didn't like to
practice the piano, but I liked to improvise and invent new pieces,
and I liked to understand. More than playing perfectly, I wanted
to understand how the pieces were made, and how can you put two
or three lines together, following each of them individually, each
beautiful, and simultaneously sounding even more beautiful. So
that was always there. In the way children who later become engineers like to dismantle stuff, I always try to understand music. At
seven or eight, I remember playing, and trying to make sense of
what I was playing.

"You talk of Mozart," he says, "but there are galaxies of difference between Mozart and me. I was no prodigy. I am almost
ashamed to be in the same sentence with Mozart. But I wrote my
first real big piece when I was twelve. I had written other little
things, but the big piece when I was twelve was sort of a turning

point. I was inspired by a story by the great Argentinean writer Jorge Luis Borges."

Perhaps his turning point was one for us too, as it broadens our concept of what classical music is, with regard not only to the diverse elements used to construct it, but also to music's ability to make a statement about diversity and outreach. The catalyst to Osvaldo's thoughts on that big subject was my question as to whether *La Pasion Segun San Marcos* can be thought of as classical music, considering the many popular elements within it, and the fact that it does not sound like classical music in the European style we know.

"To me," he answered, "classical music is not whether you play it with violins, as opposed to electric guitars, or whether you base it on popular music or abstract mental concepts. To me classical music is music that transforms the listener, that takes the listener on a journey of change. I love the architecture of classical music that allows you to construct that journey, but I also like the music itself to be fresh and spontaneous, to touch the emotions. The music I love is like that. Mozart is like that, and Mahler too. Yes, in music there is the possibility of building this huge construction, of taking this very long and transforming journey. At the same time, I want to reserve the directness of expression. In my mind, the music I write is classical music."

Perhaps the key to Osvaldo Golijov's ability to draw tears, as well as foot stomping, from his listeners lies in the words he uses to define classical music, words and phrases such as *transform, change, fresh, spontaneous, the emotions,* and *directness of expression.* Osvaldo's follow-up remarks confirm the humanism that gives so much expressive power to his music:

"I'm thinking that for me music is very much an offering, a concrete offering to concrete people. When I wrote *La Pasion* it was very difficult to think of all of Christianity, of all of Latin America, so I thought of the beautiful people from the chorus in Caracas. It is always very difficult for me to think of the abstract concept. For me it is a personal thing. I love people from different cultures who bring unique things to the world. It is a different world, the world in which we live. There is such a mixture of people in the streets of the big cities in Latin America, Europe, and

Asia. It's a new world, and music should not be different from that new world. Bach also explored the limits of the world that he knew, writing music in the Scottish style, English style, French style, Italian style, German style, everything. He wanted to explore. Same with Mozart. Today you have more access to more people, and you want to explore that too. I think this is the natural thing to do.

"I was also interested in exploring my own roots," he continued, "which happen to be varied. Then you explore what is around you. Just think of what you eat! You may have Thai for lunch, Italian for dinner, or Japanese, or Mexican. You have the world right here in Coolidge Corner! Obviously, when I was growing up in La Plata, that didn't happen, there was only Argentinean food. Why is it okay to take from Central European culture and not from Native American culture? Everything is out there, so why not? I have lived in different cultures, and I can understand different people. When I was growing up in La Plata, there were only my Jewish friends and my Christian friends. Now, I look at the friends of my children at school, and you have everything, all the nations and faiths. It's a new and much richer and more beautiful world!"

During the days that Osvaldo's *Pasion*, based on a Christian story, written by a Jewish composer, was presented to the Boston audience, it became also "a concrete offering to concrete people" far beyond the confines of Symphony Hall, reaching out to Boston's Latin community. Osvaldo spoke movingly of that experience:

"The Boston Symphony Orchestra brought middle school and high school children from Lawrence to rehearsal. I was scared every minute, thinking, 'What if they don't like it and they start making noise?' But they were really into it. Then the next day, after the premiere, we went, with several of the soloists and members of the chorus, to the kids' school. It was one of the most beautiful days of my life! Together, we started to sing sections of *The Passion*. I felt really wonderful, in the sense that there are very few times in contemporary music where the piece is premiered one day, and the next day it is sung and played at a high school. I felt good in the sense that Mozart must have felt when people were whistling the tunes from *Figaro* the day after its premiere in Prague. The music doesn't come from thin air — it comes from rich soil."

Osvaldo's riff on one of his own quotes that I quoted back to him is revealing as to where Osvaldo is coming from and where he is going. Osvaldo had said: "If I had to die tomorrow, I would like to have left music that speaks to people. I don't want to die as a 'distinguished' composer. I want to be a composer who is loved or hated, admired or dismissed as cheesy."

"In classical music, you learn to play in an elegant style, in a distinguished style. You are taught to be elevated, which is a beautiful idea, but then it becomes a stereotype, and it's stuffy. Rather than being stuffy, I'd rather be cheesy, like popular musicians are, but at least they touch people's hearts. One of my heroes, Pablo Neruda, the great poet, said you can talk about the moon, everyone has talked about the moon, or written a poem using the moon, but what are you going to talk about to avoid the commonplaces? The danger is to become self-involved. You have to use the commonplaces, and twist them, and that is what I like to do to reach people, the cheesy things."

For Osvaldo Golijov to use the term cheesy to describe his own music appears at first blush to be mildly self-deprecating, but when you think about it, it merely expresses Osvaldo's passion to reach across time, place, and style to "transform" the broadest and most diverse audience he can reach. At this very moment, that reach is extending outwards globally from Osvaldo's small studio in the heart of Brookline to embrace millions, much as the life-enhancing music of the Viennese masters did from the city on the Danube.

RAN BLAKE

*Composer, Pianist, Humanist, Citizen of Brookline
and the World*

DIVERSE BROOKLINE HAS MANY SECRETS, and one of its best-kept
secrets is noted composer, pianist, and MacArthur genius grant
winner, Ran Blake, the most passionate proponent of diversity one
could ever hope to meet. Ran's apartment and studio — his grand
piano takes up most of the living room — has been located close
to Coolidge Corner for many years. Little did I know when I first
met him (I had been assigned to interview Ran by Oral History of
American Music (OHAM) at Yale University) that meeting him,
getting to know him, and being privileged to be his friend would
so enrich to my own life. Having known him for a few years by
the time I interviewed him on Brookline Access TV the day before
Thanksgiving 2003, it came as no surprise that the unselfish and

Brookline Access TV interview, November 26, 2003.

401

self-effacing Ran would seek to deflect attention from himself, to provide to me fascinating and historical information about Brookline that otherwise would be hard to come by.

Ran Blake was a man I liked before I ever shook his hand. I arrived only seconds before the start of a concert given by microtonal Delta guitarist Scott Sandvik at the New England Conservatory, where Ran is chair of the Contemporary Improvisation Department, to meet him in advance of the OHAM interview. In those few seconds Ran was pointed out to me, but I had no chance to meet him then. I stole some looks at Ran during the first part of Scott's concert, and was moved by Ran's glistening eyes and obvious emotion as he watched his fellow musician and faculty associate perform. This struck me as unusual and atypical in a virtuoso performer of Ran's reputation, virtuosos often being sufficiently narcissistic to observe another performer more critically than generously. That fleeting impression was a glimpse into what proved to be the nucleus of Ran Blake's humanistic and accepting personality.

Shaking Ran's hand, and talking with him and his friends during the intermission of that concert, it became immediately apparent that he was little interested in himself, and far more interested in introducing me and others around him to everybody else, better to join everybody in one great human family, which, one might say, is the real ambition of his life. It has been said of Ran that he wants to introduce everybody in the world to everybody else.

That pluralistic and inclusive philosophy was on display only two months after the cataclysm of 9/11, when Ran's Contemporary Improvisation Department produced a concert at the New England Conservatory's Jordan Hall called *Supermodels: Compositions and Recompositions*, dedicated to the unlikely trio of "Anwar Sadat, Yitzhak Rabin, and New York City, especially its firefighters and rescue workers." Not only would very few people, if any, have come up with that particular combination of dedicatees, but few would have put together the eclectic combination of performers at that concert, obviously intended by Ran to start healing the wounds and bringing together disparate elements of society in the still acridly smoldering wake of the horror. Ran spoke about that concert in his unique and freely associative style:

"We had Karim Mohammed, who played some music representing Egypt and some Arab countries. Roi Raz played beautiful music from Israel. We have tried to keep that spirit alive, such as recently having music from all over Eastern Europe, and Turkish and American music. So we have all this music bringing people together. 9/11 was quite a time in history, and we just can't even imagine what the world has suffered, and the people on the flights, and in the buildings. It was wonderful for Captain O'Reilly of the Brookline Fire Department to share his grief with us at the concert."

Having been moved not only by the concert, but also by Ran's remarks recalling it, I responded with the affection and admiration I feel for him: "That concert was really you, Ran. A month or so after 9/11, with anti-Arabism and anti-Muslimism running wild, you put this concert together with elements from all over the world. You were thinking of putting things together, not tearing things apart."

It was no accident that the *Supermodels* concert was co-produced by Ran's friend and fellow faculty member at NEC Hankus Netsky, noted klezmer artist and multitalented musician, who taught at Hebrew College, on Hawes Street in the historic Longwood area of Brookline, until that site was purchased by Wheelock College a few years ago. Ran Blake spoke about Hankus Netsky:

"Hankus is incredible," he said. "He has been called one of the most successful faculty members by the students. I met him as a struggling composition student, and he was very open to jazz and improvisation. I realized what a rich heritage he came from. His parents are Lester and Rhoda Netsky, from Philadelphia. I believe his family was thoughtful about the role of Jewish music, and started a klezmer band well over twenty years ago. It really has taken off. Just incredible! Hankus still keeps interested in jazz, classical, and contemporary music. I think by the time this show airs, he will be Dr. Netsky. He is getting a doctorate from Wesleyan."

Arguably the greatest name in American music is that of Ran Blake's mentor and good friend, Gunther Schuller, former president

of the New England Conservatory, renowned as a composer, instru-
mentalist, writer, academician, and musicologist. It was Gunther
Schuller's foresight that brought Ran to the New England Conservatory more than three decades ago to form the unique Third
Stream Department (combining jazz, classical, and ethnic elements), now called the Contemporary Improvisation Department.

Gunther Schuller's statement about third-stream contemporary improvisation sounds as much like a political statement as a
musical statement, and stands as well for Ran Blake's political and
musical philosophy. Schuller said, "Contemporary improvisation is
a global concept that allows the world's music — written, improvised, handed down, traditional, and experimental — to come
down together, to learn from one another, to reflect human diversity and pluralism."

Hearing that read, Ran responded: "First of all, Gunther
should be in the White House cabinet. That is the perfect definition, and Gunther has the unique ability to put these words
together into a solid, visionary statement."

Ran Blake and Gunther Schuller were visionaries not only in
Boston, but also in Brookline, where they formed the kernel of a
little-known musical salon that existed for more than thirty years,
soirées redolent of Vienna, Mozart, and Beethoven. The patron
was Dorothy Wallace and the venue was Chestnut Place. Ran
recalled that sound world, telling why he, as an artist, musician, and
person was drawn to Brookline.

"I did want to be near the Coolidge Corner Theatre [Ran is
a big fan of *film noir*]. I did want to be accessible to Dorothy Wallace. She has a wonderful concert hall. She was the Isabel Gardner of the seventies, eighties, and nineties at Chestnut Place. I met
her through a connection. It was the fall of 1968, and she invited
me over for lunch. I said, 'This is the best dish I've had in America.' And she asked if I wanted to have some friends over next week
to enjoy this dish. And I accepted promptly.

"We began having workshops there. We had [composer and
NEC professor] George Russell and Gunther Schuller. George is
a wonderful composer. He comes to Brookline often. We had
Jimmy Giuffre, Peter Row and his sitar, and Tommy Gordon.
All kinds of music would be heard there. Dominique Eade,

Gary Joynes, Ricky Ford, James Merenda. For about thirty years there would be three concerts a month there in a big room at 11 Chestnut Place, just off Chestnut Street. Where else could you hear the new Aretha Franklins? And free jazz? Dorothy insisted on Cole Porter. She was a wonderful emcee. We have tapes from these evenings. This was an important moment in my life, and as I talk to you about events in my life, Dorothy Wallace and Gunther Schuller are probably two of the most important people in it. It was a wonderful place to socialize. Lawyers, doctors, psychotherapists, all sorts of people were there."

Naturally, having lived here a long time, Ran has a lot to say about Brookline, up and down, as seen through his artistically encompassing sensibility, forcing us to view our well loved community from a singular perspective:

"Brookline has such a great history," he says, "and marvelous people. We have the greatest library system. We have some of the most diverse restaurants. It's just so exciting to be here. But I think it's changing. One way is that it was more diverse when there was rent control, and there was room then for another view, from people who worked hard. So we had a different community in the early eighties. Now there is a much greater diversity of restaurants and people on the streets. But they often get on the 66 bus and leave! We're a little self-absorbed. I wonder how well we know our neighbors and their work. I wish there could be some networking so we could see what others are doing. I'm thinking of the Boston scene, where there is more networking. I wish there were more networks here, especially artistically. Perhaps we should have less of choice, and get to know all artists and see how all artists get started, get to know their work throughout the years, and their conclusions and their philosophy of life.

"With social problems," he continues, "peace, terrorism, storms, and weathers, there's so much to think about, and I think the arts get overlooked. I think we all want to save the arts. I know that at the end of the evening, instead of a new singer, I go back to hear Billie Holliday, Chris Connor, and Ray Charles. All three are great, and one has to visit old friends. So I wish we had more contact with each other, and also somewhere we can dwell a few minutes and hear something new. And not just a quick two-minute evaluation of 'I don't like this painter because I don't like Picasso.'

"We're all very busy. But you can still walk at nighttime, and be near parks. It's very wonderful. In spring and fall, I can walk to the Conservatory. I don't have philosophical ideas about Brookline. I think it has given me the chance to concentrate on films and music. I like knowing some neighbors, and I loved living on St. Stephen's Street in Boston, where there was a transient population, but it was good to know people. I do feel there's a little loneliness or emptiness in Brookline. I don't know if we need something like the Cambridge club scene, whether it would be superficial grazing or would it really have a big impact. We could use a couple of more places to sit and talk. But it is a fabulous community with great educational opportunities."

Perhaps the "loneliness and emptiness" that Ran sees in Brookline, as well as his pluralistic and inclusive hopes for mankind's future, are reflected in the dual aspects of his music making. Globe critic Steve Greenlee, reflecting on a 2002 concert Ran gave at the Regattabar, wrote, "He sat in a darkened corner of the stage, behind the piano, head down the entire time, a dour expression on his face. He spoke not a word. Blake may be more than forty years into his career, but he's still experimenting. A concert with Blake is an odd thing indeed — and oddly beautiful."

Only recently was Ran's duality expressed in more than one way, at the Jordan Hall tribute concert to the late jazz composer Steve Lacy on October 12, 2004, when Ran gave "the most riveting performance of the night," interpreting his own favorite, Thelonious Monk's *Round About Midnight*. Bill Beuttler, of the Globe, observed "The stage lights were dimmed so that Blake sat in darkness, alone at the piano, and improvised his way through the best-known composition of Lacy's touchstone composer, fitting it with dark, dirge-like chords in places and yet letting light trickle in by the end."

Developing that idea of duality, I suggested to Ran that his music making reflects his love of music and his view of it as an element in the overall arc of life, including history and politics. Ran responded, "Yes! I'm not sure I'm thinking that profoundly. Sometimes I see the troops coming out, there is a dark feeling, and maybe a ray of sunshine. I do think, as I play, of a running commentary. The real version should be enjoyed. I don't always pre-plan. I just see movements of images. That's what I'm doing as a solo pianist, not a forty-minute cameo with bright lights."

Certainly Ran Blake, residing and working amongst us, walking by us unobtrusively observing every day in Coolidge Corner, is living the real version in the warm rays of the sun, while being acutely aware of the dark feelings and the troops coming out, very much a profound man and artist of Brookline and the world.

BOOK XIV

PUBLIC FIGURES

BIRTHPLACE OF
JOHN F. KENNEDY

35TH PRESIDENT OF THE UNITED STATES
BORN MAY 29, 1917, ON THIS SITE
83 BEALS ST, BROOKLINE, MASS.

THIS COMMEMORATIVE PLAQUE
ERECTED BY
TOWN OF BROOKLINE, MASS.
ON SEPTEMBER 12, 1961

Photo by author.

Photo by Dan Epstein © 2004 CBS Broadcasting Inc.

MYRON "MIKE" WALLACE

60 Minutes Correspondent

WITH THE GRACIOUSNESS THAT CHARACTERIZES HIM, despite his reputation as a no-nonsense, hard-questioning journalist, Mike Wallace gave me an interview touching on the personal under hurried circumstances, when he came to Brookline High School in late October 2002, to receive the school's 21st Century Fund Second Annual Distinguished Alumni Award.

It seemed to me that the BHS yearbook for 1935 (the year of Mike's graduation) was prescient as to where life would take him. He was designated the "most prominent" boy in the class, and competed in the J. Murray Kay Speaking Contest a few times. He never won, but he remarked on my show, "I got honorable mention a couple of times, and I remember very well that I thought I had it nailed with Cyrano de Bergerac."

Brookline Access TV interview at Brookline High School, October 25, 2002.

I suggested that maybe he would have won the prize if he had worn a big nose. Perhaps so, he allowed: "Well, I have a really prominent one to begin with," he said, scrunching up his face for the camera, thereby showing us his well-known ability to communicate meaning with facial expression.

Further exhibiting the speaking skills that later made him famous, Mike delivered the class oration at graduation. I started to read it to him, but Mike asked for it and read it himself. His words to his classmates were that they should expect "hard work at any job — to grit our teeth and look ahead — climb hard, never tiring — do not gaze back until our work is done," apt words considering that his high school graduation was in the middle of the Great Depression. Mike attributed the inspiration for his words to his parents: "That sounds like my mother and father," he said. "They had pounded that into me."

I told Mike (he insisted, however, that I call him by his given name, Myron) that his oration, long forgotten and seeming somewhat over the top to him, sounded to me like my idea of Mike Wallace. Smiling, he said: "You know something? It is!"

His favorite song back then was listed as "Stardust," and I asked Mike if that had anything to do with a high school sweetheart.

"Well, you know in high school I was in love — unrequited — with a young woman, a blonde, beautiful girl with blue eyes," he recalled. "She drove a Ford Phaeton. It was like a convertible, only it was a sedan with a cloth top. And Rachel McKnight was nice to me. But she really felt deeply about a guy named Don Hartman, who was a hurdler on the track team. So I used to cry myself to sleep at night."

Mike Wallace's memories of school in Brookline remind us all of our own experiences going to school here, and how much we value that. Mike started off at Devotion School.

"I went to Devotion earlier on," he told me. "You know, Bob Kraft [the Patriot owner] went to Devotion. And John F. Kennedy went to Devotion. And Myron Wallace went to Devotion. Bob Kraft has pointed out to me that our pictures still hang there. Bob was number one intellectually. I guess his grades were the best. I was number two, and Jack Kennedy was number three. Can you imagine!"

Mike's teachers made a big impression on him too, in various ways: "I know there was Biddy Graham at the John D. Runkle School who taught me grammar, and it has never left me."

With a gleam in his eye, Mike recalls, "There was an attractive younger teacher who used to display her bosom — I never knew whether she meant to or not. She would wear a deep cut."

"That happened to me too," I told Mike. Obviously our education here was advanced by our mentors in diverse ways.

Mike goes on: "And then there was Dr. Fleming at BHS, who was an English teacher. I admired him so. He turned me on at that time to Charles Dickens' *Great Expectations*. I remember those were good days. This is a wonderful school. You and I are sitting here at Brookline High now. We had such a good time. It was a good school then and it's obviously a very, very good school now. This Weintraub guy [Headmaster Bob Weintraub] is a pistol. He is smart and capable and enthusiastic, and seems to know the first name of every student in the school. There is the same feeling here today — and I loved going to school here — that there was back then."

I asked Mike how big a role his early years in Brookline played in his becoming one of the world's leading journalists.

"Oh, I'm sure that it had a lot to do with it," he said. "I got a good education here, and if I failed to do something as I was growing up here, and afterward, I failed to analyze enough. I failed to put what I was learning into context. I could answer the questions, but what do the questions mean, and in what context should I have been thinking about these events? It took me a long time to understand that."

Although Mike Wallace was famous for many years prior to 60 Minutes, that fame derived from TV and radio jobs more in the nature of entertainment than journalism. I suggested to Mike that just as André Previn (whom I had seen conduct the Boston Symphony the previous evening) turned from Hollywood to classical music, Mike had turned from entertainment to serious journalism.

"That's right," said Mike, who then told his story in a personal and touching way:

"It took me quite some time to realize that what I really wanted to do when I grew up was to be a reporter. But I had to spend time figuring that out for myself, and spending time in the Navy and traveling a little bit. Finally, what really made the difference was when I lost my son — my nineteen-year-old boy [in a mountain accident in Greece under mysterious circumstances], who also wanted to be a reporter. And when I lost him, I thought to myself, 'Well, I used to excuse myself for doing some things that were perhaps more trivial professionally. So what I did was — in Peter's memory — I said to myself that I'm going to do something that would make him happy, that would make him proud, and that's really when I found my way. That's forty years ago." (That was when Mike joined CBS, a few years before *60 Minutes*.)

When it did all come together, I asked Mike, and did he feel that Brookline had something to do with that?

"Yes, it's a wonderful town — I mean that so much," he replied. "It's a wonderful town!"

As I write this account (April 2003), it is only three days since the passing of Pops conductor, Harry Ellis Dickson, of whom Mike had wonderful thoughts:

"I was going to Devotion at the time," he remembers, "and I believe my folks paid five dollars an hour once a week for Harry to give me violin lessons. And he was an entertaining man! I remember he had this big mark from grasping — putting his chin — on the fiddle. I didn't like to practice, and I realized I was never going to make it as a serious fiddle player, but it was a privilege to know a man like Harry Ellis Dickson. My sister's best friend was his daughter Kitty, who later became Kitty Dukakis. So what goes around comes around. Six degrees of separation."

On the subject of musicians, Mike spoke at length about his famous interview with the elusive Vladimir Horowitz, perhaps the most famous pianist of the twentieth century.

"I think my last question was, When are you going to retire? Horowitz's answer was, 'Retire? Never!'"

Almost reflexively, considering everyone's amazement at Mike's continuing energy and spark, I said, "I should ask you the same question: when are you going to retire?" (Mike was eighty-four at the time of this interview.) His ready and expected emphatic reply: "Never!"

I asked Mike about the famous longtime producer of *60 Minutes*, Don Hewitt, and Mike told the story of how he had to choose between being White House reporter for CBS when Richard Nixon took office or sign on back in New York for the yet untested and unnamed Hewitt idea for what became *60 Minutes*. "Wasn't I lucky to make the right choice!" he said.

"You were and we were," I said.

Mike ended our interview with the personal charm for which he is well known. He thanked me warmly and shook my hand. Then, looking up first to his right and then to his left (on camera), he gave a smile and a thank-you to the camerawoman and cameraman working this show.

Photo by author.

LYDIA SHIRE

Chef Supreme, Owner of Locke-Ober and Excelsior, Brookline Bred

IN BROOKLINE YOUR NEXT-DOOR NEIGHBOR may be a Nobel laureate, a governor of the Commonwealth, a renowned maestro or musician, a famous TV journalist or novelist, or a world-class chef, like Lydia Shire. As I have been interviewing Brookline personages for the last three years, nothing surprises me anymore; I am now a firm believer that Brookline attracts a wide range of talented people who live alongside the rest of us in what might be described as a perfect harmony.

Lydia, whose forebears stretch all the way back to Miles Standish and Priscilla Alden through the Coffins and Tristrams of Nantucket, a few years ago took over Boston's classic restaurant Locke-Ober, and only recently opened Excelsior, a restaurant that

Brookline Access TV interview, June 16, 2003.

combines a bold mix of color and texture with equally bold contemporary American cuisine.

Lydia's culinary career began right here in Brookline, on Babcock Street. At four years old, she was peeling garlic alongside her artistic father as he cut out recipes from *The New York Times*. No question that Lydia's mom and dad started her off in the right direction. Lydia talked about that early time in her life:

"Both my parents were fashion illustrators and book illustrators," she told me. "My mother worked at Filene's for years under Harry Wilensky, and, in fact, she was known for her furs. Nobody could paint fur coats the way my mother could. And my father worked at Kennedy's for many years doing the men's suit illustrations, and so for me, growing up in Brookline and having two parents as artists, I would say that we were straight-across-the-board middle class. But, you know, there were certain influences that meant so much. For instance, when I would go back to school I wouldn't be bought ten outfits by my mother, but instead she would go to Best and Company, up near Washington Square, and she would buy me one beautiful wool plaid skirt and a pretty white cotton blouse with a little riffraff on the edge, and Mary Jane shoes from Stride Rite on Beacon Street. And you know, it was the quality that she showed me, and so I grew up in this household where it wasn't quantity, it was quality." About as fair a statement of the genesis of Lydia's fine family and professional values as you might want!

Lydia's memories of those early days have an aroma all their own: "My father was a great cook. I would come home from school and the whole house would smell like sherry, and he would make these chicken legs with fresh mushrooms and sherry, or he would make homemade chicken Kiev, and I just remember all my friends in the neighborhood saying, 'Lydia, can we come to your house for dinner tonight?' At age four, he had me chopping with this big cleaver; he didn't have a chef's knife back then. I used to chop the garlic for spaghetti aioli. We had that every Saturday night, flank steak and spaghetti aioli."

In her teen years, Lydia could not have foreseen her bright future, but family values were bubbling, boiling, and brewing up toward Lydia's destiny even then:

"Yes, I had my first baby at seventeen," she said. "That's

worked out well, because now my daughter is thirty-six, and I have two granddaughters. There's an advantage to having children when you are so young. But, that's what I did. I mean I had three babies right in a row, and my entertainment was cooking for friends. I remember making my first veal stock. I went to a super-market and said, 'Do you have any veal bones?' and they said, 'What! Veal bones? Why would you want that?' I said, 'Well, I have to make veal stock.' So I had to order them, and then I went home and I cooked them very slowly so the stock wouldn't get cloudy. I read and read and read at that time, and just loved cooking. I loved to cook way back then."

Lydia's first step to culinary success began a little later with a position as "the salad girl" at Boston's Maison Robert. After a stint at London's Cordon Bleu Cooking School, she returned to Maison Robert, first as a line cook and then as head chef. "Luciene Robert was extremely supportive," says Lydia. "Here I was, this little American girl growing up in Brookline, and he trusted me with the restaurant, especially the fancy restaurant upstairs, which was pretty amazing way back in the early seventies. He saw something in me, and it means a lot that somebody would believe in me. So I rose to the top there, and it was pretty nice."

The rest, as they say, is history, as the award-winning Lydia continues to earn renown with her inventive recipes and menus. Not that that comes easily, as she said in response to my remark that food not only meets one of man's basic needs, but also fulfills diverse social functions both public and private: "Oh, it does. That's why every time I sit down to write a new menu, I have this big red chair in my office at home, and I just surround myself with books, old books, new books and magazines, and I never follow anybody else's recipe line for line, but it spurs my own imagination, coupled with the fact that I've traveled a lot in my lifetime. I've been to China, Vietnam, Thailand, Colombia, Morocco. And you know when I eat in those places, then I come back with these remembrances of taste. And then I concoct a dish and I try to make it taste really good. And so far, thank goodness, it's kind of worked."

Looking at the Excelsior menu, one of the starters struck my eye: "Foie Gras Steak — Extra Bitter Chocolate — Fresh Cherries." I asked Lydia about that one, saying that it sounds like "to die for":

"It is," she said. "You know that was an idea that I had that was somewhat born out of a trip to Spain. I was in Barcelona and I was sitting at this little place called La Estrella, meaning 'The Star,' and at the end of my meal I was served a crouton, a thin, thin piece of bread, that had a thin piece of chocolate, bittersweet chocolate, melted on top of it. And then they poured extra-virgin olive oil on top of it and a little sea salt, coarse sea salt. And the flavor of the olive oil, with the salt and the bittersweet chocolate, was amazing, so I thought, 'Oh my gosh, I have to do this!' But instead of olive oil, I thought that the great fat that melts from the foie gras would be great on the crouton, and then put sea salt on it. And then, I think chocolate and cherries go well, so I put summer cherries on the dish. And it's been very popular. People have loved it. It's just a great combination!"

Locke-Ober, at Winter Place, is, of course, Boston's classic restaurant, going back to the nineteenth century. Lydia has retained most of the dishes we associate with Locke-Ober, like baked Lobster Savannah and Sweetbreads Eugenie under Glass on the entrée list and Indian Pudding (Lydia's new twist is to serve it hot with a crust with vanilla ice cream underneath with the pudding) as well as Baked Alaska on the dessert list, but she adds her own flair to both the food and decor.

Brookline's own JFK has a Locke-Ober history, and the signature dish now at the restaurant is JFK's Lobster Stew. Lydia tells us that when Kennedy was running against Nixon for the presidency, every Friday "JFK would leave Congress, he would hightail it up to Boston, get off at Logan Airport and zoom over to Locke-Ober in a cab, run up to the third floor, and who was waiting for him in this room but Ted Sorensen, McGeorge Bundy, and John Kenneth Galbraith. And they would grill him for about two hours, you know, just fire off these questions. He would have to answer them, and he would always order a bowl of JFK lobster stew."

Lydia has a taste for food, for art, and for history as well, and brings them all to bear as she restores Locke-Ober to its former opulence and distinction, including the first floor Oyster Bar with its famous nude painting of Madame Yvonne, formerly a male sanctum, now open to the ladies as well:

"Locke-Ober has many floors. Three floors. Many buildings.

Four buildings sandwiched together. And Joe DiMaggio and Mar-
ilyn Monroe had dinner upstairs on the third floor in one of the
little private dining rooms," she remembers. "Now I'm so excited
that these small private dining rooms have been restored, and we're
now bringing parties in there. There is another little tiny room that
has the distinction of having had the most marriage proposals. It's
a room for two people. It has a buzzer there that says RING FOR
SERVICE, so you can shut the door, propose to your sweetheart, and
open it when you want. I went to visit John Kenneth Galbraith at
his house a few months ago, just to learn more history of Locke-
Ober. That's what I've been doing. I've been trying to get in
touch with people who have had a long history there, because I feel
it is so important that all the information I take in about this one-
hundred-and-twenty-eight-year-old restaurant be passed down to
the next generations. It's been quite an amazing journey. You
know, Locke-Ober is a once-in-a-lifetime project. It's such a magical place!"

It was a natural question to ask Lydia, who was cooking at
four, out of Brookline High School before being married at seventeen, succeeding in a big way not too long after, and still being
young, whether she intended to continue as a chef and restaurateur
indefinitely.

Her answer combined her don't-give-it-up philosophy with
humor: "I'm going to stay in the restaurant business. I joke with
[well-known chef] Jasper White, my best friend, my best cook
friend, that we should open a hot dog stand together. And we're
going to call it Fatso's."

It sounds like a good idea to go a few miles outside of Brookline's borders every now and again for a culinary and social evening
with Lydia Shire at either Locke-Ober or Excelsior.

Portrait courtesy of Liz Walker.

LIZ WALKER

WBZ-TV 4 News Anchor and Humanitarian

THE FRIENDLY AND FORTHRIGHT QUALITIES OF LIZ WALKER that
have made her one of Boston's favorite news anchors over the last
twenty years — as well as her appreciation of Brookline — were
there for all to see when I interviewed her on Brookline Access TV.

Liz, who has lived here for the past several years with her son,
Nicholas, a freshman at Brookline High School, knew early on the
value of a good education, hard won in her hometown of Little
Rock, Arkansas, in the then desegregating South.   And Liz is
delighted that it is here in Brookline that her talented son Nick is
getting the best education possible.

Liz recalls growing up in Little Rock: "I was in the first grade
when Little Rock Center High School was desegregated and when
President Eisenhower sent the troops in to Little Rock.   I remember very vividly going out with my parents to see [the Army]

Brookline Access TV interview, January 9, 2003. *Brookline Bulletin*, December
11, 2003.

because we lived quite close to Little Rock Central. [Later] it was just chaos trying to desegregate the school system in Arkansas, so by the time I got to the seventh grade, the junior high schools were being desegregated, and that's when I was part of that group that went in — but it was a very slow and painful process in Arkansas, and one I'll never forget."

Liz' father was a minister and her mother a teacher, and, she says, "Education was key for everything, so my parents really kind of hammered that into both my brother and me — that if you wanted to be someone in this country, and you wanted to get ahead, the least you had to do was to go to college."

But it was not only her parents but also a white teacher who changed her life around in the Little Rock of 1967-1968, when things still were, as she put it, "threatening and adversarial." Her "white journalism teacher took me under his wing and helped me with reading and writing. His name was Charles Lance. He was absolutely instrumental in my becoming a journalist. We were an odd couple, but he saw something in me, and he challenged it. He told me I could be a writer if I really worked hard at it."

At home, Liz was further formed by her father's concentration on religious values. On Sundays, she had to attend not only the short service at her father's church in the morning, but the Baptist afternoon services as well. As she says, "The church was everything in my youth, whether I wanted it or not."

Now it seems she certainly does want it. She recently gave up her evening anchor post at WBZ-4 to do the noon news, which gives her more quality time at home with Nick and allows her to matriculate at Harvard Divinity School, where she wants to advance her writing career.

Liz says she would like to write about her trip to Sudan, where she went in the summer of 2001 with a group of local ministers, including Reverend Ray Hammond, Gloria White Hammond, Gerald Bell, and Harvard student activist Jay Williams, to find facts on the slave trade in southern Sudan, as guests of Christian Solidarity International, an organization whose mission is to buy back slaves who have been traded in the long-term Sudanense civil war.

Going to Sudan was "such a culture shock," she says — "Visceral.

It just attacks you to see a place that has literally been blown apart by war and people who have been displaced, lamed, and hurt physically and emotionally. To be there was an extraordinary experience."

While in the Sudan, Liz shot her own footage, which was featured in a couple of news specials on WBZ-TV 4 in 2002.

After working in TV in Little Rock, then in Denver and San Francisco, Liz came to Boston in 1980, and soon became a favorite — a feeling she returns: "Boston has been very, very good to me. It's a tough town, but if Boston decides it likes you, it really holds on to you. I love Boston!"

Liz Walker did not move to Brookline immediately, but once she chose it, she became one of its most ardent supporters: "Brookline is the best because it is the best of all worlds. It's the city, but there is a little less stress than the city itself. Parking is not a problem," she says, "and you have more room. I can walk around. Brookline is very special."

Then Liz homes in on the aspect of Brookline that draws her to its center: "The schools are without peer," she says. "There is no better school system, and Nicholas has been in it since kindergarten. We started in a private school system and moved from private to public, and it was the best choice and best decision for us, so I'm very happy with the schools. I think it's a great town that people are really involved in. Brookline is one of those communities where just about everybody is involved in something, civic or educational or community oriented. It's a town that works, at least from my vantage point."

Liz mentions some of our leading educators in Brookline, like Lincoln Elementary School Principal Barbara Shea, whom she describes as "top of the line." As for Headmaster Bob Weintraub of BHS, she says, "He is one of my favorites. I'm really impressed with BHS because this is a time when a kid can get lost. There is a real sense of community over there. Not just my kid; I see it with a lot of kids. They are kind of welcomed and nurtured and embraced. I went to a high school where I was pretty much invisible, so to see young people really embraced and welcomed by the whole community is really important to me."

"When you can have public education at the quality it is in Brookline, then you really have a model. In a lot of other communities, people are saying education is not what it should be, but in Brookline it is what it should be."

Naturally, Liz's own involvement in Brookline tends to the arts, such as PALS Children's Chorus, under Johanna Hill Simpson, artistic director.

"I think we need to put more attention and more finances into arts," Liz says, "because I think that's the holistic development of a child."

It seems like Liz's ability to meet the public with her talent and goodwill may be taking son Nick to high places as well. Liz tells us that "Nicholas is a freshman at BHS, but he is the first freshman to get a lead in a drama society production — that being *West Side Story*, playing Tony, the lead male part."

In fact, Nick is so good that at the recent dedication of the Leonard Zakim Bridge (attended by one of his heroes, Bruce Springsteen), Nick "sang the national anthem a cappella," Liz notes.

Impressed that a BHS freshman would be singing by himself to a large crowd at the dedication of a wonderful new bridge in Boston, I wondered whether Nick was heading for a career in opera. Her response shows a mother's pride:

"Keep that name Nick Walker in the back of your mind — who knows where he'll go!"

BOOK XV

PROFESSIONALS

Photo courtesy of the National Park Service, Frederick Law Olmsted National Historic Site.

Longtime Brookline Resident Frederick Law Olmsted, Sr. (1822-1903),
The Father of Landscape Architecture.

DR. DAVID A. LINK

Pediatric Public Health Physician Here and Abroad,
Mozart Lover

BROOKLINE'S RICH TRADITION of reaching out and giving back to this community and the world is epitomized by Dr. David A. Link, chief of pediatrics at the Cambridge Health Alliance and Mount Auburn Hospital, and a chief collaborator in the institution of a much-needed pediatric primary care center in Dnieperpetrovsk, Ukraine, whose love of music — and most especially Mozart — betokens David's harmonious interweaving of the medical, family, and community strands of his productive and fascinating life.

Within days after arriving from his native Cleveland to begin his studies at Harvard University, David received a felicitous invitation from a well-known Brookline family that set him firmly on a course he has followed from that day to this. David told us that story:

Brookline Access TV interview, June 25, 2004.

"It was just wonderful! I didn't know anything about Brookline. I got an invitation in the fall of my freshman year from the most marvelously hospitable family, the Feuersteins. They asked me to celebrate Sabbath with them. I was raised a traditionally practicing Jew. Ever since meeting them that fall, I went there regularly from Cambridge, and I felt an astonishing connection with this community, and what a community can do, and the Feuerstein family. My host, Moses Feuerstein, was involved in Malden Mills with his younger brother Aaron, and for a very long time, the family has been supporters of many aspects of philanthropy in Jewish and non-Jewish communities. The Feuersteins invited me to Brookline as a regular guest. It was a mutual admiration society!

Today," he says, "I'm still in touch with them, and I cherish my friendship with Shirley Feuerstein. We have been friends ever since, so much so that it ended up with my family intermarrying with the Feuerstein family, so now we're relatives."

That association coming, as it did, in David's late formative years, "propelled" him (to use David's word) not only to become a longtime Brookline resident with his wife and fellow physician, Margaret, and their now three grown children, but also to opt out of private practice and into the significantly less materially rewarding work of pediatric public health, work which David describes as "a privilege." I asked David to describe how he and Margaret feel about Brookline as a town in which to raise a family:

"I cannot think of a place where we would rather be to bring up our children. The people who live here are an endlessly talented, dynamic, and hospitable group of people. Close friends are scattered through the town, lots of academics and wonderful neighbors. You don't meet a person in Brookline whom you don't want to be with. In all our years in Brookline, we've confirmed our allegiance to the town, and our sense that this is where we belong.

"What has always struck me is the level of tolerance here in Brookline. It's a hard thing to come by, and you take it for granted, but it's not always there elsewhere. It is here, and that makes a huge difference as to who lives in Brookline, all kinds of really talented, diverse, and capable people who accept and enjoy each other and get along."

Responding to my Sumner Road neighbor David's expression

of his community-mindedness, I reminded him that it was at a cookout at his home that I met the scintillating quintessential Celtic man who remains to this day my best friend: "At that party in the late seventies," I told him, "I met my next-door neighbor for the first time, Dr. John Caulfield, who at that time was a research doctor with his own lab at Harvard Medical School (known around the world for his work on the tropical parasitical disease schistosomiasis), and who now works in a top job with a pharmaceutical company on the West Coast. We became very good friends right after that, and we did lots of things together. He was here in Boston last week. You were a matchmaker! A friend is a good thing to have!"

Knowing that David had elsewhere said, "Working in the public health arena for pediatrics is a core mission," I was interested to know what compelled him to shift from the private practice of pediatric nephrology into the broader arena of pediatric public health:

"Life experiences," he answered. "When you are a pediatric nephrologist, you take care of a small number of terribly ill children. It involved a great deal of science and clinical work, and was very seductive and exciting. I was working in Cambridge in a primary care setting, and then I began working in Somerville. At that time, twenty-five years ago, neither town was as affluent as it is now. I began to be very aware of the fact that a lot of urban kids were not doing very well in terms of their health. And it became sort of a tug-of-war, whether you do a tremendously intense amount of work on a few kids, sort of retail medicine, or whether you begin to embrace the bigger picture of need and do wholesale medicine in the public health field. So I drifted away from kidneys and toward pediatric public health. I have to say, taking care of children very rapidly propels you to public health, because things like vaccines, preventive medicine, adequate nutrition, bringing up children with a decent sense of core values, and literacy are all crucial, and you have to be in the public health domain to get at those things. We focus on the less affluent population. We have an enormous influx of immigrants. Wherever there's trouble in the world, within six months those kids will start showing up, whether from Eritrea or Afghanistan or Sudan. Whenever something breaks out,

wherever there are conflicts, we'll be seeing those families who
have started to flee, and for some reason, the big arrow points to
Cambridge, Massachusetts."

Dr. David Link's particular interest in the field of immunization is perhaps symbolic of the local, national, and international
scope of the award-winning brand of pediatric public health medicine he practices. He has received community service awards
(among others) from Harvard Medical School and the Combined
Jewish Philanthropies, and David's deep and abiding concern for
the children of this world is plain when he talks about that:

"I became aware some years ago of the prevalence here and
abroad of vaccine-preventable disease. In yesterday's *Boston Globe*,
there was an article about the recurring and worsening outbreaks
of polio in central and western Africa. I remember one statistic —
I don't want to go off on that trail — but there are two hundred
kids who had paralytic polio this year alone in Nigeria. To see in
the twenty-first century kids becoming paralyzed by polio, which is
a preventable condition, is tormenting. It's unacceptable. We
can't do this. That kind of feeling propelled me into vaccine work.
I've had grants from the Centers for Disease Control, and I've
worked for a long time in vaccine work in Massachusetts. I sit on
the Department of Public Health's Vaccine Advisory Committee
here. I work with the people who run the program in Washington, D.C. I work steadily, both around Boston and in Massachusetts in general and overseas, promoting better vaccine coverage for
vulnerable children. It's been a wonderful career!

"It's the kind of thing where you can really make a difference
in the whole child population. Even in the United States, there are
parts of our country where immunization rates are only around fifteen percent. And working overseas, it's not only the immunization rates, but they don't even have the vaccines we have. I'll never
forget the images from my early trips to Ukraine, where I saw an
entire ward devoted entirely to children who had severe complica-
tions from mumps, like encephalitis and pancreatitis. Because of
vaccination, people training here now in pediatrics have never seen
a case of mumps! If a child has had encephalitis, that child is not
going to do well. It was just, *Oh, my God* . . . the most painful eye
opener in the world!"

I observed to David that there has to be a special place in heaven, not only for doctors who work with children, but also for those who go off to foreign lands where conditions like those exist and change that around. I asked him to describe his experience in Dnieperpetrovsk, to which he has made many trips over the past several years. David threw in a little history:

"The Jewish Community Relations Council asked me to go to Dnieperpetrovsk, which means Peter the Great's city, on the Dnieper River. The Dnieper is a real river — we are not talking about the Charles here. There were horrible rapids there. It was not possible to get the barges through them, so a city was constructed there so the barges could pass, that being the way to get around Russia. That city was twinned with us, a needs assessment was done, and one of Dnieperpetrovsk's highest priorities was help with healthcare for women and children. I collaborated with associates here and there to set up a pediatric primary care center, among them my dear colleague Ben Sachs, who also lives in Brookline, and is the chief of obstetrics at the Beth Israel Deaconess Medical Center.

"The goal was very simple," he said. "We established two places in a district of Dnieperpetrovsk where we replicate the kind of care we deliver in Cambridge or Brookline. It includes a large vaccine program, which we introduced, and standard kinds of examinations and screening tests, none of which was available over there, and wanted by pediatricians there. They knew that all of this was good, and better than they had, and really needed. They were very eager to work on this project together."

David's account of the introduction of hepatitis B vaccine into Ukraine might well be a paradigm for the efforts of like-minded American physicians in many parts of the world, exporting, as it were, the best of American culture at a time in our history when a large part of the world believes we are doing the exact opposite.

"Hepatitis B is a disease that can be lifelong and can lead to cancer, which is devastating. In Ukraine, it's rampant among teenagers. It's essentially a sexually transmitted disease. And if you don't get it that way, the mother can transmit it to you when you're born. There was no hepatitis B vaccine anywhere in the country. And thanks to an amazing gift from Merck, we have been able to secure the vaccine and solve the technical details of getting it to Ukraine. We have begun a vaccine program with a newborn vaccine arrangement schedule exactly like ours. So, if you had a child or grandchild, they'd get the same treatment as children do here. We had to overcome their belief that a baby is too frail to be immunized. That worked out. At that time, the state of Ukraine in which we were working approved the program because we had a lot of credibility. It worked wonderfully! We had more than ten thousand patients.

"Coming back to Russia to work in the clinic six years later, I saw posters that said, 'Mothers, be sure your baby is protected against hepatitis B.' And below that, it had all these Ministry of Health stamps and seals on the poster. And I read that — my Russian is good enough that I can read that — and I turned to Yuri, my colleague, the chair of pediatrics, and asked, 'What's this?' And Yuri said, with a big grin, 'As of 2003, the Ministry of Health voted for universal immunization against hepatitis B!' Not only that, the government centralized it so that the entire country is getting the hepatitis B vaccine as a newborn immunization program paid by the government. I'm not so grandiose as to think we did this. But they looked very carefully at our records and saw that nothing bad had happened. And we had had enough experience working over there that they said okay, and here we are seven to eight years later, and all those babies are protected from hepatitis B!"

David, in a humorous response to my remark that public health is a great thing, advised, "Don't leave home without it!" He then expanded on his quote in another forum about the "wedding of public health to primary care for children to improve the quality of life" on the home front: "For almost twenty years now, we've had a Healthy Children Task Force in Cambridge, starting out originally on a grant to bring together core agencies in the city to work to improve the well-being of children. We have a gathering of those agencies that meets twice a month and aims programs at obvious problems, like asthma, and less obvious ones, like children who are homeless, food programs in schools, and childhood obesity."

Having known David Link for more than a quarter of a century as a friend, doctor, and a fellow lover of Mozart and music, I thought it appropriate to conclude our interview with a musical and medical question. "Tell us a little bit about your love of music, Mozart, and Vienna, and whether or not it has any medical connections." This elicited from David a revealing answer about his family, his love of music, his commitment to his work, and his qualities as a man.

"That's a tough one," he said, "but I'll try to do it quickly. I'm a first-generation American. My father was Central European and my mother was English, and both always went to musical events. The house was always full of music when I was growing up, a lot of it Central European, some from Vienna. And I guess I have been hearing Mozart, probably from the time I was in my mother's womb. My father was a great opera lover and a fan of Mozart. Music was always part of my life, and it calms me down. I've had many opportunities to travel to Vienna. There I visited the Figaro House, where Mozart lived when he composed *The Marriage of Figaro*.

"Two things about Mozart have to do with my career. I always wonder whether, if one of these kids catches polio or encephalitis, did we just lose a Mozart? Was that the next creative genius? What is little known about Mozart is that he died young, at thirty-five, of kidney disease, in 1791 — December 5, to be exact. As a pediatric nephrologist, I wonder if Mozart had had the right medical attention, would we now have a thousand of his compositions instead of the six hundred pieces we do have?"

Harmony in a humanistic and musical sense lies at the center of Dr. David Link's life and practice, lending to them, as it did to Mozart, a universality that spans continents and brings men and women closer together.

Photo courtesy of Mary Nestor.

CHARLES J. KICKHAM JR., ESQUIRE

A Brookline Life

THE LONG, FRUITFUL, AND STILL VIGOROUSLY CONTINUING personal and professional life of Charles J. Kickham Jr., Esq., demonstrates the truth of what Bernard "Bunny" Solomon said, with mild hyperbole: "Brookline is a great place to live because everyone loves each other."

Charles's roots in Brookline go back to his grandfather, who settled in Brookline around 1865 via Ireland and Prince Edward Island. His father was born here in 1885 and became one of Boston's best-known doctors — indeed, he brought some of the Kennedy girls into the world. In fact, the Kennedys and the Kickhams were close friends. Charles and JFK were both born at St. Elizabeth's Hospital a few days apart in May 1917, to the consternation of both Charles Sr. and Joe Kennedy, because this resulted

Brookline Access TV interview, October 23, 2000. *Brookline Tab*, July 5, 2001. Charles J. Kickham Jr. passed away on December 27, 2003, at age eighty-six.

in both boys being shy by a few days of age five on the enrollment date for kindergarten, and both of them had to wait a year before starting school.

All lawyers respect law books, and Charles is no exception. Speaking of Dr. John Creagh, pastor for more than thirty years at St. Aidan's, he mentioned that Dr. Creagh had one of the best canon law libraries around. Cardinal Cushing, Charles tell us, persuaded Dr. Creagh to turn over his collection to St. John's Seminary in Brighton, where it still resides.

But Charles has medical stories to tell too, although his distaste for the sight of blood and the smell of ether (experienced when he went on rounds with his dad) led him to be the first Kickham lawyer. The best such story concerns Charles's obstetrician uncle, Dr. Edward L. Kickham, late of Brookline, who performed what might be described as a miracle on the high seas in a perfect calm, as opposed to the well-known "Perfect Storm." The year was 1932, and Uncle Ed was on his honeymoon on a ship to England carrying Cardinal O'Connell as well. As the story comes down to Charles, "Cardinal O'Connell was stricken by appendicitis. There was no doctor on board equipped to do the surgery, so they put my uncle to work as a surgeon and he did the operation. They had to stop the ship in mid-Atlantic so there would not be any rippling — this caught a lot of publicity in the Boston papers. The operation went nicely and Cardinal O'Connell lived many years thereafter."

Under Charles's own term, "economics," he tells us how tough it was to earn a buck as a kid during the Depression: "I had a job at the A & P on Lawton Street two to six every day and all day Saturday, at twenty-eight to thirty hours in all for two dollars a week. I figured it out, and it comes to seven or eight cents an hour. Later, just before entering Harvard Law School, I worked in the summers for Brookline Fly and Mosquito Control eight to five, five days a week, and half a day on Saturday, for twenty-four dollars a week, which comes to about fifty cents an hour. I worked with all college kids, three going to Harvard, one to Holy Cross, one to BC, and myself. We thought of ourselves as the 'elite.' "

Charles graduated BHS in 1936, and recalled (as did Mike Dukakis on my show before him) teachers who influenced him, like

Kate O'Brien, the head of the French department; Miss Snow, who taught Latin; the brother and sister combination of Mr. and Miss Bates; and John Cochran, headmaster of Packard House.

At BHS, Charles also remembers Mike Wallace, a year ahead of him: "Every day before school a lot of kids would get there early, and Mike was holding court. Precisely what he was saying, I don't know, but he was standing out on Greenough Street in front of the high school telling stories and answering questions. You could see the bent toward conversation even then, leading ultimately to what he does. Mike was always a good communicator."

Soon after Charles established his law practice in Coolidge Corner in 1954, where he still practices at the Kickham Law Offices (he just turned eighty-four), he exhibited Brookline hallmarks, such as highly skilled professionals volunteering their time and talents to Brookline, and Brookline citizens getting along with their neighbors in easy and productive association across political, personal, and religious lines. As a practicing attorney, Charles represented private parties dealing with the town, and from time to time represented the town itself. As a volunteer, Charles served on the Brookline Council for Planning and Renewal, and was a longtime Advisory Committee member. In a town replete with notable attorneys, certainly Charles is one of the most notable over the last half century. He was chosen president of the Massachusetts Bar Association 1974-1975, president of the Massachusetts Bar Foundation, president of the Norfolk County Bar Association, and delegate to the American Bar Association, bringing honor to the town by virtue of his eminence.

Charles, and his late wife, Barbara Buckley, brought up six children in Brookline.

No one now questions the value of the Larz Anderson estate to the town, but when it was willed to Brookline by Mrs. Anderson, a lot of folks were against accepting the bequest, mostly from a desire to expand the tax base. Charles, along with many other interested Brookline leaders, such as Senator Phil Bowker (later moderator of Town Meeting) and Jim Henderson, then town assessor, argued for acceptance, and that came to pass.

A little later the issue was whether the term "recreational purposes" in Mrs. Anderson's will was broad enough to allow the former Antique Auto Museum, now known as the Museum of Transportation, to take up quarters on the Larz Anderson estate. Charles represented both the selectmen and the museum in that case before the Norfolk Probate Court, and won, Charles pressing on the court that "Mr. Anderson was an antique auto collector. He even had cars with toilet facilities, for those who wanted to use them. It was easy to argue that Mrs. Anderson would have loved the museum being there."

Around 1960, Charles served as a member of the Brookline Council for Planning and Renewal, which encouraged the establishment of the Redevelopment Authority and the town taking by eminent domain the far-below code "Farm" area where the Brook House now stands. Charles believes the council is a perfect example of the "wonderful citizen participation" we have in Brookline. Charles served on that committee with Ned Dane, then president of the Brookline Trust Company; Elmer Cappers, president of Norfolk County Trust Company; Louise Castle (who later became a very highly respected selectperson); and the young Mike Dukakis, then a student at Harvard Law School, who "showed all that promise in those days. He was bright, articulate, clearly a leader of the future."

At that time, the philanthropic Brookline Friendly Society was located in a modest (if not run-down) building in the Farm, for which the town offered little in the eminent domain taking, which resulted in litigation in which Charles represented the society in its desire for higher compensation. The case involved the usual battle of opposing appraisers, but was decided by an unusual and amusing twist. Charles tells the story:

"Gus Sewall was then president of the Brookline Savings Bank and the Friendly Society, and as president of the society could testify as to value too, and came up with a higher figure than our own appraiser. The opposing lawyer cross-examined Mr. Sewall, asking, 'How can you say such a thing — you are not an appraiser,' to which Mr. Sewall, a magnificent witness, answered, 'One of my positions for the Brookline Savings Bank is to evaluate property for mortgage purposes, that's what I do.' And the jury went along with Mr. Sewall, rather than our own appraiser, and gave the amount to which he testified!"

Some of Charles's other memories paint a picture of an

earlier Brookline. He recalls a riding academy on the present Temple Emeth site, and the Weld Golf Club, which was where Hancock Village (now Westbrook Village) now stands. He also recalls the Charles River Golf Course on Fairway Road before that area was developed for residences.

Perhaps no one is better qualified to reflect on Brookline, as Charles has spent his whole personal and professional life here. He believes Brookline is a great place to live because of such things as its schools, services, the park system, public transportation, and its proximity to Boston. Beyond that, though, Charles says, "The attitude of the townspeople to be interested enough to volunteer their time and talent in behalf of various committees is remarkable. Many people are actually vying for the opportunity to work for nothing — this makes Brookline a wonderful place to live!"

Charles does see changes, especially in demographics, " . . . with many Russians, Koreans, Chinese, Japanese, and other folks coming to live in Brookline," and cites the "complete turnaround" in politics. In previous years, he said, you "could not be elected if you were a Democrat — it was Sumner Kaplan who came first and reinvigorated the Democrats, then Mike Dukakis came along."

Charles believes Brookline schools are still outstanding, accounting for the sharply higher property values in Brookline as opposed to areas of Boston just over the border. He tells a great story about what might be described as a borderline case involving a house on Risley Road in Brookline, split down the middle between Brookline and Boston:

"The issue was whether the youngster living there could go to Brookline schools without paying tuition. It was settled law that where the bedroom was determined the issue — that is, if the bedroom was in Brookline, the kid could go to Brookline schools without tuition. So there was a 'rearrangement' of the bedroom, and Brookline school population swelled by one."

Charles's fond memories of Senator Phil Bowker demonstrated how people of various stripes get along in Brookline. "Senator Bowker was a prominent Republican," Charles says. "He spent a lot of time in Coolidge Corner, being a bachelor for a long time, and would greet the people coming home off the streetcars. He got along with everyone, Republicans and Democrats."

As I have found in interviewing people like Bunny Solomon, Mike Dukakis, Owen Carle, and Charles Kickham, this spirit of getting along is a keynote for Brookline, and seems to exist here to far greater degree than practically any other place. Bunny Solomon, Jewish and a longtime Democratic political activist; Mike Dukakis, a liberal Democrat of Greek background; Owen Carle, Protestant, and a Republican of Yankee and French background; and Charles Kickham, a Catholic, and a Republican with deep Irish roots — all speak about each other with respect and affection, having interacted in cooperative and constructive ways over a long span of years.

Photo courtesy of Timothy Sullivan.

Museum of Transportation at the Larz Anderson Estate.

Photo by author.

REVEREND DAVID JOHNSON

Brookline's Religious History in the Evolution of Brookline Community

ALTHOUGH IT MIGHT BE DIFFICULT to separate the many strands of Brookline history leading to the valued community that we enjoy, listening to Reverend David Johnson of First Parish in Brookline as my guest on Brookline Access TV, one might readily believe that the religious strand is the most important one in that evolution.

Reverend David Johnson, although a latecomer to Brookline — he arrived here fourteen years ago to take over the pulpit at First Parish — has so immersed himself in our history that he is able to educate even us "townies" in a most erudite, open, and charming way.

David's goodwill immediately came across when he said, "It's fun to become aware of the larger context in which all of us live

Brookline Access TV interview, November 29, 2000. *Brookline Tab*, August 16, 2001.

religiously and as a community. It took me three years to feel that I could say anything at all about it. It is not easy to understand the many, many lifetimes that are represented in Brookline history, from the early days of John Cotton's pasturage here in the 1630s, all the way to the present. This is a long, long time."

In fact, these agricultural beginnings are reflected in the farm animals and tools shown on the town seal.

In answer to the question as to whether Brookline's religious history is intertwined with Brookline's community as we know it, David says, "Absolutely, absolutely. Everything is mirrored in the religious communities — issues that motivated them brought them together and divided them — and everything that motivated them is mirrored in the larger community too, and vice versa."

Of course, for a very long time, First Parish was the only church in Brookline, dating from when Brookline obtained its separate existence from Boston in 1705. At that time, the Great and General Court ordered Brookline to create a school as well as a "proper Puritan church." Its order also stipulated that the townspeople should "build a building, and that they should covenant a congregation."

This was well before we were known as the "wealthy towners," and money being the issue, it was not until 1717 that a church was built near the intersection of Walnut and Warren Streets, then the center of town, and still the site of the beautiful First Parish Church. Indeed, it was from the green in front of the church that Brookline's militia marched off in 1775 to engage the British. David Johnson confirmed that: "I believe there are nineteen names on the plaque on the stone monument that stands on the corner of the old Brookline common in front of the First Parish Church in Brookline."

David Johnson recalled for us the varied and fascinating history of Pierce Hall, named after Reverend John Pierce, who was pastor of First Parish from 1796 to 1849. (Pierce School was named after him, too.) Pierce was described in *Historical Sketches*, by Harriet Woods, as a man of "magnetic vitality, great powers of spiritual leadership, and an effective cultural influence in the community."

Pierce Hall is now part of First Parish, and was originally built in 1825 as a combination school and Town Hall. David tells us that after its first use, "eventually it was privately purchased, and there was a danger it might become a dance studio. The church was shocked that this might happen right next door to old First Parish, so they bought it, not really having any use for it. But eventually it became a major resource, not only to the church but also to the town. It was the site of many concerns, singing schools, temperance and lyceum lectures, all kinds of things."

"Did dancing finally come to Pierce Hall?" I asked. David tells us, "Yes, indeed, an Estonian dance group came, all kinds of children's groups, everything and anything. It has gone to uses that probably would not have been approved one hundred years ago."

Warming to his subject, David talked of Brookline's unusual ecumenical and, finally, interfaith history. It was not until 1828 that the next church came along in Brookline, the First Baptist, at which time," David said, "John Pierce went to the Baptists and said, 'Let us celebrate your starting. Let us bring our choir to celebrate together with you.'

"The same thing happened when the Harvard Street Congregational Church was founded in 1844, when Reverend Pierce said, 'Let's make this a community celebration.' "

Reverend David Johnson notes the significant differences among Christian sects, of course, but says, "Their attitude was that this is part of Brookline. This is part of who we are, and we should be together as much as we can. That spirit has a lot of continuance today."

David relates that togetherness and community to the consistent response of Brookline citizens to war: "Brookline was very early in supporting the Revolutionary cause — many, many men from Brookline served."

Nor was it any different with the Civil War, by which time Brookline had become a town of some wealth. "Nonetheless," David said, "there were very few Brookline young men who bought their way out of service, which they could have done for a few hundred dollars. They could have not served, and it is truly amazing how many chose to serve.

"I think that has been part of Brookline, the feeling that if we are committed to something, we must all be fully committed, and not pay somebody else to do it. Brookline tries to cover its convictions with its own actions and its honor, and not shirking. I think there is a religious dimension to this too, in terms of Brookline history, and that you don't have the bitter religious warfare in Brookline that you had in so many other communities."

David encountered that continuance of community spirit on taking his pulpit here: "I found that when I came here fourteen years ago, the rabbis in the Reformed Jewish community were active in the clergy community, unlike many other places, where they find barriers. The rabbis didn't find those barriers here. In fact, they created a wonderful interfaith clergy community. I think the rabbis were as much responsible as anybody else in creating a very different feeling in Brookline, an interfaith commonality — so much so that when anti-Semitic symbols were painted on walls, for example, the Brookline clergy came together to say, "This must stop. We must not have this. This is not who we are. This is not what we want. This is not our value. This is not our understanding of what we are about."

One wonders why it is that later-coming Christian denominations, then the Catholics and the Jews, did not find those barriers here, and how much that has to do with the Brookline of today, of which a previous guest, "Bunny" Solomon, said, "[It's] a great place to live because everybody loves one another."

Certainly the answer has a lot to do with the openness and acceptance of religious men like John Pierce of First Parish. who, Reverend David Johnson tells us, went to New York City to attend a synagogue, and to Montreal to attend Mary Queen of the World Cathedral, and brought the ideas he found there back to his congregation in Brookline. David is now writing a book on John Pierce, under a grant from the Massachusetts Historical Society, using as source material Pierce's voluminous letters and diaries, some recently unearthed by David himself. "There was an open attitude that prevailed all though these years," David says, "so that when the Catholic community came in [in the late nineteenth century], and when the Jewish community came in a little later, Brookline did not have barriers. Surely there were certain prejudices, but Brookline had a head start toward a greater openness, and I think we build on it."

David Johnson also talks of John Pierce's belief that music brings people together, linking that with Brookline's early openness toward women's rights and the feminist support of the temperance cause to ensure that a family's resources would not go for drink:

"These concerts took place all the time and across barriers and boundaries. Brookline very early found ways of bridging divisions that other communities found it hard to do, giving us a head start in the world we need to build. Temperance was spread by music, by the singing, by the concerts, and that bridged all kinds of barriers. Religion made no difference in temperance."

Remarking further on how religion has been key to the development of Brookline community, David Johnson says, "Brookline has had the great virtue of having its community spirit exist for a longer span of time. It's in the body politic, it's in the community, it's in the hearts of the people. Something about Brookline has kept it going all these years. It's rare to have it last the way it has here. People move to Brookline primarily to provide for their children — to give them an education, a cultural experience, and the experience of community itself, things they don't feel they will find in as full a form in any other place. If your focus is on the children, you can't go too far wrong."

Mentioning crèches at Christmastime, David cites a concrete example of interfaith community in Brookline: "Brookline has had a great deal of simple wisdom here, that if it is an offense to my brother and my sister, I will not do it. Brookline has had that sensitivity for years and years — it's wonderful! We sense we do not wish to do something that will cause pain to someone else if we can possibly avoid it, and so we have avoided it."

David goes on to describe the interfaith spirit presently in Brookline: "We do feel we are there for each other, and it has nothing to do with religious boundaries. That's the feeling among the clergy in Brookline. I love it, I absolutely love it!

"When I came to Brookline, as I've said, I think it was the rabbis, as much as anybody, who helped to knit the clergy together. They are the heart and soul of the organization. I had that feeling from the very beginning, and I loved it. I thought it was a wonderful openness, and appropriate to life in Brookline. I especially want to name Frank Waldorf at Temple Sinai. And certainly Rabbi

Emily Lipoff at Ohabei Shalom has been a wonderful supporter of the larger interfaith community in Brookline."

David Johnson talked about the third church to come to Brookline, St. Paul's Episcopal, which he described as "active in awakening us to social issues, and making us face things that Brookline didn't easily face, such as slaves here in Brookline who would do cleaning at the First Parish building, payment for which would go to the slaves' owners."

In giving St. Paul's credit for telling us of "a piece of the dark past of Brookline that St. Paul has not let us forget," Reverend David Johnson shows himself to be a true and tolerant interfaith and ecumenical messenger.

David beckons us, as he puts it, "to understand that all of our congregations have been around for a long span of time, and are part of a rich tapestry that makes Brookline's religion and its community."

The rich weave of that tapestry is shown in David's account of the combination almost thirty years ago of three churches, United Church of Christ and the Baptist and Methodist churches, into United Parish of Brookline, located at the corner of Harvard and Marion Streets.

As David says, "With great courage they came together. It was a tough call to bring the three together, showing the possibility of a much closer model of interfaith cooperation. It took vision too, the three sects saying that 'we can do more together than we can do separately,' putting aside their traditional differences for the sake of this unity, in response to their respective shrinking congregations."

David reminds us with amusement that the Coolidge Corner Theatre was the old Beacon Universalist Church, and suggests we have the manager there show us the church decorations in the upper reaches of the theater. Likewise, he reminds us that Temple Sinai was once the Second Unitarian Church, and that its organ, still there, was taken from a failed church. In these connections David recognizes that "our history is all wound together, and we need to celebrate the weave."

David, viewing Brookline's present diverse makeup, calls it "an intercultural and international world here in Brookline, and

Brookline has responded well. I am on the Brookline Domestic Welfare Round Table, where we work to get out the message in all the various languages. Brookline responds and the religious community is part of that response. I love it!"

David sees a forum for the exchange of ideas in Brookline "in the fellowship that surrounds the worship community," he says. "Any subject is fair game, including the political issues. Brookline's religious community is one of the few that has a concern for the larger community. You can raise any issue among people who are likely to care and respond. The church and the synagogue are really places now in our world where this personal interaction can occur."

For my part, without attempting a precise historical analysis, the remarks of the affable, informative, and passionate Reverend David Johnson lend credence to the notion that Brookline's religious community informed and enhanced the total Brookline community then and now, and promises to do so into our future.

Photo by author.

First Parish in Brookline.

BOOK XVI

CLUBS

Photo courtesy of Longwood Cricket Club.

Photo of The Country Club, courtesy of Arthur Cicconi.

Photo by author.

JOHN R. GALLAGHER

*Longwood Cricket Club President, Full-time Brooklineite,
Irishman, and Occasional Jew*

WE KNOW THAT BROOKLINE IS LOADED with fantastic people, but when I interviewed John Gallagher, he proved to be one of the most fantastic of all, combining, in one fell swoop, his presidency and association with Brookline's famed Longwood Cricket Club, his family life as a member of one of Brookline's oldest Irish families, his participation in Brookline community, his professional success, and, believe it or not, his occasional Jewish life.

Even that short description serves to elucidate the egalitarian views that inform John's life. Indeed, contrary to some uninformed opinion, the Longwood Cricket Club shares with Brookline traditions of diversity, openness, and equality. John puts it this way:

"When you go to schools like Baker and Brookline High School, there is no such thing as a minority or a majority, I believe.

Brookline Access TV interview, November 14, 2003. *Brookline Bulletin*, February 26, 2004

I think that in my neighborhood [South Brookline] what happens demonstrates that we all get along. Longwood itself is very similar to Brookline. We have a cross section of people from every walk of life, every color, every religion. We just are united in our love of tennis."

So how did the Irish John become a full participant at Temple Emeth in South Brookline? John's colorful story, starting when he was a young student at Baker School, and continuing to the present while raising his family in that same area of town, demonstrates vividly a well-known facet of Brookline life — the ability of people of widely diverse backgrounds to get along and interact successfully:

"If I remember correctly, I believe there were about forty-seven of us in the class at Baker, and of those forty-seven, approximately forty-four were Jewish. Now three-man baseball doesn't work very well, and since we all played together, the thing to do, occasionally, was to sneak into the Hebrew class at Temple Emeth, right around the corner, and be taught Jewish history. I got to know Rabbi Zev Nelson, who thought it was kind of unusual for me to be there. He and I got along very well. I had so many Jewish friends that I actually had a custom-made mezuzah, with a Star of David and a shamrock on it. I had my own yarmulke. I probably went to more bar mitzvahs than most Jewish people did. That actually came in very handy because I learned a lot of Jewish and Hebrew phrases and history, and I came to understand how similar we all are, which I thought was one of the best parts of living in Brookline.

"Then when we moved back to Brookline, I had an interesting experience when my youngest daughter was ready for preschool. My wife said, 'I would like to enroll Amanda at Temple Emeth for nursery school. It has an excellent reputation.' I said fine, because nursery school at Temple Emeth was designed as a nonsectarian sort of education. After that, I attended many times, and one day I happened to be the Shabbat father. I was told by the teacher that I was probably the only Irish person who could be a Shabbat father and speak Hebrew too. So that's how I became an honorary Jew, as well as Irish Catholic."

I suggested to John that his story really tells us a lot about Brookline. His reply: "I think Brookline should be celebrated for its diversity. People of all shapes and sizes live next to each other, we have a huge influx of Russians, Vietnamese, Chinese, and, of course, originally Jewish and Irish people, some Italians, and others, but we all seem to get along together, and it's a wonderful experience. My daughter's friends come from every walk of life. You've got wealthy people going to school at Brookline High with people who are not as wealthy, and everyone seems to get along very well. I firmly believe that they teach egalitarianism, not elitism, in Brookline schools."

So what about the notion that elitism reigns at the Longwood Cricket Club, where members still play on grass and tennis whites are compulsory? John thinks not:

"Well," he says, "we love our traditions, such as wearing white, and on many occasions playing with white balls on grass. We also demand respect for our fellow members and players, honesty, civility, and we don't do business. Longwood is a fun club, an oasis. We all have jobs, families, and worries, whatever they may be, but they all seem to melt away when we cross the threshold on Hammond Street. Then we see the beautiful expanse of green, players in white, people sitting around talking, not yelling, and not talking about the next big business deal.

"Sure, when Longwood was founded in 1877 on land given by the Sears family, where the Windsor School is now, opposite Beth Israel Hospital, it certainly was founded by the elite of Boston. But as Longwood continued to grow, and as interest in tennis became more popular with the public, Longwood opened up. We do have one very strict rule: You have to love tennis, and that is our only rule for admission. You don't have to be rich, you don't have to be a good tennis player, your name doesn't have to go back to the *Mayflower*. But you have to be friendly, you have to be respectful, and you have to love tennis."

It might fairly be said that the explosion of tennis on TV on the national and international scene began at Longwood when WGBH started televising the national doubles in 1963 with Bud Collins at the mike. In the following year, the U.S. Pro Tennis Championships were shifted to Longwood, and the place name for the results of those tournaments that were flashed around the world was Brookline, Mass., USA. Reminiscing about this history elicited from John remarks about several personalities well known in Brookline and tennis history.

Bud Collins: "The place name in the newspapers was always Brookline, and a lot of this came about as a result of the work and the promotion of a great member of Longwood, and a great member of the press, Bud Collins. He still plays a mean game of tennis in his bare feet, and still writes, as most everybody knows, a very interesting column in the *Boston Globe* on a regular basis about the tennis world. Bud Collins, despite what he says, is no hacker. He was a world-class amateur tennis player in his day, winning the National Mixed Indoor Doubles, and is still one of the finer players for his age."

Walter Elcock: "He was a longtime resident of Brookline who passed away only a few months ago. Walter attended BHS, became a very successful businessman, president of the Longwood Cricket Club, and was then elected to be the head of the United States Tennis Association [USTA], then head of the International Tennis Federation [ITF], the only person to ever hold all three of those posts, becoming well known around the world. Walter was a wonderful and giving guy, a longtime Brookline Town Meeting member, and a member of the Brookline Planning Commission."

Jack Steverman: "Jack was an electrical contractor in Brookline, very involved in community, family, and the Longwood Cricket Club [he became president], so the Steverman kids, like many of my own cousins and my own daughter, did participate at Longwood as ball kids, as tennis players, and as swimmers."

Bruce Wogan: "Bruce went to Baker School and was a graduate of BHS. Bruce was the voice of Longwood tennis for many years. He's still around, plays a mean game of tennis, has a left-handed serve, and for some reason was named 'Death House Wogan' by Bud Collins."

Over the last century, Longwood also has produced four national women champions — Eleonora Sears, Maud Barger-Wallach, Hazel Hotchkiss Wightman, and Sarah Palfrey Danzig.

"Hazel Wightman was an attractive woman, had a beautiful smile, great to watch, very friendly, great with children, and a wonderful teacher. She taught all the kids in the neighborhood, lived right around the corner here in Brookline, and gave her all to tennis until the day she died [in 1975]."

The first of those women champions, Eleonora Sears (1881-1968), was as liberated as they come, riding horses, driving cars, flying planes, taking long walks, and winning championships regularly: "She was probably the Martina Navratilova of her day because anything she wanted to do she went ahead and did it. She was the first lady of American tennis, probably beat most of the men that she played, and it is my understanding from some of her relatives, like John Sears, that she was quite a character her entire life."

John Gallagher's Irish family roots go far back in Brookline and Boston history. His step-grandfather is probably the most famous Boston Irishman of them all, James Michael Curley. His grandfather, Francis T. Leahy, legal counsel to the Boston Globe for many years and a longtime Brookline resident, was key in John's upbringing after his own father's early death. John reflected about that:

"Well, I guess sometimes good things come out of bad things. [When my father died] I got to move back into the Leahy house on Chestnut Hill Avenue, where I was the object of everyone's attention, being the only child in the house. The Leahys had nine children, all of whom as far as I could tell were brilliant in one way or another. The Leahy family included people who were mathematicians, artists, writers, singers, successful businessmen, and teachers. There was always a love of books instilled within everyone in the Leahy family. Grandfather Leahy could actually speak Latin and write poetry in Latin, and I grew up at his knee. I had about forty-four first cousins, many of whom lived in Brookline, and many of whom were members of Longwood. I had a lot of aunts and uncles who were like parents, and I had a lot of brothers and sisters who were actually cousins. So looking back at it, I have to say honestly that I had a wonderful childhood in the Leahy household, and I think I learned an awful lot about getting along in big families."

It seems that that ability to get along is the hallmark of John's life, a natural outgrowth of his life in Brookline, at home, in school, in the community, and at Longwood Cricket Club.

From left: Louis Newell and John Hall.

JOHN L. HALL II, PRESIDENT
J. LOUIS NEWELL JR., ARCHIVIST

The Country Club

To me the property around here is hallowed. The grass grows greener, the trees bloom better, there is even a warmth in the rocks that you see about here. And I don't know, gentlemen, but somehow or other the sun seems to shine brighter on The Country Club than on any other place that I have seen.
— Francis Ouimet, 1932

ONE MORE CONVERSANT than this writer with the social swirls that have, from time to time, converged about The Country Club is better able to discern how ironic it might be that the words above were spoken by Francis Ouimet, the former caddie and amateur

Brookline Access TV interview, January 29, 2004

from humble origins on the other side of Clyde Street who put the game of golf and The Country Club on the map when at age twenty he won the National Open Golf Tournament there in 1913, defeating world-famous golfers Harry Vardon and Ted Ray of England.

One is not likely to gainsay Ouimet's words after entering The Country Club and proceeding across its rolling greensward, its beautiful trees and shrubs in part perpetuated by legendary landscaper and original member Frederick Law Olmsted, to the eclectic, Victorian, Georgian, and classical clubhouse at the core, strikingly evolved from an 1802 farmhouse.

The words of architect James F. Hunnewell Jr. suggest not only the social and athletic elements of The Country Club, but also its firmly local character:

> *This quadrangle of buildings, arrayed around The Country Club's central oval, is very reminiscent of the classic New England village center, wherein key civic buildings of various functions surround the town green.*

John Hall and Louis Newell both commented on that.

John Hall: "I think the oval is the reinforcement of a long tradition, a welcoming enclosure that brings you around. Our dining room is on the far side of the clubhouse; some of our athletic facilities are on the other side. I see it as a sort of welcoming signal for our members, a wonderful place to congregate. It will remain that way for generations to come."

Louis Newell: "The oval is the core of the club. I think it is interesting that before my time, there were other configurations of buildings there, but that central open area surrounded by utilitarian facilities has been there forever."

Perhaps the best metaphor for the evolving outreaching stance of The Country Club is the persona of its president, John L. Hall II, his feet planted firmly astride the business world as one of the owners and managing partner of Suffolk Downs, and his home community of Brookline, where he has long been a Town Meeting member. John's comments about the cooperation between the town of Brookline and The Country Club in staging the turbulent and hugely attended Ryder Cup matches in 1999 betoken that.

"The first time that the club really ended up going public

about some of the things it does was in connection with the Ryder Cup," says John. "Before that, for whatever reason, we liked to do things very quietly. We didn't look for recognition, but we did want to be a good neighbor for the town. At that time, negotiating together, we were able to work out a situation for the Ryder Cup that made sense for both The Country Club and the town of Brookline, without an enormous amount of agony. It was a negotiation that was run in a businesslike way. I'm just very impressed with the governance of the town. Brookline had a terrific crew of selectmen with whom we worked — people like Donna Kalikow, Joe Geller, Bobby Allen, and Debbie Goldberg. They are very thoughtful, capable people who volunteer huge amounts of time. In Rich Kelliher, the town has the very best town administrator. There is no person better able to run the town than that guy! They were all great people to work with.

"When the opportunity to host the Ryder Cup came along, there was some discussion of how good a Brookline citizen The Country Club was. At that point, we became much more aggressive in laying out what, in fact, we do. We had always let Brookline High teams use the golf course, had always been supportive of activities at Larz Anderson, had been supportive of Brookline elderly and youth. No question, we tie up a substantial portion of Brookline real estate. We don't hide from that, and we want to be a solid taxpayer to the town. Putting it bluntly, we are now much more public than we used to be, more involved in Brookline community, and believe we have a good relationship with Brookline."

Louis Newell, club archivist and historian, grew up on Walnut Place at the back end of Pill Hill and attended Park School. His parents and grandparents had lived in Brookline for over one hundred years, until 1991. He spoke in the same vein about the yearly golf match between The Country Club and the Town of Brookline Golf Club at Putterham, in which my own late low-handicap father-in-law, Jacob "Jack" Raverby, competed for Putterham:

"We have an annual match with Putterham," he said. "We have a good relationship. Another part of that sharing is that Putterham was very supportive to us in terms of an alternative site during the Ryder Cup, and our groundskeeper was helpful to Putterham in its agronomy program. It's been a shared relationship."

People around the globe, as well as most of us living here in Brookline, think naturally of The Country Club and golf as one. There was Francis Ouimet's victory in the rainswept 1913 National Open, Julius Boros's playoff win over Arnold Palmer and Jackie Cupit in the windswept 1963 National Open, and the American triumph in the strife-swept 1999 Ryder Cup matches. But Louis Newell's long view demonstrates how myopic that view really is, as he recalls The Country Club's founding and the profusion of sporting endeavors there.

"When The Country Club first came into existence, in 1882," he tells us, "the property was leased from what was then called a stock farm. There was an existing little hotel there, and the farm was dedicated to the enterprise of horse racing and racehorses. That facility, already in existence, including a steeplechase and providing fox hunting, attracted some of the early members, that being their principal interest. Some of them came over from the Myopia Club in Winchester, which was started before The Country Club, where a lot of baseball was played. Many of the players wore glasses — hence, the name Myopia. Later, that club moved to Hamilton on the North Shore, and is now well known as the Myopia Hunt Club.

In the early years, there were a couple of grandstands for racing, one of them a very large edifice. Racing here was a big public event, with a lot of wagering, and people had a good time. In fact, when golf became popular, the horses were the target, and there was a battle among the members. That was resolved in the mid-thirties when racing ceased."

In fact, the catalog of sports that have been played at The Country Club rivals the catalog of conquests rattled off by Leporello to Donna Elvira in Mozart's *Don Giovanni*, their diverse national origins favorably comparing with those of the Don's damsels in distress.

Besides horse racing (and its cousin, steeplechasing), the hunt, and golf (1893), The Country Club has seen lawn tennis, indoor tennis, paddle tennis, curling, free skating, figure skating, hockey, squash racquets, skeet shooting, bowling-on-the-green, rowing, and swimming. Louis Newell spoke of a few of those sports:

"Tennis predates golf at The Country Club, as does ice skating.

There has been a long history of people who later skated in the Olympics, the most recent and noteworthy being Tenley Albright [Olympic gold medalist, 1956], who is a member. As a young boy, I remember she put on a performance here at the pond. It was fabulous and magical — she was doing all sorts of jumps. Curling is a game that was started in Scotland, as was golf. It's a game best described as shuffleboard on ice, played on a sheet of ice one hundred and forty feet long, with round flat stones, each of which weighs forty-two pounds. It's a thinking-man's game. Curling started as an outdoor game, and indoor curling was started in 1920. The Country Club built the first exclusively indoor curling rink in North America. We've had curling going on at the club for a long time, since 1898, often having major tournaments. Richard D. Sears [U.S. lawn tennis singles champion 1881-87] was an early member of the club. His racquets are housed here at The Country Club."

A theory embraced by the members of The Country Club is that its physical elements greatly enhance its mission of balancing athletics and community. To see its more than two hundred thirty acres, assembled piecemeal in the late nineteenth century from owners whose names — like Samuel and John Newell, Thomas and Joseph Dudley, Gulliver and John Winchester, and Daniel Webster — ring of Brookline and New England's Yankee past, lends credence to that theory, as do the names of recent members like Elmer O. Cappers, formerly president of the Brookline Trust Company, and F. Stanton Deland Jr., Esq., Brookline activist.

Louis Newell and John Hall spoke of that theory.

Louis Newell: "The Club was devised originally to be a combination athletic and social club. We have been true to our purpose."

John Hall: "It would have been quite easy for us to evolve into a great golf club but not into a country club. We chose not to do that. The social element of it is very important, and family is what we're interested in. We're definitely a family social club."

Whatever may have been the case in years past, it appears true that the society so valued among the members of The Country Club has evolved to sufficiently extend to the Brookline community that surrounds it in ways beneficial to each.

AUTHOR'S NOTE ON
HOW THIS BOOK WAS WRITTEN

The methodology of writing this book (quite apart from whatever merit it has) may be of interest to the general reader, as well as to interviewers, journalists, writers, and historians. Over the more than four-year period from the first tape-recorded interview with Ethel Weiss and a few months later the first television interview with Bernard "Bunny" Solomon to the completion of the manuscript, the method of writing remained roughly the same, although it became more refined as time went by, as is the case with all works in progress. It may be that the method I am about to describe is unique — although I am not sure about that — employing as it does preparation for an interview; the interview itself; transcription of the interview onto the printed page; analysis of the interview to judge how best to use the interviewee's own words in combination with my own to find the thread or threads to bring that person to life in the contexts of Brookline and the world; and finally to combine the individual stories into appropriate sections in a book in a sequence that will provide a cogent and lively overall sense of Brookline community and its people from about 1925 to the present.

This process seems interesting not only in the objective or technical sense of elucidating how the book was written, but also in the very subjective and personal sense of interacting in the intimate setting of an extended television interview. In fact, it is the juxtaposition of the professional and the personal, the objective and the subjective, the solitude of the writing and the togetherness of the interview that infuses this method with a life-simulating reality and perspective that I hope translates from the printed page in a lively and life-enhancing way into the reader's imagination.

As I mentioned earlier in the preface, I was fortunate that the idea of capturing Brookline's past through oral history by means of extended television interviews came to me and remained a constant from the time of the first television interview in September 2000 through the last one in December 2004. Along the way, I minimized, then put aside, a theme I had thought would predominate, that of Brookline community being lost in the impersonality of millennium cyberspace. Minimized, too, was the relatively amorphous idea of interviewing only longtime Brookline residents and shopkeepers. Experience proved both of those notions to be restrictive in scope, insufficient to develop what came to be my main purpose: to cover the many strands of Brookline life over the last seventy-five years or so to convey the full scope and significance of Brookline life over that period.

Of course, on public access television one does not have the luxury of a staff to obtain the guest and to do the research and background required to run a good interview. This limitation was a blessing in disguise in that it prompts, if not forces, the producer/talk-show host to insinuate himself into every facet of the creation of the interview. That process is invaluable and edifying. Further, when you think about it, that process fits exactly the original concept of public access television in a free and democratic society: to give a public voice to all segments of the community, running the spectrum from humble to exalted.

Instinctively, it was my belief that most of us want to be on television, perhaps simply to see ourselves there, but mostly to tell our own story. With that conviction in mind, I was never hesitant to contact any person to be my guest. Often easily, sometimes only with persistence, I obtained practically every guest I sought.

There was little challenge in enticing my first guest, good friend Bernard "Bunny" Solomon, well-known politico and raconteur. I knew that the test to pass with Bunny was to rein in my own talkativeness to give him sufficient space to tell his own story in the entertaining fashion I knew he would. The anticipation of that result catalyzed an interior conversation that caused me to lay down a few rules for interviewing, to which I have adhered from that day to this, rules that — at least to my observation — many well-known interviewers breach on a regular basis. Those rules can be summed up under the heading of respect for the interviewee, the natural by-product of which is usually a show that is informative and entertaining, and sometimes deeply personal.

I reminded myself to prepare thoroughly for a talk by mining all sources reasonably available, including the library, the Internet, friends and relations of the interviewee, writings of the interviewee, and the interviewee himself or herself (although in many instances, the interviewee was unavailable until the cusp of the interview). Perhaps the most important rule I taught myself during this "psyching" process was a guiding principle that somehow became emblazoned in my mind's eye, boldly proclaiming, "It's about them!" — a principle not adopted without discipline by one who is hardly a shrinking violet. Perhaps this is the conflict that most easily trips up an interviewer or talk-show host, for who but a person with a strong sense of self would attempt such an endeavor?

As I prepared for that first show with Bunny Solomon, with that principle in mind, I resolved to be a good listener: to listen to my guest without interruption, and to respond naturally to what my guest was saying, rather than with a canned next question. I tried to achieve the spontaneity of a real and relaxed conversation in which two (or more) people speak openly with one another, yet always keeping in mind a general direction in which I wanted the conversation to flow so that the significant features of the person's life would be covered. Within these bounds, it was my belief from the beginning that my role should not be limited to that of a mere questioner, but rather should go far enough to offer comments or responses sufficient to create a dynamic promoting real conversation in an artificial setting, encouraging expansion of what the guest might tell and reveal about his or her own personal life and about life in Brookline and the world. Concomitant with that objective and with an aim to develop historical as opposed to current-event information, I strove to create a low-key, noncontroversial, nonconfrontational atmosphere in which to do the interview, calculated to allow my guest to be relaxed, conversational, and expansive.

In short, that conversation I had with myself about interviewing proved to be the best one I ever had, or ever will. Upon emerging from his one-hour interview, Bunny Solomon effusively told me how much he had enjoyed the interview. His laudatory and encouraging comments firmly impelled me forward from that day to this.

To prepare for the writing of the twenty or so stories I did for the *Tab* from early 2001 to the spring of 2002, I transcribed the television programs myself in my almost indecipherable (even to me) script, a back-wrenching process, which I happily and eventually gave over to Brookline High School seniors Mariana Folco and

Samantha Cheng, computer masters both. Mari and Sam more than ably produced accurate transcriptions of a great many of my television shows. Whether done with difficulty by myself or with relative ease by Mari and Sam, the transcriptions of the marvelous and provocative words of my guests, whether precise and serious or anecdotal and funny, proved to be a mine of gold, providing me with the material to attempt to bring the Brookline of our lifetime alive for readers now and (in my dreams) in the future.

As to content, I have alluded previously to the idea of weaving together the subject's quotes with my own words to bring that person alive in the reader's mind. To do this, from the first, I naturally adopted a personal style in the writing of each story, shifting back and forth from the first to the third person, as seemed to me most suited to achieving that end. On the occasions when a relatively precise accounting of the historical record was appropriate, I employed the third person almost exclusively. Two prime examples are the stories on Richard Leary and Robert Sperber. Both gentlemen sat down with me previous to the taping of the show to thoroughly prepare me as to the significant facts of their respective tenures as town administrator and superintendent of schools. At the other end of the spectrum, I point to the story *Giuliani, Baseball, and Brookline*, in which I extensively used the first person to join my own baseball and Brookline experiences with those of Bunny Solomon, Charles Kickham, Michael Dukakis, Bob Sperber, Harry Ellis Dickson, and Owen Carle. It is my belief that this method of shifting back and forth between the first and the third person allowed me to write in a freely flowing style designed to re-create the atmosphere of spontaneity that I believe characterized the television interviews and gave life to the stories themselves.

Not inconsequentially, it would be naïve, if not disingenuous, not to suppose that the idea to adopt such a style appealed to me as a way to speak in my own voice about my experiences and ideas as a lifelong citizen of Brookline. Although I recognized from the very start that each show was about the guest, never did I think of retreating out of sight; I always believed the dynamic of two or more citizens of Brookline talking with animation in the give-and-take of a real conversation would be the best wellspring of information about Brookline of personal as well as historical relevance. In the last analysis, then, it is fair to say that this book contains a substantial autobiographical strain.

Once having decided that, indeed, I was writing a book, I took pains to invite guests representing all the disparate elements of Brookline life. When it came time to combine the stories about each of those people into appropriate groupings and sequences, I found that task to be both challenging and enjoyable. It seemed appropriate to entice and draw in the reader with stories of basic human interest in the first four Books — *Sisters, The Holocaust, Immigrants,* and *Dogs* — and then to proceed to stories combining human interest with the more serious and historical theme of Brookline's uniqueness, including the notion that Brookline community and political life represents an unusual, if not unique, microcosm of democracy. Attempting to achieve a balance in the overall arc of the book, the latter sections return to stories of basic human interest. Of course, it is my hope that all the stories read together will vivify Brookline life over this period, so that a reader now or later might say, "Yes, that is what Brookline is like!" or "So that is what Brookline was like!" It also occurs to me now that a prime facet of what I was always about in this endeavor was to try to add a tiny bit to our understanding of human nature and the human condition—an effort which I think is shared (hesitant though I am to place myself in that company) by all serious writers and artists whether or not he or she is conscious of that aim.

To add to the aura of verisimilitude which I hoped to create, I have either taken or obtained photographs as natural as possible of the subjects of the stories, to head each of them. To give historical context I have written the "Brief Overview of Brookline History" which appears at the front of this book, and assembled photographs and illustrations to head each of the sixteen "Books," as well as for the dust jacket, endpapers, the frontispiece, the page opposite the epigraph by de Tocqueville, and elsewhere.

Finally, it is useful to describe the method employed in the extensive use of quoted material. Rarely, if ever, does any person speak in a straight line in a spontaneous conversation, whether on or off television. Everyone tends to digress, repeat, contract, pause, stumble, and do all those other things with which we are all familiar in ordinary conversation. To slavishly render quotes onto the printed page would be overly testing to the reader, no matter how interesting the content. Therefore, it becomes necessary to shape the quotes into some form having literary quality, at the same time retaining the cadence, spontaneity, and feel of the person's speech. In doing that, it often becomes necessary to reorder and smooth out the quoted material, sometimes even to change words. This process can be a precarious balancing act, as one wants to retain the feel of the conversation that had taken place, but never to breach the cardinal rule of rendering precisely the person's meaning.

This is not to say that the quotes you read in this book are very far from what the person said on the television show. Probably more than ninety percent of the quotes are exactly as spoken, with punctuation added and unnecessary words deleted to provide smooth readability. As to the rest, a little more cutting and pasting was required, but the subject himself or herself will read the quotes without discerning the difference or, if discerning the difference, will accept the difference as an accurate rendering of what was said. The truth of that statement has been demonstrated by the response to my practice of submitting the story to the subject for corrections and suggestions. Most came back merely correcting a misspelling or suggesting a change in grammar or syntax. Some subjects actually extended the process I had begun, offering further changes — an indication of their agreement that the process employed was required to accurately transcribe what they had said onto the printed page in readable form. The proof of that pudding came when one subject, a writer, made extensive alterations of her own quotes to better communicate what she had said (trimming much that she had said in the vernacular, at the same time retaining her conversational tone), while leaving my first- and third-person words untouched.

Of course, it will be for others to say whether the method I have employed is unique and whether it has proved sufficient to realize the intended purpose of bringing Brookline and its residents to life on the printed page.

Brookline, Massachusetts, January 20, 2005

INDEX